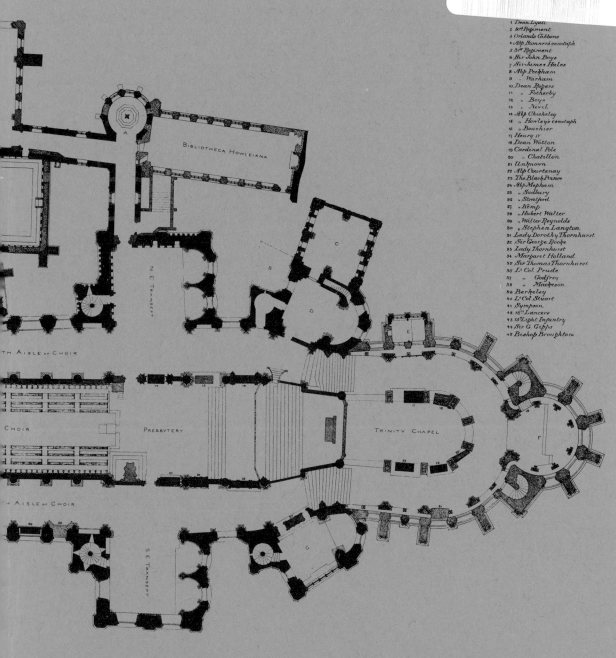

BIBLIOTHECA HOWLEIANA

N.E. TRANSEPT

TH AISLE OF CHOIR

CHOIR

PRESBYTERY

TRINITY CHAPEL

TH AISLE OF CHOIR

S.E. TRANSEPT

1 Dean Lyall
2 50th Regiment
3 Orlando Gibbons
4 Abp Sumner's cenotaph
5 31st Regiment
6 Sir John Boys
7 Sir James Hales
8 Abp Peckham
9 ,, Warham
10 Dean Rogers
11 ,, Fotherby
12 ,, Boys
13 ,, Nevil
14 Abp Chichley
15 ,, Howley's cenotaph
16 ,, Bouchier
17 Henry IV
18 Dean Wotton
19 Cardinal Pole
20 ,, Chatillon
21 Unknown
22 Abp Courtenay
23 The Black Prince
24 Abp Mepham
25 ,, Sudbury
26 ,, Stratford
27 ,, Kemp
28 ,, Hubert Walter
29 ,, Walter Reynolds
30 ,, Stephen Langton
31 Lady Dorothy Thornhurst
32 Sir George Rooke
33 Lady Thornhurst
34 Margaret Holland
35 Sir Thomas Thornhurst
36 Lt Col Prude
37 ,, Godfrey
38 ,, Macheson
39 Berkeley
40 Lt Col Stuart
41 Sympson
42 16th Lancers
43 13th Light Infantry
44 Sir G. Gipps
45 Bishop Broughton

# THE ARCHITECTURAL HISTORY OF
# CANTERBURY CATHEDRAL

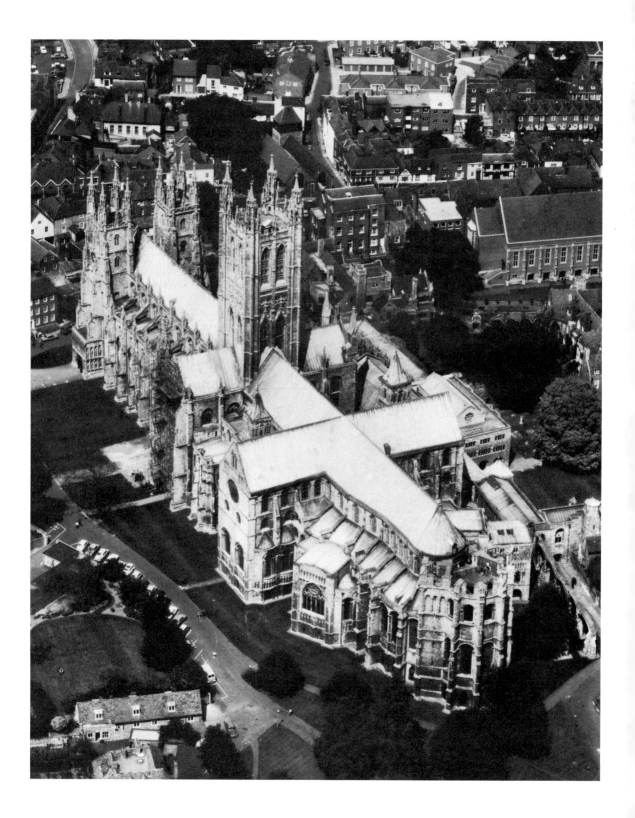

# FRANCIS WOODMAN

# THE ARCHITECTURAL HISTORY OF
# CANTERBURY CATHEDRAL

**ROUTLEDGE & KEGAN PAUL**
**LONDON, BOSTON AND HENLEY**

*First published in 1981*
*by Routledge & Kegan Paul Ltd*
*39 Store Street,*
*London WC1E 7DD,*
*9 Park Street,*
*Boston, Mass. 12108,*
*USA and*
*Broadway House,*
*Newtown Road,*
*Henley-on-Thames,*
*Oxon RG9 1EN*

*Set in Monophoto Imprint*
*and printed in Great Britain by*
*BAS Printers Limited,*
*Over Wallop, Hampshire*

*ISBN 0 7100 0752 3*

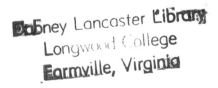

To William Urry

# CONTENTS

# FIGURES

# ABBREVIATIONS

| | |
|---|---|
| *Arch. Cant.* | *Archaeologia Cantiana* |
| *Arch. J.* | *Architectural Journal* |
| *Arch. Rev.* | *Architectural Review* |
| *Archaeol. J.* | *Archaeological Journal* |
| *Antiq. J.* | *Antiquaries Journal* |
| BM | British Museum |
| *Cant. Cath. Chron.* | *Canterbury Cathedral Chronicle* |
| *Cant. Papers* | *Canterbury Papers* |
| *J. Brit. Archaeol. Ass.* | *Journal of the British Archaeological Association* |
| *JRIBA* | *Journal of the Royal Institute of British Architects* |
| G. Smith, *Chron. Hist.* | *A Chronological History of Canterbury Cathedral* |
| Willis, *Arch. Hist.* | *The Architectural History of Canterbury Cathedral* |
| Willis, *Hist. Mon.* | *The History of the Monastery of Christ Church Canterbury* |
| Woodruff and Danks, *Mems CC* | *Memorials of the Cathedral and Priory of Christ in Canterbury* |

# PREFACE

There can never be a definitive architectural history of Canterbury Cathedral – the building withholds too many secrets that have passed away beyond our modern grasp. Yet this masterwork of man has exercised its fascination on successive generations, and has become world famous for its beauty and as a repository of the nation's heritage. Canterbury Cathedral is a textbook of English mediaeval architecture. Its importance lies not just in the variety of styles found therein but in the high quality of every component part, whether the Romanesque crypt or the Late Perpendicular central tower. Willis's comment on the cloister might well apply to the whole church: 'Consequently these walls . . . resemble those of a museum of mediaeval architecture, against which examples of all the styles have been placed for the edification of students.'[1]

1 R. Willis, *Hist. Mon.*, p. 40.

The superb quality of the architecture is, of course, a reflection of the great status that Canterbury enjoyed throughout the Middle Ages. It was the oldest of England's cathedrals, the seat of the Primate of all England, and it housed one of the richest and most powerful monasteries in the country. It was also the church of St Thomas. The cult of St Thomas of Canterbury was amongst the most popular in Christendom, and the cathedral basked in the fame and glory of its martyr. The unique combination of primatic seat, great monastery and principal shrine church of the nation has left its mark on the architecture and the arrangement of the building. It is England's most complex and rewarding church, and it is the purpose of this book to attempt some explanation of how and why this remarkable building came about.

The architecture cannot be divorced from the circumstances that determined the cathedral's fortunes, and some account of those events germane to the development of the building will be found framing the successive architectural campaigns. Its history, often lurid and bloody, has been variously chronicled since Anglo-Saxon times. Bede, Eadmer, William of Malmesbury and Gervase provide most of the information prior to *c.* 1200. Later writers tend to concentrate on the more domestic aspects of the monastic cathedral, though information from obits, deeds, accounts, etc., provide sufficient evidence for the more important developments. Antiquarian endeavour began with John Leland, the 'father of English history', whose work on Canterbury is tragically incomplete. Matthew Parker, archbishop to Elizabeth I, and Francis Godwin both wrote at length about the cathedral, though their interests lay more with its personalities than with its architecture. Outstanding among the seventeenth-century writers on Canterbury was William Somner. *The Antiquities of Canterbury*, first published in 1640, provides an invaluable insight into the contemporary state of the building, as well as some indication of the current level of research and available information. Somner had access to documents and manuscripts that were lost subsequently, and he also records the condition of the cathedral prior to its despoilation by the Commonwealth in 1642. A second edition appeared after the Restoration in 1660 and Battley published yet another, with many additions, in 1713.

Of the eighteenth-century writers, Dart and Gostling must be considered of prime importance. Dart produced the first fully illustrated book on the cathedral in 1726, while Gostling's gossipy work on the church and its precincts reveals a long and intimate knowledge of the building. The 1825 edition of his *Walk in and about the City of Canterbury* is by far the best, for it contains more illustrations and has additional material regarding the early nineteenth century restorations and repairs. Britton's remarkable prints and drawings of Canterbury Cathedral, published in 1821, have become a standard work of reference, though their accuracy should be regarded with some caution.

But of all the writers the most outstanding must be Robert Willis. His *Architectural History of Canterbury Cathedral*, 1845, was a pioneering work in the study of English mediaeval building. Much of his scholarship is faultless, but his attitudes and training were those of the early nineteenth century, and the great wealth of research and discoveries over the last hundred years has advanced our knowledge and understanding of the building. Hence his work is often narrow and, to the modern student, uninformed. Willis was primarily interested in the late twelfth-century text by Gervase concerning the burning and repair of the cathedral choir, and this interest is reflected in his book. The later phases of construction tend to be rather lightly treated – perfectly understandable within the context of the nineteenth century that had not yet come to terms with the late mediaeval Perpendicular style.

No writer since Willis has attempted to deal with the architecture of the cathedral in such detail, though many worthy and important articles have appeared by such writers as St John Hope, Jean Bony, Peter Kidson and H. M. Taylor. The present volume is written in the light of current knowledge, which is by no means finalized or conclusive. The Gothic choir, always a problem for the architectural historian, appears increasingly complex, for it is one of the ironies of Canterbury that while we have an abundance of written information – even the names of the architects – the more we learn about the development of Gothic in northern France, the less we seem to understand about William of Sens or his choir. Of the other sections of the cathedral, we are unlikely to discover more of Lanfranc's or Anselm's work in the Romanesque period, and here it is more a matter of interpretation. The Perpendicular work is less well known, largely because of the prejudice of Victorian scholarship. In recent years, the upsurge of interest in England's 'national style' has led to exciting research, with a particular emphasis on the identification of master masons and their role in the design process.

The destructions of 1540 and 1642 are tragically familiar, but must take their place in the architectural history of the building. So too, must the remains of the monastic buildings and the Archbishop's Palace, for they were built and repaired by the very masons who worked upon the church, and, quite often, reflections of lost works within the cathedral can be found in the surviving claustral offices.

The post-Reformation history of Canterbury Cathedral, itself a fascinating social and political study, has no place in an architectural treatise. The development of the building stopped dead in 1540. For nearly three centuries, the cathedral survived against all the odds, and it was only in the nineteenth century that any real effort was made to preserve its ancient fabric. In general, the Victorians did not wreak their usual havoc upon Canterbury; it was neither scraped nor academically restored. The only major loss was the old north-west tower which robbed Canterbury of its most ancient feature and its whimsical silhouette. Losses and restorations are recounted in chapter 7 on the post-Reformation, but the reader will appreciate the necessary and appropriate brevity of the account.

The preparation of this book has been a daunting challenge, even after many years of research. One is always in the shadow of Willis, and fully conscious of the considerable expertise on both sides of the Atlantic that is devoted currently to the study of mediaeval architecture, research that may one day revolutionize our understanding of Romanesque or Gothic. Until then, it is hoped that this new architectural history will extend our knowledge of this great monument and form a basis for discussion and further research.

## Technical aspects

It is necessary to call the attention of the reader to the problem of measurement and currency. The surviving building accounts of Canterbury Cathedral specify weights in tons, hundredweights, pounds and ounces as appropriate. Payments are made in pounds sterling, shillings and pence, and occasionally in marks. All units of measurement are in feet and inches: the foot being the modern one of twelve inches for the greater part of the period. It will be appreciated that all previous works on the architecture of Canterbury Cathedral were written long before the introduction of metric measurements and decimal currency into this country. Therefore some knowledge of the previous usage is essential. As all the books on the subject have discussed and measured the cathedral in feet and inches, some more accurately than others, it would appear only sensible to continue this tradition. Metric measurements follow the Imperial length.

For the benefit of those unfamiliar with the vagaries of the Imperial system, and of English mediaeval monetary units, the following table may be useful.

### Weights

16 ounces (oz) = 1 pound (lb)
14 lb = 1 stone
112 lb = 1 hundredweight (cwt)
20 cwt = 1 ton

### Lengths

12 inches (in.) = 1 foot (ft)
3 feet = 1 yard (yd)
1 inch = 2.54 centimetres (cm)

### Currency

4 farthings = 1 penny (d); e.g. 1d
2 halfpennies = 1 penny; halfpennies are usually indicated as $\frac{1}{2}$d
12 pennies = 1 shilling (1/- or 1s)
20 shillings = 1 pound sterling (£1)
$2\frac{1}{2}$ shillings = half a crown (2s 6d)
13s 4d = 1 mark
6s 8d = $\frac{1}{2}$ mark

# ACKNOWLEDGMENTS

I wish to thank Eric Fernie and Martin Johnson for reading sections of this book and for their many helpful suggestions. Also Jean Bony, Stephen Gardner, Sandy Heslop and Christopher Wilson for discussing individual points. I have been most fortunate in having the assistance of Stella Shackle of the Photographic Unit of the Department of Fine Arts, University of East Anglia, and of Robert Smith of the Centre of East Anglian Studies. I also wish to thank Shirley French for her excellent preparation of the manuscript.

I have received the greatest courtesy and kindness from the Dean and Chapter of Canterbury Cathedral, especially from Jim Brasier, Frederick Cole, Brian Lemar and from numerous vergers. My thanks to Professor J. H. Plumb for his interest and encouragement. Lastly, my deepest gratitude to my parents for their constant support.

The following figures have been prepared by Robert Smith: Figures 2, 11, 13, 23, 24, 26, 41, 43, 44, 58, 81, 82, 102, 104, 124, 150.

Most of the photographs were taken by the author over the period 1978–80 and were processed and printed by Stella Shackle. I wish to thank the following for their kind permission to reproduce photographs: The Dean and Chapter of Canterbury Cathedral, 159; the Friends of Canterbury Cathedral, 4, 27, 116, 135, 158; The Master and Fellows of Trinity College, Cambridge, 12; Entwistle of Canterbury, 6, 15, 133, 145; the *Kentish Gazette*, 3, 120, 149, 161; and Christopher Wilson, 112, 113, 128, 160. The following photographs have been reproduced by courtesy of the National Monuments Record Office, 28; and the Courtauld Institute, London, 20, 21, 75, 77, 78, 91, 98.

I wish to thank the Master and Fellows of Christ's College, Cambridge, and the British Academy for their generous financial support towards the research expenses for this book.

# INTRODUCTION

Whan that Aprille with his shoures soote
The droghte of March hath perced to the roote,
And bathed every veyne in swich licour,
Of which vertu engendred is the flour;
Whan Zephyrus eek with his swete breeth
Inspired hath in every holt and heeth
The tendre croppes, and the honge sonne,
Hath in the Ram his halfe cours yronne,
And smale foweles maken melodye
That slepen al the nyght with open eye
So priketh hen nature in hir corages;
Thanne longen folk to goon on pilgrimages
And palmeres for to seken straunge strondes
To ferne halwes kowthe in sondry londes;
And specially from every shires ende
Of Engelond, to Canterbery they wende
The hooly blisful martir for to seke,
That hem hath holpen when that they were seeke.[1]

1 Chaucer, Prologue, *The Canterbury Tales.*

When Chaucer's pilgrims trod the Kentish lanes, Canterbury Cathedral was already eight centuries old. It was a hallowed spot, the birthplace of English Christianity, and was hailed, as the city's motto proudly proclaims: 'Ave, Mater Angliae.' The English have always held Canterbury in the highest regard and the twelfth-century writings of John of Salisbury amply illustrate this enduring sentiment:[2]

2 John of Salisbury, Prefix to *Polycraticus*, trans. L. Evans, the King's School, Canterbury (unpublished).

This mother-shrine was first to sing the praises of the Heavenly King;
By her our thankful hearts we raise in honour, duty, love and praise.

The story begins with St Augustine, who consecrated the first cathedral soon after his arrival in 597. The high Altar was dedicated to our Blessed Saviour, a dedication that survived throughout the Middle Ages. In more modern times, the church is styled the Cathedral of Christ Church or, more properly, the Cathedral of the Holy Trinity, Christ Church. Both parts of this dedication can be traced back to the Anglo-Saxon period: Christ Church to at least 813 and Holy Trinity to 990.[3]

3 A. Haddan and W. Stubbs, *Councils and Ecclesiastical Documents relating to Great Britain and Ireland*, Oxford University Press, vol. 3, 1871, p. 575; Bartholomew Cotton, *Historia Anglicana* (ed. H. Luard), Rolls Society, 1859, p. 48.

After the Norman Conquest, the latter title tended to fall into disuse, even though the easternmost altar of the cathedral continued to be dedicated to the Holy Trinity, occupying the eastern axial chapel, now the Corona, a place normally associated in England with the cult of the Virgin. By the late Middle Ages the cathedral was 'dedicated' by popular acclaim in honour of its most illustrious martyr St Thomas, though this title was never formally adopted by the monks.

For the first five centuries of its existence, the cathedral presented an amalgam of different building campaigns; perhaps Romano-British, with additions from the seventh to the tenth century. Our modern knowledge of this church is almost entirely drawn from chronicles, particularly that of Eadmer the singer, who knew the Anglo-Saxon cathedral as a boy. The post-Conquest fire of 1067 prompted the total demolition of this ancient structure and the building of a new church in the Romanesque style then current in Normandy. Archbishop Lanfranc quickly completed his new cathedral, and his successor, St Anselm, replaced the small east end with a huge choir raised upon a splendid crypt. St Anselm's choir was one of the most famous buildings of its day and was decorated with spectacular stained glass and mural paintings. But in 1174, soon after the murder of Becket, this 'glorious choir' was devastated by fire and reduced to a ruin. There followed the most famous and best documented reconstruction of the European Middle Ages. Gervase, a monk of Christ Church, chronicled almost every detail of the new work, with annual reports of the

**2** Site plan of the monastery and Palace showing the development of the precincts

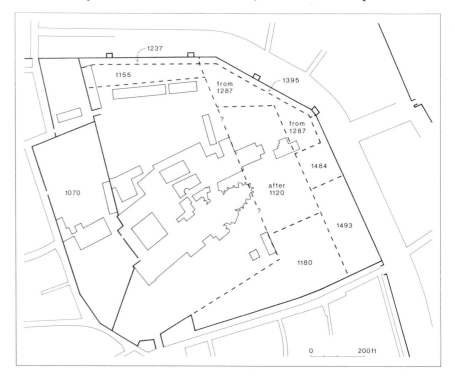

construction and an insight into the role and practices of the master masons. Canterbury is doubly fortunate in this, for not only have we the writings of Gervase, but also the building, hardly touched since its completion in 1184.

The last great building campaign at Canterbury is associated with the Perpendicular style – the final major addition to the fabric, the majestic central tower, was completed only *c.* 1504 and it is very easy to forget that few of the pilgrims who flocked to the city ever saw the cathedral as we do today. Like so many of England's churches, the present aspect of Canterbury results from the achievements of the last of the mediaeval builders – the building has come down to us virtually frozen since the days of Henry VII. The evolutionary process by which it took on its familiar form was ended abruptly by the dissolution of the monastery in 1540. Had the Reformation come to England just a few decades later, had the English permanently reverted to catholicism after 1553, the outcome might have been very different. We might have seen a late sixteenth century replacement of the famous choir or a Baroque redressing of the nave! Paradoxically the tragedy that befell the ecclesiastical architecture of England in the 1530s has provided us with one of the greatest collections of mediaeval churches in Europe, one almost entirely untainted by the influence of later styles.

The events that put an end to major church-building in England also robbed Canterbury of many of its former functions – most especially that

**3** The cathedral from the north-west, *c.* 1955

of a monastic cathedral. The combination of monastery and cathedral church was something alien to most of Christian Europe. In France, for example, the secular and regular clergy were kept separate, and bishops, as administrators of the secular church, were established in collegiate cathedrals staffed by vicars or canons who sometimes lived in common. The monasteries, ruled by abbots or priors, belonged to national or international groups, some owing allegiance to a mother church in another place if not another country. All owed allegiance to Rome and to their various temporal rulers, but the conflicting roles of bishops and monks kept the two arms of the church at some distance. Collegiate cathedrals on a continental model existed in England, e.g. Lincoln, London and Salisbury, but there were, in addition, a number of combined houses – the monastic cathedrals. Canterbury was the most influential and famous, while others existed at Bath, Durham, Ely, Norwich, Rochester, Winchester and Worcester. The bishops of these cathedrals acted as the nominal abbot of the priory, the monks performing the ceremonies and rituals of the Benedictine Order in the cathedral churches. The archbishop of Canterbury was not only abbot and bishop, but also Primate and first subject of the realm, and quite often he was appointed Lord Chancellor of the Kingdom, the most important civil post in the royal administration. With such wide-ranging and demanding duties, the archbishops discharged most of their monastic responsibilities to the prior, who accordingly rose in status and power. Throughout the Anglo-Saxon period the archbishops had lived in common with the monks, but this close relationship came to an end with the appointment of the first post-Conquest archbishop, Lanfranc, who built a separate palace for the Primate. This division between the secular and regular aspects of the cathedral became increasingly keen as the Middle Ages progressed.

The monks of Canterbury Cathedral had the technical right to elect the archbishop as they would an abbot. This right caused many disputes between the Crown and the priory, sometimes ending with open hostilities. The priors, too, increased their powers by papal grants that eventually raised them to episcopal rank. Their position even entitled them to carry out archiepiscopal visitations during the vacancy of the see. The rising authority of the priors of Christ Church inevitably led to conflicts between them and the archbishop and king, and between the priory and the rest of the church in England. But for most of the Middle Ages, a *modus vivendi* existed within the precincts whereby the prior attended to the business and economy of the cathedral while the archbishop tended his see and his other more lofty offices.

Of the sixty-eight archbishops of the mediaeval cathedral to 1558, seventeen are honoured as saints by the Catholic Church. Four archbishops met violent deaths and nine were created cardinals. Many were appointed papal legate, and from the post-Conquest period they had

**4** The cathedral from the south-west, *c.* 1950

the sole right of coronation. As the English empire in France expanded and contracted, so did the territorial primacy of Canterbury. The first five archbishops were Italian, being drawn from the band of missionaries led by St Augustine. St Theodore in the seventh century was a Byzantine Greek, while Robert of Jumièges in the 1050s was Norman French. The two archbishops following the Conquest were both Italian – Lanfranc and St Anselm – and they were succeeded by a series of Norman French prelates until 1162. St Thomas was native born but of Norman immigrant parentage, and after his murder, the archbishops were English, save for Boniface of Savoy (1245–70).

While little is known of the majority of Anglo-Saxon archbishops, the lives of the post-Conquest prelates are recorded relatively well. The archbishops professing the Benedictine Rule ended with the death of Richard of Dover in 1184. St Edmund adopted the Cistercian habit during his final exile in Pontigny, while members of the new mendicant orders occupied the throne of St Augustine between 1272 and 1292. The archbishops from the late fourteenth century to the Reformation period

**5** The cathedral from the
north-east

tended to be drawn from the members of the leading noble families:
Courtenay, Arundel, Stafford, Bourchier and Pole. Some, such as
Chichele and Warham, were men of great learning and others were astute
and successful politicians – one of the most notable being Cardinal
Morton.

The priors ruled the monastery of Christ Church between *c.* 1080 and
1540, replacing the deans of the Anglo-Saxon period. The first, Henry,
was Italian, who was succeeded by Ernulph from Beauvais and then
Conrad, who was probably German. From the late twelfth century, the
priors were of English extraction and, from 1222, at least nineteen of the

**6** (*opposite*) The cathedral
from the cloister

twenty-four priors were drawn from local families in Kent and East Sussex. After the Norman Conquest, the priorate of Canterbury became a stepping-stone to an important abbacy or bishopric – Prior Ernulph became abbot of Peterborough and then bishop of Rochester – but as the power and prestige of the priors grew, they were tempted to stay for life, unless they were expelled like Thomas of Ringmere.[4] Two priors stand out from all the others – Henry of Eastry, 1284–1331, and Thomas of Chillenden, 1391–1411. Both men dominated the precincts, and left their distinct impression upon the architecture of the cathedral and its monastic buildings.

The archbishops and priors had considerable financial resources from estates and properties and the many legal ecclesiastical fees due to them. Each laid out vast sums for the rebuilding of the cathedral, sometimes in unison and at other times not. The internal arrangement of the church was complicated by the dual role of the archbishop: as Primate he could occupy the throne of St Augustine that stood at the top of the presbytery stairs, while as abbot he was entitled to sit in the first stall: in his case a simple wooden seat on the south side of the choir. He had the right of entry into the cathedral, and by the sixteenth century the Palace was

4  Ringmere was forced to resign after quite groundless charges of corruption were made against him. See C. E. Woodruff and W. Danks, *Mems CC*, pp. 134–5.

7  (*below left*) The nave interior from the west
8  (*below right*) The crossing from the north choir aisle

connected directly to the old north-west tower of the church. The rights of the archbishop within the monastic curia were less generous. For centuries the only connection between the Palace and the monastic offices was a small door in the north-west angle of the cloister through which the archbishop could process into the church. About 1500, a new entrance was created between the nave and the cellarer's offices that provided direct access to the cloister from the new southern wing of the Palace. Few archbishops had the temerity to enter the Chapter House, which became increasingly the domain of the prior, and in the light of this unwritten law of entry it is not surprising that the archbishops paid little interest to the rebuilding schemes for the monastic buildings.

As the two administrations within the cathedral drew further apart, so too did their finances. By the end of the Middle Ages there was an absolute division between the archiepiscopal and prioral revenues, especially as the archbishop's administration gravitated towards his London residence at Lambeth.

The financing for the various building campaigns at Canterbury did not follow any clear pattern. When Lanfranc rebuilt the church after the Conquest, he clearly saw himself as both abbot and archbishop, whereas St Anselm was archbishop first, and thereafter he left the administration and rebuilding work to his successive priors. Anselm's grant of income towards the building of the new choir does suggest that the priory, not the archbishop, was funding that project. Gervase does not hint at who was paying for the reconstruction of the choir between 1174 and 1184, but the close ties that existed between the archbishop, Richard of Dover, and the Benedictine monks of Canterbury could indicate that money was forthcoming from both sources.

For the rest of the Middle Ages, architectural initiative was shared by archbishops and priors. Archbishop Sudbury began the rebuilding of the nave at his own expense, though the work was subsequently taken over by the priory with the occasional grant from the succeeding archbishops. In the fifteenth century, the central tower was rebuilt at the expense of Cardinal Morton, while the prior paid for some of the trimmings and additions. It is important to stress that archbishops, priors and monks paid for these various building projects. There was a popular myth in the nineteenth century to the effect that monks and common people actually laboured on the fabric, all working gratis for the greater glory of God. Modern research has revealed that the building trade operated much as at present, with professional architects or master masons, and a strict hierarchy of craftsmen and workers right down to the meanest of tasks.[5] All were paid fixed rates according to their skills, though the leading master masons could command fees higher than normal. A great cathedral like Canterbury would usually employ a resident master mason on a life-term. However, there were occasions when, if no work was in progress or projected, the master might leave and not be replaced for

5 See, for example, D. Knoop and G. Jones, *The Mediaeval Mason*, Manchester University Press, 1949, and L. Salzman, *Building in England down to 1540*, Oxford University Press, 1952.

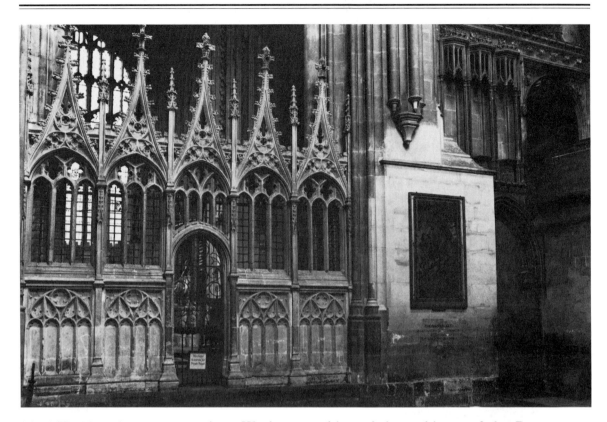

9 (*above*) The Martyrdom interior from the west
10 (*opposite*) The choir and Trinity Chapel interior from the west

some time. We know nothing of the architects of the Romanesque cathedral; indeed the incredibly full picture provided by Gervase of William of Sens and William the Englishman is the first we know of any of the cathedral masters. Odd names occur throughout the thirteenth century with little to justify any assumption that they can be associated with the designers of surviving fabric. From the early fourteenth century, a series of masters can be identified, together with something of their work and terms of employment. Two of the three masters of the Kent School at work in Westminster, Michael and Thomas, were called 'of Canterbury' and there is some reason to believe that they were successive masters at Canterbury cathedral. The mid-century saw John Box at work on the prior's buildings, and his successor, Thomas of Hoo, worked on the cathedral until at least 1398.

In the reign of Richard II, royal masters became associated with Canterbury Cathedral – Henry Yevele, Stephen Lote and Thomas Mapilton – the latter being first employed by the archbishop and only later appointed master mason by the prior. A similar situation existed for his successor, Richard Beke, who worked on the cathedral for three years before a contract for life was offered in 1434–5. The deed of employment has survived, and is one of the most detailed of the Middle Ages.[6] The only important master to have definite connections with the cathedral in the

6 Salzman, op. cit., pp. 590–1.

late Middle Ages was John Wastell, whose relationship with Canterbury was typical of that enjoyed by the leading architects of his day. He was non-resident and appeared at the cathedral only when necessary. Wastell's practice was centred in Bury St Edmunds, while most of his building work was in Cambridge. By the late fifteenth century we can see the life of the modern architect in embryo.

A list of the master masons of Canterbury Cathedral and some reference to their work can be found at the end of this book.

As the cathedral grew in size, more and more land was acquired for its expansion and for that of the monastery. The only fixed boundary to survive from the pre-Conquest period is probably the division between the monastic curia and the Archbishop's Palace, a demarcation made soon after 1070. Expansion to the north began in the 1150s, while the southern precincts were extended after a fire in a house in Burgate led to the burning of St Anselm's choir in 1174. The monks adopted a policy in the twelfth century to clear the city buildings from those parishes between the northern and eastern walls of the Curia and the near-by city walls. This policy caused great friction with the citizens of Canterbury and the monks had to wait until the 1490s to achieve the present extent of the precincts. They did not survive long to enjoy their acquisitions.

# CHAPTER 1

# THE ANGLO-SAXON CATHEDRAL,

## 597-1070

The conversion of Ethelbert king of Kent by St Augustine in 597 is one of the best known incidents in the history of England. The pope, St Gregory, had instructed Augustine to evangelize the English and to establish metropolitan sees in both London and York – the two principal cities of the former Roman province. But St Gregory's notions of Britannia were quite out of touch with the realities of Anglo-Saxon England in the late sixth century, and Augustine wisely capitalized on his initial and unexpected success at Canterbury by establishing his principal see and mission base in the royal Kentish city. The kingdom of Kent was at its most powerful, and Ethelbert overlord of much of southern England. Augustine dedicated his cathedral to the Blessed Saviour. According to legend, the building was Ethelbert's palace, which Augustine suspected had once been a Romano-British church. He also built a new foundation outside the city walls dedicated to SS Peter and Paul. In true Roman tradition, the cathedral within the city was for the living, while the church outside was for the dead. It is difficult to visualize the Canterbury of 597. It had been a sizeable town by Romano-British standards, with lavish public buildings set in spacious 'garden city' surroundings. Even in Augustine's day, the city must have been dominated by the mass of the Roman theatre, one of the largest in that part of the empire. This was the scale of Durovernum Cantiacorum and it cannot be doubted that many Roman buildings suitable for St Augustine's purpose survived into the sixth century. Bede tells us that Augustine 'recovered' an old Roman church, built, 'as he had learnt', when Romans were still in the land.[1] Such a find must have had immediate benefits for the early missionaries and, whether or not they were correct in the belief that they had repossessed an ancient Christian church, it must have been of enormous significance to them and may well have been at the heart of Augustine's decision to establish his metropolitan see at Canterbury. The antiquity of the cathedral fabric was never allowed to be questioned, and it was a powerful argument for the various archbishops who fought to preserve the status of their see. Even in the twelfth century, Eadmer the chronicler could say in all faith that the church he had known as a boy was 'that very church which had been built by [the] Romans'.[2]

1 Bede, *Historia Ecclesiastica Gentis Anglorum, Venerabilis Baedae Opera Historica*, ed. C. Plummer, p. 70. Bede places the event between letters of AD 601 and 603. It is not clear whether this defines the date of the consecration or if Bede is simply picking up the narrative where he left off.

2 *De Reliquiis S. Audoeni*; see Willis, *Arch. Hist.*, pp. 9–10.

3 A. Haddan and W. Stubbs, *Councils and Ecclesiastical Documents relating to Great Britain and Ireland*, Oxford University Press, 1871, vol. 3, p. 575.
4 *Anglo-Saxon Chronicle*, ed. B. Thorpe, Rolls Series, 1861, p. 108.

St Augustine intended that both foundations should be monastic, and the Anglo-Saxon Chronicle states that the cathedral was always inhabited by monks. In 813 the cathedral was indeed described as a monastery, but it would appear that as early as *c.* 660 the inmates were a mixture of monks and secular clerks.[3] A great plague is said to have killed all but five of the clergy in 833, forcing Archbishop Ceolnoth to make up the numbers from secular priests,[4] and this arrangement continued late into the tenth century until Archbishop Aelfric, 995–1005, obtained papal permission to reform the house and to substitute monks for the priests. The size of the community that served the cathedral throughout the Anglo-Saxon period is difficult to estimate, though Lanfranc's intention to treble the number to 150 suggests that by the mid-eleventh century there were some 50 monks in the house. Augustine had arrived with some 40 monks, which he may have divided between his two foundations.

Augustine died in 604–5, and the next four archbishops were drawn from those Italian monks who had accompanied him on his mission. King Ethelbert died in 616 and, with his death, the power of Kent declined. He was buried in the abbey of SS Peter and Paul, which was to become the sepulchral church of the Hengistian dynasty. After various vicissitudes, Christianity gained a firm hold in Kent and in the reign of Eorcemberht, 640–64, strict observance of the new religion was enforced and the worship of idols abolished throughout the realm. In 655, Deusdedit became the first English Archbishop of Canterbury.

The turbulence of that period before the reign of King Offa of Mercia appears hardly to have affected Canterbury, which had become a centre of learning and culture, particularly under St Theodore of Tarsus, archbishop 668–90, and St Adrian, the African abbot of SS Peter and Paul, 669–708. Offa, jealous of the power and prestige of the archbishops of Canterbury, attempted to establish a rival metropolitan see within his own Mercian territory. In 785 he persuaded the pope to grant archiepiscopal status to Lichfield and to deprive Canterbury of the sees of Hereford, Leicester, Worcester, Elmham and Dunwich – a move aimed specifically at lessening the power of the Kentish archbishop. The threat was short-lived and by 801 both the king and the only archbishop of Lichfield, Hygeberht, were dead. Cenwulf, the eventual successor to Offa, brought Kent firmly into the Mercian confederation and with it the see of Canterbury. Later, with the collapse of Mercian power, Kent came first under the domination and then under the protection of Wessex. During the tenth century Canterbury became one of the principal centres of ecclesiastical reform, especially under St Dunstan, archbishop 961–88. The period witnessed the growth of a major school of manuscript illumination which continued to flourish for much of the Middle Ages. Dunstan's burial 'in the midst of the choir'[5] brought more fame and glory to the cathedral, and the cult of his relics spread quickly among the English. The famed wealth of the cathedral also brought danger,

5 From Eadmer; see Willis, *Arch. Hist.*, p. 6n.

particularly as Canterbury lay close to the sea and exposed to the havoc brought by Danish raiders. The worst attack came in 1011–12, when the city was burnt, the cathedral ransacked and fired and Archbishop Alphege was dragged away to his eventual murder at Greenwich. Like the church, Canterbury drew strength from the blood of its martyrs, and in recompense for the crimes of his people, King Canute heaped further patronage and prestige on the cathedral. He completely restored the buildings and escorted the body of the martyr Alphege from London to Canterbury. Upon the saint's coffin, the Danish king laid the Crown of England.

The last great event in the Anglo-Saxon cathedral was the coronation of St Edward the Confessor by St Eadsige in 1043.[6] After Edward's death and the fall of Harold at Hastings in 1066, Canterbury lay at the mercy of William the Conqueror, and the Anglo-Saxon era was at an end.

Canterbury Cathedral was mysteriously burned in the following year. Whatever caused the fire, it marked the end of nearly five centuries of tradition. The ancient church was more than just a symbol of the 'old days' before the Conquest – it was the church of St Augustine and it linked Anglo-Saxon Christianity with the days of the Roman believers. It also contained the remains and relics of great saints – Alphege, Oda, Wilfrid, Audouen (Ouen), Bartholomew and, above all, Dunstan. The venerable cathedral was valued and loved for its very antiquity, and the aura of sanctity that surrounded its fabric must have acted as a considerable constraint on the development of its architecture.

It is remarkable that any building that disappeared without a trace over 900 years ago should still be an object of interest and speculation. That this is so of the Anglo-Saxon cathedral at Canterbury is due to its historic significance and to the writings of Eadmer, monk of Christ Church and biographer of St Anselm. Eadmer was an eye-witness to the fire of 1067 and he saw the demolition of the old church and the building of Lanfranc's new cathedral. The main purpose of Eadmer's description of the Anglo-Saxon cathedral was to detail the disposition of the various altars, shrines, tombs and relics. The architecture was also of considerable interest to him both for its antiquity and for its association with some of the leading figures of the English church. Eadmer had been to Rome, and commented that his own cathedral 'was duly arranged in some parts in imitation of the church of the blessed Prince of the Apostles Peter'. Eadmer's description of Canterbury Cathedral is as tantalizing as it is informative, for while there is sufficient information to establish the basic layout of the building, some of the most interesting areas are described only in vague or ambiguous terms. The interpretation of these areas is crucial not just for the plan but also for the date of the various parts of the cathedral. Despite these uncertainties, Eadmer's work remains one of the most important architectural texts of the period.

The following extracts from Eadmer translate only those sections relevant to the architecture of the cathedral:[7]

6 Edward had previously been crowned at Winchester.

7 A text, with interpolations from Gervase and Osbern, can be found in Willis, *Arch. Hist.*, pp. 9–14. The translation here is by H. M. Taylor, 'The Anglo-Saxon cathedral church at Canterbury', *Archaeol. J.*, 126, 1969, pp. 105–6. For Eadmer, see A. Wilmart, 'Opuscula: Edmeri Cantuariensis cantoris nova opuscula de sanctorum veneratione et obsecratione', *Revue des sciences religieuses*, 15, 1935, pp. 362–70.

This was that very church . . . which had been built by Romans, as Bede bears witness in his history, and which was duly arranged in some parts in imitation of the church of the blessed Prince of the Apostles, Peter . . . The Venerable Oda had translated the body of the blessed Wilfrid archbishop of York, from Ripon to Canterbury, and had worthily placed it in a more lofty receptacle . . . that is to say, in the great Altar which was constructed of rough stones and mortar, close to the wall at the eastern part of the presbytery. Afterwards another altar was placed at a convenient distance before the aforesaid altar, and dedicated in honour of our Lord Jesus Christ, at which the Divine mysteries were daily celebrated. In this altar the blessed Alphege had solemnly deposited the head of St. Swithin . . . To reach these altars, there was an ascent of several steps from the choir of the singers, because there was beneath them a crypt which the Romans call a confessionary. The crypt was fabricated in the likeness of the confessionary of St. Peter, the vault of which was raised so high, that the part above could only be reached by many steps. Within, the crypt had at the east end an altar, in which was enclosed the head of the blessed Furseus, as of old it was asserted. Moreover, the single passage . . . which ran westward from the curved part of the crypt, reached from thence up to the resting-place of the blessed Dunstan, which was separated from the crypt itself by a strong wall; for that holy father was interred before the aforesaid steps at a great depth in the ground, and at the head of the saint stood the matutinal altar. Thence the choir of singers was extended westward into the body . . . of the church, and shut out from the multitude by a proper enclosure.

In the next place, beyond the middle of the length of the body, there were two towers which projected beyond the aisles of the church. The south tower had an altar in the midst of it, dedicated in honour of the blessed Pope Gregory. At the side was the principal door of the church, which, as of old by the English, so even now is called the Suthdure . . . Opposite to this tower, and on the north, the other tower was built in honour of the blessed Martin, and had cloisters about it for the use of the monks . . .

The extremity of the church was adorned by the oratory of Mary, the blessed Mother of God; which oratory was so constructed, that access could only be had to it by steps. At its eastern part, there was an altar consecrated to the worship of that Lady . . . When the priest performed the Divine mysteries at this altar he had his face turned towards the east, towards the people who stood below. Behind him to the west, was the pontifical chair constructed with handsome workmanship, and of large stones and cement; and far removed from the Lord's table, being contiguous to the wall of the church which embraced the entire area of the building. And this was the plan of the church of Canterbury.

Further information regarding the history of the fabric can be gleaned from other works by Eadmer, particularly his lives of Archbishops:[8]

8  Willis, *Arch. Hist.*, pp. 2–9.

Cuthbert . . . amongst his other good works, constructed a church to the east of the great church, and almost touching it, which he solemnly consecrated in honour of St. John the Baptist.

In the days of Archbishop Oda . . . the roof of Christ Church had become rotten from excessive age, and rested throughout on half-shattered pieces: wherefore he set about to reconstruct it, and being also desirous of giving to the walls a more aspiring altitude, he directed his assembled workmen to remove altogether the disjointed structure above, and commanded them to supply the deficient height of the walls by raising them.

. . . the tomb of the blessed Oda . . . was constructed in the fashion of a pyramid, to the south of the Altar.

Archbishop Dunstan . . . was buried in the spot which he himself had chosen . . . the place, to wit, where Divine office was daily celebrated by the brethren, and which was before the steps that led up to the Altar of the Lord Christ. Here in the midst of the choir his body was deposited in a leaden coffin, deep in the ground, according to the ancient custom of the English, and the depth of the grave was made equal to the stature of an ordinary man. A tomb was afterwards constructed over him, in the form of a large and lofty pyramid, and having at the head of the saint the matutinal Altar.

It must be remarked . . . that the church itself at the time of the suffering of the blessed martyr Alphege, was neither consumed by fire, nor were its walls or roof destroyed.

After these things, and while misfortunes fell thick upon all parts of England, it happened that the city of Canterbury was set on fire . . . and that the rising flames caught the mother church thereof. How can I tell it? The whole was consumed, and nearly all the monastic offices that appertained to it, as well as the church of the blessed John the Baptist . . .

A number of facts stand out from Eadmer's writings: he firmly believed that the church he knew as a boy was the very same church that Augustine had recovered, and that it resembled in some way the basilica of St Peter in Rome. His knowledge of the layout and traditions of the Anglo-Saxon cathedral is too detailed for even the most precocious child of nine or ten – Eadmer's age when the church was burnt. The tone of his work implies years of research and gathering of information – indeed, he boasts that he talked to old monks whose memories stretched back to the days of Canute, who, in turn, had learnt the history of the cathedral from still older monks who could remember back to the reign of Edgar. Under these circumstances, it would seem unlikely that any major event concerning the fabric of the cathedral since *c.* 950 would have been overlooked, particularly if it had involved one of the greater archbishops or saints. On the other hand, literary evidence revealing earlier building operations may not have survived the fire of 1067 when many manuscripts and charters were lost, and it is notable that Eadmer has only two entries concerning the building between the time of Augustine and King Edgar's reign. Both date from the mid-eighth century and concern the church of St John the Baptist in which Cuthbert and his successor, Bregwin, were buried. The builder of that church, and the identity of the tombs therein, could have been known from architectural inscriptions. Eadmer's history of the fabric appears to rely on Bede for the earliest period, and then almost entirely on the stored memories of his fellow monks.

Willis was not the first to realize the importance of Eadmer's work, but he was able to interpret the text with the benefit of his background in architectural history. He reconstructed the cathedral as a basilica containing a choir enclosure in the Roman manner. Both the east and west ends were given apsidal plans, and half-way along the nave Willis proposed projecting towers. His idea of the crypt was arrived at without our modern knowledge of Old St Peter's, which Eadmer said it resembled 'in some part'. This model for the Anglo-Saxon cathedral remained unchallenged for over a century, though Baldwin Brown, G.G. Scott and W. St John Hope each added his own version of the crypt.[9] Scott's plan of the crypt was prophetic of the crypt of Old St Peter's in Rome, only recently discovered by excavation, while St John Hope added a great deal more of the plan of Old St Peter's to the cathedral at Canterbury, including an unbroken transept and an attached octagon at the east end.[10] All agreed that the church was basilican and that both ends were apsidal. While Eadmer is quite clear that the east end had an apse, the plan of the western oratory of the Virgin is less certain. But his statement that the archbishop's throne was built into the western wall of the church 'embracing the whole area' was taken as an indication of an apse of a standard Roman type, with an altar at the top of a flight of stairs up from the nave where the people stood to attend mass. This arrangement was seen as confirmation of Bede's story that Augustine had recovered a Roman church and that the building described by Eadmer was the very same church.

In recent years, the whole basis of the traditional plan has been challenged by different interpretations of Eadmer's text and on the assumption that nothing of the Roman structure survived to Eadmer's day.[11] A 'box' church is now proposed similar to Augustine's other Kentish churches, perhaps augmented at subsequent periods by north and south porticus chapels. Two of these may have been later extended as towers. The 'alas' referred to by Eadmer, usually translated as 'aisles', were, it is suggested, a series of connecting chapels which had grown up along the original box nave. The very notion of a Roman or later western apse is rejected in favour of either a western tower block or an internal gallery containing a more isolated oratory of the Virgin accessible only by a system of stairs. The apsidal east end is not challenged, though a date late in the tenth century is preferred with regard to the extensive building-works associated with such reformers as Ethelwold, Oswald and Dunstan. As an alternative to the ring crypt with an axial passage, a central chamber enclosed within a D-shaped ring crypt giving access to the tomb of St Dunstan has been proposed. A dedication recorded in 990, in the church of the Trinity, is cited as evidence of some rebuilding about the time of St Dunstan's death – a date preferred for the building of the east end described by Eadmer.

Thus the main areas of dissent are the plan and date of the crypt, and of the west end of the cathedral. With such fundamental differences of

9  For a summary of the various proposals, see H. M. Taylor, 'The Anglo-Saxon cathedral church at Canterbury', *Archaeol. J.*, 126, 1969, pp. 120–1.

10  Ibid.

11  R. Gem, 'The Anglo-Saxon cathedral church at Canterbury', *Archaeol. J.*, 127, 1970, pp. 196–201; D. Parsons, 'The pre-Conquest cathedral of Canterbury', *Arch. Cant.*, 84, 1969, p. 175.

11 Reconstruction of the Anglo-Saxon cathedral: A eastern Confessio with hall crypt surrounded by an annular crypt with access to St Dunstan's tomb; B eastern Confessio with annular crypt and axial passage to St Dunstan's tomb; C basilican church with eastern and western apse and projecting towers; D box church with eastern and western apse and towers above portacus chapels

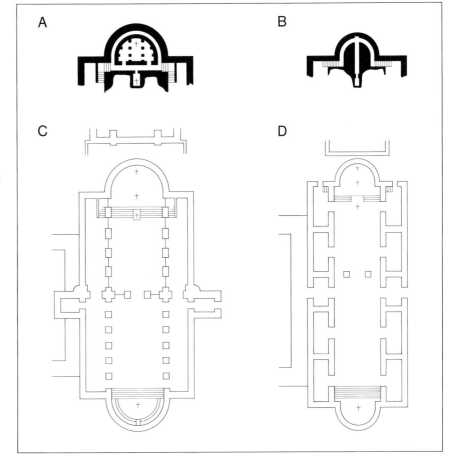

opinion, it is perhaps not out of place to propose another possible interpretation of the date of the Anglo-Saxon cathedral which would have some bearing on the likely form of its architecture (Figure 11). The east end of the cathedral was undoubtedly apsidal and there is no reason why this apse should not have formed part of the Roman building converted by Augustine as his cathedral. St Martin's church in Canterbury, a very early structure, may have had a small eastern apse, and all the churches built by Augustine had eastern rather than western apses. While it is tempting to see a western apse as the way in which Canterbury resembled Old St Peter's in Rome, it is not the parallel drawn by Eadmer – he links the eastern apse at Canterbury with the west end of St Peter's. The Anglo-Saxon cathedral of Augustine's time may have been a basilican building with a large apse springing directly from the east end; in this respect, the early church at Lydd in Kent may be of some significance, for it is regarded as seventh or eighth century. Excavations have revealed that this small church was truly basilican – that is, it had continuous aisles separated from the nave by an arcade resting on square piers.[12] A large

12 D. Jackson and E. Fletcher, 'Excavations at Lydd basilica', *J. Brit. Archaeol. Ass.*, 31, 1968, p. 19.

13  H. M. Taylor, 'Lyminge Church', *Archaeol. J.*, 126, 1969, pp. 257–60.

eastern apse opened directly from the nave, so resembling a Roman building that it has led some to speculate upon an even earlier date for the structure. The western end of the church contained a broad 'porch' flanked to the north and south by 'chambers'. The near-by church at Lyminge, built soon after 632, had both an eastern and a western apse,[13] and the proximity of both churches to Canterbury might suggest that they were modelled upon the cathedral of Augustine's day or shortly after.

If the eastern apse at Canterbury was indeed Roman, then a crypt or Confessio could have been inserted at any date, just as at Old St Peter's. A date of *c*. 988, after the death of St Dunstan, would appear to be too late, for it is highly unlikely that Eadmer would have overlooked an important and recent addition to the church, particularly if it was concerned with the tomb of Canterbury's most celebrated saint. Eadmer's information, albeit third-hand, went back to the 950s, and such an event would surely have been recalled. Certain phrases employed by Eadmer suggest that the crypt pre-dated the late tenth century, especially when he refers to the altar in the crypt which contained the head of St Furseus, 'as of old it was asserted', with its implication that the legend went back before the time of Eadmer's informants. For the crypt to post-date St Dunstan's death, the venerable altar it contained must have come from elsewhere, and the high Altar in the sanctuary above and the tomb of Oda which stood to the south must have been dismantled and re-erected at the new level.

Eadmer's description of the crypt is open to many interpretations and it is idle to speculate further. Both a ring crypt with an east-west passage or a chamber crypt enclosed by a ring crypt are acceptable within the known architecture of the Anglo-Saxon period and neither plan could determine the date of its construction.

The towers that stood half-way along the nave of the cathedral may have begun as chambers at the western end of the original building, similar to Lydd, and when the church was extended westwards they were simply left behind. A westward extension of the nave would not have been unique among the early churches of Kent; both SS Peter and Paul in Canterbury and the church at Reculver were considerably enlarged by the addition of porticus chapels and western porches in the seventh century, and at some stage a larger nave was added to St Martin's in Canterbury. About the year 620, a second church was added to the monastic complex at SS Peter and Paul and dedicated to the Virgin Mary, and it is possible that a Virgin oratory was added to the cathedral at the same time. The enlargement of the metropolitan cathedral would have required an increase of the internal space in order to house the expanding congregation, whereas such unity was not required in the purely monastic churches of SS Peter and Paul or Reculver, where the pressure was for increased tomb space and for additional cult altars which could be accommodated within additional chapels built on to the existing fabric.

Despite differences of function, the abbey at Canterbury provides evidence that the cult of the Virgin was sufficiently popular by *c.* 620 to warrant a separate oratory. The Virgin oratory in the cathedral should pre-date *c.* 750, when Cuthbert built the church of St John the Baptist to the east: while one of the functions of his church may have determined its dedication, the Virgin would have had a higher priority for an oratory than St John the Baptist, and it can be assumed that her position had been fully respected in Canterbury Cathedral some time before.

If the western oratory had indeed been added before Cuthbert's time, then an apsidal termination should perhaps be expected. An elaborate, and inevitably later, *westwerk* is certainly not ruled out by Eadmer's text but it would seem unlikely for a number of reasons. English *westwerks* appear to date from around the end of the Anglo-Saxon period, about the time of Dunstan or Oda. This would be reprehensibly tardy for the provision of the only Virgin chapel, and the memory of this important addition should have survived the half-century of Eadmer's informants. Furthermore, *westwerks* were usually raised above the main door to the church, but no such entrance existed at Canterbury where the principal entrance stood nearly half-way down the nave. The omission of a western entrance and the absence of any reference to an area beneath the oratory would suggest that the chapel stood upon a raised platform rather than high up within a tower or gallery. The Virgin oratory could function with the nave, for the people were able to stand below and attend the mass said at its altar. The position of the throne which was built into the 'embracing' wall of the western oratory is the most telling element for an apsidal reconstruction of the west end. The nave between the western and eastern sanctuaries is described by Eadmer as having 'alas', which could be aisles or wings. The latter would suggest a transept, though a true transept should not be expected at any of the proposed dates for the construction of the church. The only reference to them is in connection with the towers, which projected either above or beyond the 'alas' – though this hardly clarifies what they were. The towers must have projected beyond the alas, for it is needless to state that the towers project 'upwards' – that is the nature of towers. True aisles like those at Lydd could be proposed simply as a matter of scale, for Osbern, an early contemporary of Eadmer, states that the Anglo-Saxon cathedral was very large, 'for at that time there was no other church in these parts big enough to hold the vast numbers of people that did resort to it'.[14] While allowance must be made for the usual amount of mediaeval exaggeration, it was clear to Osbern that the cathedral was impressively large inside. The idea that the cathedral was a Roman building at the east end and perhaps early seventh century at the west would imply a junction between the two builds, and perhaps some unevenness between the two builds caused the fracturing of the high roof inherent in Oda's repairs.

Archaeological evidence concerning the Anglo-Saxon church has not

14 W. Somner, *Antiquities of Canterbury*, 1703, pt 2, p. 6. Osbern was senior to Eadmer and would have had a better knowledge of the Anglo-Saxon church.

15  D. Gardiner, *Canterbury*, London, 1923, p. 17.

16  Excavations by the Canterbury Archaeological Trust, 1978, unpublished.

17  An impression of the Anglo-Saxon seal is preserved in the Society of Antiquaries, London. For an illustration, see Woodruff and Danks, *Mems CC*, p. 16.

18  For an illustration, see ibid., p. 44.

yet answered any of the major architectural problems. Three finds stand out: the first occurred in 1737 when a deep grave was dug in the fourth bay from the west end of the present nave.[15] According to an eye-witness, a section of 'Roman pavement' and a number of 'Roman tiles' were discovered. More recently, a section of walling, either late Roman or early Saxon, was discovered near the angle of the Gothic nave and south-west transept arm. The footings apparently ran north–south, and the eastern side gave the impression of being an internal face. In 1979 a Roman mosaic pavement was discovered beneath the apse and south wall of St Anselm's chapel. One corner of a chequer pattern could be seen projecting from under the foundations on the exterior.[16] As the very position of the Anglo-Saxon cathedral is uncertain, the last two finds cannot be related to it at present.

One final piece of information is the depiction of a church on the earliest seal of Canterbury Cathedral which is attached to a document of *c.* 1102.[17] It shows a low building of basilican form, with an apse at either end, low aisles with small projecting porticus chapels at both ends and a central tower porch high enough to contain windows at an upper level while not breaking the overall height of the main roof.

It would be wrong to suggest that churches depicted on seals should be interpreted literally, but there is an uncanny resemblance between this church and the traditional reading of Eadmer's text – too close to be readily dismissed. The succeeding seal of Christ Church did attempt some outline of the major features of the mid-twelfth-century cathedral,[18] and there is a possibility that we have at Canterbury not only a rare written description of an Anglo-Saxon cathedral, but also, a complementary illustration.

# CHAPTER 2

# THE ROMANESQUE ARCHITECTURE OF CANTERBURY CATHEDRAL, 1070-1174

The Romanesque architecture of Canterbury Cathedral covers the century from 1070 and provides a microcosm of the English architecture of the period. The time was one of intense building activity at Canterbury, with the erection of Lanfranc's new cathedral from 1070, the building of St Anselm's choir from 1096 and the enlargement and modernization of the monastic buildings by Prior Wibert in the 1150s and 1160s. The plan and structure of the Romanesque cathedral are crucial to the understanding of the development of Canterbury Cathedral throughout the Middle Ages, but as it is often difficult to relate the sequence of building to the present fabric, an overall picture of the period will be given before describing the individual campaigns in detail.

While not the first Romanesque building in the country,[1] Lanfranc's cathedral gave great status to the style, and its combination with monastic reform made Canterbury a model for the new Norman hierarchy. While stressing the importance of Normandy to England's first post-Conquest cathedral, the strong stylistic influences from other sources should not be overlooked – influences that caused differences between the new church and its Norman predecessors. Canterbury was no 'mirror-image' of Lanfranc's Benedictine abbey of St Etienne at Caen, begun c. 1068. It developed the basic design, while parting company with St Etienne in several important ways. The differences between the two churches may provide a clue to the origin of the designer of the works at Canterbury, a man who freely employed the cushion capital, a form quite unknown in Normandy at such a date. The use of Caen stone also post-dates the very first phase at Canterbury, for the lowest work in the west wall of the crypt contains Quarr with associated rubble and Roman brick, but no Caen. While this stone was introduced rapidly to replace Quarr, the use of the latter and the re-use of native Roman materials including tufa suggests a man well versed in English building techniques.

Certainly, many English masons and sculptors received their basic Romanesque training at the Confessor's abbey at Westminster and one should not look automatically to Normandy for Lanfranc's architect. Several elements of the design of the first Romanesque church at Canterbury indicate a lack of awareness of the later stages of St Etienne,

1 It was preceded by Edward the Confessor's Abbey at Westminster, Harold's Waltham Abbey and Odo's church of St Martin le Grand at Dover.

or perhaps a deliberate disregard; this is most evident at the west end where the twin towers form a vigorous and articulated group around the nave west gable, quite different from the block-like *westwerk* at Caen. In decoration, Canterbury employs motifs of Imperial origin, most notably the spiralled columns in the dormitory.

The crypt of Lanfranc's cathedral provides one of the earliest links with Normandy, though not with St Etienne. In plan it resembled that in the cathedral of Bayeux and in the church of La Trinité at Caen,[2] with the addition of a central entrance at the west. If, however, the present west responds in Anselm's crypt were re-used from Lanfranc's time, then capitals of Imperial form were in use at Canterbury from the outset.

This is not to diminish the vital elements that did originate in Normandy; the triple storey elevation, the insistent articulation, the tribunes and their transept bridges, the arch mouldings and the monastic layout all speak a Norman language. How much of this – possibly all of it – had already entered England through Westminster is now impossible to discover.

Anselm's work must have succeeded Lanfranc's almost without a break. In style, there are indications that the same hand was at work, or at least the same workshop tradition. By the late 1090s, better techniques in stone-cutting and structure led to greater experimentation and a dramatic improvement in sculpture. Anselm's choir highlights the Anglo-Norman blend of the styles of Normandy and of the Empire. It was a giant Imperial church stretched and broken apart for a 'pilgrimage' apse and ambulatory plan. The curious mixture of the Germanic eastern towers and the Franco-Norman ambulatory was unique in its day, a combination that might reflect both the origins of the architect and the aspirations of the monks. Yet many individual features of the choir were shared by its English contemporaries. An arcade of cylindrical piers with tau cross capitals was employed in St John's Chapel in the Tower of London, and capitals similar to those in Anselm's crypt have survived from the Romanesque cathedral at Worcester. But other elements in the design at Canterbury are quite outside the mainstream of English building, particularly the form of the eastern transept tribune bridge that formed a direct continuation of the main arcade. The only known parallels would be Bayeux and Jumièges in Normandy, St Trond and Orp-le-Grand in the Empire,[3] and Pisa Cathedral.

At the close of the eleventh century, both the English and French strove for new constructional methods and designs. The rib vault experiments at Durham and Caen are exactly contemporary with St Anselm's choir, and while the removed nook-shafts in the aisles have led to speculation that Canterbury was also investigating the potential of rib vaulting, the choir was essentially an experiment in spatial and lighting effects. The aisle windows of St Anselm's choir were conspicuously bigger and more adventurous than others of their date and it was the

2  Bayeux, mid-eleventh century, the rest of the choir is unknown; see J. Vallery-Radot, *La Cathédrale de Bayeux*, Paris, 1958. The crypt at La Trinité evidently formed part of a rebuilding programme post-1080; see M. Bayle, *La Trinité de Caen*.

3  For Bayeux and Jumièges, see R. Liess, *Der Frühromanische Kirchenbau* (many references, especially Figs 1 and 12). For St Trond and Orp-le-Grand, see L. Genicot, *Les Eglises mosanes du XIe siècle*, pp. 27–32, 76–7.

intention from the outset to fill the church with the most lavish and expensive stained glass. Whatever St Anselm's work may have lacked in architectural innovation was more than compensated for by the quality and fame of its decoration. The painting, glass and sculpture of the choir became a yardstick for the twelfth century, indeed it was probably never equalled.

The decoration of the choir must have occupied many years and the debt was crippling. The finances of the priory remained at a low ebb for some time and it was only with the economic reforms of Prior Wibert that new building work could be contemplated. Wibert was truly the Augustus of Canterbury Cathedral. Hardly anything was left untouched in the monastery: he rebuilt and extended existing buildings and erected whole new ranges. His architecture is curiously conservative, yet it laid the groundwork for the arrival of William of Sens at the cathedral in 1174. Wibert's buildings contain two strains of architecture – a well-established style with its roots firmly planted in St Anselm's choir, and a new style with close connections with northern France. The threads are wound together in an arbitrary fashion, so that capitals resembling those on Anselm's crypt some half a century earlier can be found on the same building as advanced waterleaf designs related to proto-Gothic sculpture in France. Wibert's architect shows an especial grandeur that almost approaches a Roman tradition. His buildings are conscious of the spaces around and underneath them, and several are elevated upon open undercrofts. The Aula Nova presented a monumental facade to the curia – with a loggia basement and an elegant arcaded exterior stair. The basic design of the stair is deceptively simple for it is architecture in the round, the fretting of the side walls with attenuated arcading and the relative narrowness of the structure allowing full play of light and shade and complex cross-vistas to great effect. English Romanesque of the mid-twelfth century had become a sophisticated and versatile style, displaying an interest in spatial qualities paralleled in early French Gothic, and rejoicing in the elaboration that was to be the hallmark of English architecture for centuries.

The same architect designed the great barrel-vaulted gate, perhaps modelled on one of the Roman city gates then still in use. The most insistent motif on all Wibert's buildings is the triple arcade with a larger central arch, constantly recalling the Roman triumphant arch. Some of Wibert's works incorporate re-used Roman columns, probably robbed from ruins in the city.

During Wibert's priorate appeared the first signs at Canterbury of the new Gothic style of France. Proto-Gothic details appear to be in use in some of the earliest of his works, with waterleaf capitals in the Infirmary Chapel, dogtooth in the Aula Nova stairs and the Water Tower, leaf spur bases in the Aula Nova undercroft and deeply undercut chevron against roll mouldings in both the arcades of the Aula Nova stairs and the Water

Tower. The latter also demonstrates Wibert's use of rib vaults – the first tardy appearance of this motif in the cathedral.

The period also saw the introduction of many specific elements to be employed later by William of Sens in the new choir, including the use of polished dark marble shafts. These were much loved by Wibert's architect for cloister arcading, and angle nook-shafts and their popularity extended through much of east Kent. Dark Tournai shafts can be found at Rochester and St Augustine's, while several different colours were lavished on the Royal Abbey at Faversham in the mid-century. The great cloister at Canterbury, the principal achievement of Wibert's priorate, presented an extraordinary array of different coloured shafts and polished floor slabs, almost Italian or Byzantine in inspiration.

Whatever the background of William of Sens might have been, he appears to have fully assimilated the indigenous style of Canterbury, and the decoration of Wibert's buildings is an essential factor in a full understanding of the new Gothic choir that was to follow.

## Lanfranc's cathedral

The Norman Conquest of England in 1066 heralded a period of tense uncertainty for Canterbury Cathedral. The vast monastic estates that were the foundation of its wealth were left relatively intact and for some years the see continued to be held by the troublesome Archbishop Stigand. The city and its monastic houses seethed with anti-Norman feeling, and William the Conqueror had to tread very carefully in his moves against the archbishop and in his attempt to secure the loyalty of the cathedral community. It was only after a papal commission in 1070 that the king was able to deprive Stigand of his various sees[4] and put Lanfranc, the Italian-born Abbot of Caen, in his place. Lanfranc was already about sixty-five and did not welcome his departure from the Abbaye aux Hommes, or St Etienne, at Caen, which was still under construction as a model reformed Benedictine house. He regarded the English with some disdain, yet his astuteness and piety was to make him one of the greatest and best loved of archbishops. He wisely refrained from instituting immediate or sweeping reforms at Canterbury, nor did he flood the house with Norman monks. His one questionable decision on assuming this difficult position was to bring with him a fellow Italian, Henry, to be dean and later prior of Christ Church.

Several important developments that were to affect the status of the archbishop occurred at this time. The most notable was the Accord of Winchester of 1072 by which Lanfranc finally wrested the English supremacy from the claims of York – with the word 'Concedo', Thomas, archbishop of York, signed away the assumed title of the northern see. Lanfranc used all the influence and political manoeuvring at his disposal

4  Stigand held several ecclesiastical offices in plurality.

and resorted to some highly dubious activities to secure his success. Many of the Anglo-Saxon archives of Canterbury Cathedral had been consumed in the fire of 1067. Charters, rights and privileges that had been won or assumed over the centuries evaporated into dense smoke. The proof for all the jealous claims of the cathedral were lost in a few minutes, but Lanfranc showed no hesitation in rectifying matters. The lost documents were replaced by blatant forgeries; an action guaranteed to please the monks and the only course open to the archbishop anxious to assert his undoubted rights. William the Conqueror wanted Lanfranc to reform the English church and in turn, Lanfranc wanted written confirmation that no one else, especially his rival York, could stand in his way. The right of coronation was also secured for the archbishops of Canterbury or, in their absence, their chief suffragan the bishop of London. Lanfranc's single-minded character also left its mark on the city of Canterbury. He decided that the archbishop and Primate of all England should not have to live in common with the monks, something that doubtless pleased both factions so soon after the Conquest. Lanfranc determined to carve out a site for a new palace beginning at the north-west corner of his new church and running northwards alongside the old curia wall (see Fig. 2). This involved the destruction of twenty-eight buildings in the city and the shifting of an entire street line – and in a single stroke, a great slice of the city disappeared into the cathedral precincts for ever.[5] The creation of the palace enclosure divided the precincts between the monastic curia and the archbishop's domain and while each had their own separate access to the cloister and the church, no other connection existed between the two. This sharp physical partition emphasizes the increasing isolation and occasional antagonism that came to exist between successive archbishops and the priory.

The architectural history of the present cathedral may be said to begin on 29 August 1070, the day of Lanfranc's enthronement. Lanfranc had come to reform and refashion the English church and Canterbury was to be for England what Caen was for Normandy. His reformation was made easier by the mysterious fire that had gutted the old church in 1067. The enthronement ceremony took place in a temporary shed within the blackened ruins and Lanfranc immediately began the realization of his vision of a greatly enlarged and strictly reformed monastic church.

First, he carefully removed the bodies and relics of the Saxon saints from the old church, even though he doubted the sanctity of some and the very existence of others. According to Eadmer,[6] the bodies were safely stored in the west end of the ancient cathedral, after which the eastern apse was demolished to make way for the new church. As the exact position of Lanfranc's cathedral can be determined, Eadmer's information would suggest that the east end of the Anglo-Saxon church stood somewhere to the east of the present central tower. In time, the western end of the old church was also demolished to make way for the advancing

5  See Figure 2. The southern boundary is uncertain at this date.

6  For Eadmer, see Willis, *Arch. Hist.*, and R. Southern, *St Anselm and his Biographer*, Cambridge, 1963.

work, and once again the relics were moved, not into the new east end but into the monastic refectory which had escaped the fire of 1067. Evidently the Anglo-Saxon church was much shorter than the new work, for the old west end was destroyed before Lanfranc's choir could be brought into use. It was to be a 'few years' before the itinerant relics were brought back into Lanfranc's cathedral and even then, only the north transept of the church was available to the monks.

Lanfranc's cathedral was 'rendered almost perfect' within a space of seven years; the word 'almost' doubtless covering a great deal of unfinished work. When the cathedral was consecrated on 4 October 1077,[7] it probably consisted of only the choir, transept and two or three bays of the nave. The greater part of the nave, together with the central and western towers, probably occupied the builders for many more years.

Little remains of Lanfranc's cathedral, yet it has left an indelible mark upon the church. The ground plan was to determine the layout of the western part of the cathedral for the rest of the Middle Ages, but no sooner had the church been completed than the whole area east of the central tower was deemed to be too small and was demolished to make way for the great new choir of St Anselm. Thus Lanfranc's ritual choir was unknown

7   Woodruff and Danks, *Mems CC*, p. 32. There were consecrations in both the churches of Caen in the autumn of 1077. Is this just coincidence?

12   The Waterworks Drawing, MS.R.17.1, Trinity College, Cambridge

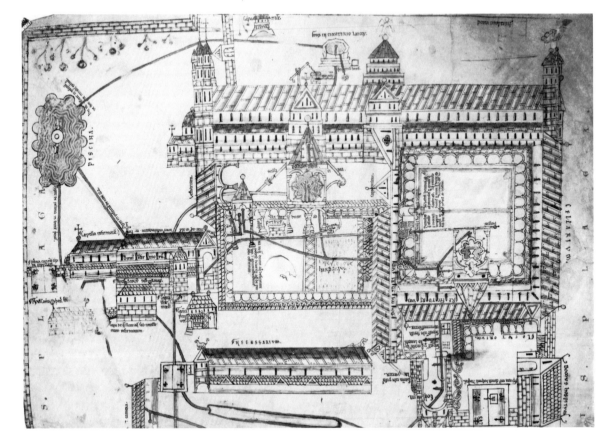

8  Gervase, chronicler of Christ Church, professed monk of Christ Church 1163. Variously published, see Willis, *Arch. Hist.*, pp. 37–41.
9  Gervase, *Of the Burning and Repair of the Church of Canterbury*, in Willis, *Arch Hist.*, pp. 32–62, also *Cant. Papers*, no. 3, ed. C. Cotton, Friends of Cant. Cathedral, 1930.

10  Extracts from Willis, *Arch. Hist.*, pp. 37–41 (modified).

to Gervase,[8] who sought in vain for a description of it, and only the nave and western crossing could be detailed in his preface to 'The Burning and Repair of Christ Church'.[9] Almost as a complement to this text, the Waterworks Drawing of *c*. 1160 provides an exterior view of the nave from the north (Figure 12), and the evidence from this can be added to Gervase to gain an overall view of the church. In the following extract from Gervase it is essential to remember that he refers to the various divisions of Lanfranc's church as they were in the second half of the twelfth century and not as in the 1070s.[10]

I will first describe the work of Lanfranc; beginning from the great tower, not because the whole of this church has been destroyed, but because part of it has been altered. The tower, raised upon great pillars, is placed in the midst of the church, like the centre in the middle of a circle. It had on its apex a gilt cherub. On the west of the tower is the nave or *aula* of the church, supported on either side by eight pillars. Two lofty towers with gilded pinnacles terminate this nave or *aula*. A gilded *corona* hangs in the midst of the church. A screen with a loft, separated in a manner the aforesaid tower from the nave, and had in the middle, and on the side towards the nave, the altar of the holy cross. Above the *pulpitum*, and placed across the church, was the beam, which sustained a great cross, two cherubim, and the images of St. Mary, and St. John the Apostle. In the north aisle was the oratory and altar of St. Mary . . . The aforesaid great tower had a cross from each side, to wit, a south cross and a north cross, each of which had in the midst a strong pillar; this sustained a vault which proceeded from the walls on three of its sides; the plan of the one cross is exactly the same as that of the other. The south cross was employed to carry the organ upon the vault. Above and beneath the vault was a *porticus* extended towards the east . . . The north cross similarly had two *porticus* . . .

Between this space [the entrance to the north aisle of the later crypt] and the aforesaid *porticus* [the north transept chapel] is a solid wall, before which that glorious companion of martyrs, and guest of the Apostles, the holy Thomas, fell . . . This place of martyrdom is opposite to the door of the cloister . . .

The pillar which stood in the midst of the cross, as well as the vault which rested on it, were taken down in process of time out of respect for the martyr, that the altar, elevated on the place of the martyrdom, might be seen from a greater distance.

The nave and transept of Lanfranc's church are pictured in the Waterworks Drawing. The artist shows an unusual interest in the depiction of architecture, and it is possible that the drawing is the work of the engineer responsible for the installation. Lanfranc's church is seen on the right with the great eastern extension built by St Anselm to the left. The twin western towers have tiers of windows and are topped by pyramidal spires and cockerel vanes. The artist is most careful to give visual explanation to the western gable of the nave that stands between the two towers. The nave is shown with far more windows than it can reasonably have possessed, but the general disposition of the exterior elevation is clear. The north aisle has small windows that peep over the roof of the cloister while the larger windows above denote the presence of an upper aisle or tribune. The tribune roofs slope up to the clerestory windows, and like all the roofs of the church they are covered with lead sheeting drawn in some detail. The north transept is seen gable end on, and has a stepped outline, similar to the central tower – resplendent with its pointed roof and gilded cherub from which it took its name, the Angel Steeple. The Waterworks Drawing is a product of its time and contains many conventions of contemporary illumination, but it is remarkable that wherever it is possible to compare features against the surviving fabric, the drawing is surprisingly accurate.

The interior of the nave was divided into nine bays – the most westerly being between the twin towers (Figure 13). In Lanfranc's day, the monastic choir stalls occupied the three eastern bays, while a fourth bay

**13** Lanfranc's cathedral: the plan. Extant areas shown in black

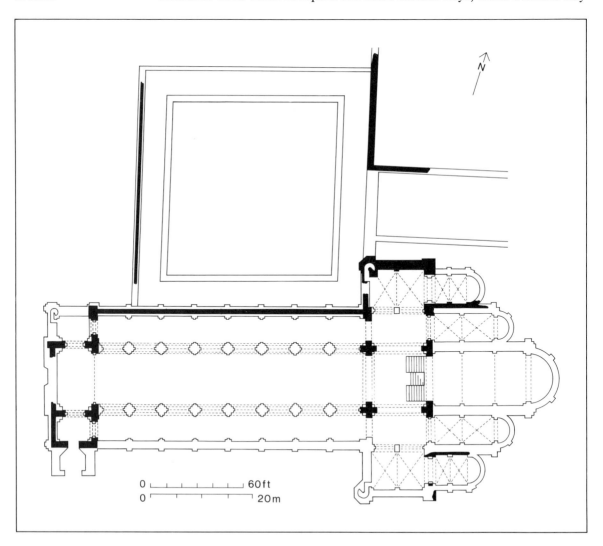

0 ⊢⊣⊣⊣⊣⊣⊣ 60ft
0 ⊢———————⊣ 20m

**14** The north entrance to the crypt with Lanfranc's north choir aisle respond

11 Canon Scot-Robinson, report, *Arch Cant.*, 18, 1893, p. 253; also Woodruff and Danks, *Mems CC*, p. 30.

12 The excavations were not properly recorded or published. See Woodruff and Danks, *Mems CC*, p. 30, and a letter to St John Hope in the Society of Antiquaries of 1895.

was blocked by a pulpitum screen. The altar of the Holy Cross stood to the west of the screen, while the north aisle flanking the monks stalls contained the main Lady Chapel. The unusual position of this chapel, blocking the access to the northern transept arm, may relate to the position of the former oratory of St Mary in the Anglo-Saxon cathedral. The crossing and transept provided a major break in the interior with four great arches supporting the tower and cross-vistas to the north and south. The matutinal, or daily, altar stood on a low platform immediately beneath the tower, with steps from the nave and transept, and two flights leading eastwards, to the ritual area of the high Altar, divided by a central stair leading down to the crypt.

Each arm of the transept contained a tribune bridge supported by a central column. The bridge filled only the projecting bay of each arm and did not cover the aisles. Two-storey chapels projected eastwards from each arm, so that the tribune bridges acted as *atria* for the chapels at the higher level. The northern chapels were dedicated to St Benedict (lower) and St Blaise (upper), while the southern were St Michael (lower) and All Saints (upper). It is at this point that the evidence of Gervase and the Waterworks Drawing ends. It will be seen that the ground plan indicated by Gervase corresponds to that now surviving in the western section of the church. Evidence for the elevational design must be sought within the fabric, and despite the Perpendicular character of the nave and transept, significant fragments of Lanfranc's cathedral remain hidden away behind work of later centuries. This surviving evidence is scattered throughout the church and some important sections are no longer visible. The following summary begins in the present crypt and proceeds westwards.

An apsidal foundation was found under the north aisle of the crypt in 1895. The excavation, in the fourth bay from the western end of the aisle, suggested that the choir aisles were apsidal inside and out.[11] Further sections of Lanfranc's north choir aisle remain at the present entrance to the crypt from the north-west transept. The great pier at which St Thomas fell was preserved throughout the Middle Ages by the erection of the Altar of the Sword's Point against its western face. Thus the pier became trapped amid the later alterations of the immediate surroundings. The base and shaft at the western end of the crypt entrance are bonded into and are structurally part of this great pier, and thus mark the beginning of Lanfranc's north choir aisle (Figure 14). This evidence fixes the floor-level of the aisle as that in the transept and nave, an important clue in any reconstruction of the lost east end. Further excavation in the crypt revealed a rather shapeless termination for the choir proper,[12] which was interpreted at the time as an apse – indeed, any other plan would be unlikely at this date, given that the aisles were also apsidal. The sanctuary was raised upon a crypt, the ghost of which can still be seen against the western wall of the present crypt (Figure 15). St Anselm's smoother and more refined stonework can be seen resting on the haunches of three

arches which descended to rectangular piers. The aisles were slightly narrower than at present and the walling is a mixture of rubble and coarse ashlar. There is evidence of a narrow western entrance to the crypt from the crossing above, with the scar of one step remaining beneath the present crypt floor.[13] Small sections of the north and south walls of the early crypt also survive running a few feet east from the terminal wall – their sharp vertical junctions with Anselm's later work being particularly conspicuous. These joints may mark the western jambs of doorways which once led up to the choir aisles. The narrow crypt underlying only the ritual sanctuary of the choir recalls the crypt of Bayeux and of La Trinité at Caen. The apparent difference between the floor-levels of the sanctuary and the lateral aisles at Canterbury poses problems for the design of the choir elevation which can be discussed profitably only when the various heights within the rest of the cathedral have been established.

The northern arm of the transept is the best place to begin. Both the angles of this survive relatively intact, including a Romanesque stair-turret in the north-west corner with several blocked doors that relate to Lanfranc's church (Figure 16). The eleventh-century section of the turret rises to a height of 68 ft 2 in. – 2,078 cm – above the transept floor, at

which point there is an obvious junction with a later mediaeval extension.
The turret is lined with alternate layers of Caen stone and tufa, each
several feet high. The original stairs break off at a height of 65 ft 2 in. –
1,986 cm. Doors leave the stair at 26 ft 9 in. – 815 cm (east), 28 ft 2 in. –
858.5 cm (south) and 45 ft 8 in. – 1,392 cm (east). A fourth exit which
does not appear to be original leads to a passage over the western window
of the transept with a floor-level at 49 ft 10 in. – 1,519 cm.[14] A section of a
similar late mediaeval passage exists in the opposite wall of the north-west
transept, built over the present entrance to the north choir aisle. The floor-
level is approximately 48 ft – 1,463 cm – above the transept. The exterior
of the transept arm retains a considerable amount of Lanfranc's
stonework, which can be distinguished by the smallness of its square
blocks and their more advanced state of deterioration. A series of
horizontal string courses cut across the western face of the transept,
dividing it into four tiers. The string courses are all restored and some
may not relate to any particular height on Lanfranc's building. The
strings occur at 49 ft 6½ in. – 1,510 cm, 58 ft 5 in. – 1,780.5 cm – and 72 ft
10 in. – 2,220 cm. The present roof gutter height is approximately 82 ft
9in.–2,522cm–above the internal floor-level of the transept (Figure 17).[15]
On the far side of the transept away from the cloister, Lanfranc's
stonework rises to only 59 ft 2 in. – 1,803 cm, and the various string

courses on the north-east angle are difficult to equate with those on the cloister side.

The most notable feature of Lanfranc's church on the transept facade lies between the two lowest string courses on the western face. Tucked in against the projecting angle of the corner turret (see Fig. 16) are the remains of an arch springing out towards the nave – its present curvature being sharper than that indicated by Britton in 1821.[16]

The eastern wall of the north transept arm retains several sections from the double-storey chapel, which are now trapped within the fifteenth-century Lady Chapel. A half-shaft, now exposed in the southern wall of the chapel, may relate to the springing of a transverse arch higher up in the chapel roof. This arch fragment divides two sections of a barrel vault, indicating that the Romanesque chapel had a two-bay plan. Evidence at the eastern end of the vault fragment signifies the existence of a rubble semi-dome over an apse. The dimensions of the Romanesque chapel were 28 ft 9 in. – 867 cm – by 16 ft 4 in. – 498 cm – internally. The vault fragments retain traces of red ashlar painting on a white ground.

The southern arm of Lanfranc's transept has been substantially rebuilt and contains little evidence of the Romanesque church. The eastern chapel was rebuilt in the fifteenth century, though retaining its original two-storey form. The Romanesque stairs to the upper chapel still serve its replacement and it is possible to establish from them that the original upper floor-level was between 28 ft – 853 cm – and 28 ft 7 in. – 871 cm – above the transept floor. The west wall of the upper chapel also preserves a section of the Romanesque entrance arch which formerly led out on to the raised tribune bridge in the transept. The underside of the arch rises to a maximum height of 13 ft – 396 cm – above the chapel floor. Above the arch and within the thickness of the transept wall lies a fifteenth-century passage with a floor-level some 48 ft – 1,463 cm – from the transept floor. A similar passage at 51 ft 5 in. – 1,567 cm – exists within the western wall opposite, serving as access from the angle stair turret to the roof-space above the south aisle of the nave. One other fragment of Lanfranc's southern transept arm appears on the exterior at the south-east corner adjoining the transept chapel, where a series of rebated pilaster buttresses has become trapped amid the later rebuilding (see Fig. 134).

The Perpendicular crossing piers under the central tower are commonly believed to encase their Romanesque counterparts, though investigation of this theory has so far proved inconclusive. One cushion capital was found attached to a section of shafting some 45 ft – 1,372 cm – up on the transept side of the north-west pier. No further capitals were discovered when similar openings were cut in the other piers, and this one rather shapeless fragment poses more questions than it can usefully answer. Some sections of Lanfranc's crossing tower still survive above the piers and within the present roof of the nave. They reveal that the exterior angles were clasped by half-shafts, one of which can also be seen on the outside under the north-west corner of the present tower.

16  See Britton, *The History and Antiquities of . . . Canterbury*, Pl. IV. The distances between the various string courses on the transept exterior are not shown correctly.

**18** The north aisle of the nave: interior of the roof-space showing the angle of the Martyrdom and the north arcade wall of the nave, with a fragment of the clerestory retaining arcade from Lanfranc's cathedral

**19** The north aisle of the nave: interior of the roof-space showing the angle of the north-west tower and the north aisle wall of the nave

17 Buckler's drawings are in the Society of Antiquaries, London.
18 The tower is measured in Imperial lengths.

A short section of a stair turret can be traced in the north-east angle of the tower, indicating that access to the upper parts of the central tower was from the north choir aisle tribune. Stair turrets may have risen from both aisles of the choir, as at St Augustine's, Canterbury, and Norwich Cathedral, while only one stair continued up the belfry stage. The lower stair turrets were replaced by the existing straight stairs at the western ends of the aisles during the building of St Anselm's choir from 1096. The surviving fragment of the north-east angle stair at the base of the tower must have been subjected to extensive alterations in order to provide the relevant access-points for the elevated choir of St Anselm; later, William of Sens must have carried out another reconstruction of the stair to accommodate the increased height of the Gothic choir. The stair was finally abandoned and filled with rubble when the existing south-west angle stair was begun.

Further sections of Lanfranc's work can be seen within the roof-space of the present aisle vaults of the nave. At the eastern end of the north aisle and at the western end of the south aisle there are fragments of arches similar to that on the exterior of the north-west transept, and springing from the same height – approximately 54 ft 6 in. – 1,661 cm – above the nave floor (Figure 18). The fragments appear to be part of a series of over-arches that once ran the length of the nave and around the transept facades. They seem to relate to the bay divisions of the nave, with a span of about 19 ft – 579 cm, and a clear height of 64 ft – 1,951 cm – above the floor. The three arch fragments play a vital part in the reconstruction of Lanfranc's cathedral, though there are certain inconsistencies associated with them. The angle between the nave and the north-west tower is relatively intact. The tower survived until the nineteenth century, when the exterior sides were rebuilt leaving the greater part of the eastern wall trapped against the nave. The masonry under the present aisle roof is Lanfranc's, yet there is no indication of an arch springing eastwards along the nave arcade wall. This suggests that on the north side, the over-arches were discontinued somewhere along the length of the nave.

The western towers provide the final evidence for a reconstruction of Lanfranc's cathedral. The old north-west tower of the nave was drawn and measured in the nineteenth century by Buckler before its destruction,[17] and his observations are a valuable source of information (Figures 20 and 21). The towers were divided by a series of string courses, much like the transept facades.[18] They occur at 13 ft 9 in. – 419 cm; 30 ft 9 in. – 937 cm; 52 ft 11½ in. – 1,614 cm – and 73 ft 3½ in. – 2,234 cm. Internally, two possible floor-levels existed in the lower part of the tower, at 30 ft 9 in. – 937 cm – and 49 ft 6 in. – 1,509 cm. Considerable sections of the eastern walls of both Romanesque towers survive within the nave aisle roofs. Each contains an arch with cushion capitals and half-shafts. In the south tower, the arch is centrally placed, while that on the north is pushed up against the outer wall of the aisle (Figure 19). Both arches were approximately 7 ft 9 in. – 236 cm – wide, with a clear height of some

**20** (*above*) Lanfranc's cathedral: Buckler's drawing of the old north-west tower

**21** (*above right*) Lanfranc's cathedral: Buckler's cross-section through the old north-west tower

19 E. G. Carlson, 'Excavations at Saint-Etienne, Caen', *Gesta* (New York), 10, no. 1, 1971, p. 23.

15 ft 6 in. – 472 cm – above the present aisle vaults. Many of the prints and drawings of the old north-west tower speak of its sturdy character and austere lines, and some indicate a gradual reduction in bulk as the tower rose. This was achieved by means of set-offs at the various string-course levels with a consequent reduction in the wall thickness from the exterior.

Much of this evidence was not available to Willis in 1845. Yet, from his observations, he was able to propose that Lanfranc's cathedral at Canterbury was a replica of his church at Caen, now known as St Etienne. However, recent excavations of the east end of that church have added to the differences between the two which are worthy of closer examination before any comparisons can be made.[19] The choir of St

Etienne was demolished in the thirteenth century and has only been partially recovered. The side aisles terminated in parabolic apses on the interior, which were squared externally. The 1895 excavation at Canterbury revealed that the northern apse was semi-circular both inside and out. There is no suggestion that the choir at Caen was raised upon a crypt, whereas the remains at Canterbury indicate a crypt at least under the high Altar. The crypt at Canterbury would raise the sanctuary above the floor-level in the rest of the church which would, in turn, affect the elevational design, whereas at Caen the various levels in the nave could have continued into the choir without major alterations. The treatment of the towers at the western end of the two churches was also different in approach – at Caen the towers rise from a massive *westwerk*, whereas at Canterbury they were specifically twin corner towers with the gable-end of the nave placed in between. In this respect the west end of Lanfranc's cathedral bears a closer resemblance to Bayeux and to La Trinité at Caen. Any comparison between the east end of Canterbury and these two Norman churches is made difficult by a total lack of information regarding the plan or elevations of the choir at Bayeux, though the choir of La Trinité may well represent a close approximation of the interior of the first Romanesque choir at Canterbury. Lanfranc's cathedral should therefore be seen as an amalgam of several strands of contemporary Norman Romanesque and not as a mere reproduction of St Etienne exported across the Channel.

The Waterworks Drawing indicates that the nave at Canterbury had tribunes above the aisles, and their existence in the transept is confirmed by Gervase (see Fig. 12). It would be natural to assume that they also existed above the choir aisles, and perhaps contained chapels. There is still an indication of tribunes in the Romanesque choir at St Etienne, for the present Gothic choir has large tribunes matching those in the nave and transept. La Trinité does not now have tribunes but a blind triforium ranging between the nave arcade and clerestory. But while the nave elevation at Canterbury was probably like that of St Etienne, the ritual sanctuary may have been similar to La Trinité with its solid walls dividing it from the aisles. The only openings through the walls are the small side doors with steps down into the aisles, and the high clerestory windows. A similar elevational scheme in the choir at Canterbury would have had several advantages, for the intervention of the crypt under the high Altar would have raised the floor-level higher than at Caen, where the crypt compensates for the falling ground-level. The inevitable difference between the floor-levels of the sanctuary and its lateral aisles at Canterbury and the resulting disjunction of the proportions resulting from any continuation of the nave elevation east of the crossing could have been overcome by the employment of solid walls between the sanctuary and its aisles. This would not rule out the possibility of tribune openings looking down on to the altar below, though such an arrangement would

20  For example, Cerisy-le-Forêt in Normandy.

be difficult to parallel in England.[20] Such a reconstruction of the east end would have an added advantage in that the tribune openings of the nave could be continued east of the crossing without any diminution, which would not be possible with the equivalent arcade opening below.

The exact design of the elevation of the east end can only remain a subject for speculation, but the nave and transept are surer ground, for they retain considerable remains which allow accurate measurements and comparisons to be made. The most important evidence is within the stair turret of the north arm of the transept. The original door at 28 ft 2 in. – 858.5 cm – must represent an entrance on to the tribune bridge within the transept, and this level can be confirmed by the surviving floor of All Saints Chapel in the southern arm. The equivalent tribune height at St Etienne is 28 ft 4 in. – 863.5 cm. Within the old north-west tower on the west front of Lanfranc's church at Canterbury there appears to have been a floor-level at 30 ft 9 in. – 937 cm – which may reflect the tribune floor-level at the western end of the nave, or possibly there were three steps up from the tribune into the tower.

The blocked exits within the transept stair turret above 28 ft 2 in. – 858.5 cm – are less helpful. The passage through the western wall at 49 ft 10 in. – 1,519 cm – relates to a fifteenth-century re-ordering though there is always the possibility that it follows the line of a former Romanesque passage. The door at 45 ft 8 in. – 1,392 cm – (east) does appear to be original. No further doors survive within the stair turret, but at approximately 60 ft 8 in. – 1,849 cm – there is a Romanesque arch set within the stair vault which suggests a support for a top landing. The turret lining continues to be Lanfranc's for a further 8 ft – 244 cm, though the steps are cut off at 65 ft 2 in. – 1,986 cm. The absence of higher doors available for clerestory passages is puzzling, for they might have been expected between 50 ft – 1,524 cm – and 55 ft – 1,676 cm (see Fig. 16). The exterior walling of the transept at this height consists of sections of thick wall into which the Perpendicular clerestory windows have been set. But at the springing of the present clerestory arch moulds, the thick wall ends abruptly, to be replaced by a thin inner skin that leaves a few unsightly buttress tops. The thick wall sections may have formed part of Lanfranc's clerestory walling. The evidence of the surviving sections would point to a transept without clerestory passages.

The existence of passages in the nave is also uncertain. The Buckler drawing of the old north-west tower of the nave, with plans at various levels, gives no indication of any passage connecting the interior of the tower with a clerestory passage. The angle between the tower and the nave arcade wall survives within the north aisle roof of the present nave, but shows no evidence of any internal or external walkway, and on the basis of this one area it would appear that the nave, and perhaps the choir, of Lanfranc's cathedral did not have a passage at clerestory level. This would be a major departure from the nave elevation of St Etienne at

Caen, where a clerestory passage existed even before the construction of the present high vaults and would place Canterbury with an earlier group of churches in Normandy, such as Bernay and Jumièges.

The only indication for the position of the clerestory at Canterbury would appear to be the remains of over-arches now trapped beneath the present aisle roofs and left exposed on the north transept arm over the cloister. Their original height was around 64 ft – 1,951 cm – above the nave floor, and as no work from Lanfranc's church can be found above 68 ft 2 in. – 2,078 cm, it must be assumed that these arches framed the clerestory windows. As over-arches, they must have supported some superstructure and a corbel table for the high roof which could well bring the overall height up to the level of Lanfranc's work in the north transept stair turret (see Fig. 18). A top height of 68 ft 2 in. – 2,078 cm – for the nave walls of Canterbury Cathedral would compare with 68 ft 10 in. – 2,098 cm – at St Etienne at Caen. If the over-arches did indeed contain the clerestory windows, then the apertures could not have exceeded 64 ft – 1,951 cm – above the nave floor. This would suggest a sill height of between 51 ft – 1,554 cm – and 53 ft – 1,615 cm. It may be significant that a range of windows existed on the old north-west tower of the nave with a sill height of 52 ft 11½ in. – 1,614 cm – above nave floor-level.

From these various heights it is possible to propose a complete scheme for the interior of the nave of Lanfranc's cathedral: an arcade of 28 ft 2 in. – 858.5 cm, a tribune storey not exceeding 23 ft 10 in. – 726.5 cm – and a clerestory of approximately 17 ft – 518 cm (Figure 22). This would compare with 28 ft 4 in. – 863.5 cm, 24 ft – 732 cm – and 17 ft – 518 cm – at St

**22** (*below left*) Lanfranc's cathedral: reconstruction of the nave elevation. A exterior; B interior

**23** (*below right*) Comparative cross-sections through the nave: A as at present; B Lanfranc's nave

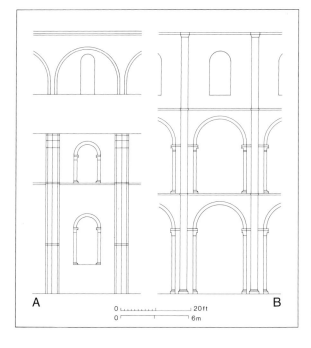

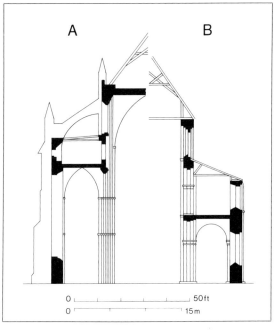

Etienne at Caen. On the exterior, the aisle and tribune wall could reach approximately 44 ft 6 in. – 1,356 cm – at Canterbury, compared with 46 ft 4 in. – 1,412 cm – at Caen, where the aisles may have been subject to later alterations associated with the subsequent construction of the high vaults. The nave of Lanfranc's church must have been austere and sombre (Figure 23). The intervention of the tribunes and of the cloister against the north aisle would have seriously reduced the illumination, with the south aisle brighter than the rest. The clerestory windows would have thrown some light on to a wooden roof that may have been exposed or boarded over. The screens that crossed the nave and enclosed the monastic stalls probably presented a substantial barrier such as can still be seen at Norwich. Only the south aisle of the nave was available for public access to the eastern part of the cathedral, because of the Lady Chapel in the north aisle.

The transept would have been relatively well lit, except the area beneath the north tribune bridge where St Thomas fell. This section would always have been gloomy, on account of the proximity of the Chapter House and the likely intrusion of a night stair. The upper part of the transept was lit by tiers of windows that must have streamed sunlight towards the crossing, which, like Caen, may have been augmented by a lantern. The arrangement of the stairs under the central tower was complicated by the blocking of the north aisle of the nave, so that the only access from the northern arm of the transept to the rest of the church was either across the matutinal altar platform or by traversing the crypt. The isolation of the northern arm was even more frustrating, as it contained the principal entrance to the church from the monastic buildings. However, the remoteness of this area had the advantage of keeping the general public well away from the cloister.

From the altar platform beneath the crossing, stairs led up to the high Altar sanctuary and down into the crypt. The raised choir contained not only the high Altar, the Trinity altar and the archbishop's throne, but also innumerable shrines, and given the increased size of the community and the retinue of the archbishop, it is little wonder that the cramped and congested east end of Lanfranc's cathedral was doomed to destruction within twenty years of its completion.

The new cathedral was only one of Lanfranc's projects within the precincts. He also provided for the needs of the monastic community with a new Chapter House, cloister, dormitory and all the other offices necessary for his new and enlarged monastery. Everything was thought of and strictly attended to, and his *Regularis Concordia*, intended primarily for the reform of the English monasteries, was doubtless written with Canterbury in the forefront of his mind.

Lanfranc's decision to increase the number of monks at Christ Church demanded a new and ordered monastic layout, and this he undertook with as much vigour and speed as he expended upon the church. The regular

**24** The monastic plan of Christ Church:
1 Campanile; 2 Christ Church gate; 3 buildings of the Archbishop's Palace; 4 Palace Court; 5 Palace boundary wall; 6 Almonry Chapel; 7 great gate; 8 Aula Nova; 9 Prior's Mansion; 10 Meister Homers; 11 infirmary; 12 vestiarium; 13 Prior's Chapel; 14 infirmary cloister; 15 Water Tower; 16 dormitory; 17 slype passage; 18 necessarium; 19 Prior's Lodgings; 20 Chillenden Chambers; 21 kitchen; 22 refectory; 23 cellarer's hall; 24 cellarer's office; 25 great cloister; 26 Chapter House

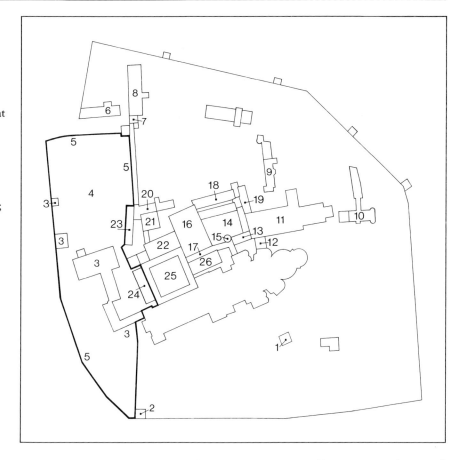

plan came from Cluny, with the most important offices arranged around three sides of a rectangular cloister built against the side of the nave (Figure 24). The placing of the claustral buildings on the north side reflected the Anglo-Saxon arrangement at Canterbury and was, in any case, dictated by the position of the surviving refectory, utilized by Lanfranc as his temporary cathedral, and by the lack of open space to the south of the church. Lanfranc's cloister was identical in size and disposition to the present one, with the Chapter House and great dormitory on the east, the cellarer's range along the west, and the refectory and kitchen buildings arranged around the north side. No doubt Lanfranc provided infirmary and reredorter offices and all the other buildings necessary for a monastic community, but they have left little trace. Most of his offices were rebuilt, and some re-sited, during the considerable enlargement of the monastery in the mid-twelfth century. The basic claustral layout survives from Lanfranc's day, and some idea of its appearance *c.* 1160 can be gained from the Waterworks Drawing. The principal buildings to survive from Lanfranc's priory lie along the east cloister walk, including the great dormitory and part of the Chapter House facade. Despite later reconstructions, the general dimensions of the Chapter House are unlikely to have changed save for the substitution of a square end in place of the Romanesque apse. The Chapter House facade above the cloister roof preserves the springing of an arcade, lower than that on the adjoining dormitory, suggesting the presence of a raised gallery leading from the first floor of the dormitory across the Chapter House and into the north transept of the church. The gallery arrangement would thus conform to the standard night stair of the period. The Waterworks Drawing shows the west gable of the Chapter House with a globe-like finial, and, between it and the church, a curious wedge-shaped structure that was interpreted by Willis as the extension of the night-stair gallery into the church. The only other section of Lanfranc's Chapter House to survive is the north wall, which is common to both the Chapter House and the adjoining dormitory. The night-stair gallery would have passed from the Chapter House over the original slype passage, which in Lanfranc's plan lay between the Chapter House and the transept. The old slype was abandoned long before the Waterworks Drawing was made, when the cathedral was extended eastward. Its position is now occupied by the Warham Chantry. The former slype led around the north transept and out into the open fields beyond, and despite the almost total enclosure of this exit, the eastern end of the old slype remained open until the recent erection of an electrical installation in its path.

The great dormitory is the most substantial and evocative building to survive from Lanfranc's day (Figure 25). Its mammoth size, 148 ft – 4,511 cm, by 78 ft – 2,377 cm, and the strength of its construction, stand witness to Lanfranc's determination to enlarge the community and to provide for it spacious and durable buildings. Sadly, many interesting architectural features were lost during the building of the Victorian library in 1867, including evidence indicating the layout of other buildings of the primitive plan.[21]

The dormitory was raised upon a vaulted undercroft, six bays wide and eleven long, originally supported by forty free-standing columnar piers and a central spine wall that ran the length of the building from north to south. The spine wall supported the main columnar arcade of the chamber above – remains of which were destroyed in 1867. The dormitory chamber was covered with two pitched roofs placed side by side and running north–south. Each had its own end gable – those on the south rising above the shared north wall of the Chapter House.

The divided crypts of the undercroft must have presented a splendid sight, each with three rows of column piers supporting the groin-vaulted ceiling. The piers at the southern end retain their elaborate decoration, with chevron, lozenge and spiral patterns. Many other piers in the undercroft appear to have been similarly decorated, though now weathered or rotted away.[22] The southern piers are preserved because the crypt was later subdivided when the new slype passage was formed. This

21  For the condition of the ruins in 1869, see Willis, *Hist. Mon.*

22  Not all the piers in the open ruins of the dormitory were found *in situ* – some had found their way into the adjoining archdeacon's garden and were replaced only in this century. This may account for the inconsistency of the surviving decoration.

25 The dormitory ruins from the south-west. Some of the columns were recovered from the archdeacon's garden after the Second World War

was achieved by the partitioning of the southernmost alley of the undercroft and by cutting an arch through the central spine wall. The partition immured one row of piers which remained concealed until recently. The date of this alteration remains uncertain, but it occurred before *c.* 1160, as the slype was already in this position when the Waterworks Drawing was made.

The piers supported keeled capitals like those in Gundulph's crypt at Rochester; indeed the surviving section of the dormitory may give some idea of the appearance of Lanfranc's crypt in the cathedral. The original vaults were built of light tufa, soft enough to preserve the marks of the boards used for the centring during construction. Three features of the cloister side of the dormitory are named on the Waterworks Drawing; two doors and an intervening window. The first door, replaced in the fifteenth century, served the new slype passage, though on the drawing it is labelled *hostiam locutorii* or parlour door. The parlour, as its name suggests, was a place of unrestricted verbal communication and was often a vaulted through-way of some importance within the monastic layout. To the north of the door, a double window opened under the cloister roof. It was fitted with elaborate ironwork which is depicted on the drawing in a contemporary style. In the next bay north was an iron-bound door, represented by the existing lavish doorway, though its architecture is somewhat later than Lanfranc. The intervening double window was blocked up in later centuries, and all trace of it finally disappeared in 1867.

On the far side of the dormitory, opposite the cloister wall, was a similar window opening, one bay from the southern end, and to the north was an exit door. Thus the iron-bound door in the cloister, an opening through the central spine wall and the door on the east wall were all in one line, suggesting a through passage. Fragments of walling recorded by Willis indicate that at least one other building ran eastwards from the dormitory. It was either a broad building with a southern aisle, or a narrower structure with an adjoining cloister walk to the south.[23] The axis established from the iron-bound door continued through the lost building and off to the east. A building in this position would usually be a reredorter, perhaps with an adjoining passage leading to the infirmary ranges. The iron-bound door in the cloister served another important function, for it stood at the base of the dormitory day stairs that were cut through the undercroft vault. The duplication of the doors from the undercroft into the cloister suggests that at least by 1160 they served different functions and were not necessarily alternative exists from the same internal space. It may be that the three southern alleys of the undercroft were originally used as the parlour with the iron-bound door providing the only access from the cloister. The parlour gave access to both the dormitory and the infirmary ranges, and was lit by large double windows – one on to the cloister, the other overlooking the herbarium. At some later date the southern end of the parlour was partitioned to form the new slype, with doors provided at either end. A new slype was needed to cope with the general enlargement and rearrangement of the monastic buildings in the twelfth century, during which the old 'infirmary passage' and its approach through the dormitory undercroft were abandoned. Henceforward, the major part of the parlour may have returned to the undercroft, while only the southern bay formed the new *locutorii*. Whatever happened, the changes were probably effected by about 1160.

The upper level of the great dormitory would have presented a vast hall divided by a row of cylindrical columns and round arches supporting the weight of the roof. Tall windows were provided wherever possible, certainly on the gable ends and over the cloister, and probably on all the other unobstructed walls. Four windows remain over the cloister incorporated into the modern library facade. They are grouped into a continuous arcade, with alternating windows and blind arches. Each is flanked by nook-shafts with cushion capitals which support arch mouldings of two orders. The arched-corbel table below the windows

23  See Willis, *Hist. Mon.*, Fig. 5.

probably represents the original line of the old cloister roof. The northern end of the dormitory was partly buried by gardens after the Reformation, but has been subsequently cleared. A large section of the vaulting survives, though in a deteriorating condition, together with evidence of the window splays at undercroft level. The north-east corner preserves two more windows of the upper level, much altered when subsequent structures were built against them.

Lanfranc died in 1089 and for the next four years William Rufus indulged himself on the fruits of the see. And then in a fit of panic for his life, he was persuaded to nominate the abbot of Bec to the throne of Canterbury. St Anselm had been drawn to Normandy from his home in Aosta by the reforming movement begun by William of Volpiano. Anselm, a disciple of Lanfranc and one of the greatest minds of his century, did not concern himself with the detailed daily life of the priory, which assured him of the approval of the monks. He had the wisdom to appoint Ernulph of Beauvais as prior and their partnership launched Canterbury upon a new Golden Age. The flowering of Canterbury under Anselm emphasized the inadequate size of the new cathedral for its burgeoning community, its growing number of relics and as a suitable setting for the primatic throne. Lanfranc had intended that the priory should house between 140 and 150 monks and by the beginning of Anselm's archiepiscopacy there were already over 100. Their numbers were rapidly outgrowing the space provided for their stalls in the eastern bays of the nave. The choir had to be enlarged.

The building of an entirely new choir was made possible by the sudden rise in the monastic income supplemented by the revenue granted by St Anselm from his estates at Petham.[24] By the time of Domesday, 1086, the annual monastic land revenue was about £730, but the explosion in land values late in the century took this income to around £1,000, and the ever-increasing wealth of the monastery found expression in the new and grandiose additions to the monks' church.

The builders of the new choir were probably transferred straight from another part of the priory where work on the completion of Lanfranc's buildings was still in hand. Indeed, the commencement of St Anselm's choir appears to have been regarded as a continuation of the giant building-era inaugurated by Lanfranc rather than as a new beginning.

## St Anselm's choir

St Anselm's choir was an extraordinary building. It was begun in 1096 and construction continued until about 1110, while the extensive decoration dragged on for many more years. In 1124, William of Malmesbury commented: 'Nothing like it could be seen in England, either for the brilliancy of its glass windows, the beauty of its marble

24 Eadmer, *Historia Novorum in Anglia*, p. 25. Variously called 'Petham' or 'Peckham'; Eadmer called it 'Petteham'. Petham, near Canterbury, is perhaps more likely.

25  William of Malmesbury, *De Gestis Pontificum*, p. 138.

pavements, or the many coloured pictures which led the wandering eye to the very summit of the ceiling.'[25] The enormous painting cycles and great glittering stained glass windows created a dazzling prospect and the remains of its extravagant mural and sculptural programme still convey the strength of its exotic, almost byzantine, fascination. The organization of the work was in the capable hands of Ernulph, a former pupil of Lanfranc when still abbot of Bec. Ernulph had joined his old master at Canterbury soon after 1070 and became a widely respected theologian and lawyer. But it is for his contribution to the fabric of his adopted cathedral that he is chiefly remembered. According to William of Malmesbury, the high roof of the new choir was already being painted when Ernulph became abbot of Peterborough in 1107. If true, then the major constructional work had been accomplished in the remarkably short space of twelve seasons. Matthew Paris refers to a consecration at Canterbury in 1114.[26]

26  Matthew Paris, *Historia Anglorum*, ed. F. Madden, Rolls Series, vol. 1, 1866, p. 219.

The new choir was the project of both St Anselm and Prior Ernulph, while the legendary decoration is usually accredited to Ernulph's successor, Prior Conrad – indeed, the whole work is sometimes known as 'Conrad's glorious choir'. While this is somewhat unfair to Ernulph and Anselm, it was undoubtedly Conrad who supervised the production of the famous glass windows and who was responsible for the general brilliance of the interior. Conrad was a man of expensive tastes. He spent voraciously and always bought the biggest, if not the best. The five great bells he purchased required sixty-three men to ring them, and one cope made for him out of gold thread was covered by 140 silver bells interspersed with precious stones. It is little wonder that by the time Conrad was translated to the abbacy of Benet Hulme in 1126, the monastic finances at Canterbury were sliding down a perilous slope.

The variety and profusion so evident in the enrichment of the new choir was merely a reflection of its singular architectural form. The interior was burnt in 1174 and the arcade walls and much of the ambulatory were torn down subsequently for the new Gothic choir. But from the remaining aisles, and the following account from Gervase, the whole layout and something of the elevational details can be determined (Figure 26).[27]

27  Extract based on Willis, *Arch. Hist.*, pp. 42–7, with amendments indicated*.

Let us begin therefore with the aforesaid great tower, which, as already explained, is placed in the middle of the whole church, and proceed eastwards. The eastern pillars of the tower projected as a solid wall, and were formed each into a semi-pillar. Hence in line and order were nine pillars on each side of the choir, nearly equidistant from each other; after these, six in a circuit were arranged circularly, that is, from the ninth on the south side to the ninth on the north, of which the two extreme ones were united by the same one arch. Upon these pillars, those in a straight line as well as those in the circuit, arches were turned from pillar to pillar; above these was a solid wall* broken by small dark openings*. This wall (on either side) bounding the choir met the corresponding

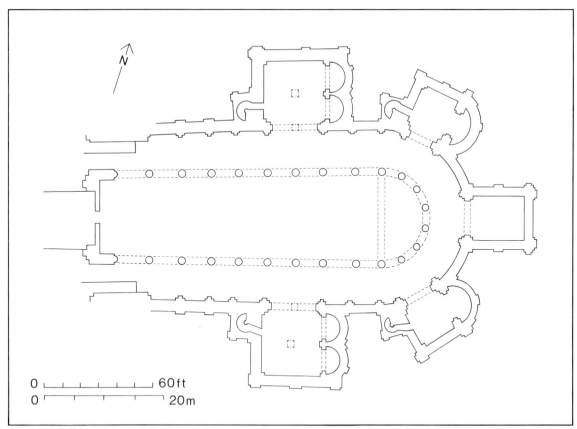

**26** St Anselm's choir: the plan

0 |___|___|___|___|___|___| 60 ft
0 |___|___|___|___| 20 m

one at the head of the church in that circuit of pillars. Above the wall was the passage which is called *triforium*, and the upper windows. This was the termination upwards of the interior wall. Upon it rested the roof and a ceiling decorated with excellent painting. At the bases of the pillars there was a wall built of marble slabs, which, surrounding the choir and presbytery, divided the body of the church from its sides, which are called aisles. This wall enclosed the choir of the monks, the presbytery, the great Altar dedicated in the name of Jesus Christ, the altar of St. Dunstan and the altar of St. Alphege, with their holy bodies.

Above the wall, in the circuit behind and opposite to the altar, was the patriarchical seat formed out of a single stone, in which, according to the custom of the Church on high festivals, the archbishops were wont to sit during the solemnities of the mass, until the consecration of the Sacrament; they then descended to the Altar of Christ by eight steps. . .

At the eastern horns of the altar were two wooden columns, gracefully ornamented with gold and silver, and sustaining a great beam, the extremities of which rested upon the capitals of two of the pillars. This beam, carried across the church above the altar, and decorated with gold, sustained the representation of the Lord, the images of St. Dunstan and of St. Alphege, together with seven chests covered with gold and silver, and filled with the relics of divers saints. Between the columns there stood a gilded cross, of which the cross itself was surrounded by a row of sixty transparent crystals. In the crypt, under this altar of Christ, stood the altar of the holy Virgin Mary, to whose honour the entire crypt was dedicated. Which crypt occupied precisely the same space and compass in length and breadth as did the choir above it. In the midst of the choir hung a gilded corona carrying four and twenty wax lights. This was the fashion of the choir and presbytery. But the exterior wall of the aisles was as follows. Beginning from the martyrium of St. Thomas, that is to say from the cross of Lanfranc, and proceeding towards the east as far as the upper cross, the wall contained three windows and no more. Opposite to the fifth pillar of the choir, the wall received an arch from it, and turning towards the north it formed the north cross. The breadth of this cross extended from the fifth to the seventh pillar. For the wall proceeding northwards from the seventh pillar as from the fifth, and making two apses, completed the cross of the eastern part. In its southern apse was the altar of St. Stephen, under which, in the crypt, was the altar of St. Nicholas. In the northern apse was the altar of St. Martin; and under it, in the crypt, the altar of St. Mary Magdalene. At the altar of St. Martin two archbishops were laid, to the right, Vulfred, to the left, Living; and similarly at the altar of St. Stephen, to the left Athelard, and to the right the venerable Cuthbert . . .

From this apse of St. Stephen, the aforesaid wall proceeding eastward had a window opposite to the side of the great Altar. Next after came a lofty tower, placed as it were outside the said wall, which was called the tower of St. Andrew because of the altar of St. Andrew which was therein, below which, in the crypt, was the altar of the Innocents. From this tower the wall proceeding, slightly curved and opening into a window, reached a chapel, which was extended towards the east at the front of the church, and opposite to the high seat of the archbishop. But as there are many things to be said of the interior of this chapel, it will be better to pause before its entrance until the south wall with its appurtenances had been traced up to the same point. This south wall, beginning from the apse of St. Michael in the cross of Lanfranc, reaches the upper cross after three windows. This cross at its eastern side, like the other, had two apses. In the southern apse was the altar of St. Gregory, where two holy archbishops were deposited; to the south St. Bregwin, to the north St. Plegemund; underneath in the crypt was the altar of St. Audoen, archbishop of Rouen. In the other apse was the altar of St. John the Evangelist, where two archbishops reposed; to the right Athelgar; to the left Aelfric; underneath in the crypt was the altar of St. Paulinus, where Archbishop Siric was buried. Before the altar of St. Audoen and nearly in the middle of the floor was the altar of St. Katherine. The wall proceeding from the above cross had a window opposite to the great Altar, and next a lofty tower, in which was the altar of the Apostles Peter and Paul.

But St. Anselm having been translated there and placed behind the altar gave his name to the altar and to the tower. From this tower the wall proceeding for a short space and opening into a window in its curve, arrived at the aforesaid chapel of the Holy Trinity, which was placed at the front of the church. An arch springing from each wall, that is from the south and from the north, completed the circuit.

The chapel placed outside the wall but joined to it and extended towards the east, had the altar of the Holy Trinity, where the blessed martyr Thomas celebrated his first mass on the day of his consecration. In this chapel, before and after his exile, he was wont to celebrate mass, to hear service, and frequently to pray. Behind the altar there lay two archbishops, to the right St. Oda; to the left St. Wilfrid, archbishop of York; to the south, close to the wall, the venerable Archbishop Lanfranc, and to the north Theobald. In the crypt beneath, there are two altars, on the south that of St. Augustine, the apostle of the English, and on the north that of St. John the Baptist. Close to the south wall Archbishop Ethelred was deposited, and Eadsin against the north wall.

In the middle of this chapel there stood a column which sustained arches and a vault, that came from all sides . . . [it was] the place where the blessed martyr Thomas was buried, on the day after his martyrdom . . .

And now the description, as concise as I could make it, of the church which we are going to pull down, has brought us to the tomb of the martyr, which was at the end of the church; let therefore the church and the description come to an end together; for although this description has already extended itself to a greater length than was proposed, yet many things have been carefully omitted for the sake of brevity. Who could write all the turnings, and windings, and appendages of such and so great a church as this was?

The new choir was virtually a cathedral in its own right, with nave, transept, choir, apse and ambulatory. It was as if the monks were abandoning Lanfranc's church to the laity, for the requirements of that most English of institutions, the monastic cathedral, must have engendered continual conflicts between two such opposing groups. Men brought up in the claustral quiet of Bec, such as Anselm and Ernulph, must have found the public clamour of Canterbury quite intolerable. The new choir was to be a fortress of spiritual calm deliberately remote from the distractions of the crowd. The physical divisions it imposed have survived to the present day and have become the most characteristic feature of Canterbury Cathedral. The principal means by which the new work was insulated from the old church was the extensive crypt. The whole enormous structure of the choir was raised upon an undercroft, so large as to become a lower church with at least eight altars. The plan of the crypt reflected that of the church above but with additional arcades under the central vessel to support the choir floor. The overall plan resembles that of a pilgrimage church, an apse and ambulatory with radial chapels, a short aisled chancel, a large transept with eastern chapels and an aisled nave. The main arcade continued without a break across the entrance to the transept, quite divorcing it from the choir proper. A matutinal or daily monastic altar may have stood under the eastern crossing, though Gervase does not refer to one. Beyond the high Altar stood the throne of St Augustine, which was raised on steps within the main apse. This, and the high Altar platform, represented the only major change in the floor-level throughout the choir, save for the central aisle between the monastic stalls where the floor was slightly lower as at present. The stalls occupied the five bays between the new eastern crossing and Lanfranc's old transept and central tower. It was here that the difference between the level of the new work and the old was most apparent, for the choir was raised over 10 ft – 310 cm – above the floor-level of the nave, which necessitated the provision of additional stairs from the old matutinal altar platform under the central tower up to a new pulpitum screen that formed the entrance to the new choir. The western entrance to the crypt was abandoned and an entirely new system adopted within the entrances to the choir aisles, with stairs down into the crypt and up into the choir – an arrangement that survives today on the southern side.

The plan of St Anselm's choir was unique amongst mediaeval churches. When linked with Lanfranc's nave, it formed a vast church with double transepts, and an apse and ambulatory layout of unusual form with the two radial chapels carried up as great towers that cant inwards towards the axial chapel. The overall appearance, to judge from the Waterworks Drawing, was one of a double-ended church with towers at either end. The plan was probably Imperial in origin, though it combines significant features that have their roots in the Anglo-Norman tradition. The creation of an upper church raised upon an enormous crypt was probably modelled on Speyer in the Rhineland, where the eleventh-century crypt lies under the east end and the eastern transept. The most telling features for an Imperial provenance are the eastern

**27** The crypt interior from the south-east

towers, standing as tall as the central and western towers. While they suggest the employment of such towers throughout the Empire, their siting on the angle of an ambulatory aisle is without precedent. The apse and ambulatory plan was comparatively rare in the Empire, though it was common in both Norman and post-Conquest English building. Its inclusion in St Anselm's choir illustrates the diversity of influence current at Canterbury, and the desire of the cathedral to combine the best of all architectural worlds. The result of this eclecticism was monumental and a little bizarre.

The crypt of St Anselm's choir has survived remarkably intact and provides the most evocative Romanesque interior in Canterbury, if not in England (Figures 27 and 28). The ranks of columns with their elaborately carved capitals and the complex cross-vistas with sudden bursts of daylight recall the mysterious interior of Cordoba or the cavernous cisterns of Constantinople. The central nave, 157 ft – 4,785 cm – long and 38 ft – 1,158 cm – wide, is subdivided by two rows of columns, and bounded on the north and south by an arcade of massive rectangular piers which are drawn together around the apsidal east end. Beyond the arcade is a wide ambulatory which provides a spacious processional path with

**28** The crypt plan

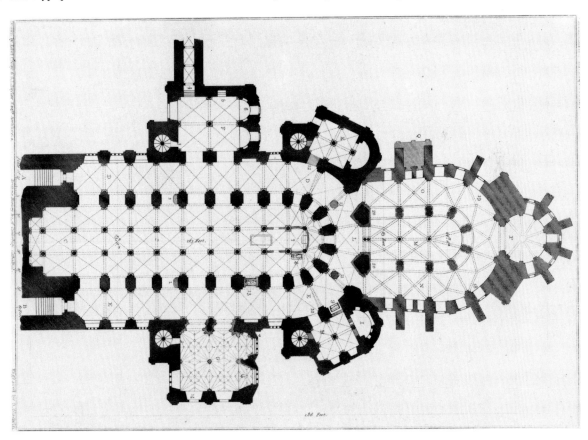

access to a series of separate chapels – two under each arm of the transept, and three radiating from the east end. The groined vaults of each chapel are supported by a single central column which divides the interior into four bays. The only major loss to St Anselm's crypt is the eastern axial chapel, originally dedicated to St Augustine, which was demolished for the rebuilding of the Trinity Chapel after 1180.

Despite the predominance of the surviving Romanesque work in the crypt, the interior today is somewhat misleading. The original windows were mostly replaced by larger Perpendicular ones which have transformed the appearance of the aisles, though some impression of the original lighting can still be gained from the radial chapels, and from the area underneath the northern transept arm. The simple round-headed windows of St Anselm's time would not have allowed much light to enter the aisles, and little could have filtered through to the central nave, particularly if they contained a high proportion of stained glass. Moreover, the mural and vault paintings of the crypt are almost completely lost, together with the colouring of the carved capitals. The fragments in St Gabriel's chapel suggest that the whole crypt was a riot of colour, the greater part of which could have been glimpsed only by candlelight. The loss of these rich painting cycles has robbed the crypt of much of its original flavour. The chapel of St Gabriel, under St Anselm's chapel, illustrates something of the appearance of the crypt in the twelfth century (Figure 29). The plan, repeated in the northern Holy Innocents' Chapel, is a rectangle containing four groin-vaulted bays supported by a central column. On the eastern wall are twin entrances divided by a column, leading to a shallow apse. The semi-dome over the apse has extensive remains of high-quality frescoes depicting scenes from the birth of St John the Baptist, and less distinct scenes from the birth of Christ. High up in the top of the semi-dome, Christ is seen in glory surrounded by flying angels. The single axial window of the apse was subsequently blocked, but its position remains visible. The walls and vaults of the main area of the chapel also retain traces of painting, with one relatively complete bay of the vault. Post-Reformation plaster may conceal more original decoration, traces of which can be seen around both window openings. The divided entry into the apse is noticeably constricted, and there is evidence to suggest that the present narrowness is the result of an alteration which probably occurred during the construction of the main level chapel and tower above. The whole eastern wall of the chapel, and the two rear buttresses within the apse, have been inserted into the previous layout, resulting in the diminution of the apse entrance arches and the blocking of original features of the apse, especially the first aumbry. The imposition of this strengthening wall has resulted in the curious appearance of the adjoining transverse arch, which now dies away into the wall before reaching its supporting capital. When the vault was first built, the apse entrance arches were more spacious and, in order to

29 St Gabriel's chapel:
interior from the south-
west

compensate for this, the vault was raised by means of stilting. A similar
strengthening was carried out on the opposite Holy Innocents' Chapel. A
date for this alteration of $c.1100$ can be proposed from the appearance of a
broken billet string course across the new work, a motif employed on the
exterior of the main level chapels, and the continuity of the base plaster of
the paintings in the apse – that is, the plaster post-dates the strengthening
of the chapel. The reason behind the underpinning of the chapels was the
instability of the great eastern towers above, for the differential settlement
between the great weight of the tower structure and the relatively light
ambulatory aisles led to a tilting of the towers away from the church,
especially to the north-east and south-east. The early propping-up of the
eastern towers proved insufficient to consolidate the southern tower
above St Gabriel's chapel, and within a few decades the whole apse had to
be walled up to prevent the collapse of the superstructure. This happened
prior to 1163, by which time no altar existed in the chapel. The

abandonment of the apse in the Holy Innocents' Chapel opposite was not necessary, due to the buttressing provided by the adjoining vestiarium, built after 1151, but the very preservation of this chapel led to the modernization of its eastern window and the post-Reformation destruction of its painted decoration. However, nothing could halt the continued decline of the eastern towers, and both were taken down before 1336.

The chapel of St Gabriel is a foretaste of the sculptural richness of the whole crypt. The apse entrance capital is vigorously carved, and there are traces of the original colour, and of painting on the column. The central vault support is perhaps the most elaborate of all, with its spiralled column shaft and fantastic animal musicians on the faces of the cushion capital. The style and cutting of this capital is so distinct that other work by this master can be distinguished in the crypt, and his work forms a marked contrast to the style of the capitals in the opposite Holy Innocents' Chapel, which must be exact contemporaries (Figure 30). The 'Gabriel master' allows his subjects to move freely on each face of the capital, with only their sinuous bodies to suggest the inherent cushion shape of the whole. The 'Holy Innocents' master' adopts an entirely different approach, favouring a lower relief and a strict division between the vertical and angled planes of the cushion. This he achieves with rather naive twisted rope borders, and sprays of leaves at the angles. The 'Holy Innocents' master' does not appear again in any other surviving capital of the crypt.

The aisles of the crypt are mostly devoid of sculptural decorations; only two carved half-capitals occur at the western end of the south aisle, and the cushion capitals throughout the aisles may have had only simple painted decoration. The chapels under the eastern transept have similarly lost all their decoration, both painted and sculptured. The capital supporting the vaults under the northern arm was replaced by a stiff-leaf design some time after 1174, and the southern chapels were transformed into the Black Prince's chantry in the fourteenth century. The northern transept arm does retain its original layout with two shallow apses with horseshoe entrance arches and austerely plain window openings.

The central nave of the crypt is rightly famous for its series of historiated capitals (Figure 31). The original sequence along the two rows of columns was an alternating pattern with carved column shafts and plain cushion or scalloped capitals, and plain shafts supporting carved capitals. Six of the columns have become engulfed in the later screen work of the eastern chapel of Our Lady Undercroft, and though the columns with their deep spiral patterns appear to be Romanesque, the capitals have been replaced. Behind the eastern screen of the chapel the corners of the lost Romanesque capitals still stick out from the plaster, and carved fragments may survive underneath. Several sculptor hands may be detected in the capitals of the crypt – the 'Gabriel master' in the Wyvern

**30** (*above left*) Capital in the
Holy Innocents' Chapel
**31** (*above right*) Crypt capital

and Dog scene, while another sculptor was fond of repeating a single pattern on all four sides, as on the capital immediately opposite. The 'Gabriel master' is the most assured hand of all: his sense of design and vitality outstripping his fellows. He always retains a regard for the original cushion shape, emphasizing it by the hollowing of the back plane whilst leaving a ridge along its perimeters. This distinguishes him from the second 'master', whose patterns flow over the angles of the capital, reducing the block to a funnel shape. The stress he places on the angles by the introduction of corner heads creates the impression of a historiated volute capital rather than a cushion. The unfinished capital towards the western end of the crypt appears to be by this hand. A 'naturalistic master' was attracted to genre scenes and to isolated animals recalling pages from a mediaeval bestiary. The freest of his designs are the faun, and the horse-rider near the western end, which have little of the formalism and stylization of his contemporaries. The 'Corinthianesque master' has three capitals in the crypt, the so-called Lanfranc capital, and two half-capitals in the south aisle. This hand is frequently found in the exterior arcade under the main windows of the choir, particularly near the east end. There is the possibility that more than one sculptor worked on a single capital, for the tumblers on the reverse of the Wyvern and Dog capital would appear to be the work of the 'naturalistic master', whereas the fantastic battle that gives the capital its name is probably the work of the 'Gabriel master'. This poses the whole question of the date and method of manufacture of these capitals. There can now be little doubt that the bulk of the Romanesque carving at Canterbury was produced in the workshop and is contemporary with the construction of the building – not carved *in situ* at some later date. Hence, the crypt sculpture should be dated to 1096–*c.* 1100. Further, the argument that the sculptors must have derived their inspiration from the products of the Canterbury scriptoria debases the skill and imagination of the masters concerned, for the quality of the design and execution of the capitals speak for themselves. The monks who illustrated books had far easier access to the crypt than the sculptors had to the monastic library.

The sculpture workshop appears to have been concentrated into two production lines: one for the external, the other for the internal capitals. The requirements of the exterior sculpture far outnumbered those in the crypt, for an interlaced arcade ran around the entire choir exterior between the crypt and choir aisle windows. The arcade repeated the alternating pattern within the crypt, but the capitals were generally simpler in order to avoid weathering. At the eastern end of St Anselm's choir much sculpture can still be seen, especially around the apsidal chapels of the eastern towers. Many of the colonnettes have been replaced or lost, but the alternating pattern can still be traced with either volute capitals, some 'feathered', or cushion capitals, and some with deeply incised angles such as those in the crypt (see Fig. 35). It is notable that the exterior sculpture runs out as the choir progresses westwards, surely an indication of the great speed of the building campaign and the relative inability of the sculpture workshop to keep up. The westernmost bays of the choir, both on the north and south, are devoid of all external sculpture in the interlaced arcade. A similar situation is evident within the crypt, for not only does the decorative programme break down as the building moves westwards, but obvious intrusions can be found whose introduction must have been dictated by the sheer lack of finished material. Thus two volute capitals of the 'Corinthianesque master' have found their way into the south aisle of the crypt, though probably intended for use in the exterior interlaced arcade. The most celebrated intruder is the unfinished capital near the west end, where only one face was completed and another marked out, while the two remaining faces were left blank. The urgency that prompted the use of any available sculpture, whether finished or not, may be responsible for the mistakes in the laying out of the western end of the crypt where the bay widths suddenly jump to quite staggering lengths before crashing into the west wall of Lanfranc's crypt. The only explanation would appear to be that the new work proceeded as far west as was possible without destroying the previous short choir.[28] Eventually a point would be reached where the old structure, now wrapped within the shell of the new, had to be pulled down and the gap made good. Errors in layout and any lack of ready sculpture are highly likely to make themselves felt at such a juncture.

While the crypt survives relatively intact, the choir above was largely destroyed as a result of a great fire on 4 September 1174. According to Gervase, it was reduced almost to ashes, but even the most casual glance

28 The new aisle walls stood outside the choir aisles of Lanfranc's east end, so that they could have been built around the old work.

32 (*above left*) The north aisle of the presbytery: interior from the west with the entrance to St Andrew's chapel and the blind arch set against the adjoining stair turret

33 (*above right*) St Anselm's chapel: exterior from the south showing the remains of the great tower-chapel with its decorative arcading and the Oxenden window of 1336. The stair turret giving access to the upper stages of the tower is seen on the left

29 Willis, *Arch. Hist.*, p. 78.

at the choir aisles is enough to confound his claims (Figure 32). The Gothic choir of the two Williams was carefully slotted into the shell of its predecessor, and the only major demolition of the perimeter walls of the building was in the upper parts of the transept and in the ambulatory between the two eastern towers – the latter to make way for the present Trinity Chapel. The two Williams made no attempt to disguise the earlier work in the aisles, though the second William did overlay the interior elevations of Anselm's transept. Nevertheless, the greater height of the Gothic choir and the requirements of its comprehensive vaulting forced the first master, William of Sens, to adapt and, in some cases, to demolish and rebuild sections of the outer walls, so distorting or obliterating their original design. While Willis went too far in his suggestion that William of Sens raised the height of the old aisle windows and meticulously replaced the original heads at a higher level,[29] William of Sens did show a considerable respect for the Romanesque fabric, then some seventy-five years old. There is more than a suggestion from Gervase that this conservation policy was in order to placate and reassure the anxious monks, who were loath to lose even a stone of their 'glorious choir'.

The principal surviving sections of the choir above the crypt occur in the aisles between the western and eastern crossings, in the lower walls of the eastern transept, in the short presbytery aisles and within the main level chapels of the eastern towers. Great caution must be exercised in any investigation of the latter, as it is evident that substantial alterations were made in the radial chapels prior to the fire of 1174.

The surviving radial chapels present extremely complex problems, for they have undergone at least three major renovations since their inception (Figure 33). The first alteration came during the construction and may have been related to the strengthening of the chapels underneath them. At a very early stage, the original window design was abandoned in favour of much taller openings and, possibly, a central division of the aisle entrance arch was eliminated. The evidence for the alteration of the chapel windows is most clear in the west wall of St Anselm's chapel, where the chip-carved voussoirs of a previous opening have been crudely cut through for the increased height of the present window. While this indicates a design change, it does not necessarily imply a raising of the whole choir interior. The windows within the apse of the southern chapel give no indication that they have ever been shorter than at present, so that the design change may have come before the initial construction of the major arches into the apse and aisle. That the evidence for the alteration of the windows does exist on the west wall of that chapel probably indicates that the section nearest the stair turret was in advance of the rest of the work. The height of the adjoining aisle and ambulatory was determined the moment that the aisle entrance arch into the chapel was built, for its span dictates the present proportions. Furthermore, there is no evidence that the windows in the aisles have been altered. The original scale of the chapel windows may have been directly related to the weight of the tower above.[30] Their enlargement represented a considerable risk, and the generous dimensions of the various arches and windows provide a clue to the subsequent history of the tower-chapels, for the spaciousness of the various arched openings proved too ambitious for the great weight of the structure above, and considerable underpinning was necessary within a few decades (Figure 34).

We have already seen that strengthening walls had to be added in the crypt chapel below, probably as early as *c.* 1100, but the gradual shift continued and further action became essential in order to prop up the ailing towers. In St Anselm's chapel, the inner order of mouldings on both the apse and aisle entrance arches, together with their shafts and capitals, can be seen as additions to their earlier work, with decorative designs of the mid-twelfth century. It was also necessary to remove the old groined vault, or perhaps it fell, and it was replaced by a lighter and stronger rib vault – the rib profiles would link the work to the priorate of Wibert, 1153–67. The arches in the opposite chapel, St Andrew's, were similarly strengthened and a rib vault inserted, but otherwise St Andrew's preserves more of its original appearance because of the building of the vestiarium against the north wall. The window apertures

30   The evidence within St Andrew's chapel suggests that the northern chapel was in advance of the southern. The west window shows evidence of raising, as in St Anselm's, but in addition, the southernmost window of the apse contains another abandoned arch head. The level of the original openings suggests that the aisle level chapels were to be lower than at present, perhaps with subdivided apse and entrance arches. This would have facilitated the arrangement of the ambulatory vaults. Additional chapels may have been planned for the tribune level, as at Gloucester, and their abandonment during construction may have encouraged the enhancement of the aisle level chapels.

34 (*above left*) St Andrew's chapel: interior from the north-west showing the additions of *c.* 1160

35 (*above right*) St Andrew's chapel: exterior from the north-east showing the apse flanked by the vestiarium to the right and Henry IV's chantry to the left

in this wall still can be seen, at least in outline, and their blocking as early as *c.* 1160 further discredits the theory, proposed by Willis, that William of Sens raised all the other windows to their present height. The radial chapels were only one level of the great eastern towers that must have stood to a height of about 120 ft – 3,658 cm – without their spires (Figure 35). Access to the upper levels was by means of a small stair turret on the western side which also communicates with the crypt chapel. The stair turrets were lopped off when the towers were demolished, but the southern turret still displays evidence that it once continued to a further chamber above the present vault-loft of St Anselm's chapel. The Waterworks Drawing shows a major chamber above the radial chapels, and two belfry stages above that. The upper chambers are not referred to by Gervase, so we may assume that by 1163 they had no practical purpose, and any intention to use them must have been thwarted by their instability. The stair turrets now terminate at the level of the vault-space above the main chapels. The loft above St Anselm's has been severely mutilated with much of the southern wall cut back in 1336 to lessen the weight above a new window. The western wall was rebuilt in the nineteenth century, but the opposite apse wall contains a blocked relieving arch that once led into the half-conical roof over the apse. The northern wall of the loft contains a passage, the so-called 'Watching Chamber', though it is actually part of William of Sens's aisle triforium design. The opposite vault-loft, above St Andrew's, has been used as a store for many years and has a concrete floor. The walls show considerable signs of burning, which may indicate that the floor of the lost chamber above was wooden and that it caught fire in 1174. The southern wall over the choir aisle contains a doorway which formerly led above the vaults of the Romanesque ambulatory and now forms an entrance to the William of Sens aisle triforium. The adjoining stair turret was gutted during the rebuilding of the Audit House, and its present internal appearance is mostly modern.

The eastern axial chapel is lost, but its appearance can be gauged from the Waterworks Drawing and from the account by Gervase. It was a two-storey structure, rectangular in plan and without an apse. The vaults at crypt-level were supported by a central column, at the foot of which St Thomas was buried after his murder in 1170. Hence it became the principal object of his cult, but its size and relative remoteness from the rest of the church sealed its fate and it was torn down for the present much larger chapel after 1180. The chapel above contained the altar of the Holy Trinity and various tombs and shrines. It must have been the brightest of the ambulatory chapels, with tall windows on three sides. Between the axial chapel and the eastern towers there was sufficient wall for a single window bay, so that there was an alternating pattern around the ambulatory of windows and chapel entrance arches.

The plan of the ambulatory gives rise to a number of problems (see Fig. 26). Gervase states that there were six columns forming the apse – indeed, six piers survive in the crypt below, but there the bay divisions around the ambulatory remain fairly constant due to the subdivision of the radial chapel entrances (see Fig. 28). This allows an even disposition of the aisle responds. In the ambulatory above, such uniformity was not possible, as the entrance arches into the tower-chapels were not subdivided and this must have forced a wide variation in the placing of the aisle responds. The result must have been a series of irregular and awkward ambulatory bays, not dissimilar to the later antics of William of Sens.

The exterior of the ambulatory chapels is decorated with an extension of the interlaced arcade design beneath the windows, which is repeated above, doubtless related to the lost windows of the upper chambers. The crypt window-openings are quite plain, while the main level windows are set back beneath a chip-carved arch mould, those on St Anselm's chapel having further orders which may represent later strengthening. The window jambs contain freestone shafts and plain cushion capitals which support a roll arch moulding. The walls are enriched with broken billet string courses and tiers of scallops curved straight into the surface. The aisle exteriors share most of the decorative arrangements of the

**36** (*opposite*) The south-east transept arm: exterior from the south-west showing the arcading and aisle-level windows of St Anselm's period. The work above is by the two Williams while the decorated stages of the stair turret dates from *c*. 1160

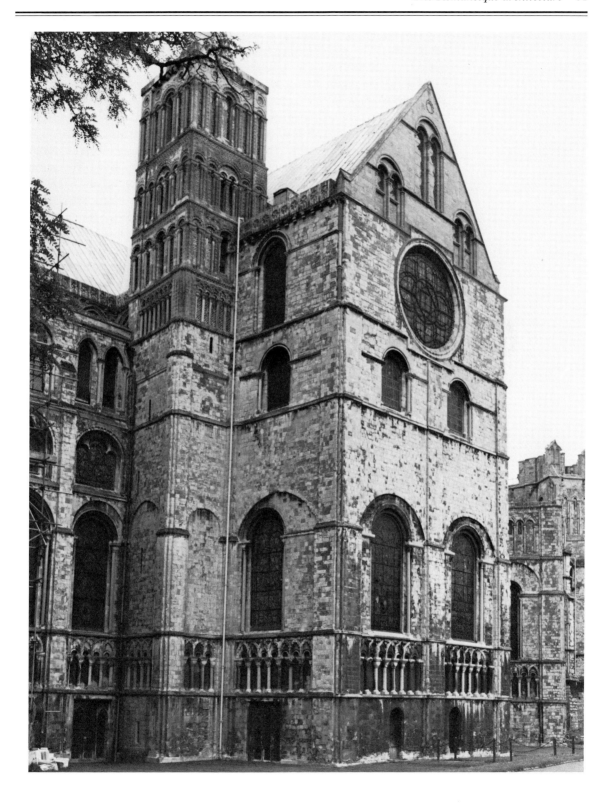

31  The upper sections of the transept stair turrets were built *c.* 1160, see p. 83.

radial chapels with interlaced arcades, chip-carved arch moulds, nook-shafts, etc. The transept facades represent the largest surviving section of St Anselm's choir, and are also the most misunderstood (Figure 36). The only area that can be accepted with any degree of confidence is confined to below the sill-level of the middle range of windows, and includes the crypt, the interlaced arcade, the main level windows and the four apses. To this can be added the stair turrets to the height of the second interlaced arcade.[31] Everything else is the result of alterations and extensions carried out by the two Williams after 1174. The original sections of the transept have the same severity and strength as the eastern chapels, with their clasping buttresses, segmental relieving arches and blank expanses of masonry. A sudden and quite remarkable change occurs in the sculpture of the exterior interlaced arcade on the southern and western walls of the south transept arm, and on the northern wall of the opposite arm. The additional sculptural enrichment of these sections begins as abruptly as it ends. The capitals, which are well preserved on the northern side, are every bit as spirited and elaborate as those within the crypt, but their style is more advanced. This has led to suggestions that they were not cut earlier than about 1150, but the complex abacus mouldings are identical to those in the interior aisle arcading and several points of comparison can be drawn between the better preserved capitals and some of the crypt sculpture.

The choir aisle facades are now seen as part of a multi-storey construction with windows at crypt, aisle, an upper aisle or 'triforium' level and, on the south side, a tribune (Figure 37). The latter came into existence after 1174, while the 'aisle triforium' level may represent an original feature of St Anselm's choir. The exterior of the choir aisle west of the transept is divided into three window bays flanked by the transept stair turret to the east, and the later chapels of the western transept. The central window bay is wider than its neighbours, so creating an A–B–A arrangement emphasized by the pushing of the axis of the lesser windows towards the central bay. The upper parts of the slim clasping buttresses were rebuilt by William of Sens to give more support to his new aisle vaults.

Internally, the aisles of the choir and presbytery are rich in architectural evidence. St Anselm's work is again distinguishable by the presence of the Romanesque arcade beneath the windows, though in the transept the arcades are Gothic replacements (Figure 38). The aisle bays are articulated by pilasters and half-shafts, which now rise to the level of the aisle triforium passage where they have William of Sens capitals. Some impression of the original height of these supports can be found where the coursed masonry shafts end and the later single block shafting begins. The shafts formerly supported transverse arches crossing the width of the aisle and resting on the capitals of the main arcade. The first design allowed for additional flanking shafts in the angles of the pilasters, a scheme that was soon abandoned. The string courses along the top of the

**37** The south choir aisle: exterior from the south. The lowest windows date from the fifteenth century. The arcading and aisle windows are from St Anselm's choir. The trefoil windows light the aisle triforium of the William of Sens choir and replace tribune windows of the earlier choir. The coupled lancets represent the first design of William of Sens for a lit tribune throughout the choir

**38** The north choir aisle: interior from the east. The windows and wall arcades remain from St Anselm's choir, while the aisle responds are Anselm below, changing to William of Sens towards the top. Note the fragment, extreme right, of the original abacus moulding from the capital of the transverse arch carried across the blinded arch against the transept stair turret

wall arcades have been extended to cover the gap originally left for these shafts, but the bases were never removed (Figure 39). The intention to provide nook-shafts has led to some speculation that the aisles were to be rib vaulted. The capitals of the window jamb shafts are at a higher level than those supporting the transverse arches, so creating a syncopated rhythm along the aisle with the lower transverse arches breaking up the space into a series of oblong units. The reason behind this somewhat unorthodox arrangement was the extreme width of the aisle in relation to the window bay. The semicircular transverse arches had to rise over 9 ft – 275 cm, plus the thickness of the vault itself, and this determined the level

**39** The north choir aisle vault respond base. The grouping of the aisle respond bases intended that three shafts should support the vault, a design that was abandoned almost immediately. The presence of the additional bases has led to speculation that the aisles were to be rib vaulted

32 An early door to the central tower survives at the western end of the present north clerestory passage in the choir. Straight joints beneath this, now within the north choir aisle roof-space, may relate to straight stairs that once led up from the north tribune of St Anselm's choir.

from which the arches could spring. On the other hand, the windows could, and did, rise to the level of the crown of the arcade arches opposite. The arrangement of the aisle elevation and height of the surviving chip-carving above the windows would indicate the thinnest of vaults, dying away into the upper walling of the transverse arches. In these last two respects, the design closely resembled the aisle elevation of the nave of St Augustine's from *c.* 1090.

At the western end of the choir aisles a major change in the floor-level occurs within the transition bay from Lanfranc's narrower church to the extra width of St Anselm's. The retention of Lanfranc's transept chapels to the west restricted the aisle width in the link bays, whereas the main arcades of the choir continued to the western crossing in a straight line, and were linked to the narrower crossing arch under the central tower by right-angled walls which survive substantially intact. The link bays between the two buildings had to accommodate stairs rising some 10 ft 2½ in. – 311 cm – from the transept floor, and secondary stairs dropping 4 ft 11½ in. – 151 cm – down into the crypt. The outer walls of the bays belong to Lanfranc's choir aisles, though considerably refaced. The northern wall at choir aisle level displays a blind arch, 11 ft 6 in. – 350 cm – high and 7 ft 6 in. – 229 cm – wide, with an overall height of 26 ft 6 in – 808 cm – above the old floor-level. The arch is something of a puzzle, for while the masonry setting appears to be Lanfranc's, the string course set into it at the level of the present choir floor must be Anselm's. On the south side a similar arch exists, though blocked up. There the string course at choir floor-level continues straight across the infilling. But the presence of the arches must be related to the straight stairs which are contained within both walls and give access to the upper chapels of the western transept. The stairs are Anselm's, though the doorways were rebuilt and possibly repositioned by William of Sens. The upper parts of the walls within the link bays must have been extensively cleaned or refaced after 1174, for they show no trace of their original vaults. Built into these upper walls are further stairs which now lead from the passages in the aisle triforium up the the present aisle roof-spaces. Their original purpose has been concealed by alterations and additions during the building of the Gothic choir – possibly they continued to the clerestory level in the western transept, and to yet higher stairs giving access to the central tower.[32]

The outer walls of St Anselm's choir can still give some idea of the appearance of the aisles, but what of the interior elevation, the main arcades and upper walls? Gervase describes the choir interior with numbers of columns, etc., and the disposition of altars and shrines, and while this contributes towards a reconstruction, it does not help with a detailed examination of the elevation. The basic points in Gervase can be augmented by the exterior view in the Waterworks Drawing, where the whole choir is depicted on a base pattern of brickwork. No such feature has ever existed on the building, but the artist gives several indications that the brickwork represents the crypt. He makes this most clear with his depiction of the crypt-level door at the foot of the north-east transept arm which stands within the Water Tower passage. In order to show this door, he elevates the brickwork pattern around the Water Tower roof into which he inserts an open door, which is labelled '*Hostium Cripte*'. Further evidence that the pattern represents the crypt comes at the east end, with the towers and the axial chapel. Only the main level windows are shown on the eastern towers, while the axial chapel, known from Gervase to have been two-storeyed, is shown with only the brick pattern and one range of windows above. The evidence of the brickwork pattern is crucial for a reconstruction of St Anselm's choir, for if it indeed represents the crypt, then the elevation of the choir would read as: crypt, aisle, tribune, tribune roof, clerestory and high roof. If, however, too literal a reading is being forced upon the drawing and the pattern refers to nothing more than a base for the whole church concealed to the west by the cloister, then one element of the elevation must be removed – namely, the tribune. Evidence for two very different elevations must therefore be sought within the surviving structure, and from the description by Gervase.

Inside the choir, Gervase states that the old arcade resembled the new, only it was not so high. This implies that St Anselm's arcades consisted of alternating round and polygonal piers. Gervase then compares the number of triforia or walkways within the new choir and those in the old, saying that the Gothic choir has one over the aisle and two over the arcade, whereas St Anselm's choir had only one in the arcade wall. Unfortunately the description of the choir elevation, written by Gervase more than twenty years after its destruction, is ambiguous on this point and the arrangement of the upper parts is open to differing interpretations. Gervase states that arches were built upon the columns, and upon them rose a solid wall that was broken by small dark openings. He then breaks his description of the elevation to comment that this wall continues all round the choir and meets at the head of the apse. Returning to the elevation once more, he continues that above the solid wall, broken by the openings, is the triforium and the upper windows. The phrasing of the Latin: '*via erat quae triforium appellatur, et fenestrae superiores*', might suggest that the two elements were connected, i.e. a clerestory passage of standard Anglo-Norman form, with the passage-level somewhat lower than the clerestory sill. In his reconstruction of 1845,[33] Willis adopts a different solution for the elevation; for him, the '*murus solidus parvulis et obscuris distinctus erat fenestris*' constituted nothing more than a decorative blind arcade above the arches of the main arcade, but Gervase is clearly indicating something of greater architectural significance than that – he passes over all the other blind arcades within the choir without a word – and he certainly seems to indicate that the wall was broken by openings into some dimly-lit area. This could be either a roof-space or a

33 Willis, *Arch. Hist.*, p. 42.

tribune with only small exterior windows. Willis did not consider the possibility of the existence of a tribune or of any major feature of the elevation between the arcade and clerestory and so, for him, St Anselm's choir was a squat ill-proportioned building, with arcade walls rising barely 50 ft – 1,524 cm – above the floor. But if Gervase is alluding to a tribune, then the whole choir must be raised to a greater height, one befitting its generous width.

A close examination of the surviving sections of St Anselm's choir can reveal important evidence concerning the various floor-levels within the arcade wall. Most important are the stair turrets of the eastern transept, which preserve several doorways relating to Anselm's church, some of which have been adapted by William of Sens for his Gothic choir. Two doors up to the present clerestory passage appear to be Romanesque, and in both cases their original floor-levels can still be discovered. Figure 40 illustrates the relationship between the original door-levels and the passages to which they now give access. It can be seen that the lowest door provided an access point over the original aisle vaults at a height of 28 ft 4 in. – 864 cm – above the choir floor – the same height as Lanfranc's tribune floor in the nave. The wide doors are preceded by a groined vaulted lobby and a complete break in the spiral stair for a platform. The next door faces east and may have been inserted by William of Sens to provide a passage around the transept and into his tribunes. The present passage floor is 37 ft 4 in. – 1,138 cm – above the choir floor, but the original sill level within the doorway was only 34 ft 8 in. – 1,057 cm. The highest doors within the original sections of Anselm's work are at a height of between 52 and 54 ft – 1,585 to 1,646 cm – above choir floor-level. These doors also cause a break in the stairs for a platform within a vaulted lobby, and the walls on the aisle side of the turret have been slightly set back in order to squeeze the doors into the corner. The doors now lead down to the Gothic clerestory passage at a height of between 50 ft 6 in. and 51 ft – 1,539 and 1,554 cm – above the choir floor. The original limit of Anselm's work within the turrets is best seen on the northern side, where the spiral stair is abandoned after reaching a height above the choir floor of 63 ft 4 in. – 1,930 cm. Above this, the turret extension of *c.* 1160 is fitted with wall stairs and a minute angle spiral at the very top. The southern turret was similarly extended during Wilbert's priorate but now contains a vaulted spiral stair to the top – the dating evidence for this stair is confusing, for it may have been inserted only after 1174.[34] The highest work of Anselm's period within the southern turret stops at 61 ft 9½ in. – 1,883 cm – above the choir floor, or 72 ft – 2,194 cm – above Lanfranc's nave floor-level.

How does the stair-turret evidence affect Willis's reconstruction of St Anselm's choir? Willis made one fundamental decision about the height of the choir which was based on a simple mistake in his translation of Gervase. This concerned the number of vaults built by William of Sens in

34  The inner lining of the southern turret supporting the stair extension is not bonded to the shell of the tower. See the vertical joints in each window opening. In addition, the present entry into the vault-space above the south-east transept arm appears to be an original entry through the stair-well. This entry can only be part of William the Englishman's project of *c.* 1179.

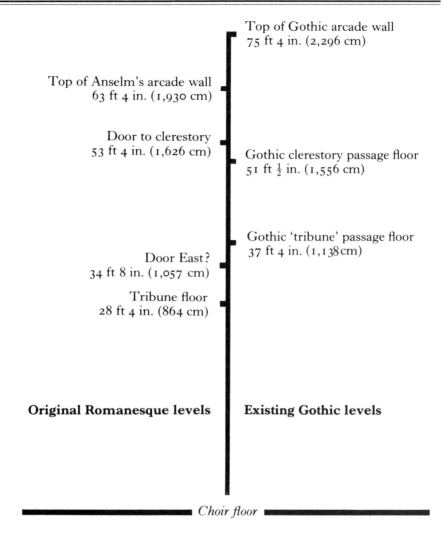

**40** St Anselm's choir: floor-levels within the north-east transept stair turret. The 'Romanesque' door at 34 ft 8 in. may be a William of Sens insert adapted by William the Englishman

Top of Gothic arcade wall
75 ft 4 in. (2,296 cm)

Top of Anselm's arcade wall
63 ft 4 in. (1,930 cm)

Door to clerestory
53 ft 4 in. (1,626 cm)

Gothic clerestory passage floor
51 ft ½ in. (1,556 cm)

Gothic 'tribune' passage floor
37 ft 4 in. (1,138 cm)

Door East?
34 ft 8 in. (1,057 cm)

Tribune floor
28 ft 4 in. (864 cm)

**Original Romanesque levels**    **Existing Gothic levels**

*Choir floor*

a certain year either side of the crossing. Willis translated the phrase as two vaults each side, whereas Gervase implies one vault either side of the crossing. The upshot of this was that Willis believed that all the present vaults, and hence the Gothic clerestory windows in the eastern transept, were built by William of Sens, and he was puzzled by the odd alignment of the intermediate range of windows immediately below the Gothic clerestory (see Fig. 83). For Willis the answer was simple, though the final implications led him to an untenable conclusion. The middle-range windows of the transept were, to Willis, the former clerestory windows of St Anselm's choir. This satisfied his anxiety over the odd relationship between them and the clerestory above, which he believed was by William of Sens. The height of the middle-range windows determined all his thinking about St Anselm's choir, and led him to reconstruct the building as a low, dimly-lit structure, broader than it was high. Hardly the glittering interior of William of Malmesbury. Willis then found that the fixed height of his clerestory sill did not allow sufficient room for the pitch of an aisle roof, and he was forced to propose that William of Sens had raised all the aisle walls and heightened the old windows to match. Thus he was able to cut over 3 ft – 91 cm – off the present Romanesque walls and to squeeze a pitched aisle roof beneath his clerestory windows. In Willis's mind there was no room for a tribune and, for him, the top of St Anselm's choir was marked by the present clerestory passage floor-level, about 50 ft – 1,524 cm – above the choir floor, or 60 ft – 1,829 cm – above the nave floor. According to Willis, the choir was at least 5 ft – 152 cm – lower than the lowest possible height for Lanfranc's nave, despite the fact that it was raised over 10 ft – 311 cm – above the floor-level of the church. Quite clearly, St Anselm's choir must have equalled the height of Lanfranc's church; indeed, there is evidence to suggest that it was taller than his predecessor's work.

An alternative reconstruction to that proposed by Willis can be based on the evidence within the transept stair turrets and on the Waterworks Drawing (see Fig. 40). The latter illustration suggests the presence of a tribune, and Gervase hints at the same with his description of small and dark openings above the brilliantly lit aisles. The existence of tribunes would automatically raise the overall height of the church as well as ex-plain some of the present anomalies of the choir, especially the triforium built by William of Sens over the old aisle windows. The aisle triforium passage provides access between the eastern transept stair turret and the upper levels of the western transept, and may once have led to the central tower. The existence of this unique passage suggests that similar access had existed in St Anselm's choir, namely through tribunes over the aisle vaults. A second storey over the aisle would also explain the continuation of the main arcade across the transept in St Anselm's choir, for a bridge could have carried a tribune processional path over to the eastern section of the building. The tribune-level is almost certainly indicated on the Waterworks Drawing by the second range of aisle windows, and its outer wall height is now represented by the aisle triforium of William of Sens; indeed the beginning of the earlier walls can still be traced within the western ends of the triforium passages, and near the eastern transept stair turrets. The relatively low outer wall, less than 10 ft – 300 cm – high, would have limited the available window space and would explain the shadowy nature of the tribune when compared with the aisles below.

The presence of a tribune poses the question of the middle-range windows in the transept, accepted by Willis as St Anselm's clerestory. The windows relate to a passage inserted by William of Sens at a level now some 3 ft – 91 cm – higher than the access-level in the turret. The mouldings, capitals and bases of the middle-range windows are all by

William of Sens and the windows appear to be part of William of Sens's original intention to provide a lit tribune-level throughout his new Gothic choir (see Fig. 69). If the windows are post-1174, what then did the door at 34 ft 8 in. – 1,057 cm – lead to? A tribune bridge would eliminate the need for a wall passage at this height. Once William removed the bridge, a wall passage becomes essential. The doors may have provided access to a lower passage around the transept, one built by William, but raised by his successor as part of a new design of *c.* 1179. The exterior of the transept is not helpful on this point, for the arrangement of the string courses was altered by William of Sens, and differences exist between the northern and southern arms. The present Gothic clerestory passage above may well represent the level of the earlier clerestory sill, which was entered by the door from the transept stair turret. If the height of Anselm's work surviving in the northern turret marks the height of the whole building – 73 ft 6½ in. – 2,242 cm – above nave floor-level – then a 13 ft – 396 cm – clerestory could be fitted above a reasonably pitched roof over the tribune (Figure 41). This is also the overall height of the exterior of the stair turrets as they were first built, and the junction between their two periods of construction is marked by a string course at about 73 ft – 2,225 cm – above the nave floor.

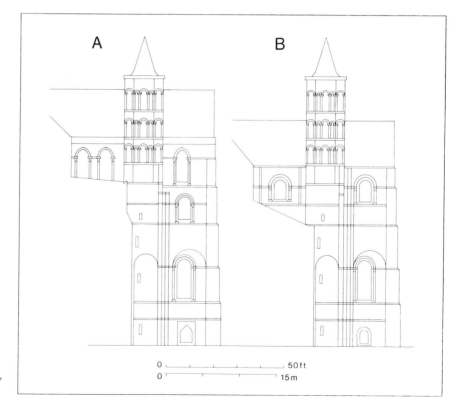

**41** St Anselm's choir: reconstruction of the south-east transept exterior from the west: A facade as at present; B suggested appearance by *c.* 1170

**42** The north side of the choir beneath the crossing seen from the Chapter House roof. The Martyrdom appears on the right, the choir on the left. The lower section of the Martyrdom buttress, with the circular aperture, appears to be Romanesque. It adjoins the tribune wall of the first design of William of Sens, converted by him to an exposed *mur boutant* and superseded by his later design seen on the left. Above the former tribune wall and within the angle of the crossing can be seen the two intersecting arches and the plinth level picked out in white that appear to form part of St Anselm's choir

Further evidence that St Anselm's choir rose to a height of at least 73 ft can be found under the central tower (Figure 42). Above the western bay of the choir there is a curious section of the church, best seen on the north side from the Chapter House roof. Immediately under the central tower and in the angle of the choir and western transept are a pair of interlocking arches. Higher still, a distinct plinth runs between the tower base and the first buttress of the choir clerestory. This buttress is thicker and cruder than any further to the east, and does not appear to relate in a structural way to the Gothic vault support which now abuts onto it. The southern side of the choir is less clear, following the imposition of a flat roof and more extensive rebuilding later in the Middle Ages (see Fig. 64). Nevertheless, the odd, thicker buttress is again present against the clerestory wall, together with the plinth. The impression given by the north side with its interlocking arches is that St Anselm's choir rose above the level of Lanfranc's transept, and that the taller arch originally traversed the gutter-level of the adjoining transept and came to rest on the thickness of its wall. The arch seems unlikely to have been a clerestory window since it was so close to the central tower, and it is now connected with a system of stairs that once may have led from the choir tribune up into the Angel Steeple. The lower parts of these stairs may have been lit by the oculus cut through the foreground buttress.

One major difficulty is presented by a reconstruction of St Anselm's choir with a height of 73 ft – 2,225 cm – and that is the thickness of the clerestory wall. The upper parts of Anselm's stair turrets are decorated with an exterior interlaced arcade. The present clerestory walls built by William the Englishman smash into these arcades in a way that was clearly not intended in the original design. The previous clerestory should have occupied the lower 13 ft – 396 cm – of the same area, and must have been sufficiently slim on the outside to have allowed the last arch of the arcade to be completed. This would inevitably result in a slight step back at clerestory sill-level. Something of this stepped arrangement is hinted at in the Waterworks Drawing. An alternative reconstruction would be to eliminate the clerestory passage altogether, though the existence of the original doors at this level and the comments by Gervase would render that argument difficult to uphold.

St Anselm's choir was not the gloomy barn as proposed by Willis, but a brilliantly lit and airy building swathed in the multicoloured radiance of its stained glass and paintings. The interior elevation was almost as high as the nave, about 63 to 68 ft – 1,920 to 2,073 cm – but as the main vessel of the choir was wider, the high canted roof may have matched the height of that in the nave (Figures 43 and 44). The aisles were equal in height to their nave counterparts, though their proportions were somewhat unconventional. The shortfall between the elevational height of the nave and choir was made within the tribune, while the clerestory openings were probably similar in size to Lanfranc's work. The high roof was covered by a canted ceiling, perhaps in five planes, covered with painting 'to the very summit'. At the head of the choir stood a great arch which led into the apse. The Waterworks Drawing makes it plain that the apse was lower

**43** (*below left*) St Anselm's choir: reconstruction of the interior elevation. The three reconstructions have cylindrical arcades and tau cross capitals:
A represents the largest possible opening for a tribune; B coupled tribune openings with a continuous clerestory passage arcade; C twin tribune openings without the retaining arch allowing for a low-level clerestory passage and a more substantial clerestory arcade

**44** (*below right*) Comparative cross-sections through the choir: A St Anselm's choir; B choir of William of Sens

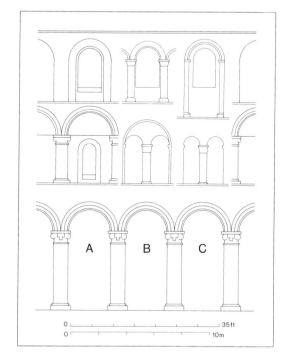

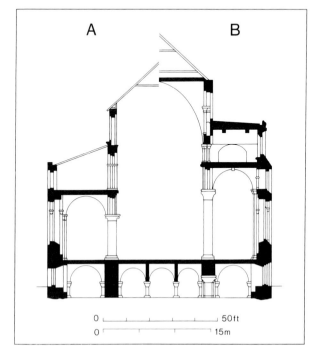

than the choir, and the roof must have rested against a gable wall raised upon the great arch.

The interior contained several unusual features: the uniformity of the drum piers lacking any bay articulation related to the upper levels, and the continuity of the main arcade across the transept. The latter poses several major questions about the nature of the transept. Was it just the arcade that continued, or were the higher elements of the arcade wall carried across as some sort of screen? Was there a second pier within the transept opening to support a tribune bridge the full width of the aisle? And what of the transept arm? Did it rise unobstructed to its full internal height or did it too contain a tribune floor akin to Lanfranc's transept further west? Was the transept in fact a giant two-storey construction open only at the crossing? Gervase is not forthcoming on any of these points, indeed, they were not relevant to his argument. But the transept highlights the problem of which tradition lay behind the curious plan and elevation of St Anselm's choir.

The addition of St Anselm's choir to the transept and nave of Lanfranc's cathedral created a double transept church, with the larger crossing furthest east. The resulting plan has been linked to several churches, including Cluny III in Burgundy and St Benoît-sur-Loire (Loiret). The great abbey church of Cluny, begun c. 1088, had an enormous choir with an apse and ambulatory surrounded by five radial chapels. The church had two transepts, one at the commencement of the ambulatory and a much larger one at the junction of the nave and choir. Both carried crossing towers, while only the western transept was extended at the full height of the nave – the eastern crossing being at the full height across the aisles, thereafter continuing at a much reduced level. It has been proposed that the plan of St Anselm's choir was suggested to the archbishop during his visit to Cluny, but that occurred only some four years after the beginning of the Canterbury choir. In addition, the weight of argument over the dating of the east end of Cluny would point to a later date for the completion of the choir of the abbey than for St Anselm's choir. The reduced eastern transept at Cluny may have its origins at St Benoît, perhaps better known as Fleury. The Fleury choir is earlier than St Anselm's, and in plan it foreshadows that at Cluny. However, the eastern transept is very different in its relationship with the choir, being more of a tower-chapel placed at the springing of the ambulatory than a true crossing. The main arcade wall continues across the opening with hardly any reference to it, and the aisle roof divorces the projecting arms from the upper parts of the choir elevation. The 'tower-chapels' at Fleury provide a better parallel for the ambulatory chapels at Canterbury than for its great east transept. Such 'tower-chapels' may have common origins in the Empire, and there is probably no need to seek any direct reference to Fleury in the design of St Anselm's choir.

The Imperial connotations of St Anselm's choir are very strong: the

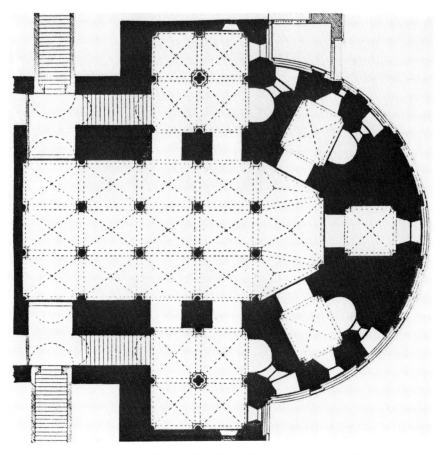

**45** Cologne, S. Maria im Capitol

eastern towers, the emphasis placed on the stair turrets, the decoration and the whole relationship between the crypt and upper church. One particular Imperial building appears to have exerted a considerable influence upon the plan of St Anselm's choir: the small mid-eleventh-century church of S. Maria im Capitol in Cologne (Figure 45). The crypt of S. Maria, consecrated in 1065, provides a close parallel for some of the peculiarities of the Canterbury plan, though the latter was expanded on to a giant scale. The Cologne crypt underlies the apse and ambulatory, the transept and even part of the nave. The east end of the crypt has a very thick outer wall which is the depth of the whole ambulatory aisle in the choir above. Gouged out of this wall are three radial chapels, two rectangular with eastern apses lying on the angle of the ambulatory, and a rectangular chapel on the eastern axis. The similarity to Canterbury is striking – particularly in the eastern chapel, for an apse on the Cologne chapel is omitted due to the limitations of the wall thickness, whereas at Canterbury, with its projecting axial chapel, no such limitations existed, yet the apse still did not make an appearance (see Fig. 26).

The elevation of the choir displayed a more complex mixture of

**46** The crypt: interior of the Romanesque ambulatory showing a re-used pier from St Anselm's choir. The two piers built within the ambulatory by William of Sens to support his new presbytery arcade are made up of re-used blocks from several Romanesque piers salvaged from the demolition of St Anselm's choir. Some of the abacus fragments are curved, suggesting that they originated in the apse above

Imperial and Anglo-Norman forms. The columnar arcade is not uncommon in the Empire – St George in Cologne, Hersfeld, Utrecht, etc. – and similar arcades can be found in England, though few perhaps at this early date. One particular example, in the chapel of St John within the Tower of London, is slightly earlier than St Anselm's choir, and its drum piers and tau cross capitals are very similar to the piers formerly in the choir but re-used by William of Sens in the crypt ambulatory (Figure 46). St John's also lacks vertical bay divisions, probably a feature of St Anselm's choir, for Gervase describes the continuous wall that ran around the choir above the main arcade that was broken only by the small dark openings and the clerestory unit. The lack of bay articulation suggests the horizontal 'layered' tradition of the Empire seen in such churches as Gernrode, Limburg an der Hardt, Hildesheim and Susteren. Three-storey elevations were, however, more common in Anglo-Norman architecture than in the Empire, though examples can be found at St Cyriac at Gernrode and at Soignes.

Parallels for the transept arrangement at Canterbury are hampered by the lack of information concerning the extent of the division. Complete two-storey transepts, open only at the crossing, are very rare, though two examples formerly existed, at Jumièges and Bayeux. The evidence of the transept stair turrets at Canterbury, however, suggests that the transept arms were open to their full height, and that only the aisle was obstructed by a tribune bridge or a simple continuation of the main arcade. Parallels for such a design would be very scarce, though something of this nature exists in the west block of St Cyr at Nevers, a very Imperial building, and in the transept at Pisa. The west block at St Pantaleon at Cologne may be a distant relation, and the original eastern transept of that church may also have been hidden by a continuation of the main arcade.

While St Anselm's choir was to its contemporaries an object of admiration and delight, the influence exerted by its architecture appears to have been limited. The nave of Southwell, begun *c.* 1110, may reflect St Anselm's choir with its strong aqueduct interior free from any vertical articulation. One other building, outside England, appears almost as a northern version of Canterbury – Dunfermline Abbey in Scotland. The abbey was founded by Queen Margaret, who asked Lanfranc to send monks from Canterbury to form a community. The first church was superseded by a larger abbey built after 1128 by King David, who also took an active interest in Canterbury. He was present, with Henry I, at the great dedication of St Anselm's choir in 1130. Two years earlier, he had persuaded Geoffrey, then prior of Christ Church, to leave Canterbury and become abbot of Dunfermline. The new church was begun a few months later.[35] The nave, which remains substantially intact, exhibits the same horizontal emphasis as St Anselm's choir, being totally devoid of any vertical bay articulation. The arcade consists of tall columnar piers, some decorated with chevron. The aisle walls have a socle arcade. The tribune has much smaller openings than the arcade arches, and only limited lighting from single windows. The clerestory is similar in size and contains a wall passage. While the work is admittedly crude when compared with Canterbury and the church far smaller in scale, the basic design of the elevation is that of St Anselm's choir, with one or two updated features.

St Anselm did not live to see the completion of the choir that bears his name. His death, on the Tuesday of Holy Week 1109, was touchingly recorded by his biographer Eadmer: 'with the whole family of his children being gathered round him he slept in peace'. The body of the saintly archbishop was laid to rest in the nave next to the tomb of his predecessor Lanfranc. A cult quickly grew up and the tomb became the object of veneration. Some time before 1124 it was decided to enshrine his remains and to place them in the chapel of SS Peter and Paul, the southern tower-chapel of the choir ambulatory. Devotion to the saint continued, and the chapel soon became called St Anselm's.

35 T. Boase, *English Art, 1100–1216,* p. 149.

The great new choir was formally dedicated on 4 May 1130, long after the completion of the fabric. The delay is something of a mystery, though the whole procedure of consecrations and dedications at this time is far from clear. Politics appear to have played an important role in the occasion, for both William I and David of Scotland were present at the event. Both kings were eagerly promoting the claims of Matilda as heir to the English throne, and their principal supporter, Archbishop William de Corbeuil, may have staged the ceremony for some political advantage.

The scale and magnificence of the event was later recaptured by Gervase:[36]

The Church of Canterbury thus founded and finished by Lanfranc, but enlarged by Anselm, was dedicated by Archbishop William with all respect and liberality on the 4th of May. At this dedication were present Henry I King of England, David King of Scotland, and all the Bishops of England. So famous a dedication has never been heard of on earth since the dedication of the Temple of Solomon.

St Anselm's choir was an expensive oddity. It catered for the unique requirements of an extraordinary foundation. It combined a monastic church, a metropolitan seat, a pilgrimage church and a vast repository of tombs into one extravagant and unlikely building. Its architecture was quickly superseded, especially in those areas experimenting with high vaults. It was also the last great cathedral church to be planned during the Romanesque period in England and, as such, the opportunity for emulation was never to arise.

## 1130–74

The years from the dedication of the new choir up to the priorate of Wibert in 1153 were relatively quiet for Canterbury Cathedral. The enormous expenditure upon the fabric and its decoration, and the large outlay necessary for the splendid dedication, had put a heavy strain on the monastic finances. The wars of Stephen and Matilda following the death of Henry I did not provide a suitable background for any long-term building projects and, for a time, the monks were content with their 'glorious' new choir. After the departure of Prior Conrad in 1126 there followed a succession of short priorates of between two and eight years, ending with the brief and inauspicious reign of Walter Parvus. Inflation coupled with some unwise long-term fixed leases had brought about a considerable decline in the monastic revenues, and it was Wibert, first as sub-prior, then as prior, who put the House back on a firm financial footing.[37] His fourteen-year priorate witnessed a new building campaign which at once modernized, enlarged and rationalized the monastic buildings in a scale befitting the great church. Despite this considerable expenditure, Wibert was also able to extend the curia precincts, and to introduce the famous waterworks system.

36   Gervase, *Actus Pontificum*, quoted in *The Historical Works . . .*, vol. 2, p. 386.

37   For a study of the finances of Canterbury Cathedral, see R. A. L. Smith, *Canterbury Cathedral Priory*.

The building of St Anselm's choir had fundamentally changed the relationship between the cathedral and its monastic buildings. Formerly, they had enjoyed a close proximity in which the claustral layout provided the shortest route between the principal offices and the monastic choir in the eastern bays of the nave. After *c.* 1110, the new monastic choir lay east of the central tower while the high Altar stood on what had been open ground in Lanfranc's time. The monastery had been left behind, dwarfed by the now vast and majestic church. One of the first additions made to the priory buildings was a new night passage running from the east face of the dormitory to the north-east transept of the new choir (see Fig. 1). The new route was so obvious that it may have been adopted during Conrad's priorate, but the present structure is not contemporary with the building of the choir. The night passage is raised upon an open arcade that forms an extension of the new slype passage under the dormitory (Figure 47). The

**47** The Water Tower and central tower from the infirmary garden. The upper stages of the Water Tower were remodelled by Prior Chillenden *c.* 1400. The night passage stands to the right, above it can be seen the roof of the Chapter House of *c.* 1410, and the gable end of the Martyrdom of *c.* 1475. Immediately to the left of the Water Tower, a single buttress from the Prior's Chapel remains to indicate the proportions of that building. The existing first floor of the chapel dates from the late seventeenth century. Above can be seen the gable end of the north-east transept as remodelled by William of Sens and William the Englishman, 1175–81

architecture is severe and rather ponderous, with undecorated scallop capitals and small, plain window apertures. Its date remains uncertain, but its association with a new slype, which contains work of Wibert's period, might suggest that it was one of his additions.

The remaining buildings associated with Prior Wibert extend all over the northern precincts of the curia. They include the Water Tower, the vestiarium, the infirmary chapel, the Aula Nova and the adjoining great gate, the cellarer's hall and Prior's Gate, as well as additions to the cathedral fabric (see Fig. 24). These extensive works were not built all at once, but by the time of the Waterworks Drawing (*c.* 1160), most had been completed. The earliest appear to be the infirmary chapel and the Aula Nova block. However, dating must rely on style, which can be very misleading at this time as more than one stylistic tradition is in evidence. The infirmary chapel is depicted on the drawing with an apsidal termination which appears to have been replaced by the present square end some time in the 1160s. The remaining south arcade has sculpture of high quality much in the tradition of Anselm's crypt capitals, but now sadly mutilated and in need of preservation or removal. The arcade has square piers with attached half-shafts supporting elegant arches with roll mouldings. The clerestory windows have jamb shafts while the later chancel windows retain elaborate chevron decoration. Much of the rubble at present supporting the flowerbeds by the side of the chapel came from the south aisle. The fragments show that the aisle windows were also decorated with chevron patterns and that some of the jamb capitals had crude waterleaf designs. The main hall of the infirmary was separated from the chapel by a solid wall and is of unknown date. The remaining south arcade is so devoid of stylistic evidence that it could be *c.* 1100 or 1150 (see Fig. 89). The similarity between the pier and capital form in the hall and those of Wibert's famous Norman entry stairs may point to a mid-twelfth-century date for its construction, but its awkward relationship with Wibert's vestiarium must leave the date of the hall in some doubt. Lanfranc must have provided some infirmary offices, and the size of the surviving hall, 148 × 66 ft – 4,511 × 2,012 cm – without the chapel suggests a development on a scale similar to his great dormitory. If the present remains are later than Lanfranc, then a previous hall, possibly on another site, must have been demolished. The infirmary and the new night passage were grouped around a second cloister which included other Wibert buildings, but whether all the buildings surrounding the new infirmary cloister should be seen as dating from the 1150s must depend upon some stylistic comparison between the various works. Certainly, the remains of the exquisite arcade that forms a narthex to the west door of the infirmary bear little relationship to the sombre style of the hall, but its waterleaf capitals can be related to the chapel sculpture further east. Possibly the hall belonged to an earlier plan related to the lost eastward extension of the dormitory that was abandoned for the formation of a second cloister with the new Water Tower as its focal point. Only one section of Wibert's infirmary cloister arcade survives – that at the western end of the infirmary, which was formerly linked to the east wall of the dormitory by a northern alley (Figure 48). The cloister garth is shown on the Waterworks Drawing with a central division made of wicker, and with a wooden pentise leaning against the east wall of the dormitory. The arcading of the whole cloister is depicted as uniform, but the surviving sections show that this was not so. The southern arcade supporting the night passage is quite unlike the eastern arcade with its complex pattern of alternating plain and spiralled columns, the simplest of arches and, originally, a lean-to roof. The capitals are either scalloped

48 The infirmary cloister arcade. The coupled columns are of Purbeck or Bethersden marble. The single columns are of jasper and may be Roman

or crude waterleaf, and the variation in size and height may indicate that the scallop capitals have been re-used from an earlier structure. Similarly, the bases exhibit different designs and the scallop capital columns have crude bases of *c.* 1100, whereas the twinned spiral columns with waterleaf capitals have the more advanced undercut bases found on other Wibert buildings. The plain shafts are polished jasper,[38] and there is a suggestion that they are re-used Roman colonnettes robbed from the city. At the south-east corner of the new infirmary cloister stands the vestiarium, more commonly called the treasury, standing upon a four-bay undercroft open to the churchyard to the east and the stillitory on the west, thus enabling the circuit around the outside of the choir to be maintained. It may have replaced an earlier structure of unknown size and purpose built up against the north wall of St Andrew's tower. The exterior walls of the vestiarium (Figure 49), much restored, are finely decorated and articulated, while some of the best carved work of the period can be found on the angle shafts of the undercroft vault. Roman columns made of jasper have been re-used on the western face of the undercroft. The interior of the vestiarium is one of the hidden delights of Canterbury, a great eight-part dome with ribs springing from the angles and the mid-points of the walls and rising to an improbable multi-faced central boss (Figure 50). The structure, unique in England, has been compared with the tower vaults of Bayeux and Montivilliers, both in Normandy.[39]

38 Jasper is a stone from the area of the Red Sea that will cut into freestone columns and will take a high polish.
39 J. Bilson, 'The Norman school and the beginnings of Gothic architecture: two octopartite vaults: Montivilliers and Canterbury', *Archaeol. J.*, 74, 1917, pp. 1–35.

**49** (*below left*) The vestiarium: exterior facade from the east. The upper stage was added by Henry of Eastry in 1292, and was later rewindowed

**50** (*below right*) The vestiarium: interior showing the octopartite dome, also the painted decoration of the fourteenth (?) century

The Water Tower is another of Wibert's specialized buildings, being the main supply point for the circulation of fresh water (Figures 51–3). It consisted of a raised cistern encased within an arcaded circular structure on an open undercroft with elaborate rib vaults. Most of the lower capitals are variations of the scallop, though one of the central core has a highly accomplished foliate spray. The interior of the cistern chamber above was heavily decorated, with considerable use of chevron patterning.

Wibert also expanded the curia to the north by the purchase of a strip of land running parallel to the city wall. On part of this site he built a raised hall and a new great gate (see Fig. 2). The hall has mostly vanished, but sufficient of its undercroft exists together with excavated remains to show its general form and something of its decoration.[40] The east facade of the hall on the Green Court stood upon an open arcade with simple roll moulded arches supported by square piers with angle shafts. None of the present capitals is original, though one base is intact and has leaf spurs at the angles. The undercroft was groin-vaulted throughout, and arranged in three aisles – a section at the southern end survives as the King's School Memorial Chapel. After the fifth bay from the south the arcade ceased and the block continued northwards upon solid walls. The lost western facade onto the Mint Yard almost certainly presented a walled basement, for it served as part of an important boundary line between the curia of the archbishop and that of the priory. The upper facade of the Aula Nova was

40 Excavation 1978 by the Canterbury Archaeological Trust, as yet unpublished.

51 (*below left*) The vault of the night entry passage and Water Tower

52 (*below right*) The Water Tower: interior arcade trapped against the Prior's Chapel

richly decorated, judging from the excavated fragments of the period. The windows had elaborate arch mouldings, some decorated with dogtooth. The hall was rebuilt or remodelled on several occasions, the last by Prior Chillenden in *c.* 1400 who added exterior buttresses to sections of the undercroft, in which many fragments of the twelfth-century upper hall were re-used. The showpiece of the Aula Nova was never replaced – the famous Norman entry stairs (Figure 54). The entrance stair consists of diminishing arcades preceded by a square bay with steps on three sides. The capitals and miniature arcades are richly carved, as once were the slender shafts. At the top of the stair, originally within the hall, are the remains of waterleaf (?) capitals. The great gate at the southern end of the Aula Nova is perhaps the most monumental of all Wibert's works. The high barrel-vaulted gate originally supported a gabled upper chamber, later rebuilt by Prior Chillenden who also inserted the dividing arches into the western archway to facilitate the use of smaller gates. The great portal arches, the high vault and the decoration of the portal spandrel still stand as witness to the grandeur of Wibert and of his monastery. The portal is flanked by tall freestone shafts supporting heavy overhanging capitals, some with fantastic animals. The arch mouldings above are variously decorated with grotesques and foliage, and the occasional scene.[41] One repeated design, a pattern of leaves radiating from within a wheel, is found on several of Wibert's buildings. The eastern face of the gate is less ornate and more restored.

41  The sculpture of this portal has been considerably restored. However, comparison with other unrestored Wibert sculpture indicates that the style and detail are generally reliable.

53  The Water Tower: detail of the exterior arcade with arrow-heads, dogtooth, chevrons, etc

54  The Norman entry stairs from the south-east. The roof is modern. The remaining sections of the Aula Nova basement arcade can be seen on the left

Within the cathedral church, Wibert seems to have made a further attempt to prevent the collapse of the great eastern towers. The main-level chapel vaults were removed, or perhaps they fell down, and were replaced by lighter rib vaults while the arches into the aisles and apse were thickened by the addition of extra orders. The sculpture associated with these reinforcements is particularly poor and resembles the interior capitals of the vestiarium. In contrast, Wibert's other additions to the fabric of the church are the two exquisite transept stair turrets (Figure 55). Anselm had left them unfinished at the height of the new choir arcade walls, and they must have had some temporary covering at this level. They were not prominent features of the building and were omitted from the Waterworks Drawing. Wibert's extensions employ an entirely new design for the exterior facades with broad pilaster buttresses scooped out with arcades and chevron circles like those on the great gate. Everywhere, the triple arcade motif dominates, and the wall surfaces are fretted away. Internally, the north turret has only wall stairs plus a tiny top spiral, while the southern turret now contains an extension of the broad spiral stair from below.

One major work that was probably carried out during Wibert's priorate is known only from fragments – a new great cloister. Wibert's reorganization of the slype was only one part of a scheme for the replacement of Lanfranc's cloister arcades, and for the provision of new access doors. The remains of the arcading suggest that the new work can

**55** The north-east transept stair turret: exterior from the north-west, showing extension by Prior Wibert *c.* 1160

hardly have been equalled in northern Europe, with a rich use of polished coloured marbles for both arcades and flooring. From the fragments, the arcades can be reconstructed with coupled shafts made up of marble columns linked by intermediate stone shaft rings. The bases were also coupled and had leaf spurs. The evidence suggests that several bays were grouped together within stone piers that may have supported over-arches. The columns were variously coloured and some were decorated with spirals, chevrons or other incised designs. No capitals have come to light – perhaps they were too big for later re-use and were consequently broken up for rubble. The arches were also marble with chevron decoration on both sides and a profile of two roll mouldings answering the coupled columns below – some fragments also contain decoration between the rolls, some foliate, some free-standing chevron. The arches were topped by dripstones of Caen with carved headstops. The spandrels, perhaps inside and out, contained a series of magnificent roundel plaques with grotesque or biblical heads of superb craftsmanship (Figure 56). The flooring was of polished marble, blue and brown and the whole ensemble must have presented a marvellous spectacle. It is not possible to date the fragments to any particular part of Wibert's priorate, for the sculpture is of the highest quality only rarely seen in his other works. The architectural elements are much more standard for the period, though nowhere else can they all be found in marble. Doubtless, the cloister formed the principal project of Wibert's priorate and employed the best of his sculptors (Figure 57).

Wibert's controlling hand can be seen in the earliest of the city rent rolls preserved in the cathedral library, and in the reformation of the entire monastic central financing system, which was to remain almost unchanged for the rest of the Middle Ages.[42] His priorate also saw the advent of Thomas Becket.

The story of St Thomas of Canterbury races across the pages of English history. For a brief eight years he held the attention of Europe. To the citizens of Canterbury he became almost a Christ-figure, though his residence in the city can be counted only in months. The impact of his murder and the miraculous powers of his body caused a sensation throughout Christendom, and the enigma of his life and the devotion

42  For the rent rolls of the twelfth-century cathedral, see W. G. Urry, *Canterbury under the Angevin Kings*; a remarkable study in the social history of the period.

**56**  (*below left*) The cloister finds: fantastic mask probably from a cloister by Wibert, *c.* 1160

**57**  (*below right*) The Prior's Gate: right-hand capital from the exterior first-floor window, *c.* 1170

**58** Romanesque base profiles:
1 St Anselm's choir, aisle respond; 2 St Anselm's chapel additional work; 3 St Anselm's chapel, vault respond; 4 dormitory night passage; 5 Water Tower; 6 vestiarium undercroft; 7 vestiarium; 8 dormitory, door to cloister; 9 Infirmary Chapel; 10 Infirmary Chapel

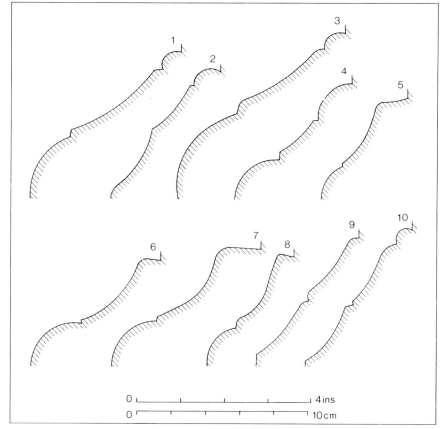

inspired by his cult have kept the memory of St Thomas alive in the popular imagination. Throughout the Middle Ages a multitude of the devout and worldly flocked to his fantastic shrine. Some came in hope of cure, some for penance, many just to gawp. The panoply that engulfed his relics outstripped all other shrines and his cult was at once religious and profane, spiritual and commercial. The lure of the shrine of St Thomas is the perfect example of the inseparable religious and worldly sentiments of mediaeval man. For the cathedral, possession of the saint's relics brought even greater fame and glory, though the mere presence of the shrine did not bring the fabulous wealth to the monks with which it is so often associated.

In the immediate aftermath of the murder, the cathedral stood closed and desecrated. The penitential acts of Henry II, the canonization of the martyr by Alexander III and, above all, the miracles performed at his tomb, gripped Christendom with a feverish adulation. St Thomas was everywhere – from Salamanca to Monreale. His tomb at Canterbury, now a shrine, lay in the easternmost chapel of the crypt, well served by the great Romanesque ambulatory but far removed from the monks and their daily devotion. Everything and everywhere associated with the saint became precious: the floor spattered with his blood, the shattered sword that struck the glorious blow, the altars at which he had prayed. The whole church abounded with the relics of his life and death. Now all these had to be presented to, and protected from, the crowds that flocked to seek the intercession and miraculous powers of the saint. But how were the monks to accommodate the stream of pilgrims both rich and poor that clamoured for access to the saint's remains, and how could the cathedral physically embody the glorification of their martyred archbishop? The answer came most dramatically on 5 September 1174. In mid-afternoon a fire swept through St Anselm's choir, 'hitherto delightful like a paradise of pleasure'. Soon it 'lay contemptible in the ashes of the fire'. Whether the work of man or of devil, the burning and repair of Christ Church provided the monks of Canterbury with an opportunity which at first they hardly realized.

**Note**

Temporary display lighting in the north choir aisle early in 1981 revealed the following evidence: the aisle responds could be clearly seen as additions to the Romanesque window jambs from above the level of the original transverse arch springing. The coursing of the extensions in the two responds between the windows is well matched (see Fig. 38), they being the earliest work on sculptural evidence. The others, both east and west, together with all the respond extensions in the south choir aisle, have far more casual bonding alignment. This would not have been so had William of Sens raised the windows as well (as suggested by Willis). Window II in the north aisle was damaged when the Romanesque vaults were removed in 1174 – one chip-carved voussoir being replaced with a block of a different design. The vault scars were then made good with re-used Romanesque masonry.

# CHAPTER 3

# THE GOTHIC CHOIR, 1174-84

Henry II was not anxious to fill the vacant see of Canterbury after the murder of Becket. When finally he was forced to allow an election he disputed the result. The monks chose Richard, prior of St Martin's, Dover, a cell of the cathedral, and eventually he was compelled to go to Rome in order to gain papal support for his election. Archbishop Richard, unlike others in the convent, sought to play down the political implications thrown up by the increasing devotion to the martyr, and by 1173 the monks were seriously divided over the question of what should be done with the body of St Thomas. The saint's tomb in the eastern crypt chapel was convenient for the pilgrims and had in any case assumed a sanctity of its own. Any thought of translating the body into a new tomb in the choir was firmly resisted by the archbishop, for both reasons of tact and the overcrowded conditions already prevalent around the sanctuary. But Prior Odo, later the abbot of Battle, saw things quite differently. Why waste this great asset that fortune, or God, had put their way? In an era when relics were of increasing importance, the body of the holy and blissful martyr was far too significant to lie in such obscurity. No details survive concerning the proposed site for a new tomb; it may not have been in the choir at all, but it is quite clear that not everyone was content to leave the body where it had been so hastily buried on the night of the murder.

Richard returned from Rome armed with his papal confirmation on 4 September 1174. On the following day, disaster struck – the most fortuitous disaster in the long history of the cathedral. A house caught fire, perhaps that of Lambin Frese the minter that stood somewhere at the western end of Burgate near the south-west tower of the cathedral. A common event in any mediaeval town, but one that has been enshrined in the literature of the Middle Ages. The fire spread to several houses, the sparks flew, and the great choir caught light. Conrad's glorious choir, the church of the blessed Anselm and of St Thomas was consumed. The story of the fire and the subsequent rebuilding, as told by Gervase, is full of mediaeval hyperbole, gross exaggeration and biblical parallels, but it also exhibits an unusual and keen understanding of the process of building. Gervase knew about architecture, and with the advantage of hindsight, he realized that he had witnessed the construction of Europe's newest and most dazzling shrine-house. Unfortunately, Gervase was also fond of telling half-truths – he records only what he wants us to know, and his account must be read with some insight into the mediaeval mind. All his statements concerning the burning and rebuilding of the choir must be compared with the structural evidence. For, remarkably, we have at Canterbury not only a detailed account of how a building was put up in the twelfth century but also the very same structure hardly touched in eight centuries.

As a monastic chronicler, Gervase was responsible for recording the dedications and positions of all the altars and tombs, but, in addition, he was fascinated and perhaps even directly involved with the building of the new choir. From him we learn something of the process of decision-making. What did a great cathedral do after a serious fire? The answer at Canterbury was a kind of symposium with leading master masons from both England and France gathering to offer their advice. It is interesting that they came from both countries, for Canterbury had already absorbed an amount of French influence by the middle of the century and was evidently open to new ideas. Predictably there was no consensus of opinion, probably because the damage was not as serious as Gervase insists and many of the masters were in favour of simple repair work. The circumstances by which William of Sens was appointed master mason are glossed over, indeed there is more than the slightest hint that Gervase and William did not get on. Nevertheless, all the others were dismissed and William was left to brood upon the options available to him.

But how did William procure such a position? Who was he and where did he come from? Gervase calls him 'of Sens', and that may well have been his native city. No place on earth possessed such magic in Canterbury as the city of Sens – it had been the refuge of St Thomas during his years of exile and it was the only other church to have major relics of the martyr, particularly his mass vestements. The very name of Sens would open doors in Canterbury and there may have been some personal intervention on William's behalf from the French archbishop. The monks of Canterbury dismissed all the other masters upon William's arrival, even though it was some time before he told them what he intended to do with the old choir. He either came to them with references from an impeccable source, or some previous work of his recommended William to the convent. Gervase speaks of his 'lively genious and good reputation', though this might mean anything in a mediaeval context.

Before William could begin, he had to persuade the monks that most of the old choir should be demolished. The crypt was sound, and the aisle walls were deemed to be re-usable. The major demolition involved the arcade walls and the tribune bridges across the transept opening. William was able to build his new choir into, and on top of, St Anselm's, and the retention of so much of the Romanesque structure was an important factor in the design of the early stages of the work. The remark by Gervase that as much as possible of the old choir was left in order to please the monks is seriously flawed, for they were clearly not bound by any conviction about the sacred associations of the building. By 1180 they were perfectly willing to demolish the old Trinity Chapel that contained one of the most important altars in the growing cult of St Thomas, and – in its crypt – the shrine itself. The original argument for retaining as much of the old choir as possible was probably financial, including the advantage of constructing the new work on the top of the existing crypt.

Work proceeded rapidly until, in 1178, William fell from the scaffolding and was seriously injured. He tried to control the work from his sick-bed with the help of a monk – perhaps Gervase himself. However, this partnership caused bitterness and jealousy, and eventually William went home to France. He was replaced by another William, styled 'the Englishman' by Gervase, and quite plainly the monk preferred this native architect to the Frenchman. Work proceeded even more quickly under the second William, seeing the completion of the high vaults of the choir and transept and the building of the new Trinity Chapel. The only break in the work occurred in 1183, due to lack of funds. This is no reflection on the wealth of the cathedral, but rather an indication of the great speed of construction and the costly materials lavished on the building. By 1184, just ten years after the fire, the fabric was completed and the long process of decoration and embellishment began.

The work of the two Williams at Canterbury Cathedral is of paramount importance for the development of Gothic architecture in England. For the first time, a major English ecclesiastical patron sought to emulate the new style of France. Various Gothic elements had percolated into Canterbury during the middle of the century, but now, for the first time, a French master was chosen to build a Gothic church in England.

Unlike the architecture of the Romanesque period at Canterbury, the Gothic choir survives virtually untouched and can be studied as a standing building rather than as a subject for hypothetical reconstruction. Therefore the choir is described in two sections – first the work of William of Sens, 1174–9, with a discussion of its place in contemporary French Gothic, followed by the work of the second William, 'the Englishman', whose remarkable work covers the period 1179–84.

## The work of William of Sens, 1174–9

The choir of William of Sens is the earliest surviving Gothic building in England and was by far the most significant influence over the dissemination of that style throughout the southern half of the country (see Fig. 10). The choir is divided into three, roughly equal, sections. The choir proper containing the stalls for the monks occupies the five western bays between the central tower and the eastern crossing. William of Sens abandoned the old continuous arcade across the transept and widened the crossing beyond its Romanesque limits (Figure 59). The presbytery occupied the four bays east of the crossing, with the high Altar raised upon a few steps and flanked by the altar-shrines of SS Dunstan and Alphege. The last and most elevated bay of the presbytery contains the throne of St Augustine. Beyond lies the work of William the Englishman – the new Trinity Chapel with two bays plus five more in the apse, flanking aisles and an ambulatory. The chevet has no radial chapels save a single axial tower-chapel, the Corona.

The choir elevation has three storeys with great emphasis placed on the main arcade. The triforium level is diminutive but is the subject of considerable enrichment, while the clerestory is almost concealed within the high vaults which spring from the level of the 'triforium' capitals. The clerestory is set back within a passage and is glimpsed through a polished marble arcade. The design of this and the triforium is adjusted according to the irregular widths of the arcade bays. The aisle elevation has two storeys; Anselm's great round-headed windows below, with rather squat trefoil windows above, set into the rear wall of a passage. The aisle vaults spring from the floor-level of the upper passage.

**59** (*below left*) The eastern crossing from the north choir aisle

**60** (*below right*) Interior of the choir and Trinity Chapel from the east

The high vaults of the choir follow a sexpartite plan which is expressed on the arcade wall by an alteration of the vault support shafts. The first bay west is quadripartite due to the uneven number of the bays, and is preceded by descending pointed barrel vaults which originally assisted the transition from the lower crossing arches to the new high vaults.

The presbytery narrows as it moves eastwards in order to avoid the Romanesque ambulatory tower-chapels (Figure 60). It exhibits a greater degree of decoration and a variety of pier designs. The Trinity Chapel beyond the presbytery follows the main lines of the choir, though the proportions are radically altered by the raising of the floor-level. The aisle walls are entirely Gothic, being beyond the ambulatory of St Anselm's choir.

William designed his new choir in such a way that it could be built within the greater part of the Romanesque shell of St Anselm's work. He was able to re-use the outer walls and leave the crypt intact, but he also proposed to enlarge the eastern axial chapel which had become the focal point of the growing cult of St Thomas. The work proceeded rapidly from 1175, and we can do no better than to refer to the narrative by Gervase.[1]

1 Translation according to Willis, *Arch. Hist.*, pp. 34–6, 48–62, with amendments indicated*.

### The operations of the first year

Bethink thee now what mighty grief oppressed the hearts of the sons of the Church under this great tribulation; I verily believe the afflictions of Canterbury were no less than those of Jerusalem of old, and their wailings were as the lamentations of Jeremiah; neither can mind conceive, or words express, or writing teach, their grief and anguish. Truly that they might alleviate their miseries with a little consolation, they put together as well as they could, an altar and station in the nave of the church, where they might wail and howl, rather than sing, the diurnal and nocturnal services. Meanwhile the patron saints of the church, St. Dunstan and St. Alphege, had their resting-place in that wilderness. Lest, therefore, they should suffer even the slightest injury from the rains and storms, the monks, weeping and lamenting with incredible grief and anguish, opened the tombs of the saints and extricated them in their coffins from the choir, but with the greatest difficulty and labour, as if the saints themselves resisted the change.

They disposed them as decently as they could at the altar of the Holy Cross in the nave. Thus, like as the children of Israel were ejected from the land of promise, yea, even from a paradise of delight, that it might be like people, like priest, and that the stones of the sanctuary might be poured out at the corners of the streets; so the brethren remained in grief and sorrow for five years in the nave of the church, separated from the people only by a low wall.

Meantime the brotherhood sought counsel as to how and in what manner the burnt church might be repaired, but without success; for the columns of the church, commonly termed the pillars, were exceedingly weakened by the heat of the fire, and were scaling in pieces and hardly able to stand, so that they frightened even the wisest out of their wits.

French and English artificers were therefore summoned, but even these differed in opinion. On the one hand, some undertook to repair the aforesaid columns without mischief to the walls above. On the other hand, there were some who asserted that the whole church must be pulled down if the monks wished to exist in safety. This opinion, true as it was, excruciated the monks with grief, and no wonder, for how could they hope that so great a work should be completed in their days by any human ingenuity.

However, amongst the other workmen there had come a certain William of Sens, a man active and ready, and as a workman most skilful both in wood and stone. Him, therefore, they retained, on account of his lively genius and good reputation, and dismissed the others. And to him, and to the providence of God was the execution of the work committed.

And he, residing many days with the monks and carefully surveying the burnt walls in their upper and lower parts, within and without, did yet for some time conceal what he found necessary to be done, lest the truth should kill them in their present state of pusillanimity.

But he went on preparing all things that were needful for the work, either of himself or by the agency of others. And when he found that the monks began to be somewhat comforted, he ventured to confess that the pillars rent with the fire and all that they supported must be destroyed if the monks wished to have a safe and excellent building. At length they agreed, being convinced by reason and wishing to have the work as good as he promised, and above all things to live in security; thus they consented patiently, if not willingly, to the destruction of the choir.

And now he addressed himself to the procuring of stone from beyond sea. He constructed ingenious machines for loading and unloading ships, and for drawing cement and stones. He delivered moulds for shaping the stones to the sculptors who were assembled, and diligently prepared other things of the same kind. The choir thus condemned to destruction was pulled down, and nothing else was done in this year.

As the new work is of a different fashion from the old, it may be well to describe the old work first and then the new. Eadmer, the venerable singer, in his Opuscula, describes the ancient church built in the Roman manner, which Archbishop Lanfranc, when he came to the see, utterly destroyed, finding it in ashes. For Christ Church is recorded to have suffered thrice from fire; first, when the blessed martyr Alphege was captured by the Danes and received the crown of maryrdom; secondly, when Lanfranc, abbot of Caen, took the rule of the church of Canterbury; thirdly, in the days of Archbishop Richard and Prior Odo. Of this last conflagration, unhappily, we have not read, but have seen it with our own eyes. . . .

The Master began . . . to prepare all things necessary for the new work, and to destroy the old. In this way the first year was taken up. In the following year, that is, after the feast of St. Bertin [5 September 1175] before the winter, he erected four pillars, that is, two on each side, and after the winter two more were placed, so that on each side were three in order, upon which and upon the exterior wall of the aisles he framed seemly arches and a vault, that is, three keys* on each side. I put keys* for the whole vault* because the key* placed in the middle locks up and binds together the parts which converge to it from every side.* With these works the second year was occupied.

In the third year he placed two pillars on each side, the two extreme ones of which he decorated with marble columns placed around them, and because at that place the choir and crosses were to meet, he constituted these principal pillars. To which, having added the key-stones and vault, he intermingled the lower triforium from the great tower to the aforesaid pillars, that is, as far as the cross, with many marble columns. Over which he adjusted another triforium of other materials, and also the upper windows. And in the next place, three keys* of the great vault, from the tower, namely, as far as the crosses. All which things appeared to us and to all who saw them, incomparable and most worthy of praise. And at so glorious a beginning we rejoiced and conceived good hopes of the end, and provided for the acceleration of the work with diligence and spirit. Thus was the third year occupied and the beginning of the fourth.

In the summer of which, commencing from the cross, he erected ten pillars, that is, on each side five. Of which the two first were ornamented with marble columns to correspond with the other two principal ones. Upon these ten he placed the arches and vaults. And having, in the next place, completed on both sides the triforia and upper windows, he was, at the beginning of the fifth year, in the act of preparing with machines for the turning of the great vault, when suddenly the beams broke under his feet, and he fell to the ground, stones and timbers accompanying his fall, from the height of the capitals of the upper vault, that is to say, of fifty feet. Thus sorely bruised by the blows from the beams and stones, he was rendered helpless alike to himself and for the work, but no other person than himself was in the least injured. Against the master only was this vengeance of God or spite of the devil directed.

The master, thus hurt, remained in his bed for some time under medical care in expectation of recovering, but was deceived in this hope, for his health amended not. Nevertheless, as the winter approached, and it was necessary to finish the upper vault, he gave charge of the work to a certain ingenious and industrious monk, who was the overseer of the masons; an appointment whence much envy and malice arose, because it made this young man appear more skilful than richer and more powerful ones. But the master reclining in bed commanded all things that should be done in order. And thus was completed the ciborium between the four principal pillars. In the key-stone of this vault the choir and crosses seem as it were to meet. Two vaults,*, one each side*, were formed before the winter; when heavy rains beginning stopped the work. In these operations the fourth year was occupied and the beginning of the fifth. But on the eighth day from the said fourth year, on the idus of September, there happened an eclipse of the sun at about the sixth hour, and before the master's accident.

And the master, perceiving that he derived no benefit from the physicians, gave up the work, and crossing the sea, returned to his home in France. And another succeeded him in the charge of the works; William by name, English by nation, small in body, but in workmanship of many kinds acute and honest. He in the summer of the fifth year finished the cross on each side, that is, the south and the north, and turned the ciborium which is above the great Altar, which the rains of the previous year had hindered, although all was prepared. Moreover, he laid the foundation for the enlargement of the church at the eastern part, because a chapel of St. Thomas was to be built there.

For this was the place assigned to him; namely, the chapel of the Holy Trinity, where he celebrated his first mass, where he was wont to prostrate himself with tears and prayers, under whose crypt for so many years he was buried, where God for his merits had performed so many miracles, where poor and rich, kings and princes, had worshipped him, and whence the sound of his praises had gone forth into all lands.

The master William began, on account of these foundations, to dig in the cemetery of the monks, from whence he was compelled to disturb the bones of many holy monks. These were carefully collected and deposited in a large trench, in that corner which is between the chapel and the south side of the infirmary house. Having, therefore, formed a most substantial foundation for the exterior wall with stone and cement, he erected the wall of the crypt as high as the bases of the windows.

Thus was the fifth year employed and the beginning of the sixth.

### The entry into the new choir

In the beginning of the sixth year from the fire, and at the time when the works were resumed, the monks were seized with a violent longing to prepare the choir, so that they might enter it at the coming Easter. And the master, perceiving their desires, set himself manfully to work, to satisfy the wishes of the convent. He constructed, with all diligence, the wall which encloses the choir and presbytery. He erected the three altars of the presbytery. He carefully prepared a resting-place for St. Dunstan and St. Alphege. A wooden wall to keep out the weather was set up transversely between the penultimate pillars at the eastern part, and had three glass windows in it.

The choir, thus hardly completed even with the greatest labour and diligence, the monks were resolved to enter on Easter Eve with the new fire. As all that was required could not be fully performed on the Saturday because of the solemnities of that sacred day, it became necessary that our holy fathers and patrons, St. Dunstan and St. Alphege, the co-exiles of the monks, should be transferred to the new choir beforehand. Prior Alan, therefore, taking with him nine of the brethren of the church in whom he could trust, went by night to the tombs of the saints, that he might not be incommoded by a crowd, and having locked the doors of the church, he commanded the stone-work that enclosed them to be taken down.

The monks and servants of the church therefore, in obedience to the Prior's commands, took the structure to pieces, opened the stone coffins of the saints, and bore their relics to the *vestiarium*. Then, having removed the cloths in which they had been wrapped, and which were half consumed from age and rottenness, they covered them with other and more handsome palls, and bound them with linen bands. They bore the saints, thus prepared, to their altars, and deposited them in wooden chests, còvered within and without with lead; which chests, thus lead-covered, and strongly bound with iron, were enclosed in stone-work that was consolidated with melted lead. Queen Ediva also, who had been placed under the altar of the holy cross after the fire, was similarly conveyed to the vestiarium. These things were done on the night preceding the fifth feria before the holy Easter; that is, on the sixteenth kalend of May. On the morrow, however, when this translation of the saints became known to the whole convent, they were exceedingly astonished and indignant that it should have been done without their consent, for they had intended that the translation of the fathers should have been performed with great and devout solemnity.

They cited the prior and those who were with him, before the venerable Archbishop Richard, to answer for the slight thus presumptuously cast upon themselves and the holy patrons of the church, and endeavoured to compel the prior and his assistants to renounce their offices. But by the intervention of the archbishop and other men of authority, and after due apology and repentance, the convent was appeased; and harmony being thus restored, the service of Holy Saturday was performed in the chapter-house, because the station of the monks and the altar which had been in the nave of the church, were removed to prepare for the solemnities of the following Easter Sunday. About the sixth hour the archbishop in cope and mitre, and the convent in albs, according to the custom of the church, went in procession to the new fire, and having consecrated it, proceeded towards the new choir with the appointed hymn. At the door of the church which opens to the martyrium of St. Thomas, the archbishop reverently received from a monk the pix, with the Eucharist, which was usually suspended over the great Altar. This he carried to the great Altar of the new choir. Thus our Lord went before us into Galilee, that is, in our transmigration to the new church. The remainder of the offices that appertain to the day were devoutly celebrated. And then the pontiff, standing at the Altar and vested with the infula, began the Te Deum laudamus; and the bells ringing, the convent took up the song with great joy, and shedding sweet tears, they praised God with voice and heart for all His benefits.

The convent was ejected by the fire from the choir, even as Adam from paradise, in the year of the Word 1174, in the month of September, on the fifth day of the month, and about the ninth hour. They remained in the nave of the church five years, seven months, and thirteen days. And returned into the new choir in the year of grace 1180, in the month of April, on the nineteenth day of the month, at about the ninth hour of Easter Eve.

### Remaining operations of the sixth year

Our craftsman had erected outside the choir four altars, where the bodies of the holy archbishops were deposited, as they were of old, and as we have above described. At the altar of St. Martin; Living, and Wilfrid. At the altar of St. Stephen; Athelard, and Cuthbert. In the south cross at the altar of St. John; Aelfric, and Ethelgar. At the altar of St. Gregory; Bregwin, and Plegmund. But Queen Ediva, who before the fire reposed under a gilded *feretrum* in nearly the middle of the south cross, was now deposited at the altar of St. Martin, under the *feretrum* of Living.

Moreover, in the same summer, that is of the sixth year, the outer wall round the chapel of St. Thomas, begun before the winter, was elevated as far as the turning of the vault. But the master had begun a tower at the eastern part outside the circuit of the wall as it were, the lower vault of which was completed before the winter.

The chapel of the Holy Trinity above mentioned was then levelled to the ground; this had hitherto remained untouched out of reverence to St Thomas, who was buried in the crypt. But the saints who reposed in the upper part of the chapel were translated elsewhere, and lest the memory of what was then done should be lost, I will record somewhat thereof. On the eighth idus of July the altar of the Holy Trinity was broken up, and from its materials the altar of St. John the Apostle was made; I mention this lest the history of the holy stone should be lost upon which St. Thomas celebrated his first mass, and many times after performed the divine offices. The stone structure which was behind this altar was taken to pieces. Here, as before said, St. Oda and St. Wilfrid reposed for a long period. These saints were raised in their leaden coffins and carried into the choir. St. Oda, in his coffin, was placed under the feretrum of St. Dunstan, and St. Wilfrid under the feretrum of St. Alphege.

Archbishop Lanfranc was found enclosed in a very heavy sheet of lead, in which, from the day of his first burial up to that day, he had rested untouched, in mitre and pall, for sixty-nine years and some months. He was carried to the vestiarium in his leaden covering, and there deposited until the community should decide what should be done with so great a Father. When they opened the tomb of Archbishop Theobald, which was built of marble slabs, and came to his sarcophagus, the monks who were present expecting to find his body reduced to dust, brought wine and water to wash his bones. But when the lid of the sarcophagus was raised, he was found entire and rigid, and still subsisting in bones and nerves, skin and flesh, but somewhat attenuated. The bystanders marvelled at this sight, and placing him upon a bier, they carried him as they had done Lanfranc, to the vestiarium, to await the decision of the convent. But the rumour began to spread among the people, and already, for this unwonted incorruption, many called him St. Theobald. He was exhibited to some who desired to see him, and they helped to spread the tale among the rest.

He was thus raised from his sepulchre in the nineteenth year from his death, his body being incorrupted, and his silk vestments entire. And by the decision of the convent was buried in a leaden coffin before the altar of St. Mary, in the nave of the church, which place he had wished for while living. The marble tomb was put together over him, as it was before. But Lanfranc having remained, as before said, untouched for sixty-nine years, his very bones were consumed with rottenness, and nearly all reduced to powder. The length of time, the damp vestments, the natural frigidity of the lead, and above all, the frailty of the human structure, had conspired to produce this corruption. But the larger bones, with the remaining dust, were collected in a leaden coffer, and deposited at the altar of St. Martin. The two archbishops who lay to the right and left of St. Thomas in the crypt were taken up, and placed for the time in their leaden coffins under the altar of St. Mary, in the crypt.

The translation of these Fathers having been thus effected, the chapel, together with its crypt, was destroyed to the very ground; only that the translation of St. Thomas was reserved until the completion of his chapel. For it was fitting and manifest that such a translation should be most solemn and public. In the mean time, therefore, a wooden chapel, sufficiently decent for the place and occasion, was prepared around and above his tomb. Outside of this a foundation was laid of stones and cement, upon which eight pillars of the new crypt, with their capitals, were completed. The master also carefully opened an entrance from the old to the new crypt. And thus the sixth year was employed, and part of the seventh. But before I follow the works of this seventh year, it may not be amiss to recapitulate some of the previous ones which have either been omitted from negligence or purposely for the sake of brevity.

It has been above stated, that after the fire nearly all the old portions of the choir were destroyed and changed into somewhat new and of a more noble fashion. The differences between the two works may now be enumerated. The pillars of the old and new work are alike in form and thickness but different in length. For the new pillars were elongated by almost twelve feet. In the old capitals the work was plain, in the new ones exquisite in sculpture. There the circuit of the choir had twenty-two pillars, here are twenty-eight. There the arches and every thing else was plain, or sculptured with an axe and not with a chisel. But here almost throughout is appropriate sculpture. No marble columns were there, but here are innumerable ones. There, in the circuit around the choir, the vaults were plain, but here they are arch-ribbed and have keystones. There a wall set upon pillars divided the crosses from the choir, but here the crosses are separated from the choir by no such partition, and converge together in one keystone, which is placed in the middle of the great vault which rests on the four principal pillars. There, there was a ceiling of wood decorated with excellent painting, but here is a vault beautifully constructed of stone and light tufa. There, was a single triforium, but here are two in the choir and a third in the aisle of the church. All which will be better understood from inspection than by any description.

This must be made known, however, that the new work is higher than the old by so much as the upper windows of the body of the choir, as well as of its aisles, are raised above the marble tabling.

And as in future ages it may be doubtful why the breadth which was given to the choir next the tower should be so much contracted at the head of the church, it may not be useless to explain the causes thereof. One reason is, that the two towers of St Anselm and of St. Andrew, placed in the circuit on each side of the old church, would not allow the breadth of the choir to proceed in the direct line. Another reason is, that it was agreed upon and necessary that the chapel of St. Thomas should be erected at the head of the church, where the chapel of the Holy Trinity stood, and this was much narrower than the choir.

The master, therefore, not choosing to pull down the said towers, and being unable to move them entire, set out the breadth of the choir in a straight line, as far as the beginning of the towers. Then, receding slightly on either side of the towers, and preserving as much as he could the breadth of the passage outside the choir on account of the processions which were there frequently passing, he gradually and obliquely drew in his work, so that from opposite the altar, it might begin to contract, and from thence, at the third pillar, might be so narrowed as to coincide with the breadth of the chapel, which was named of the Holy Trinity. Beyond these, four pillars were set on the sides at the same distance as the last, but of a different form; and beyond these other four were arranged in a circle, and upon these the superposed work [of each side] was brought together and terminated. This is the arrangement of the pillars.

The outer wall, which extends from the aforesaid towers, first proceeds in a straight line, is then bent into a curve, and thus in the round tower the wall on each side comes together in one, and is there ended. All which may be more clearly and pleasantly seen by the eyes than taught in writing. But this much was said that the differences between the old and new work might be made manifest.

### Operations of the seventh, eighth and tenth years

Now let us carefully examine what were the works of our mason in this seventh year from the fire, which, in short, included the completion of the new and handsome crypt, and above the crypt the exterior walls of the aisles up to their marble capitals. The windows, however, the master was neither willing nor able to turn, on account of the approaching rains. Neither did he erect the interior pillars. Thus was the seventh year finished, and the eighth begun.

In this eighth year the master erected eight interior pillars, and turned the arches and the vault with the windows in the circuit. He also raised the tower up to the bases of the highest windows under the vault. In the ninth year no work was done for want of funds. In the tenth year the upper windows of the tower, together with the vault, were finished. Upon the pillars was placed a lower and an upper triforium, with windows and the great vault. Also was made the upper roof where the cross stands aloft, and the roof of the aisles as far as the laying of the lead. The tower was covered in, and many other things done this year. In which year Baldwin bishop of Worcester was elected to the rule of the church of Canterbury on the eighteenth kalend of January, and was enthroned there on the feast of St Dunstan next after . . .

Gervase paints a picture of an ordered and efficient programme, well defined, and with all the major decisions made at the outset and adhered to until completion. Apart from the accident to William of Sens in 1178, things went smoothly and according to plan with the whole choir reaching completion within the remarkably short space of ten building seasons. The building tells a different story. One of complex problems, of uncertain techniques and apparently a complete change of plan halfway through.

William of Sens's decision to preserve the original aisle windows led him to one of the most unusual features of his choir – the double-storey aisle elevation (see Fig. 38). William raised the roof-line of his choir from about 73 ft – 2,225 cm – to around 85 ft – 2,591 cm – by raising the main arcade 12 ft – 366 cm – higher than Anselm's. Thus the present aisle vaults spring from the floor-level of Anselm's tribune, combining the previous aisle wall with the height of the former tribune wall. It was the decision to retain the access at the old tribune level that determined that the additional height within the new aisle should contain a passage to connect the eastern transept stair turrets to the various levels of Lanfranc's church further west. To this end, William removed the exposed section of the old tribune wall and replaced it with a wall containing an interior arcaded wall passage (see Fig. 37). The new walls are almost completely voided by the trefoil-headed windows of a most unusual design, one more at home in

Mosan metalwork than in architecture. Had William been able to abandon the access at the old tribune level, he doubtless would have replaced the former aisle windows with lancets rising the full height of the new aisle.[2]

Thus the proportions of the new arcade were determined by the existing height of the old aisle and tribune walls – a relationship probably forced on William of Sens by the problems of buttressing his proposed high vaults (Figure 61). The history of French Gothic for much of its first century is dominated by one problem – how to support the high vaults. The final answer was the flying buttress, but that solution was not available to William in 1174. The repertoire of vault-support systems current at that time was restricted: either vaulted tribunes requiring external buttressing, transverse barrel-vaulted tribunes or buttressing walls carried transversely over the aisles. William would probably have favoured the first option, which had been used in several of the earliest

2 The choir of the near-by abbey of St Augustine, burnt in 1168, was rebuilt in this way. It also exhibited other remarkable similarities with the work at the cathedral, especially the design of the vault ribs. This has led to some speculation that one of the Williams may have worked on the remodelling of the abbey. The date of the work is unsure.

**61** The south arcade wall of the choir

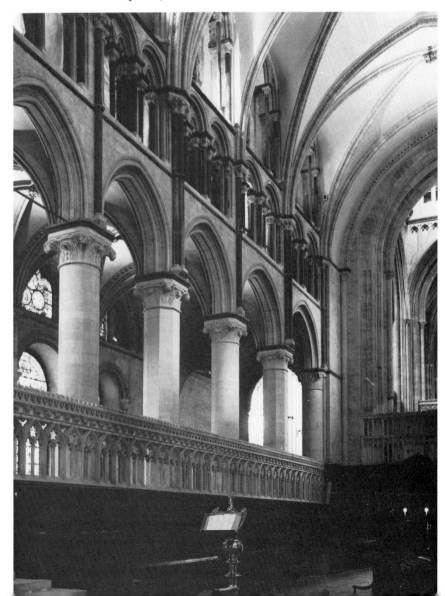

**62** Vaulted tribune of the
south choir aisle during
the absence of the organ
pipes in 1978

3  The barrels were covered in a
thick layer of plaster, which was
renewed in 1978. Details of their
construction are no longer visible.

**63** Exterior elevation of the
south choir aisle tribune

Gothic buildings in France. However, it presented almost as many
problems as it solved, for at Canterbury the possibility of providing the
necessary exterior buttressing was extremely limited. The elevational
design of Anselm's aisle walls presented a severe restriction on William's
choice, for the sheer unbuttressed walls rising above the crypt have
minimal wall space between the large windows (see Fig. 37). It would
have been impossible for William to add sufficient buttressing for a rib-
vaulted tribune without obstructing the existing windows. But while the
design of the aisle excluded the addition of significant buttressing, the
very thickness of the old walls could provide a firm base for transverse
barrel-vaults, and this was to be William's first choice (see Fig. 44).
According to Gervase, the northern and southern sides of the choir
proceeded at the same pace, but this was evidently not so. The southern
side was plainly in advance of the northern flank by the time the high vault
supports were commenced. The southern side maintains the original
vault-support system, at least between the central tower and the eastern
crossing. The northern side was begun with the same design as on the
south, only to be abandoned in favour of a different solution. The barrel-
vaulted tribunes above the south choir aisle rest on transverse arches
which not only support the barrels but also assist in countering the thrust
of the high vault. The barrels are slightly pointed and are made of roughly
cut ashlar, with two semicircular stiffening ribs towards the centre
(Figure 62).[3] The supporting transverse arches have depressed segmental
openings forming a through passage. An open arcade of clustered shafts
grouped into twin openings by two semicircular over-arches looks down
into the interior of the church. The columns are made of polished marble
and the capitals have a variety of foliate carving. Inside the tribune, the
northern end of the barrel-vault rests on a single over-arch which frames
the marble arcade. The first bay west, the earliest, has a thicker over-arch
supporting the barrel and while this was dropped in favour of the slimmer
arches further east, springing stones for the former width were provided
throughout. This may signify that all the transverse arches were built at
once, and only later received their barrel-vaults.

The supporting over-arches rise higher than the top of the tribune level
as expressed by the upper string course on the interior elevation. They
actually cut above the floor-level of the clerestory passage which sits
directly upon the marble arcade. As if to emphasize the constructional
complexity of this section, William voided the area between the clerestory
passage floor-level and the underside of the barrel-vault support so that it
is possible to see the passage above from the tribune. The over-arch
supporting the end of the barrel also carries the window wall of the
clerestory above – both the upper passage and the clerestory window wall
are supported by oversailing. The exterior facade of the south tribune
contains pairs of lancets and a horizontal parapet (Figure 63). There is no
evidence of drainage spouts between each bay so that the relatively flat

roof over the tribune may represent an original arrangement. One further structural feature of the southern tribune is visible only from this roof. Each transverse arch carrying the barrel-vaults below also supports a triangular buttress wall which rises to a pilaster placed against the exterior wall of the clerestory (Figure 64). These buttress walls just break through the flat tribune roof-line.

The design of the south tribune has several advantages: it does not require additional exterior buttressing because of the north–south alignment of the barrels; it also provides an intermediate band of daylight between the interior main arcade and the upper clerestory windows, a lighting-scheme first favoured by William of Sens. But these advantages were more than outweighed by the disadvantages – the most obvious being the restriction upon the level of the support for the high vault. The form of a transverse barrel-vault will provide the highest level of support where it is least required, namely, under the centre of the clerestory window. The maximum support from a barrel-vault is down at the level of the intersection of the barrels which could be raised only by further raising the clerestory in advance of the vault-apex. The barrel-vaults were necessarily heavy, but their weight hardly justified their support. Finally, the interior lighting at tribune level was intermittent, with large sections blacked-out by intervening structures associated with both transepts (Figure 65).

While the southern tribune was carried to completion between the western and eastern transept, the northern tribune was abandoned at an early stage. Only the small half-bay furthest west and the adjoining whole bay received their barrel-vaults, and the latter was then demolished in favour of a different design.

The very notion of a tribune over the aisle was dropped, and the north aisle received a standard pitched roof resting directly on the top of the aisle wall (see Fig. 42). Beneath the roof, the transverse arches remain as on the south side, complete with their redundant springing blocks for the

**64** The clerestory above the south choir aisle tribune

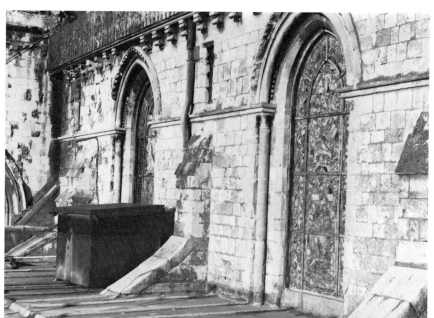

**65** (*opposite*) The south choir aisle tribune from the choir floor during the absence of the organ pipes, 1978. The uncovering of the exterior windows of the tribune allowed daylight to stream through the tribune arcade for the first time in many decades. The lighting is very strong and quite transforms the appearance of the elevation

barrel-vault. But instead of vaults, the transverse arches support only the triangular buttress walls which now break through the pitched roof-line to be visible on the exterior. The first buttress wall at the western end is a survivor from the barrel-vault scheme, here exposed to view. The rest are of a more developed design with a slimmer wall topped by a heavy stone brace. The ends of the transverse arches which now project through the lower section of the roof have become slab-like buttresses supported by oversailing carried by the transverse arches of the aisle vault.

Once again, the northern vault supports have their good and bad points. They have removed unnecessary weight from above the aisle vaults and from the old aisle walls. The new design allows the sill of the clerestory windows to be lowered by as much as 10 in. – 25 cm – and it creates a uniform, if dark, band throughout the interior. The disadvantages are confined almost entirely to the external appearance, though the roof of the north aisle could be seen only from the adjoining roof of the Chapter House (Figure 66). Gervase makes no mention of this change of heart, or of the demolition of completed sections above the new north choir aisle. According to him, the 'triforium', clerestories and high vaults of the whole section between the two transepts were built in a single season. If so, then the change of plan and its execution must have been rapid. The clerestory design introduces yet another puzzle into the make-up of William of Sens, for it contains that most English of elements, an internal wall passage. Clerestory passages are almost unknown in northern French Gothic, though they do have a long tradition in Anglo-Norman architecture. It is sometimes asserted that William gave in to local pressure from the monks at Christ Church over this feature, but the inclusion of an internal passage does have some benefits related directly to the support of the high vault. The thickness and structure of the wall passage provides for the vaults an internal buttress practically independent of the exterior vault-support systems. Again this goes back to the problems arising from the re-use of the old aisle walls, and the inclusion of a clerestory passage may well have formed an integral part of William's strategy from the outset.

Each bay of the clerestory contains a single lancet window – those on the north somewhat deeper than on the south. The internal passage is enclosed within a triple arcade that rests on the string course above the tribune arcading. The whole weight of the outer clerestory wall is carried on the haunches of the transverse arches of the aisle. Gervase states that the marble employed for the clerestory passage shafts differs from that used in the 'triforium' – a difference not evident today.

The high vaults over the choir proper are arranged in three bays – the most westerly with a quadripartite vault and a series of pointed barrels effecting the transition to the crossing arch. The two other bays are spanned by sexpartite vaults which spring from an alternating series of single and grouped marble shafts that reflects the intermediate and

principal ribs of the vault. The shafts rest directly upon the abacus of the main arcade capitals as in contemporary French buildings, i.e. Laon (Figure 67). The piers marking the entrance to the eastern transept are decorated with a cluster of marble shafts reaching from the floor to the high vault springing. The lower tier of shafts adds visible support to that at tribune level which wraps round the transept angle to form substantial clusters.

William's work in the eastern transept was limited almost exclusively to the elevations over the choir aisles which conform in their main lines to the bay design in the choir (Figure 68). They are, however, considerably broader, reflecting the width of the aisle, and William introduced a number of adjustments as compensation. The aisle arches are semi-circular in order both to span the aisle and to reflect the similar profile of the aisle vault transverse arches. The clerestory windows are doubled with a single tall marble shaft supporting the wall passage arcade. William had already adjusted his standard bay design for the last bay of the choir, which is narrower because of the retention of the Romanesque transept stair turrets. The widening of the transept opening was achieved by moving the entrance piers respectively west and east of their predecessors. The diminution of the last bay of the choir proper necessitated the elimination of the subdivision of both the tribune arcade and

**66** (*opposite*) Exterior of the north choir aisle

**67** (*below left*) The north arcade of the choir
**68** (*below right*) The north choir aisle from the presbytery

clerestory passage. In the crypt immediately below, additional support had to be introduced for the new crossing piers as they were now quite out of sequence with their Romanesque forebears (see Fig. 28). William inserted thick polygonal half-piers, with grotesque waterleaf capitals, to ensure the stability of the western piers of his new crossing.

In 1178 he built the quadripartite vaults over the aisle bays adjoining the transept, but his only other contribution to the transept design was the provision of windows at tribune level. They must be early works of *c.* 1176–7, for they are part of the initial plan for a lit tribune throughout the choir – an idea dropped in 1177 (Figure 69). The mouldings, capitals and bases of the intermediate range of windows in the transept are all of William of Sens's period, though their round arch-heads, and their axial relationship with the large Romanesque windows below, speak of an unusually sensitive approach to the problem of fusing the new with the old. In order to provide a passage at tribune floor-level around the transept interior, William made, or re-used, doors from the angle stair turrets.

**69** The south-east transept: exterior from the south-east. The lower work is Anselm's, while the middle range windows above the apse roofs appear to be by William of Sens. The trefoil windows over the aisle light the aisle triforium, replacing Anselm's tribune wall. Above can be seen the 'glazed flying buttress' against the transept east wall

William rejected the former arrangement of the crossing with the transept cut off from the choir proper by a continuation of the main arcade. He appears, however, to have intended to preserve as much of the Romanesque transept interior as possible, and his round-headed windows at tribune level would seem to be an attempt to reconcile his additions with the older work. He pre-empts the transition from the Romanesque forms to the gothic by the use of rounded elements in both the aisle arches and in the tribune openings at the entrance to the transept (see Fig. 68).

The building of the presbytery proceeded at an increased pace and in the year 1178 all ten piers were built, together with the aisle vaults, the tribune and clerestory. While the basic bay design was continued from the choir William gave fresh reign to his decorative talents in the treatment of the piers of the four bays of the presbytery (Figure 70). The first pair forming the eastern crossing piers are encased in marble shafts, the second are plain cylindrical piers, followed by octagonal piers with attached marble shafts on the cardinal faces, twin coupled columns with

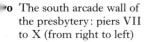

**70** The south arcade wall of the presbytery: piers VII to X (from right to left)

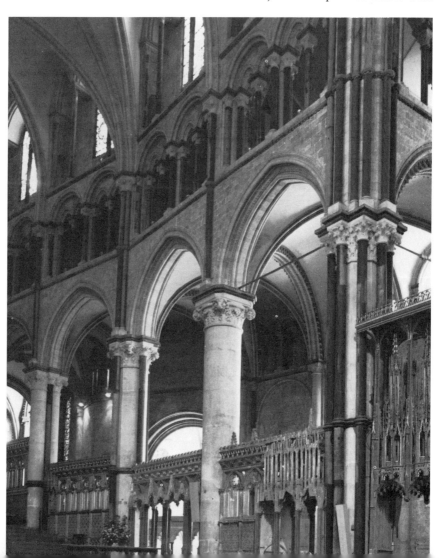

**71** (*above left*) The vault of the south presbytery aisle: the five-part vault adapting two bays of the Romanesque aisle to a single bay of the new arcade

**72** (*above right*) The north entrance to the Trinity Chapel. The arcades form part of William of Sens's design for an aisled eastern chapel at the same floor-level as the choir aisles. His socle arcade can be seen dying into the stairs added by William the Englishman after 1179

flanking marble shafts and finally a curious design which begins octagonal but changes half-way up to become circular. This eccentric display is matched by the design of the adjoining aisle vaults, for William not only pushed his main arcade line eastwards through the curve of the old ambulatory but also reduced the number of bays so that the arcade no longer related to the articulation in the old aisles. The principal problem arose in the first bay of the presbytery where William's single arcade bay had to be related to two bays of the aisle wall. With a certain amount of shifting of aisle responds, he was able to throw a five-part vault over the aisle, succeeded by a series of variously distorted quadripartite vaults each attempting to accommodate the ever-decreasing width of the aisle (Figure 71). Gervase goes to some length to explain why this should occur. William did not wish, or was not allowed, to demolish the great eastern towers above St Andrew's and St Anselm's chapels. Yet he did wish to extend a new aisled Trinity Chapel beyond these obstructions. As the towers formed part of the old ambulatory, William had no choice but to squeeze his new work through a gap formed by knocking down everything that stood between, and east of, the towers. He then skinned the nearside of each tower apse in order to gain the maximum possible width for his new aisles. This presented quite a gamble, for the towers were far from stable, and, to compensate, he blocked up the contiguous wall within each apse. In an attempt to conceal the strong angle that they had previously formed with the ambulatory, he added new outer orders to

**73** Detail of arcade pier base, north choir aisle. The incised band was for an iron clamp

**74** Detail of tribune arcade base, south-east transept aisle bay

4 The pattern is broken by pier IV on the north side of the choir, which is an octagonal pier, though the bell within the capital is round.

J. Bony, 'French influences on the origins of English Gothic architecture', *J. Warburg and Courtauld Insts*, 12, 1949, pp. 1–15. Also J. Bony, 'Origines des piles gothiques anglaises à fûts en délit', *Gedenkschrift Ernst Gall*, pp. 95–122. For Cambrai, see R. Branner, 'The transept of Cambrai Cathedral', ibid., pp. 69–86.

the tower-chapel entrance arches set obliquely to the Romanesque arches. William lined the sections of the chapel apses, now inside the aisle, with a wall arcade, continuing the scheme of the former choir, though now 'Gothic' (Figure 72).

The architectural background to the style of William of Sens has been sought in his native city and throughout northern France. His architecture is seen as regional rather than 'mainstream' Gothic, and his work at Canterbury – his only known work – presents a curious blend of French Gothic and native English, or at least Kentish, work. The clues that can be gleaned from his choir provide an increasingly diverse picture of William's training and traditions, and the exact role of the monks of Canterbury in the process of decision-making remains a constant problem (Figure 73). The strands found within William's architecture can be divided into several groups: the general scheme of the elevation, the main arcade sculpture, the structural solutions deemed necessary to support the high vaults, and the decorative repertoire (Figure 74). The first two could be said to be Parisian in inspiration, except that William found means of avoiding the fourth storey employed in several early churches such as Noyon and Notre-Dame-de-Paris. The latter groups within William's choir form an extension of the 'Channel school' connections that had existed in Canterbury over the last twenty years, and to a certain extent the new choir was a natural development of an established relationship. What was new to Canterbury were the Parisian elements in the arrangements of the elevation, the sophistication of the arcade sculpture and the high rib vaults.

The overall design of the choir elevation at Canterbury is a curious blend of Laon and Paris, and churches like St-Germain-des-Prés and Vézelay, which are themselves reflections of the original design of St-Denis. The main arcade follows the pattern of Notre-Dame-de-Paris – large columnar piers with massive capitals upon which stand all the vault-support shafts (see Fig. 61). This imbues Canterbury with the same feeling as Paris and Laon, where the structure seems almost propped up on an arcade that has little to do with the building above. The piers are round and octagonal in alternation, a theme that is mostly taken up in the shape of the bell within the capitals.[4] The employment of a columnar arcade distinguished Canterbury from another major group of early French Gothic churches that have major–minor pier alternation such as Noyon and Sens.

The piers from the crossing into the presbytery are rich and varied. The crossing piers, wreathed in their dark shafts, represent an early essay in this design that also make an appearance in the aisles of Notre-Dame-de-Paris, in the nave at Laon and the transept at Soissons. Their earliest use in France may have been at Cambrai *c.* 1175, but many earlier examples in England have been cited by Jean Bony.[5] The sudden elaboration of the pier designs in the presbytery may have facilitated

the introduction of an arcaded screen, vestiges of which remain further east (see Fig. 70). The final design of pier IX, with four attached shafts on the cardinal faces of an octagonal pier, foreshadows the *pilier cantonné* solution found at Chartres from 1194. William's last pier, XI, at the junction of the choir and the Englishman's Trinity Chapel, is extremely odd. Polygonal for the lower half, and round above – the faceted nature of the lower section made the addition of the screen much simpler, and the attached capitals and shafts from the screen can be seen partially buried within the new floor-level to the east.

The capitals of the main arcade can be divided into two groups. Those in the choir proper, with the exception of the last piers (VI north and south) and the last capital but one on the south side (pier V south), are characterized by broad and flat leaf forms that at times resemble high Romanesque carving, or the proto-Gothic sculpture of Noyon (Figure 75). The second group, from pier V south and VI north, through to piers XI north and south at the end of the presbytery, are more 'classicizing', with pronounced angle volutes and great depth of carving. The appearance of one of this later group on the south side of the choir proper may be another indication that the construction of the south arcade was in advance of the north. Individual parallels with French sculpture for the capitals of the first group have ranged from the hemicycle piers of St-Remi at Reims and pier III south, and St-Leu-d'Esserent (Oise) and Notre-Dame-de-Paris with pier II north (Figure 76). The later group extending throughout the presbytery at Canterbury has been linked with Arras, as well as further capitals from Notre-Dame and St-Leu, and others at Champeaux (Seine-et-Marne) – especially pier V south with Arras, pier VI south with the aisle capitals of Notre-Dame, pier VIII north (Figure 77) with the south aisle of the nave of Notre-Dame, St-Leu and Champeaux, and pier X north and south with both Arras and St-Leu (Figure 78). The wide-ranging influence detected in the arcade capitals at Canterbury speaks of a workshop well versed in the sculptural developments of Paris and the north, and once again the Arras–Cambrai area must have been the melting-pot for this rich mixture.

The vault responds at Canterbury rest directly upon the top of the main arcade capitals. The shafts are trebled under the main transverse arches of the high vault, while single shafts support the intermediate transverse arch of the sexpartite vault. This system follows Paris and Laon rather than Sens and Noyon, where the alternation of the vaults finds expression in the major–minor pattern of the piers.

William's first design for the choir elevation included transverse barrel-vaulted tribunes above the aisle vaults – a curiously archaic throwback to Romanesque techniques. Vaulted tribunes did have a respectable place in contemporary French Gothic, though hardly as squat and primitive as at Canterbury. The classic example, Laon, may have been well known to William, but there the tribune is rib-vaulted and plays an important part in the elevation and lighting of the church (see Fig. 44). It is quite unlike the cavernous and crouching aspect provided by the Canterbury tribunes. William's design may have resembled the system at Arras cathedral, from *c.* 1171, where the choir exterior was surrounded by a series of gables at tribune level – the external gable on each bay may denote the presence of pointed transverse barrel-vaults[6] similar to those over the south choir aisle at Canterbury, though they may equally have been ramped rib vaults. The Canterbury tribunes are screened both inside and out, creating a 'triforium' facade within the choir elevation with dark polished colonnettes rippling along the interior. The thought behind these concealed tribunes is only apparent once the unique constructional difficulties of Canterbury are appreciated, but the prospect it presents is unfortunate, and as soon as the tribune was deemed to be unnecessary, it was quickly abandoned (see Fig. 65).

William's second vault-support system, found on the north side of the choir, employed the pitched aisle roof divided by exterior buttressing walls. This scheme satisfies the demands of the high vaults without placing unnecessary weight upon the old aisle walls. It also enabled

6 Mantes has similar barrel-vaults, though the tribunes there are well lit.

William to enlarge his clerestory windows. Internally, the tribune has become a dark roof-space, glimpsed through the 'triforium' screen. The polished colonnettes now merge into the background rather than catching the daylight that filtered through the tribune windows. The second scheme, abandoning the lit middle storey, changed the elevational design from three to two illuminated tiers, divided by a dark band. Its French counterparts would be Sens, Vézelay, St Germain-des-Prés, and very probably the choir of St-Denis. What was new at Canterbury was the division of the aisle roof by boldly projecting buttress walls which compartmentalized the roof to an unprecedented degree (see Fig. 42). Smaller and lower buttressing walls had already appeared in Flanders, most noticeably at Cambrai and Arras, but at Canterbury they are allowed to dominate the aisle roof. It may be said that their size was permissible above the north aisle where they are obscured by the Chapter House, but it is evident that William intended to continue this design east of the choir crossing, where they would have been clearly visible.

The relationship between the cathedrals of Sens and Canterbury has been a favourite topic for many years. In the nineteenth century, the design of Sens was attributed to William himself, but the early dating of that cathedral, from *c.* 1130, and the many differences that exist between the two structures should finally eliminate that possibility. More recently, attempts have been made to isolate those parts of Canterbury Cathedral that are 'Sens derived'.[7] The elevational proportions, the base and archivolt profiles, the alternation in the presbytery and, most of all, the double columns with attached colonnettes, have all been cited as evidence that a new appraisal of William's debt to his native city has become necessary. The proportions of the choir elevation may well resemble that of Sens, but the outcome at Canterbury was conditioned strictly by the preservation of the Romanesque aisles and the requirements of the high vaults. While any final similarity with the elevation at Sens may not have displeased William, the evolutionary development of Canterbury would suggest that any likeness was providential rather than intentional. More important, the elevational type intended for Canterbury was very different from that of Sens, which has an arcade, triforium openings into the roof-space and a thin-walled clerestory. William's design for Canterbury involved an arcade, vaulted tribune and a thick-walled clerestory, and while the ultimate rejection of the vaulted tribune resulted in a closer resemblance to Sens, it had not been William's original intention.

Evidence surviving on the base of pier IX (the third pier east from the crossing) has been taken as proof that William intended to introduce a pier pattern in the presbytery modelled on that at Sens, which has compound piers alternating with single columns (see Figs 70 and 113). But the additional bases that allow for attached shafts on the angles of the octagonal piers exist only on the eastern faces, and are complemented by

7 K. Severens, 'William of Sens and the double columns at Sens and Canterbury', *J. Warburg and Courtauld Insts*, 33, 1970, pp. 307–13.

**79** Vault respond capital: north presbytery aisle. The arch mouldings flanking the respond are Anselm's. Above can be seen the details of the vault ribs and the aisle triforium passage from William of Sens's choir

the scooping of the capital necking. This arrangement shows that the piers were not to be duplicates of the crossing piers, but an asymmetrical design with a cluster of shafts restricted to five faces of the column. There is no evidence to suggest that the coupled columns that follow these extraordinary piers were intended by William to be the first of a hemicycle modelled on that at Sens and to be built along the line of the Romanesque apse (see Fig. 72). The aisle responds opposite are closest to the style of the earliest of the arcade capitals and would appear to pre-date the construction of the presbytery arcade, yet they precipitate the advent of an aisled Trinity Chapel beyond the limits of the old choir (Figure 79).

However, coupled columns with attached colonnettes were employed at Cambrai after 1161 where the shafts were executed in dark Tournai marble – providing a far closer parallel for the piers at Canterbury than the monochrome appearance of the earlier design of the hemicycle piers at Sens. The use of polychrome elements at Cambrai and at Canterbury is significant, for it radically changes the appearance and the visual understanding of the pier. The dark colonnettes stand out dramatically from their faint background, making obvious the fact that they were freestone shafts. At Sens, the shafts would merge into their neighbours giving the overall impression of rather slim compound piers which could equally have been built with integrated coursing. If, on the other hand, the attached shafts at Sens were a subsequent addition to the coupled piers, it may indicate that the influence of Cambrai had already reached northern Burgundy – the choir of Vézelay, begun *c.* 1165, also contains several references to Cambrai.

While it would be foolish to rule out Sens completely as a possible source of influence on Canterbury, particularly as it was William's native city, the parallels that can be drawn are insufficiently exact to eliminate the possibility of a common source. What, for example, did the 'triforium' arrangement look like at Cambrai, and how did the mouldings at Arras compare with Canterbury? The one occasion where Sens would appear to provide a reasonable source would be at the very beginning of William's work – the half-capitals on the arcade responds adjoining the piers under the central tower, pier I. They are quite unlike any others of the main arcade, but they do resemble some of the hemicycle capitals at Sens. Yet several decades must separate the execution of the capitals and, once again, there is the possibility of a lost intermediary.

The most important difference between Canterbury and Sens lies in the constructional technique. The elevation of Sens is executed in the standard thin-walled method common to many early Gothic buildings in France: that is, the whole depth of the arcade wall right up to the top of the clerestory is carried directly by the main arcade piers. Thus there is insufficient depth of wall to include an internal wall passage at clerestory level if one were required. William's choir elevation at Canterbury stems from a different tradition, that of thick upper walls supported on the aisle side by oversailing; the extra thickness of the upper wall is carried on the haunches of the transverse arches of the aisle and tribune (see Fig. 44). In this respect, Canterbury follows the techniques of Laon, with the additional complexity that the clerestory is deep enough to include an internal passage. This motif is commonly cited as an Anglo-Norman element in William's work, but its construction differs from the Romanesque passages of England and Normandy which are simply channelled through the thickness of the masonry and rubble. William's elevation is composed of two skins, laid one against the other, a balancing act that in turn helps to support the high vaults. William may have gladly accepted, or even have suggested, such a passage as part of his system of vault support. Once again, the difficulty of constructing a new vaulted choir within the shell of the old work may have dictated the use of this important stylistic element.

This is not to say that William of Sens was ignorant of or indifferent to the native traditions of Canterbury. Far from it. His decorative repertoire is dominated by motifs which can be found in many of Wilbert's buildings of the previous two decades (see Fig. 79). The extensive use of chevron and undercut roll mouldings on the vault ribs, the lavish employment of dogtooth, the frequent use of polished marble shafts and the waterleaf capitals in the minor arcades all link William's work with the preceding generation of Romanesque builders at Canterbury. Part of this continuity could be accounted for by the presence of the same sculptors and masons who had worked for Wibert before 1170, and there is evidence of at least one sculptor who carved capitals on the Prior's Gate

8 One capital in the north tribune of the choir proper is decorated with a strip of flattened rings – typical of capitals from the late years of Wibert's priorate.

9 Bony also cites Amblény, near Soissons, as 'the nearest approximation' to the complicated mouldings of the arcade at Canterbury; see 'French influences . . .', p. 8.

**80** Capital from the tribune: south-east transept aisle bay

and who also worked on the earliest phase of the new choir.[8] However, this overlap should not be taken as an indication that William's decorative detail was either Romanesque or English, for Wibert's architectural repertoire was almost as French as it was indigenous. The 'Wibert' style at Canterbury has its counterpart around Beauvais, Soissons[9] and Paris, and possibly it was transmitted to east Kent through Cambrai and Arras. Evidence from Dover, Faversham and Rochester would suggest that in the mid-twelfth century east Kent formed part of a 'Channel school', and William of Sens's readiness to employ this stylistic repertoire may itself indicate the area of France in which he trained. So many of the design features in the choir of Canterbury point to the Cambrai–Arras area, and the loss of these two important French cathedrals may have destroyed additional information regarding the transition from Romanesque to Gothic in England. Cambrai employed a system of detached shafts encircling a columnar pier in the early 1170s. The shafts may well have been of dark Tournai marble. William of Sens used a similar motif on his crossing piers in 1177. Arras utilized five-part vaults around the ambulatory before 1177, William used them over the difficult presbytery aisles in 1178 and Arras also had coupled column piers used by William in the same year. The elevation at Arras also contained coloured Tournai shafts, which can be found throughout the 'Channel school'. While not all of William's design motifs emanate from Cambrai and Arras, sufficient links can be made to suggest that he had more than a passing knowledge of that area (Figure 80).

Perhaps the most intriguing problem in the whole history of Canterbury Cathedral concerns William's original project for a new east end. What had William proposed in his original design? Quite plainly, he planned an aisled axial chapel, for he had cut back the old eastern towers and had begun the new aisle walls (see Fig. 72). He did not intend to raise the floor-level, and consequently was prepared to maintain the previous level of the crypt vault. This might suggest that he did not intend to demolish the old axial chapel at crypt level which contained the saint's tomb. As this chapel was square-ended, the most likely plan for a new chapel above would also be rectangular, enclosed within a similar ambulatory aisle. At crypt level, the new aisle could have boxed in the old chapel, and access arches could have been cut through the side walls. At choir level, William could have built two more bays as an extension of the presbytery arcade, standing them on the top of the old crypt chapel (Figure 81). A single arch could have spanned the old eastern wall, which would open into the eastern aisle of the ambulatory. Thus William's new choir could have occupied the same length as Anselm's, with the sole addition of an eastern terminal aisle (Figure 82). It would, however, abandon the old apse and ambulatory plan and push the new arcade through a gap cut between the eastern towers. Doubtless the new axial chapel was to be dedicated to the Holy Trinity and perhaps it was

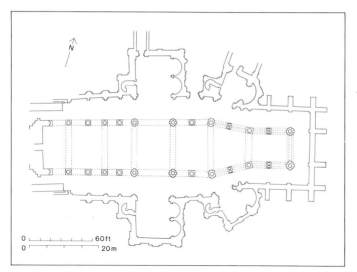

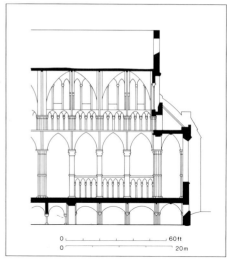

**81** (*above left*) Proposed ground plan for the William of Sens east end
**82** (*above right*) Proposed cross-section through the William of Sens east end

intended to place the old and venerated altar from the previous chapel in the new east end. Whatever plan William of Sens had proposed in 1174, there are at least two indications that his east end was not to be as extensive as the present chapel. The first is that William's original plan did not involve the wholesale clearing of the surrounding monastic cemetery which had to be done before William the Englishman could even lay out the foundations of the present chapel. Second, the iconography of the clerestory windows had to be expanded towards the end of the programme.

There can be little doubt that the glass from the western end of the new clerestory is coeval with the building, and that it was already in place when the new choir was brought into use in 1180. The clerestory contains a genealogy of Christ made up of 84–88 figures, two in each window. The ancestry is that taken from Luke beginning with God the Father and Adam in the most westerly window on the north side and ending with the Virgin and Christ directly opposite. The sequence continued round the choir and transept in chronological order, though with one or two omissions. One consequence of starting in the western bay and progressing eastwards was that the cycle was manufactured from both the beginning and the end and worked uniformly towards the middle. Such a cycle would have been worked out at an early stage, and the choice of characters dictated by the original number of windows in the first plan. If during construction the plan was enlarged, there should be some indication of an alteration of the iconography of the glass. Faced with a sudden increase in the number of clerestory windows, the master glass-painter could either fill out the middle of his ancestry in the correct order but of necessity drawn from another source, or he could fill out the middle with something else altogether. The only other solution would be to rescaffold the choir, take out some of the finished windows and rearrange them with new additions. What happens in Trinity Chapel is that eight additional figures taken from Matthew have been inserted in the correct order following Nathan. While the three windows of the apse containing the life of Christ may always have been intended, at least four windows, or two bays, have been added to the original scheme of iconography. The elimination of these extra bays from the present plan would allow for a square end resting on the walls of the old crypt chapel. A square end within a similar ambulatory would be difficult to parallel in contemporary France, though it could often be found in twelfth-century England.

## The work of William the Englishman, 1179–84

There is no suggestion from Gervase that the second master had been the assistant of William of Sens, or that William the Englishman had any previous association with Canterbury. The continuity of certain features in the later work may be due to simple expediency and the continuation of the previous workshop. Nevertheless, William the Englishman made his own distinctive mark upon the building. In his earliest work, the completion of the eastern transept, there is a disregard for his predecessor's design (Figure 83). The Englishman stripped the transept interior and superimposed upon it tier upon tier of arcades, galleries and windows. In the transept chapels, the Englishman introduced round

**83** (*below left*) The north-east transept: interior of west wall. The middle range of windows were part of the lit tribune of the first design of William of Sens. The present arcade is by William the Englishman, apart from the first arch on the extreme left where William of Sens began an arcade with capitals at a lower level. William the Englishman has simply proceeded with his own design, though springing from this half-built arch. The result is a little exotic

**84** (*below right*) The north-east transept: St Stephen's chapel, remodelling by William the Englishman

**85** The north-east transept vault and upper levels by William the Englishman

abacus and base forms unknown in the Frenchman's works (Figure 84). The clerestory windows above were positioned not by any axial alignment with the existing windows below but by strict mathematical placing within a regular sexpartite vault. Here, too, new forms are introduced to Canterbury, with the notable stilting of the intermediate transverse rib allowing a greater flow of light and a more elegant line (Figure 85). William the Englishman's major contribution to the design of the transept was the gable end rose – a great circular hole punched into the terminal wall of each arm, perhaps the largest undivided area of glass of its time. But then, almost maliciously, he partly obscures the rose with the tall arcade of the clerestory passage, leaping over the rose but still dissecting it with its attenuated shafts.

While the sexpartite vault over the high Altar bay was prepared by

William of Sens before his accident, it was erected only by his successor. At this juncture, William the Englishman took the opportunity to abandon the previous vault-support system. William of Sens had intended to continue his buttress walls beyond the eastern transept even though they would then have been plainly visible from below. He built the first two buttress walls, in tufa as before, but William the Englishman appears to have cut them down to below the level of the aisle roof, and replaced them with flying buttresses. The junction of the presbytery aisles and the eastern transept is complicated by the Frenchman's decision to illuminate the aisle roof-space by turning the lean-to roof against the east wall of the transept. This presented a cross-section view of his vault-support system which he transformed into a curious double window sympathetic in style to the mid-range windows of the transept. The result is almost a glazed flying buttress (see Fig. 69).

By the spring of 1180, the second William had completed the vaulting over the presbytery bays, and had erected a temporary east wall between the third piers. The new Gothic choir was solemnly entered on Easter eve 1180, less than six years after the fire.

It was about this time that the convent came to an important decision. The tomb of St Thomas down in the extremity of the crypt should be moved, or rather elevated. A new shrine would be built directly above the old tomb to form the centrepiece of a new chapel poised above the level of the choir. William of Sens had not intended to raise the floor-level beyond the presbytery and so by implication did not propose to alter the level of the old crypt vault. He may well have planned to leave this most sacred chapel intact; indeed he utilized part of it to support his easternmost presbytery piers. The monks who were so unwilling to lose any of their old church in 1174 would hardly have agreed at that time to the destruction of the most venerated area of the church. But by 1179–80 attitudes may well have changed. St Thomas had become a cult figure, pilgrims flocked to his tomb in increasing numbers, the king and all manner of important personages were now regular visitors, and in 1179 the king of France himself arrived in fulfilment of a vow. Louis VII brought a new international prestige to the tomb, not to mention a legendary treasure, and the thought of the glory and honour that a great and worthy shrine would confer upon the church and convent seems to have diminished any sentiment still held for the old building.

The Trinity Chapel introduced several new elements to Canterbury Cathedral while maintaining the broad themes of the choir. William the Englishman was free to design his own aisle elevation from the ground, untrammelled by the Romanesque work that had so restricted his predecessor and he felt able to raise the floor-level within the chapel, though he could hardly lift the high vaults above those in the choir at such a late stage.

The plan of the new Trinity Chapel is something of a puzzle, for the aisles are not parallel and the arcades in both the crypt and chapel above bow outwards from the confines imposed by the final presbytery bay of William of Sens. The plan is like a long balloon, half inflated, with the Corona as that bit on the end that resists until the last (see Fig. 1).

The decision to raise the new shrine above the level of the high Altar dictated the provision of the lofty crypt – more of a lower church. Its walls are massive and their supporting role is everywhere expressed in the architecture; sharp lancets set in deep unmoulded splays and coupled drum piers with a total absence of applied decoration (Figure 86). It is a simple yet grand opening statement in the story of English Gothic. The unadorned rib vaults descend on to a pair of elegant polished marble columns. The great piers of the arcade and apse are thoroughly English, all the forms are rounded and plain, speaking of a Romanesque tradition stretching back to Durham and Gloucester (Figure 87). Only in the crypt of the eastern tower, the Corona, is decoration allowed to make an appearance in the form of a rich foliate boss which draws together the mass of vault ribs.

The connection between the new crypt and the Romanesque ambulatory to the west is complicated by the remaining masonry from the old axial chapel which supports the last of William of Sens's piers. In

**86** (*below left*) The eastern crypt: interior from the west. The double columns in the entrance still have square pedestals and abacus mouldings. William the Englishman abandoned these in the interior of the crypt and in the remodelling of the north-east transept chapels

**87** (*below right*) The eastern crypt: interior of the south aisle from the west

addition, the Frenchman re-used two piers from the old choir above, made up from several piers, in order to provide support for the presbytery arcade which here stands on top of the crypt ambulatory vault (see Fig. 46). So many obstructions can hardly have been welcome to the vast concourse of pilgrims who streamed along the aisles of the crypt towards their sacred goal.

The interior of the Trinity Chapel above is one of the most beautiful in England (Figure 88). The austerity of the crypt is replaced by an opulence that only the shrine itself would rival. A variety of richly coloured marbles, lavish sculpture and brilliant stained glass are all combined in one glittering setting. The raising of the floor-level radically changed the proportions of the bay design, perhaps for the better. The clerestory and

**88** The interior of the Trinity Chapel. The high Altar and St Augustine's throne were restored to their mediaeval positions in 1978

triforium levels are continued exactly as before, the shortfall being entirely absorbed within the arcade, with the loss of 7 ft 9¾ in. – 238 cm. William the Englishman grasped the opportunity afforded by the new proportions to introduce a more human scale into his work. Everything is on an intimate level, the aisle windows bring the miracles of St Thomas down within easy reach, the slender columns of the arcade and apse carry meticulously carved foliate capitals from which tiny heads emerge. The reduction of the capital size by the simple coupling of the columns produced a totally different response from the sculptors than had the great piers of the earlier work.

The tall passage that voids the aisle wall, separating the vault-supports from the outer skin, invites human participation in the architecture (see Fig. 96). It is the most dramatic innovation of the English William. He abandons the Frenchman's stated intention of extending the socle wall arcade in favour of a giant arcaded passage rising the full height of the aisle. The vaults are supported not by wall responds but by a sequence of thin free-standing piers alternating with daringly slim single marble shafts. The aisle wall stands back at some distance and it is possible to walk between the outer wall and the seemingly independent vault supports. Visually, the passage creates a sense of weightlessness, which is greatly enhanced by the size of the windows. This feeling is just as strong on the exterior, where the glass almost completely replaces the wall. This

**89** The exterior of the Trinity Chapel from the north. In the foreground can be seen the remains of the Prior's Lodging, the stair turret of the Chequer building, the south arcade of the infirmary, the upper chamber of the vestiarium built in 1292 and the stump of St Andrew's tower

skeletal construction was made possible only by William's adoption of the flying buttress, which are among the earliest datable examples in existence (Figure 89). They are kept low, though not out of sight. Their profile is dependent upon the correct level of abutment necessary for the height of the high vaults and their relatively modest appearance is indicative of the shortcomings of the system adopted by William of Sens rather than of any embarrassment or apprehension (Figure 90). Had William the Englishman been free to choose his own level from which to spring the high vaults, he doubtless would have raised them higher, but his desire for internal and external unity made that impossible. William maintained the transverse arches hidden beneath the aisle roof as part of the Trinity Chapel vault-support and this additional buttressing enabled him to remove excess weight from the triforium wall (Figure 91).

In his new work, William the Englishman had a distinct advantage over his predecessor, as the Trinity Chapel was free from the restrictions imposed by the old aisle walls upon the provision of external buttresses. The stability of the flying buttresses built by William the Englishman depends entirely upon the dramatic exterior buttresses which project from the aisle walls, and it is the contrast between their solid massiveness and the brittle glasshouse walls of the aisle that makes the exterior of the Trinity Chapel as remarkable as the interior.

The Englishman introduced several changes into the upper parts of the bay design. He abandoned the remnants of the old 'tribune' in favour of a true triforium passage; that is, a passage built within the thickness of the wall. He also abandoned the coupling of the triforium openings, replacing it with an arcade of lancets running uniformly over the straight bays and

**90** (*below left*) The flying buttresses of the Trinity Chapel from the north-east transept roof

**91** (*below right*) Roof-space of the Trinity Chapel ambulatory. To the left and right can be seen the buttressing arches under the aisle roof. The wall is the exterior of the triforium passage, which can be entered by the central door. The upper relieving arches support the clerestory windows. Most of the infill material is tufa

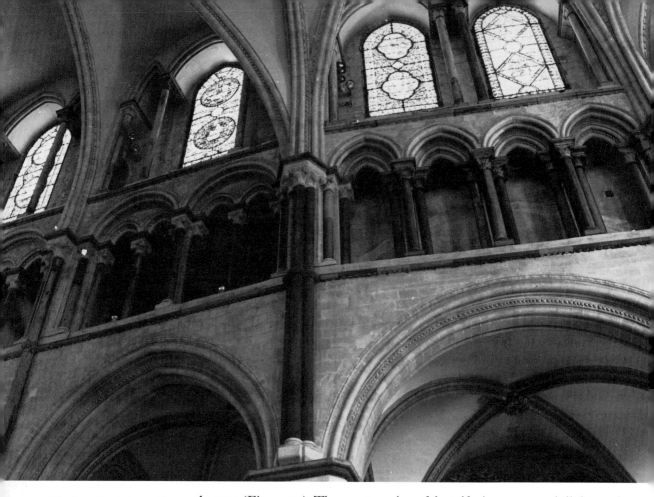

**92** The junction between the work of the two Williams, north side

10 The vaults round the ambulatory are ramped outwards, as are the equivalent vaults in the eastern crypt.

the apse (Figure 92). The construction of the triforium passage is lightened by a relieving arch set into the back wall which supports the clerestory wall above. The area below this arch is infilled with light tufa. the clerestory windows are doubled in the straight bays of the chapel, while in the apse the single windows virtually fill the available wall space.

The decision to build an apsidal termination for the chapel interrupted the sequence of sexpartite vaults, and William erected a single quadripartite vault over the first straight bay followed by an eight-part apse vault in the current French manner. One notable feature of the apse vault is the degree of stilting which is not vertical but horseshoe.[10]

The interior of the eastern axial chapel, the Corona, is luminous and rich. The tall polygonal chapel is detached from the main body of the apse by the ambulatory aisle and its purpose and original design remain unknown. It is a unique feature in the Gothic architecture of the period, and it may have been specifically related to the cult of St Thomas (Figure 93). It is not even clear whether it was intended to be a tower – the present top being an eighteenth-century concealment of an abortive Tudor extension. An eastern axial tower could have complemented the two Romanesque radial towers which William of Sens had gone to great lengths to preserve, and the Corona is flanked by slim angle stair turrets similar to that on Anselm's tower. There is certainly sufficient buttressing for additional height, and the twin stair turrets serve little purpose at present. A tower in such a position might have had precedents in Anglo-Saxon architecture, but would these still be known to William the Englishman in 1180? The interior design of the Corona is virtually a summing-up of the Englishman's work in the transept and in the Trinity Chapel, with the attenuated wall arcade, large windows, tiers of arcaded galleries and the brightly lit vault (Figure 94). A head-shrine existed in the Corona before 1220, which was believed to contain that part of the skull of St Thomas severed during his murder. The chapel has always been called the Corona or Becket's Crown, and possibly the possession of this relic determined the placing and shape of the chapel.

As one might expect from this extraordinary building, the architecture of William the Englishman is perhaps more truly French than that of his predecessor. His work reveals a deep knowledge of contemporary French building, especially Reims and Laon, and his architecture introduces a fragile note into Canterbury with an interest in skeletal construction and a proper understanding of flying buttresses. In his first work, the transept interior, William inherited his predecessor's middle range of windows which had been intended as an extension of the lit tribune into the transept (see Fig. 83). William of Sens appears to have constructed the outer walls at this level but the passage arcading within is the work of the

**93** (*below left*) The Corona exterior from the east. The battlements are eighteenth century
**94** (*below right*) The interior of the Corona

11 There are obvious bonding breaks
between the outer wall containing
the window openings and the
inner skin with the arcade and
passage vaults. Possibly the
William of Sens passage was to be
lower, hence the raising of the
arcade level and part blocking of
the access door.

Englishman,[11] who also returned to the lower levels of the transept
interior to introduce angle vault shafts, blind arcades and new entrance
arches into the apsidal chapels. There, for the first time, round capitals
and bases are employed – perhaps the most English trait in all his work.
The bases are raised upon high round pedestals which are decorated with
attenuated foliage designs in low relief (see Fig. 84). The round abacus
mouldings above are slightly uncomfortable, being rather small for the
arch mouldings and vault ribs. The great round windows of the transept
terminal walls are also to the Englishman's design: devoid of infilling,
they depend entirely on their complex armatures to hold the glass in place
(see Fig. 47). Transept gable roses were relatively new to France, the
earliest perhaps being at Beauvais, while those at Laon were still under
construction when the transept at Canterbury was built. This conflicting
acceptance and rejection of current French ideas, such as the rose and the
round capital and base form, highlight the complexity of the background
of William the Englishman. The transept vaults exhibit a refinement over
the earlier vaults of William of Sens with their stilted rib profile ensuring a
lightening of the vault, both visually and physically (see Fig. 85). Such a
flattening of the rib curvature was still a recent Parisian innovation, best
seen at Mantes, on the Seine.

William the Englishman's new design for the Trinity Chapel would
appear to be greatly indebted to St-Denis. It is raised high above the choir
floor, with the main arcade reduced to a more intimate scale, and it shares
a similar feeling for the importance of direct lighting, casting a
shimmering backcloth of colour behind the shrine (Figure 95). The Trinity
Chapel is transparent architecture, where the very structure dissolves
away. Four other ambulatory designs may have exercised some influence
on Canterbury: Arras, Sens, St-Remi at Reims and the original east end
of Laon. One might point to Arras, Sens and Laon for an ambulatory
without radial chapels, while either Sens or Arras can provide prototypes
for the ambulatory pier design. The comparison with Sens would seem to
end at that point, and the duplication of the design elements between Sens
and Arras would obviate the necessity to include the former at all.
Visually, Sens and the Trinity Chapel are worlds apart and nowhere is
this more evident than in the treatment of the aisle wall (Figure 96). The
extraordinary attenuation of the wall arcade that frames the windows of
the Trinity Chapel is without precedent. Rising from floor to vault, it
denies the solidity and mass of the vault-support pier while inviting the
onlooker to penetrate into the wall itself. This is Gothic of an advanced
nature, as up to date as anything in France. William the Englishman had
already shown his interest in spatial complexities in the design of the
transept terminal walls, where the view of the gable-end roses is
deliberately interrupted by an arcade stepping high up to the vault apex.
The arcaded passage is employed as in the Trinity Chapel, but in the
latter it breaks up the outer wall when seen from the angle of approach,

**95** (*above left*) The Trinity Chapel: north aisle of the ambulatory

**96** (*above right*) The Trinity Chapel: north aisle wall

whereas the gable-end roses can be seen only frontally. This encouraged William to overlay two conflicting designs to ensure the desired effect. The result recalls a similar deliberate obstruction to the windows at the west end of St-Remi, a contemporary work. The whole notion of a detached wall arcade is thought to have originated in Reims with the ambulatory of St-Remi. This was, however, only just high enough to walk under and it was integrated not into the ambulatory wall design but into the entrance arches of the radial chapels. The wall arcades in the Laon transept are closer, and they and the wall arcades within the west end of St-Remi are perhaps the best contemporary parallels. This may be another pointer to the area in which William the Englishman received his basic training. Certainly the exterior of the St-Remi choir, with its broad lancets filling the wall space between the deep buttresses, bears the closest resemblance to the exterior of the Trinity Chapel (Figure 97).

The main arcade wall of the Trinity Chapel is strikingly different from the earlier choir bays, yet it continues most of the major themes established further west. The most immediate change is in the scale of the main arcade, and the abandonment of the heavy single column piers in

**97** (*opposite*) The Trinity Chapel exterior from the south

**98** Capital from the apse arcade

favour of a coupled design executed in an array of coloured marbles. The first piers even have marble capitals. The arcade arches remain acutely pointed and become increasing stilted; all, that is, except the westernmost bay which is semicircular. The embryonic capitals supporting the inner arch mouldings have been seen as evidence that the coupled capitals at Canterbury are directly related to those at Sens, where intermediate shafts have been removed leaving capitals similarly 'stranded' (Figure 98).

The Canterbury design, however, utilizes these capitals for the visual effect afforded by their support, and are plainly designed as corbels. The sculptural parallels for the Trinity Chapel capitals again lie between Reims and Arras, and there is little to indicate that a new sculpture workshop replaced that of William of Sens after 1179.

Above the arcade, another recent French innovation makes an appearance – the true triforium passage. By replacing the sombre roof-spaces of the earlier choir with a slim wall passage, William the Englishman took his work forward into a new phase of architecture that would eventually abandon the middle tier altogether. It was a daring but wholly appropriate move, for the reduction in the bay height made the presence of a broad central element undesirable. The dark roof-spaces are still there, but are now concealed behind the rear wall of the passage. The twin bays of the former design gave way to a continuous lancet passage that ripples around the chapel and facilitates the transition into the narrower bays of the apse.

The clerestory design is also simplified, with twin windows in the straight bays and single windows in the apse. The difference between the vaulting techniques employed by the two Williams is best seen at the junction of the 'throne' bay and the western bay of the Trinity Chapel (see Fig. 92). While both vaults were erected by the second William, the last bay of the choir was doubtless prepared by the predecessor, for it displays the long curved profile of the diagonal ribs found in all his previous vaults.

The Englishman's vault is so stilted that it springs out at a noticeably higher level, so illuminating the interior and demonstrating his complete understanding of the techniques and possibilities of flying buttresses. This technical mastery is so advanced that it is difficult to find a contemporary parallel in France, for at the time when William the Englishman first built flying buttresses at Canterbury in 1179, no French building can be cited that incorporated them in its original design. Flyers were added to existing churches in France around 1180, but their exact dating remains a matter of dispute. Similarly, the triforium passage within the Trinity Chapel places Canterbury in the vanguard of French Gothic, with only Juziers near Mantes and the lost church of St-Vincent at Laon as possible French counterparts. How William the Englishman achieved such superiority in design, and precisely where he trained, may never be discovered. Reims is constantly recalled in his architecture, but the parallels are not always entirely convincing and the choir of St-Remi is not well dated. A number of important buildings of the mid-twelfth century have been completely lost – what did the cathedral at Reims look like, and perhaps more significant, the cathedral of Amiens? It must also be that vital clues to the development of Gothic architecture at Canterbury and Reims were lost in the revolutionary dust at Cambrai and Arras.

## Note

The display lighting in 1981 (see p. 86) revealed that the vault responds in the north choir aisle between the three window openings were the first work of 1174–5. Their sculpture related to the half capitals of pier I against the western crossing, while those to the east and west relate to the next phase of the main arcade capitals, beginning with pier II. The earlier responds have diagonal implantation, answering the aisle vault ribs; the later responds do not. The south aisle responds match those to the north, with diagonal implantation between the windows, even though the respond capitals are all of the second sculptural phase. Thus the north choir aisle was begun first, and was slightly ahead of the south in 1174–5.

CHAPTER 4

# THE ARCHITECTURE FROM RICHARD I TO EDWARD III, 1184-1376

## 1184–1285

William of Sens and his successor revolutionized the architecture of England. Previously there had been only occasional references to the new French style, but the prestige of the choir at Canterbury ensured that the idiosyncracies of the work of the two Williams would be a formative factor in the development of English Gothic. The enormous cost of the new choir acted as a natural restraint upon further large-scale work within the monastery. One limited operation doubtless prompted by the fire of 1174 was the vaulting of the cellarer's hall to the north of the monastic kitchen. Nothing survives of the vault except the finely-wrought bases that supported the central columns. Their style and profiles suggest the work of the two Williams. The height of the vault necessitated the lowering of the Romanesque door, which was achieved by the introduction of a typanum supported by a segmental lintel. The tympanum has the remains of a figure of St Thomas and a representation of the Trinity. The style of the work, particularly of the jamb capitals, would indicate a date of *c*. 1180. Important sculptural fragments of a similar date have come to light from various sources. A collection of carved quatrefoils containing half-figures, some crowned, has been discovered over the last two centuries.[1] One of the earliest finds, now in the Royal Museum in Canterbury, is believed to have been re-used as rubble in the rebuilding of the Aula Nova in the late fourteenth century. Other similar pieces were re-used in the rebuilding of the cloister, mostly between 1396 and *c*. 1400. The quality of their workmanship places them among the very finest sculpture from the English Middle Ages, and it is perhaps natural that they should be associated with the work of the two Williams. The blocks have all been reshaped at a later date so that their reverse sides could be used as ashlar. This seemingly callous treatment has preserved some of the sculpture that would surely have been destroyed had it been left exposed.[2] The original disposition of the quatrefoil blocks appears to have been as a horizontal frieze under a string course – suggesting a flat-topped border to a wall or screen. It is plausible that they formed part of William the Englishman's pulpitum screen between the eastern crossing piers which

[1] Some of the fragments are on show in the crypt (1980), one is in the collection of the Royal Museum in Canterbury, another in the Victoria and Albert Museum, London.

[2] T. A. Heslop has suggested that the sawn-off angles on some of the blocks represent an original feature.

3  Two fragments preserve vestiges of the pallium. One fragment, containing the chest and arm of an archbishop, was used as a doorstop in the home of the author's mother at 10, The Precincts. The two others came from the vault packing of the west cloister walk.

4  Hackington lies just north of the mediaeval city and is now called St Stephen's.

5  It may also have been to forestall any attempt by Baldwin to remove the body of St Thomas to Hackington.

probably survived intact into the 1390s – the time when the fragments were re-used. Three other pieces of a quite different design have also come to light, two re-used in the cloister. They are parts of full-length seated figures set into painted vesicas – at least two were figures of archbishops.[3] The drapery style again suggests a date of *c.* 1180, and the seated figures may have flanked a central door in a pulpitum. The original height of the figures must have been about 2 ft – 62 cm.

The death of Archbishop Richard in 1184 plunged the monks of Christ Church into a lengthy struggle over the right of election, coupled with the successive threats to remove the archiepiscopal throne – first to Hackington,[4] and later to Lambeth. While many of the fears harboured by the monks were groundless, the furore was such that it involved both Henry II and Richard I, King Philip II of France and several popes. The long and tangled episode began with the monks' refusal to elect Baldwin of Worcester as archbishop. Henry II, accusing Prior Alan of setting himself up as a pope in England, supported Baldwin and the suffragan bishops in their choice, and the battle-lines were drawn: Baldwin, the bishops and the king versus the monks of Canterbury Cathedral and the king of France. With the rapid succession of popes, Rome swayed back and forth and the college of cardinals was sharply divided. The claims of the monks that only they could elect the archbishop of Canterbury were further complicated by Baldwin's provocative attempt to build a collegiate church at Hackington just outside the city. The monks seized upon this as proof that the archbishop intended to move the throne of St Augustine to his new foundation, and nothing would placate them until it was demolished. In the midst of all the chaos, the monks applied to the pope for permission to translate the relics of St Thomas to the new Trinity Chapel. This move, which could hardly have taken place in the circumstances of 1185, was doubtless another barb with which to sting the aged Henry II.[5] Finally, after a seige of over eighteen months during which the monks locked themselves up in the cathedral, a temporary truce was established through the intervention of the pope. Baldwin's next move was to transfer his college from Hackington to Lambeth, and the fight began all over again. Richard I became embroiled in the long-running dispute, and even after Baldwin's death in the Holy Land, his successor, Hubert Walter was thrown into the fray. Nothing would convince the monks that the archbishop's intentions at Lambeth were honourable – even Walter's commencement of a new palace at Canterbury.

By the end of the twelfth century, a *modus vivendi* had been established within the cathedral precincts, and for the last years of his archiepiscopacy the aged Hubert Walter won the affection of the convent. He lies buried in the new Trinity Chapel, near the site of the shrine of St Thomas – the first person awarded that honour.

The disruption of the monastic life had affected the progress of the decoration of the new choir, for the fabric was hardly finished when the fight began, and the siege and the temporary loss of monastic revenues postponed the work for many years. By 1199 the monks were again continuing with the decoration and were even asking the archbishop for financial assistance.[6] It was about this time that Gervase wrote his famous account of the fire and rebuilding, probably to explain the curious design of the choir in the continued absence of its focal point – the new shrine. It would appear that much of the surviving glass, together with the lost painting cycles of the choir, dates from the relatively quiet years at the end of the century.[7]

The calm merely preceded a longer and more bitter struggle. Once again it was sparked off by the election of an archbishop. On the death of Walter, King John nominated Roger, the abbot of Walden. The pope, however, chose Stephen Langton, one of the most learned and worthy men of his time. The monks elected Langton without recourse to the king and thus new battle-lines were drawn. This time it was the monks, the archbishop, Philip II of France and the pope versus the king. The result was inevitable, but John was prepared to fight it out even at the cost of his throne. The ensuing struggle saw the exile of Langton, the expulsion of the monks for six years, the seizure of their lands and property, the capture of Canterbury by the French and, finally, the interdict placed upon the country by the pope. John was forced to submit and to sign the Magna Carta in the presence of Archbishop Stephen Langton in 1215.

The monks had returned from exile two years earlier after six years spent mostly at the abbey of St Bertin near St Omer. Langton had spent his exile at Sens and Pontigny following in the footsteps of St Thomas. Work upon the decoration of the choir at Canterbury was taken up once again, and in 1216 the new shrine of St Thomas was begun.[8] Langton completed the great Palace Hall, begun by his predecessor, in time for the great celebrations that surrounded the translation of the relics of St Thomas in 1220. The Palace was the first major building work within the precincts since the departure of William the Englishman and it was one of the most splendid and important buildings within the cathedral complex.

The work was under way before Walter's death in 1205. Langton, prevented from occupying his see until 1213, completed the Hall in time for the translation in 1220. The cost, including the great feast given by the archbishop on 7 July of that year, came to some 22,000 marks.[9] Inevitably, Langton avoided payment of this astronomic sum as did several of his successors, and it was left to Archbishop Boniface, 1245–70, to clear the debt: 'My predecessors built this Hall at great expense, they did well indeed, but they laid out no money about the building, except what they borrowed. I seem indeed to be truly the builder of the Hall, because I paid their debts.'[10] The Hall was probably erected on the site of Lanfranc's Palace, of which little is known. The new Hall lay on an east-west axis with a broad north and south aisle (Figure 99). It measured

6 *Chronicles and Memorials of the Reign of Richard I*, ed. W. Stubbs, vol. 2, Rolls Series, 1865, p. 499, letter 534.

7 See Appendices I and III.

8 Sacrist's Accounts for 1216, Canterbury Cathedral Library.

9 W. Gostling, *A Walk*, 1825, p. 143. He is quoting W. Somner, *Antiquities of Canterbury*, 1640. See also F. Grose, *Antiquities of England and Wales*, vol. 3, p. 3.

10 Grose, op. cit., pp. 3–4.

**99** (*above left*) The
Archbishop's Palace:
north porch

**100** (*above centre*) The
Archbishop's Palace:
interior of the south wall

**101** (*above right*) The
Archbishop's Palace:
window in the north-west
bay

11 Unfortunately the source is vague.
'The Great Hall of the
Archbishop's Palace at
Canterbury', *Arch. Cant.*, 43,
1931, pp. 298–300, under
Miscellaneous notes. I suspect
that it was written by the editor,
A. MacDonald, who was a master
at the King's School.

12 Gostling, op. cit., p. 143; Grose,
op. cit., p. 3.

168 ft × 69 ft – 5,121 × 2,103 cm, the aisles having an internal width of 20 ft
– 610 cm – and the nave 29 ft – 884 cm. Excavations have revealed side walls
4 ft – 122 cm – thick and an arcade base at the eastern end.[11] The evidence
from the north aisle suggests that the Hall was eight bays long, with the
surviving porch entering the aisle three bays from the west end.

A newel stair with an external entrance was discovered in the south-east
corner near to the archbishop's door into the monastic cloister. In the
eighteenth century, sections of the east end of the Hall were still standing,
including two 'canopies' of Sussex marble supported by pillars.[12]
Remains of both the north aisle and the south wall are preserved within
subsequent structures and indicate the presence of an internal wall arcade
of paired trefoil arches with a triangular wall pier supporting the central
colonnette (Figure 100). The trefoil arches have foliate crockets projecting
from the angles, while the upper arch is semicircular – the resulting shape
recalls the aisle triforium windows of William of Sens. The surviving
nook-shafts have intermediate shaft rings and moulded capitals and
bases. The style still speaks in the language of the Trinity Chapel. The
coupled wall arcade is reflected in the exterior bay design. The projecting
buttresses divided the Hall into bays some 20 ft – 610 cm – long. Each bay
contained two twin-light windows separated by a slim wall pier. The
windows were among the most advanced of their time and it is fortunate
that one has survived intact (Figure 101). The lancet shape of each window
is subdivided by a mixture of plate and quasi-bar tracery. The arch
mouldings of the individual lights and the long freestone mullion are
constructed in 'bar' tracery, while the quatrefoil set into the head is mostly
cut from plate tracery – that is, it gives the effect of having been punched
out of an existing wall. The lowest section of the window was divided by a
horizontal transom, perhaps to accommodate wooden shutters for

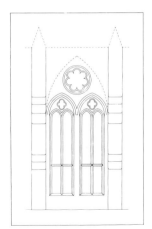

**102** The Archbishop's Palace: reconstruction of bay exterior, some parts uncertain

13 *Calendar of Close Rolls of Henry III, 1243*, PRO Publications, London, 1915, p. 23. It does not refer to a 'King's hall', only to 'the Hall'. It is unlikely that Canterbury castle had any large hall at this date.

14 Matthew Paris, *Historia Anglorum*, ed. F. Madden, Rolls Series, vol. 2, 1880, p. 242.

15 For the history of the shrine, see pp. 224–5.

ventilation. Evidently English masons were experimenting with the possibilities of 'bar' tracery at much the same time as the French.

The surviving window bay, near the west end of the north aisle, also preserves the outer frame of a second window – the springing can be seen behind a Georgian outbuilding. The basic design of the individual windows was expanded into the major theme of the bay design. The coupled windows were contained within an over-arch and the resulting typanum pierced by a circular window which enclosed some foiled shape (Figure 102). The result is characteristically French and might be seen as an exploded version of the Chartres clerestory.

Little can be recovered of the internal appearance of the Hall save for the wall arcades. The piers were probably composed of clustered marble shafts while the gable-end walls may have contained oculus windows. A clerestory would seem unlikely, e.g. Winchester Castle Hall, and the roof was probably built in a single span embracing both aisles, with a scissor-brace construction resembling other aisled halls in East Kent. The Hall was gutted by fire in 1544 and only partly rebuilt in 1559. It was undoubtedly a splendid and majestic structure, spacious and full of light. The windows were a notable development; they evidently caught the attention of Henry III, who ordered that they should be the model for the windows in his new hall in Dublin Castle: 'with windows and casements in the style of the Hall at Canterbury, which they have had a good look at'.[13] One suspects they were not the only ones.

The decoration of the Gothic choir continued throughout the period that the Palace was under construction. The troublesome archiepiscopacy of Baldwin must have frustrated the work, but his successor agreed in 1199 to take over the financial responsibility for 'perfecting' the monks' choir. Everything came to a halt for the six years under King John that the monks spent in exile, but efforts were redoubled after their return in 1213 and there can be little doubt that the decoration was completed in time for the translation of the relics in July 1220. The new shrine was begun as early as 1216 under the direction of Elias of Dereham, canon of Salisbury, and Walter of Colchester, sacrist of St Albans, 'by whose council and invention everything necessary to the making of the shrine, to its setting up and translation was done without cause for blame'.[14] The lavish shrine was raised about 5 ft – 152 cm – upon stone or possibly marble arches. The wooden coffin was clad in metal-work and covered by a canopy that could be raised and lowered by means of a pulley fitted into the central boss of the chapel vault.[15]

The shrine overshadowed even the splendid decoration of the Trinity Chapel – perhaps the richest shrine in Christendom – 'the meanest part of it was gold'. The removal of the relics from the old tomb in the crypt was surrounded by some of the greatest panoply known to the English Middle Ages. The coffin was carried by the young king, Henry III, Stephen, now Cardinal Langton, the papal legate and the archbishop of Reims, who also celebrated the mass. The ceremony was attended by all the suffragans of Canterbury 'save three, of whom one was dead and two excused by reason of sickness'. The time chosen, the seventh hour of the seventh day of the seventh month, also occurred during the fiftieth anniversary of the martyrdom, so providing the monks with a jubilee every fifty years. The offerings attained their peak in this year, some £1,142, though this was less than the cellarer was obliged to pay out for the entertainment of so many important guests. In the same year, the priors of Canterbury Cathedral won the right to wear the episcopal ring and mitre.

Other works were undertaken in the early years of the reign of Henry III, probably in association with the impending translation of the saint's remains. The great Martyrdom door in the cloister is one of the most sumptuous survivals from the early thirteenth century (Figure 103). The large central arch doubtless enclosed the Romanesque door through which the saint went to his death. The jambs are made up of clusters of Sussex marble shafts, the stiff-leaf capitals are delicately gilded, while the voussoirs above are elaborately carved and painted. The side arches frame concave niches, with evidence that they formerly contained large figures. The arches are vigorously cusped and the outer orders are stopped with fine heads. The spandrels above are filled with demi-angels. No evidence has yet been discovered to reveal the exact date of the Martyrdom doorway, and the best available guide would appear to be the base mouldings under the detached shafts (Figure 104). These correspond to those on the refectory arcade, and while that work was begun in 1221, there would be every reason to assume that the new Martyrdom door was completed in time for the translation in 1220. The location of the Martyrdom with its important Altar of the Sword's Point must have provided the monks with considerable inconvenience. The transept arm was the principal means of access between the cloister and the church, and the flood of pilgrims to the site of the martyr's death necessitated a general rearrangement of the area.

16  See p. 29.

17  This had already occurred by the time that Gervase wrote his account of the fire.

The tribune bridge surviving from Lanfranc's church,[16] and the central column that held it up, had been cleared away by the end of the twelfth century in order to provide a better view of the sacred place.[17] A further improvement involved the construction of an inner wall forming a passage from the cloister door to the steps under the central tower (see Fig. 136). At this time the steps under the crossing did not project as far as the western piers of the central tower so that it was still possible to traverse the crossing at nave floor-level. The new inner wall turned eastwards along the north side of the crossing to the steps leading up into the north aisle of the choir, which were also reconstructed with the present platform extended over the adjacent crypt entrance. The pointed barrel-vault from the Martyrdom to the crypt survives from this reordering and the line of the wall that enclosed the transept arm is preserved within the later 'bridge' forming part of the present pulpitum stairs (Figure 105). The

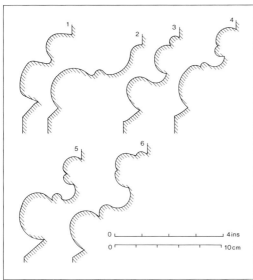

**103** (*above left*) The
Martyrdom door to the
cloister, with the cloister
vault respond of *c.* 1395
and the later door of *c.* 1500
**104** (*left*) Base profiles
from thirteenth-century
work at Canterbury:
1 Archbishop's Palace
south arcade, *c.* 1215;
2 refectory main door
inner jamb, *c.* 1221;
3 refectory cloister arcade
type I of *c.* 1225;
4 refectory cloister arcade
type II of *c.* 1225;
5 Martyrdom door to the
cloister, left jamb of
*c.* 1220; 6 Martyrdom
door to the cloister, right
jamb of *c.* 1220

**105** (*above*) The entrance
to the crypt from the
Martyrdom. To the left
stood the Altar of the
Sword's Point. The criss-
cross work within the
passage appears to be
Romanesque. The upper
tiers have been
reassembled from
demolished work,
probably from the original
stair up to the north choir
aisle

section of the new screen wall in front of the cloister door collapsed in 1734 during the digging of a grave. It formerly contained the famous Red Door which was the monks' entry into the Martyrdom, on which was painted: '*Est sacer intra locus venerabilis atque beatus, Praesul ubi Sanctus Thomas est martyrizatus.*' Public access to the sacred spot can then have been only from the crypt, the present tunnel under the crossing stairs being a fifteenth-century improvement. The arch into the crypt entry has fine head-stops, and rich mouldings similar to those in the Prior's Chapel and refectory. It is reasonable to assume that this general reordering of the Martyrdom pre-dates the translation in 1220.

The new dignity accorded to the prior in the same year may have prompted the building of a private chapel set apart from the cathedral church. The Prior's Chapel is first mentioned in 1222,[18] when it was described as new. The running expenses occur regularly from the following year, and carpentry work in the chapel appears in the accounts under 1236 (see Fig. 47). The site chosen, between the Water Tower and the infirmary, involved the replacement of a section of the infirmary cloister which was rebuilt twice the original width and projecting out into the garth. Until the seventeenth century, the undercroft was vaulted in two alleys, the vaults resting on a series of piers long since demolished. The chapel was raised in order to maintain the circulation beneath, and so that it would be at the same floor-level as the choir. It was destroyed after the Commonwealth, and only the west door and a small section of the east end survive within the present building.[19] The design of the new cloister facade is rather unusual and is a development of the internal wall arcade of the Archbishop's Palace (Figure 106). Each bay of the cloister contains a single over-arch enclosing twin lancet openings divided by a central shaft. The lancets spring from a curious half-arch with coiled leaves sprouting from its base, a feature of the Palace arcades. The result is an assymmetrical trefoil but mirrored by its pair to regain its overall symmetry. The chapel above was supported by deep buttresses of which only the westernmost remains.

The west door of the chapel, in the angle of the night passage, has deeply carved mouldings (Figure 107). The shafts are flanked by parallel grooves terminating in small foliate spurs. Little is known of the internal appearance of the chapel save that it contained paintings of St Thomas, Pope Alexander III and King Louis VII of France.[20] The chapel was extensively remodelled by Prior Roger of St Alphege, c. 1260.[21]

The monks were also concerned for their own accommodation at this time, especially with their refectory, which must have appeared dwarfish and cumbersome next to the Archbishop's Hall. The new refectory was begun in 1221 and completed in 1239.[22] It occupied the site of its Romanesque predecessor, filling the whole length of the north arm of the great cloister. The existing remains are incorporated into the eastern wall which was common with the dormitory, as well as a section of the south

18  Sacrist's Accounts.

19  The chapel was damaged by fire in 1580, and left a ruin.

20  Somner, *Antiquities of Canterbury*, 1703, p. 96. Alexander III canonized St Thomas in 1173.
21  Mentioned in the obit of Roger of St Alphege, in *Anglia Sacra*.

22  Extensive documentation in the Sacrist's Accounts.

**06** (*above left*) The Prior's
Chapel undercroft
**07** (*above right*) The Prior's
Chapel west door

wall contained within the cloister. John Pikenot is frequently mentioned in the accounts for the work, though whether he acted as master mason or simply as an overseer for another is unclear. Nearly £500 was spent, which accounts for the decorative richness of the work still evident from the remains. Some feeling for the original appearance of the building can be gained from the wall arcade within the cloister which survived the rebuilding and vaulting of the fifteenth century, though the Perpendicular vault supports did disturb the rhythm of the thirteenth-century wall arcading. The original design alternated groups of four arches with single arches – the pattern divided by wall piers (Figure 108). This was perhaps a reflection of the Wibert cloister. The arcade is supported by slender shafts with circular capitals and bases. The arches are broken into trefoils outlined by a continuous string course, once again a reflection of the Palace Hall interior arcade. Two doorways survive, one at the eastern end formerly leading under the raised dias to the kitchen court, and the main entrance further west, which contained steps up to the floor-level within the refectory. The principal entrance has elaborate mouldings, clustered marble jamb shafts and stiff-leaf capitals.

The interior of the refectory is now a private garden. The south wall has been bricked over but a section of the east wall is still visible, with a blind arcade over the original dais platform (Figure 109). The arcade

**108** The refectory: south wall
arcade within the cloister

**109** (*below*) The refectory: east
wall arcade

follows the general lines of that in the cloister. The rebuilding of the refectory may have provoked a more general reconstruction of the adjoining cloister alley, for there are payments in 1239 for work on the cloister with windows timber and carpentry, and 26s 1d for whitewashing the cloister.[23]

Nothing else survives in the cathedral from the period up to 1285. A new tower is mentioned in 1279, though whether this was in Canterbury or at the prior's new house in London is uncertain.[24] The century from 1184 was not one of the great epochs for the architecture of the cathedral church; the monks and the archbishop were concerned for once with their own welfare. The great Hall of the Archbishop's Palace, the principal achievement of the thirteenth century in Canterbury, must count as the saddest loss sustained within the cathedral precincts – its early date and the outstanding design of its windows emphasize the vital importance of the scant remains. Later in the century, while the monks ate contentedly in their new refectory and the prior spent even more money on his private chapel, the abbey of St Augustine was preparing the ground for a whole new onslaught upon English architecture. While the cathedral slumbered, the energetic rebuilding of the rival Benedictine house led to the establishment of the so-called 'Kent school'. This important school of masons was to become the backbone of the royal workshops of the Edwardian period, with the Eleanor Crosses, St Stephen's chapel, Westminster, and the creation of Perpendicular. As so often happened, it was the building activity over the city wall that prompted another period of enrichment at the cathedral.

## 1285–1376

In the late thirteenth century building activity increased both at St Augustine's and at Christ Church, during which the seeds of this last great style of English Gothic were sown. As usual St Augustine's took the initiative, with various works from the 1270s and 1280s, culminating with the majestic Fyndon Gate in progress in 1301. The 'Kent school' of masons, as they are called, gave England two great masters – Michael and Thomas of Canterbury, both royal master masons and involved in the building of St Stephen's chapel, Westminster.[25] This, the most important royal work of the period, is almost entirely lost, and it is only at Canterbury that the skill and significance of the early stages of this workshop can still be appreciated.

The first work of the Kent school in the cathedral occurred after the election of Henry of Eastry as prior of Christ Church in 1285. His election was surrounded by rather odd circumstances, for his predecessor, Thomas of Ringmere, had been forcibly deprived of the position. The priors had become powerful figures in their own right, but Thomas had

23 Ibid.

24 Lambeth Palace MS. 242.

25 Work began in 1291.

evidently overreached his authority and was dismissed by John Peckam, the first Franciscan archbishop. Eastry ruled the house for forty-six years, and like Wibert long before him, most of his energy was expended upon the monastic buildings. His list of achievements included extensive additions to the Prior's Lodgings, bells, a great clock, the rebuilding of the Chapter House, a great mass of gold and jewels for the shrine of St Thomas and vestments and ornaments for the high Altar.[26] His additions to the fabric of the cathedral church were restricted to the fittings – most notably the new choir stalls and screens. The half-century of Eastry's priorate stretched from the warring reign of Edward I to the civil turmoil surrounding the overthrow of Edward II. The events at Canterbury were somewhat calmer – the marriage of Edward I to Margaret of France on the steps of the Martyrdom door in 1299 and the archiepiscopacy of that most venerated prelate Robert Winchelsey, who died in 1313. His tomb in the south-east transept became the object of considerable devotion and, despite the fact that he was never canonized, the memory of his saintliness ensured the destruction of the tomb in 1539. The wars of Edward II were an increasing nuisance to the ageing prior, particularly the frequent visits of Queen Isabella, whose numerous dogs evidently caused havoc in the priory.

Few of the works listed in Eastry's well-known obituary[27] survive; they would have been of only peripheral interest. His major addition to the church – the new choir screens – remain substantially intact, while his work in the Chapter House has been subject to later alterations.

The account rolls indicate that work on the new choir stalls was in progress in 1298 and so there is every reason to suppose that the elaborate screens were similarly in hand.[28] The entry under 1304–5, recording over £800 spent on the screens and the Chapter House, would appear to be a final reckoning of work already accomplished. The new choir screens enclose the whole of the monastic choir and originally extended across the eastern transept and on up to the last bay of the William of Sens choir. The presbytery was closed to the east behind the Archbishop's throne by a tall iron grill topped by a wooden cornice modelled on the adjoining stonework.[29] Similar iron screens with wooden cornices were fitted at the summit of the stairs from the south-west transept arm, and presumably a matching screen was built at the top of the Martyrdom stairs. All the iron screens have gone, though parts have been re-used.[30] The stone screens have been broken into at various points for the building of tombs.

The stone screens have solid dado walls with pierced twin light openings above (Figure 110). In the choir proper the screens sit directly upon the low side wall built by William of Sens, for Eastry's screens were designed to form a solid backdrop to the new wooden stalls which did not have canopies. The walls may have been painted with drapery patterns. The openings above have ogee-headed arches and delicately cusped cinquefoils. The spandrel lights are pierced, as are the trefoils in the

26  Willis, *Hist. Mon.*, pp. 185–7.

27  Obit of Eastry, Reg. I, f. 212 ff., Canterbury Cathedral Library, and *Anglia Sacra*, vol. 1, p. 141.

28  W. Caröe, 'The choir of Canterbury Cathedral', *Archaeologia*, 62, 1911, pt 2, pp. 353–66.

29  Shown in several seventeenth-century depictions of the choir, i.e. in ibid.

30  Now divided among several gates in the church; i.e. the gates to the Trinity Chapel.

**10** The Eastry choir screens, north side

31 A. Reader-Moore, 'The liturgical chancel of Canterbury Cathedral', *Cant. Cath. Chron.*, 73, 1979, pp. 25–44. It is suggested that this area of the screen formed part of a sedelia.

32 There is no clear evidence as to the existence of return stalls in Eastry's day.

33 See Willis, op. cit., p. 99.

embattled cornice. The sections of the screen that are thought to be part of the enclosures for the shrines of SS Dunstan and Alphege are elaborately decorated with convex and concave patterns infilled with split cusp motifs and six-part flowers.[31] One original doorway survives on the north side within the crossing, with a delicately painted inner vault and hanging bosses with naturalistic foliage (Figure 111). Other foliate motifs occur within the screen tracery where the overlapping of screen and pier is blurred by climbing plant forms. Of the west door, only the innermost section survives embedded in the later Perpendicular work (see Fig. 144). The east face of the pulpitum screen was even more sumptuously decorated and traces of the original colour scheme remain behind the present stalls (Figure 112). The background was diapered with square flowers, and the scars of lost canopies or niches survive either side of the entrance arch.[32] In Eastry's time this screen must have backed onto the pulpitum built by William the Englishman *c.* 1180.

The style of the Eastry screens is advanced for *c.* 1300, especially the reverse side of the south presbytery screen with its grid-like tracery, yet it also contains fascinating throwbacks (Figure 113). The bases throughout the screens are, as Willis pointed out, remarkably similar to Anselm's aisle respond bases of two centuries before.[33] After the contradictions of the choir screens, Eastry's work in the Chapter House is even more of a

puzzle. Both are mentioned in the year 1304–5, but the first impression upon entering the Chapter House is of much earlier work (see Fig. 129). The lower walls are lined with simple arcading in grey Sussex marble and unadorned arches. A date in the 1220s would seem more appropriate, recalling the grander and more elaborate refectory. On closer inspection, the arcade bases are seen to be proto-Perpendicular though not perhaps as advanced as other Kent school works of *c.* 1300. Here is no Romanesque revival but high stepped pedestal bases taken directly from Rayonnant architecture. Eastry reshaped the Chapter House completely, abandoning the old apse and extending the building in a rectangular form. He rebuilt the south wall adjoining the Martyrdom and created an interior 60 × 35 ft – 1,823 × 1,067 cm. The surviving work along the east wall is particularly fine, with gables and pinnacles above the arcading. The repainting, though mechanical, is said to have been based on the substantial remains of the original colours that were still visible in the late nineteenth century.[34] The centrepiece of this remarkable room is the Prior's throne – gilded and enamelled, a tryptich but one out of all proportion (Figure 114). Indeed it was a 'frame' that once contained a Crucifixion scene cruelly scraped off during the Commonwealth. With the quality of English painting *c.* 1300, and the splendour of the throne, the ensemble must have presented a dazzling spectacle. Even now, the canted gables retain their enamel insets and original colour scheme.

Unfortunately Eastry's windows have been replaced. The tracery patterns of this period of experiment and innovation would have been most revealing, especially with regard to the precocious windows of the Carnary Chapel in Norwich of *c.* 1316.[35] All the windows in the Chapter House were remodelled by Prior Chillenden after 1400. The north and south walls of Eastry's rebuilding appear to survive to their full height and now contain bundled wall ribs with moulded capitals and bases, and are surmounted by castellated cornices in the contemporary Court school mode.

The Chapter House is an impressive monument, but the work of the early fourteenth century is strangely stiff and angular when compared with the subtlety of the Eastry screens. Can they really be contemporary works, or are the accounts of 1304–5 a summary of work undertaken during the first twenty-one years of Eastry's priorate? If the choir screens date from 1298–1304, then a date closer to 1290 would seem more appropriate for the Chapter House, especially when it is compared with the Peckam tomb in the Martyrdom of *c.* 1292, which shares the same richness of form, and an equally modest approach to that most dangerous element creeping into English art – the ogee. Ogee arches are almost totally absent from the Chapter House, whereas they abound within the choir screens.[36]

36 Ogees occur only in the spandrels of the throne canopy.

14 The Chapter House: the prior's throne

37 He died in 1327; see F. Woodman, 'Two tombs in the south choir aisle', *Cant. Cath. Chron.*, 69, 1975, pp. 15–22.

38 The expenditure was meticulously recorded, see Willis, *Arch. Hist.*, p. 115.

39 Willis, *Hist. Mon.*, p. 185.

40 The steps of the Meopham tomb of *c*. 1330 stood proud of the chapel floor. The base of the Bradwardine tomb of 1349 is flush to the chapel floor. Original evidence destroyed in 1979.

At his death in 1331, Henry of Eastry left the cathedral secure and considerably enriched. He had spent nearly £4,000 upon the monastery and he was the first prior to be accorded the honour of a standing monument in the church. He was buried in the south aisle of the choir, and his tomb, like that of Archbishop Walter Reynolds beside it,[37] contains several indications of the current development of Perpendicular.

The Kent school of masons had evolved a new uncluttered style that was to sweep away the heavy luxuriance of the Decorated. The window in St Anselm's chapel, one of the best examples of Kent school tracery, is an amalgam of Eastry motifs with hanging pendant bosses, split cusps and almost every conceivable variety of foiled shape (see Fig. 33). It was built by Eastry's successor Richard Oxenden in 1336.[38] The exterior face of the tracery has been unfortunately refaced and in more recent times the window has been filled with painted glass of a rather lurid nature. Nevertheless, the window is superb, and doubtless was related to the design of the lost east window of St Stephen's chapel, Westminster. The very existence of the Oxenden window is an indication that another project had been completed at Canterbury – this time a demolition. The window all but fills the south wall of the Romanesque chapel and above the vault the upper wall has been extensively robbed to alleviate the downward pressure upon the tracery. Obviously the great tower that formerly rose above the chapel had disappeared. When this occurred is unclear, priors being less anxious to claim credit for their destructions. One clue to the date of the demolition of the opposite northern tower may be the building of the room above the vestiarium in 1292,[39] as this would have been built against one wall of the tower had it still been standing (see Fig. 89). As the only access to this room involves a straight stair cut completely through the thickness of the tower's north wall, there is a strong suggestion that the massive superstructure had already been destroyed. The unstable southern tower may have survived a little longer for there is some indication that the floor of St Anselm's chapel was lowered some time between *c*. 1330 and 1349, and this may have formed some part of the lightening of the structure after the loss of the upper sections.[40]

Another unrecorded work probably dates from the 1330s – the remodelling of the Infirmary Chapel (Figure 115). A single and remarkably beautiful Kent tracery window survives from this work in the north wall. In 1342, early in the priorate of Robert Hathbrand, the small infirmary hall was added to the north aisle of the main hall, which survives in a rather restored state and now forms part of the old Choir School House. The north window facing the present Deanery must be one of the most perverse creations of the Kent school. Another work of Hathbrand's priorate survives shut up behind the disused prior's doorway in the east walk of the infirmary cloister. The elegant door with jambs lined with reticulated panelling leads into a minute lobby, exquisitely vaulted – the

**115** The Infirmary Chapel:
north window of *c.* 1330

scale and delicacy of the work is more like that of a tomb canopy. What is particularly important is the pattern, or rather mesh, that spiders its way along the tiny room. It follows directly in the line from the Gloucester south transept vault and the Aerey Porch at Windsor. It probably dates to around 1350 and may well be the work of John Box, who was in the service of Prior Hathbrand in that year. Box subsequently became king's master mason at Westminster Palace and at the Tower, and was one of the leading figures in the dissemination of the Perpendicular style until his death in 1376. Edward III's acquisition of the prior's master mason was only one example of the intimate relationship that grew up between the masters of the cathedral fabric and the royal workshops.[41] This partnership went back at least to the 1290s and was to be maintained beyond the middle of the fifteenth century.

The emergence of Perpendicular at Canterbury was far less dramatic than the first appearance of Gothic had been centuries before. The new 'Court style' of Edward III had its roots firmly planted in Kentish soil and its rapid acceptance at Canterbury reflects not only the local origins of its creators but also the lack of any strong indigenous Decorated tradition in the city. The earliest fully Perpendicular work in Canterbury, the tomb of Archbishop Stratford made *c.* 1340, exhibits such maturity of style that it must have been the product of one of the king's master masons (see Fig. 160).[42] Its delicate filigree screenwork was well liked in Canterbury

41 *Calendar of Close Rolls of Edward III, 1349–54*, p. 226.

42 As the Stratford tomb was the first to breach the Eastry choir screens, it was likely to have been negotiated if not erected prior to the archbishop's death in 1348. This was the standard practice of the archbishops of Canterbury.

and it was to exert a strong influence over the later works of native Perpendicular in the cathedral.

In 1349 the Black Death swept England and one-third of the population perished. While the plague was no less virulent in Canterbury, the cathedral community seem to have escaped the worst of its ravages. It carried off Archbishop Ufford even before his enthronement, but otherwise only four monks are known to have died. This relative immunity could be attributed to the cleanliness of Prior Wibert's water supply. The mid-fourteenth century also saw the reawakening of royal interest in Canterbury that had been lacking for so long. Edward III sent two of his sons to be educated at the cathedral under the tutorship of Prior Hathbrand. In view of the later benefactions to the church, it is assumed that one son was Edward of Woodstock – the Black Prince. Of his many visits to the shrine of St Thomas the best remembered is that of 1356, when the prince was accompanied by King John II of France recently captured by the English at Poitiers. The Black Prince founded a chantry chapel in the crypt of Canterbury Cathedral in 1363, in fulfilment of one of the conditions laid down by the pope to allow the prince to marry his cousin, Joan, Duchess of Kent. Two priests were to say daily mass for the repose of the souls of his grandparents and, after their deaths, for Edward III and Philippa of Hainault.

The chapel was constructed in the crypt of the south-east transept which was transformed from its sombre Romanesque appearance into the first major Perpendicular interior in the cathedral, heralding the great age of rebuilding that was just a few years away (Figure 116). The chapel was built close to the intended site of the prince's tomb and is a gem of early Perpendicular, with tiny colonnettes, lierne vaulting and richly sculptured bosses. The whole interior is conceived as vaulting springing from near the floor, where every architectural element is subservient to the regularity and design of the spreading ribs. All the former Romanesque heaviness has miraculously vanished. The robust vault support has been replaced by a cluster of slim shafts, with miniature capitals and bases, all executed in Bethersden or Purbeck marble, and originally polished. The use of the marble reflects the same interplay of materials employed on the Stratford tomb. The Romanesque apses have become polygonal and the east and west windows have been replaced by three light windows with sharply pointed heads. On the exterior, the windows are square framed with cusped trefoils filling the spandrels. The windows flood the interior with light, illuminating every facet of the vault and avoiding any suggestion of weight which might have been incurred by the relative lowness of the undercroft.

The brilliance of the chantry stands in sharp contrast to the second undertaking associated with the Black Prince – the chapel of Our Lady Undercroft (Figure 117). This chapel, hidden in the depths of the crypt immediately beneath the high Altar, contained one of the principal cult

**116** The Black Prince's chantry

**117** The chapel of Our Lady
Undercroft. The twisted
piers and the groin vault
are Anselm's

43 The offerings at the altar of Our
Lady Undercroft show a
remarkable increase between 1320
and 1370; see p. 220.

44 R. Hussey, *Extracts from Ancient
Documents*, p. 12.

altars in the cathedral and appears to have taken precedence over the nave chapel as the main Lady Chapel of the church.[43] It was chosen by the Black Prince as his place of sepulture, though his wishes were ignored after his untimely death. The western approach to the chapel was formerly closed by a great iron screen which was paid for between 1378 and 1380.[44] This appears to be the only dating evidence for the transformation of the chapel which may have been prepared by the prince before his death in 1376, or by Lady Mohun, another great benefactor to the church, who founded a chantry at this altar and whose tomb stands on the south side of the chapel. The style and many of the individual motifs employed in the elaborate screenwork owe a great debt to the Stratford tomb, especially the panelled tracery, the open-work gables, and the dark polished tone of the main supports. The only major departure from the earlier work is the design of the base moulding which abandons the polygonal pedestal in favour of an elongated bell – a design which also appears in the chantry chapel. The two-bay Lady Chapel is enclosed within a lattice-work of stone screens. The side screens have solid bases, originally with stone benches flanking a central doorway. The panels are infilled with trefoils standing on sub-arches, with transoms above and gabled niches surmounting the doors. The gables are slightly ogeed and are profusely decorated with crockets and finials. The east wall of the chapel is richer still, though it follows the basic design of the side screens.

The lower panels are blinded and once formed part of the altar reredos. In the centre of the upper section of the screen is a three-part niche formerly containing the figure of the Virgin. The canopies contain miniature vaults but are otherwise sadly mutilated. Of the flanking canopies, only that on the north side is original. The architect of this and the near-by chantry chapel is likely to have been John Box, who was in royal service until 1376.

The Romanesque columns of the Lady Chapel were retained in the new work, though their capitals were altered and the groin vaults were smothered with painting. The eastern vault depicts the heavens, with a multitude of stars once containing convex mirrors that twinkled in the dim candlelight of the chapel. The screen work on the south side was seriously interrupted by the insertion of the tomb of Lady Mohun, built in 1395.

All the early Perpendicular works at Canterbury share the same intimate scale and have that finely wrought and miniaturized quality so apparent in the design of the Chapter House of Old St Paul's from 1331. It is a style infinitely suited to the requirements of tombs and chapels rather than the enormous volumes of naves or choirs. The transformation of Perpendicular into a monumental style was concurrently being attempted at Gloucester and not with complete success. Unlike Gothic in the twelfth century, Perpendicular did not burst upon the architectural world as a radical and inevitable solution. The design system whereby whole interiors – wall surfaces, doors, windows and vaults – could be regularized and harmonized by the imposition of a single repeated motif was an aesthetic rather than a constructional choice and the success and eventual popularity of the style depended much upon its associated patronage and prestige. The Royal works laid the groundwork for the development and acceptability of the style at Canterbury, and the completion of the chapel of Our Lady Undercroft was a prelude for the ambitious projects that were to occupy much of the late Middle Ages, indeed an attempt to rebuild the entire nave was made in 1369, but money was short and the attempt failed. It was only with the election of Simon Sudbury as archbishop in 1375 and the death of the Black Prince in the following year that the funds and the inspiration to rebuild in a grand scale came together. The funeral cortege of the Black Prince was the last great procession to pass through Lanfranc's nave, which was deemed to be ruinous and in need of complete reconstruction. Within two years the ancient walls were being torn down and a new nave was rising in its place. And so the last great phase of the architectural history of Canterbury Cathedral began.

# CHAPTER 5

# THE PERPENDICULAR CATHEDRAL, 1377-1485

## The nave

The century from 1377 embraces one of the most important periods for Canterbury Cathedral both historically and architecturally. The burial of the Black Prince in the Trinity Chapel stimulated fresh interest from the Crown that was to continue under the Lancastrians, though for very different reasons. Richard II and Henry IV were both generous in their contributions to the various rebuilding projects, as were the small group of powerful families that formed the nucleus of the Court. In 1375 Simon of Sudbury had been elected archbishop, and he soon turned his energy and financial resources towards the rebuilding of the nave. A subscription list for donations had previously been opened by Prior Hathbrand in 1369 to coincide with the forthcoming jubilee of 1370 to celebrate the third centenary of the martyrdom of St Thomas, but the fund-raising effort ended in failure and the new prior, Richard of Gillingham, closed the account in 1371 with less than £50. But by the end of 1378, Archbishop Sudbury had issued a mandate to the clergy of the diocese urging them to promote the rebuilding of the nave. He himself had already financed the demolition of the old nave, which was said to be 'in a notorious and evident state of ruin'. Payments towards the work from various sources began in 1379 and by the time of Sudbury's murder in 1381, over £2,000 had been expended from the archbishop's revenues upon the rebuilding of the north and south aisles.[1]

The murder of Simon Sudbury by Wat Tyler and his rebels was not the only sinister event that was to cast its shadow over the new nave. In the following year, on 21 May, an earthquake shook southern England. It occurred at the opening moment of Wycliff's trial for heresy, a coincidence not overlooked by champions on either side. The damage inflicted on the Cathedral Priory appears to have been curiously local, affecting the Infirmary Chapel, the Chapter House and cloister, and the free-standing clocarium. Later in the year, Richard II issued an order for the impressment of masons 'in Kent, Surrey and Sussex for the immediate repair of Christ Church Canterbury which had been damaged in a recent earthquake'. The cost of the repairs, £35 5s 9d, would hardly justify a reaction of such proportion.[2]

[1] Willis, *Arch. Hist.*, p. 117.

[2] R. C. Hussey, *Extracts from Ancient Documents*, p. 13.

William Courtenay, who succeeded Sudbury as archbishop, was no less generous to the work, and with the election in 1391 of Thomas Chillenden, 'the greatest builder of a Prior that ever was in Christes-chirche',[3] the nave progressed at greater speed. In 1396 Pope Boniface IX offered an indulgence to all who made donations towards the work, and when Archbishop Courtenay died on 31 July of that year, the new nave was rapidly approaching completion.

The election of Thomas Arundel as archbishop brought with it the patronage of his powerful and numerous relations, among whom was the future Henry IV. The murder of Richard II and the seizure of the throne by Henry Bolingbroke hardly affected the progress of the new work at Canterbury, despite the intimate relationship that had existed between the former king and his metropolitical cathedral. Henry IV was devoted to St Thomas and to the cathedral that enshrined his relics – he was the only English monarch to commit his body for sepulture within its walls. His patronage, and that of his uncle Archbishop Arundel, secured the completion of the high vaults of the nave by 1405.[4]

The rebuilding of the nave of Canterbury Cathedral, projected in 1369, did not begin until after the election of John Finch as prior in 1377. The old nave was demolished, save for the western towers, the crossing arches and central tower, and possibly the core of the north aisle wall adjoining the cloister (see Fig. 8). Work on the new aisles was under way by the Christmas of the following year, at which point Simon of Sudbury urged the clergy to collect more funds for the fabric. The custodians of the Corona and of Our Lady Undercroft provided £66 13s 4d from their collections for the work upon the fabric of the church, and on 3 July 1379, the young king, Richard II, granted the archbishop the possessions of the deprived archdeacon of Canterbury, Aymer de la Roche: 'in consideration of the great expense of the work which the Archbishop had done upon the Cathedral church where the King's father lies.'[5]

The earliest reference to the builders of the nave occurs in 1380, when Thomas of Hoo, Richard Cook, Richard Weyland, John Asshe, Geoffry atte Well and James Aylot, 'masons of Canterbury at work on the fabric of the church', were granted two years' exemption from jury service.[6] A further 100 marks was supplied by the custodians of the two shrines in this year, which was paid directly to 'Fratri John Goodnestone' and 'John Ropere', described as superintendants of the new work upon the nave of the church. Goodnestone was probably the sub-prior of that name who died in 1397, while Ropere was a monk of some ability who served on the king's commission for the repair of the walls of Canterbury in 1385.

The murder of Sudbury in 1381 does not appear to have materially affected the progress of the nave. The door 'leading to the cloister' which was paid for in that year may be that in the north aisle which bears Sudbury's arms – a seated dog. According to his obit, the archbishop had

3 J. Leland, *Itinerary*, pts VII and VIII, vol. 4, p. 41.

4 Ibid., p. 40.

5 *Calendar of Patent Rolls*, 3 June 1379.

6 Ibid., 10 July 1379.

spent over £2,000 on the work and was responsible for the rebuilding of the north and south aisles. This suggests that the aisle walls may have been undertaken before the demolition of the old arcade walls and high roof. The earthquake of 21 May 1382 caused only limited damage, which was under repair within two years, while work on the nave continued, though at a slightly reduced cost. In the year of the earthquake, mention is made of the wall adjoining the Martyrdom, perhaps the north aisle.[7] In 1383 Goodnestone and Ropere received their usual contributions from the custodians of the Shrine, but in the following year, constructional and financial attention seems to have been concentrated on the repairs from the previous earthquake. Dating evidence for the expenditure on the nave for the rest of the 1380s is retrospective – recording only that Archbishop Courtenay had been granted a chantry chapel in 1390 for having raised 1,000 marks from the king and others of his friends for the building of the nave. In the same year, the archbishop donated £20 towards the cost of a new window in the nave to be dedicated in honour of St Alphege. This gift would suggest that at least one aisle was completed, if not vaulted, possibly the south which contains Courtenay's arms on a central boss.

The work was considerably advanced by 1391, when Chillenden was elected, for in the preceding year it is recorded that no money was paid into the treasurer's coffers from 'the trunk in the nave because the Lord Prior has it for the fabric of the church'.[8] That collections were going on at all within the new nave is some indication of its state of completion at this time. The loss of the treasurer's accounts after 1383 may however conceal a short break in the construction. A distinct junction is visible in the piers of the main arcade some 2 ft – 60 cm – above the mid-height shaft rings, above which the stone takes on a buff colour, indicative of a new bed being worked at source. Whatever significance may be attached to this break, it does demonstrate that the arcades were built uniformly along the length of the nave and not with any eastern bias, as might be expected.

The election of Thomas Chillenden marked a new phase in the construction. Expenditure increased dramatically, averaging some £400 annually, save in 1395 when only £280 was spent, 'because of decorative work in the choir'. The nave must have been nearing completion by then, for as early as 1392–3 the altar of the Holy Cross at the east end was already back in its place.[9]

Archbishop Courtenay, who died in 1396, bequeathed £200 for the pane of the cloister from the Archbishop's Palace to the church, that is the west walk, which presumes that the south walk adjoining the new nave was already built.[10] Courtenay had intended to bestow the income of the manors of Westwell and Godmersham upon the monastery to augment their building funds, but was prevented from so doing by his death. His successor, Thomas Arundel, drew up the necessary deed, which he prefaced with the following statement:[11]

7 For the cloister door and the wall adjoining the Martyrdom, see Hussey, op. cit., p. 13.

8 E. Woodruff, 'The Sacrist's Rolls of Christ Church, Canterbury', *Arch. Cant.*, 48, 1936, p. 47.

9 Chartae Antiquae, Roll C166, Canterbury Cathedral Library.

10 In 1396 the door from the Palace into the cloister was that in the north-west angle. The south-west door arrangement appears to be part of Morton's extension of the Palace.

11 Willis, *Arch. Hist.*, p. 118.

Simon of Sudbury, formerly archbishop of Canterbury, and our predecessor, had caused the nave of our church to be taken down to the foundation and demolished at his own expense, for the purpose of re-erecting the same, as he intended, and fervently desired, to do, but was prevented by his violent death; and that the prior and convent had laudably expended upwards of five thousand marks out of their common property, upon the construction of the said nave and other necessary works about the church. Also, that six thousand marks would be too little to finish the work as begun, and others that must be done about the prostrate cloister and the chapter-house, which is thought to be in a dangerous state.

The preface provides an accurate and vivid account of the state of the building work and an exact picture of the extent of the project as conceived at that time – the work involved only the nave, Chapter House and cloister, and not the western towers or the transept. In the year of Courtenay's death, the king remitted £160 in tax due from the convent 'in satisfaction of a sum promised to them by the King on account of the heavy expenditure on their works in the front'.[12] This last would seem to pinpoint the date for the construction of the west window and upper gable. The volatile relationship between Richard II and Thomas Arundel that led to the archbishop's exile had no affect on the generosity of either towards the work. Arundel especially wished to boost the building funds to secure its speedy completion in case, 'by the loss of the present Prior' or anything else, it be brought to a halt.[13] Such was the association even then between Chillenden and the new nave. Arundel donated another 1,000 marks from his own funds, as well as five bells known subsequently as the Arundel ring. By 1398 the whole nave appears to have been finished save for the completion of the high vaults, for in this year, the glazier was paid £9 2s for his work and then he 'went his way'.[14]

The high vaults were still under construction in 1401 when Arundel, recently returned from exile, gave a further 1,000 marks towards 'the building of the vault of the church'. The heraldic bosses of the vault would indicate that it was completed before 1405. The new king naturally assisted in the completion of the church that he had chosen as his place of sepulture, and Leland recalls that 'the King, Henry IV, and he [Arundel] helped to build up a good part of the body of the chirche'.[15]

By 1405, the nave was structurally complete and at least temporarily glazed. The interior faces of the western towers had been transformed with a matching Perpendicular skin, and Lanfranc's crossing arches had been recased and raised to the level of the nave vaults, which was achieved without the destruction of the old central tower above. The transepts were hardly touched, only parts of the bays next to the crossing arches being 'Perpendicularized'. In the southern arm, the lower section of the western bay was refashioned when the adjoining south-west crossing pier was recased – the upper blind clerestory being a later addition, while the opposite bay, containing the entrance to the south choir aisle was rebuilt only after the main campaign on the nave.

The rebuilding of the nave occupied no more than twenty-eight years.

12  Public Record Office, Memoranda Rolls E159/172.

13  Somner, *Antiquities of Canterbury*, 1703, p. 62.

14  Treasurers' Accounts, Feast of the Birth of St John the Baptist, 1398, in Canterbury Cathedral Library.

15  Leland, op. cit., p. 171.

The south aisle was probably vaulted first, then the north aisle, *c.* 1397, followed closely by the high vaults which were completed before 1405. The new nave follows the exact plan of its Romanesque predecessor with eight bays and a further bay between the western towers. The aisles are exceptionally high in relation to the overall dimensions, with the result that the clerestory appears somewhat diminished. This imbalance is exaggerated by the present lurid and unsympathetic clerestory glazing. The high airy cross-vistas presented by the aisles have frequently been compared with the friars' churches, and while these certainly influenced the direction of late Gothic building in England, the general proportions of the nave of Canterbury appear to derive from more practical considerations. Sudbury's initial intention was to rebuild the nave alone – the western towers and the projecting arms of the transept did not form part of his project and were not undertaken until the fifteenth century. Hence the new nave had to slot into the existing network of passages and access points within the towers and the transept. This dictated the retention of at least one passage above the aisle vaults – especially important for the south-west bell tower, which does not appear to have had any direct access from the nave floor below. A passage level had to be chosen within the increased height of the new nave which was raised to the level of the choir roof – an aesthetic rather than a practical decision. The various levels within the old nave were at tribune and clerestory height – the latter possibly an external walkway along the roof. The old tribune level at 28 ft 2 in. – 858 cm – above the floor was obviously too low for the increased height of the Perpendicular nave, and it was decided to adopt the base of the old clerestory as the level at which the east–west access would be maintained. This was not to be a passage within the thickness of the wall, but a roof-space contrived above the aisle vault. Thus the new aisles combine the height of the previous aisle and tribune, rising to approximately 50 ft – 1,524 cm – above the nave floor (see Fig. 23). The passage was screened externally by an extension of the aisle wall so that the overall height of the aisle approximated that of the choir aisles further east. The combination of Lanfranc's aisle plus the tribune within the new aisles was exactly paralleled by the coupling of Anselm's aisle and tribune by Williams of Sens two centuries earlier.

The principal liturgical entrance to the nave is by the west porch, which is, however, rather subdued, perhaps in deference to the south-west door which was the traditional entrance for the public (Figure 118). The west gable elevation recalls the earlier west front of Winchester. The slight projection of the porch is concealed within the later buttresses of the western towers, so that the rectangular entrance facade now appears as a screen. The main arch is flanked by cusped panels and tall niches, while the interior has an elaborate lierne vault containing one of the many 'portraits of the dead Henry Yevele'.[16] The rib pattern contains references to both the aisle and the high vaults of the nave.

On entering the west door, the sheer and luminous interior is unfolded.

16  J. Harvey, *Henry Yevele*, p. 49.

**118** The west porch; the niches were added *c.* 1460 and have been heavily restored

The effect would be even more striking were silvery glass restored to the clerestory. The vertical emphasis of the architecture is perfectly balanced by the diagonal vistas achieved through the arcades into the brightly-lit aisles. The piers are a triumph of harmony and elegance, with strength beyond question, yet astonishing in their slenderness. The projection of the angle bracket mouldings and the vault responds beyond the spandrel plane creates a series of recessions that add a hint of uncertainty to the exact relationship of the upper walls and clerestory. A similar ploy is seen in the aisles, where the large four-light windows are set so deep into the walls as to be quite out of sight when the aisle is seen axially. All this is in marked contrast to the surface clarity of the earlier Perpendicular choir of Gloucester, the only major interior in this style that could have influenced the new nave. The diagonality of Canterbury appears to be almost as important as its verticality, suggesting a debt to Rayonnant works like the nave at St-Denis or St-Ouen at Rouen. Yet, despite the important role played by the aisles, their design is the complete antithesis of the arcade walls. Plain to the point of severity, the large windows are surrounded by blank walling over a dado devoid of any decoration. Only the tripled vault responds break the monotony of the ashlar – their capitals, shaft rings and bases adding a solitary note of colour. The use of polished marble for these elements echoes the earlier employment of such materials in the first Perpendicular works at Canterbury.

The tracery of the aisle windows points back to Gloucester with subarcuated main lights supporting staggered gables and three reticulated lozenges (Figure 119). The twin transoms below syncopate the horizontal divisions of the adjoining vault responds, a motif visible only when viewed frontally. The aisle vaults have simple stellar patterns with liernes replacing the transverse ridges. The great height of the aisles, 49 ft – 1,493 cm – to the vault apex, is enhanced by the slender proportions of the arcade piers which have the bundled quality of Lincoln or Westminster. The lozenge piers measure only 6 ft 1 in. by 6 ft 6 in. – 185 cm by 198 cm, yet they rise over 36 ft – 1,097 cm – from floor to capital. The arcade arches are suitably slim and four-centred, with cinquefoil cusps and trefoils filling the spandrels. The vault shafts rise from high pedestal bases to a height of 57 ft – 1,737 cm – and are punctuated by two sets of shaft-rings – halfway up the piers and at the springing level of the arcade arches. Only the broad bracket moulding on the diagonal of the piers is allowed to flow uninterrupted from base to vault apex.

The triforium level, representing the roof-space passage above the aisle vaults, is merged into the clerestory design in such a way as to appear to be a blinded section of the window – an effect emphasized by the outer panels of the clerestory which are similarly blinded. The design of the triforium is a simple rectangle divided vertically into five tall panels with

**119** (*below left*) The south aisle of the nave: exterior
**120** (*below right*) The west front. Mapilton's tower is on the right. The left tower is nineteenth century

cusped arch heads. The clerestory above continues the five-part division and completely fills the vault lunette. Every panel terminates in a cusped arch surmounted by a top-heavy cinquefoil 'dagger' light. Only the three central panels form the window, and the thin-walled construction allows no clerestory passage. The net result of the combined triforium and clerestory is a little puzzling – after all, a double-pitched aisle roof in the French manner would have eliminated the need for the middle storey while preserving the height of the aisle walls and the internal roof passages. Evidently the false triforium was considered an acceptable, if not essential, part of the elevation.

All the details of the arcade elevations speak of the Court school of Perpendicular which had been centred on London for most of the fourteenth century. The arcade capitals are plain polygonal bells with moulded abaci. The polygonal bases are high-stepped, with basement, bell, pedestal, and double bell mouldings. Only the shaft-rings of the vault responds and the cardinal points of the piers strike an odd and archaic note.

The west window forms an architectural set-piece which completely fills the interior of the gable-end wall (Figure 120). It is divided into seven lights by mullions that soar up from the nave floor to the main arch moulding. The main lights are formed into a grid pattern by a series of transoms, which also appear in the upper tracery where the lights are subdivided. The simplicity of the west window tracery marks a change in taste away from the complex over-laid subarcuated windows of the aisles, and would point to a design date nearer that of its construction – that is, of *c.* 1396 rather than 1377.

The high vault of the nave is incomparable for its poise and finesse. The visual success is absolute, yet its plan is deceptively simple and, on paper, unattractive (Figure 121). The basic quadripartite plan is never lost, nor is it excessively emphasized. The transverse ribs, so apparent on the plan, are not easily distinguishable when seen from below and it is the lesser tierceron ribs that transform the appearance of the vault. The tiercerons are emeshed in a pattern of liernes which form a pointed cross in plan and arrow-heads project inwards from the clerestory – the latter motif harking back to the vaults of the Black Prince's chantry. By restricting the liernes to the upper sections of the ribs, they diffuse the awkward junctions of the various vault planes and provide the necessary activity along the axial line – blurring the rigid bay divisions throughout the length of the nave. At the same time, the 'arms' of the lierne crosses transform the vault into a series of serrated cones that echo the form of fan vaulting. The conoid effect is assisted by the doubling of the tiercerons against the transverse ridges, where the outer ribs force back the plane of the webbing beyond the line of the main diagonals. One other reason for the overwhelming success of the nave vaults is the scale of the bosses, which are never allowed to interrupt the linear flow or to upset the ethereal suspension of the whole by any excess of heaviness or arresting detail.

**21** (*above left*) The nave interior from the west

**22** (*above right*) The north aisle of the nave: exterior from the Chapter House roof

Whereas the interior of the nave is majestic and brilliant, the exterior is solid and sensible (Figure 122). The aisle walls are so high that they almost conceal the clerestory windows, and the stepped buttresses rising free of the walls cast deep shadows along the length of the nave. The aisle design is even more astringent on the outside than within – plain ashlar and an absence of decoration. The aisle windows have rather small and insignificant dripstones, while the expanse of wall above is broken only by crisp square openings, lighting the internal walkway above the vaults. The clerestory is similarly austere, and the only real concession to decoration on the exterior are the gabled niches on the buttresses of the south flank. The panelled buttress extensions support substantial flying buttresses which are virtually concealed by the upward extension of the aisle walls – an arrangement recalling the choir of Westminster Abbey.

But it is Winchester that has become the standard comparison with the nave of Canterbury Cathedral. The new nave of that church was initiated before 1366 when Bishop Edington reconstructed the west front in the new Perpendicular style. The main campaign that was to transform the Romanesque interior was not begun before 1394, when the nave of Canterbury was approaching completion. The arcade walls of the two naves differ in many respects; as the overall height of the nave at Winchester was not increased, the present clerestory corresponds exactly with its Romanesque predecessor. The aisles do not, as at Canterbury, represent the combined height of the former aisle and tribune, for the downward extension of the Perpendicular clerestory unit at Winchester occupies the upper section of the old tribune. The recasing of the old piers at Winchester has led to a heaviness not found at Canterbury and the interior lacks the airy cross-vistas made possible at Canterbury by the slender proportions of the arcade. The inherited mass of the structure at Winchester also causes the 'balcony' effect, as Willis dubbed it, where the entire wall plane moves backwards at triforium level.[17] The slim walls of the Canterbury arcade are able to maintain a uniform depth, thus avoiding the disharmony of the two tiers. While there are close connections between the two clerestory designs, the dating evidence would suggest that it originated at Canterbury. In its re-use at Winchester, a harsh angularity is introduced so typical of the later work in that church and at Oxford – its architectural offshoot.

The nave of Canterbury Cathedral is widely held to be one of the finest products of the English Middle Ages. It is therefore not surprising that the identity of the architect has been the subject of much research and discussion over the last half-century. The name of Henry Yevele has become inseparable from the building, yet the evidence to support this attribution is slight and inconclusive. Yevele was a royal master mason of some standing who succeeded John Box at both Westminster Palace and at the Tower. Box had worked at Canterbury Cathedral from at least 1350 and his services may have been retained until his death in 1376. Yevele's first known association with Canterbury was in 1385 – some ten building seasons after the commencement of the new nave – when he served on the king's commission for the repairs to the city walls. The other commissioners were Lord Cobham, William Topclyf and John Ropere of Canterbury. Topclyf was a local agent for the king who had been responsible for the impressment of masons for the repair of Canterbury Cathedral after the earthquake in 1382. Ropere was a monk of Christ Church and one of the superintendents of the construction of the new nave. Yevele and Lord Cobham subsequently participated in an agreement with the cathedral in 1386 for the repair of those sections of the city walls for which the Priory was held responsible. Throughout these negotiations, Yevele was concerned only with the city defences, though this did bring him into contact with at least one person who was directly concerned with the new nave.

In 1396–7, Yevele supplied lead and stone to the prior of Canterbury Cathedral to the value of £96 16s – material that is normally assumed to have been for the nave. But Yevele had entered into an agreement with the prior over the city defences within the precincts; work which involved the construction of a new set of bastion towers which were completed only

17 Willis, *The Architectural History of Winchester Cathedral*, London, 1846, p. 67.

*c.* 1409. It was probably for this work that Yevele received Livery from the prior in 1398 and his name appearing first in the Livery List may indicate no more than a respect for his status as the king's master mason. These are the only references to connect Henry Yevele with Canterbury Cathedral and all would appear to relate to the agreement concerning the city walls drawn up in 1386.[18]

18 For the latest discussion on the role of Henry Yevele, see A. D. Mclees, 'Henry Yevele, disposer of the King's Works of masonry', *J. Brit. Archaeol. Ass.*, 36, 1973, pp. 52–71.

Other names on the prior's Livery List of 1398 include Stephen Lote, John Roper, Thomas Hoo, John Wolward (a warden of the new work in the nave), Simon Carpenter from London, John Bulstrode and John Kent – all connected with building work. The inclusion of Thomas of Hoo is surely not without significance. As early as 1380 he was named first amongst those exempted from jury service while 'at work on the fabric of Christ Church Canterbury' – an exemption granted for a further two years from February 1390.[19] His place-name suggests that he may have worked with John Box at Queenborough in Kent, where Edward III built a new castle, and the strong implication behind his long association with Canterbury Cathedral suggests that Hoo may have succeeded Box at Canterbury after 1376. As the new nave was begun in the following year, his claim to be its designer would seem to be the strongest. His relatively low position in the prior's Livery List of 1398 might indicate that he had already retired in favour of a younger man who, from later Livery Lists, would appear to be Stephen Lote. Only two lists survive from the early fifteenth century – those for 1412 and 1416 – and, in both, Stephen Lote heads the list of masons and artificers.[20] When viewed objectively, the documentary evidence would suggest that Thomas of Hoo controlled the work at Canterbury, at least during the vital period 1377–92 which covers the construction of the aisles and apparently much of the nave arcade.

19 *Calendar of Patent Rolls, Richard II*, 10 July 1380.

20 Tanner MS. 165, Bodleian Library, Oxford.

The stylistic evidence within the fabric can throw more light on the problem of authorship, for there is evidence within the work suggesting that either one master mason expanded and explored the possibilities of his style during a single campaign – an option which could accommodate the significant changes of detail within the nave – or that a number of successive masters were engaged upon different parts of the structure. The order of building can be determined from the evidence already stated: the aisles, west porch and arcades, the clerestory, west window and, finally, the vault. The crossing piers were probably re-cased during the building of the upper parts of the arcade walls. The design of the aisles contains a number of archaic features which were not taken up in the remainder of the nave. The tracery recalls that at Gloucester from the 1330s, while the use of marble shaft-rings points to an even earlier period when Purbeck was fashionable for such details. The particular stimulus for their employement at Canterbury may have been the new nave campaign at Westminster which endeavoured to capture the essence of the earlier work of Henry III, though similar marble details were employed in all the Perpendicular works at Canterbury during the master masonship of John Box. When the second phase of the nave was begun, new tracery patterns were introduced in the west window and in the clerestory that tend towards simpler vertical divisions at the expense of complicated subarcuations. The aisle walls are devoid of all enlivenment, whereas the west wall and the triforium area under the clerestory are enriched by the downward extension of the window mullions.

The base moulding profiles throughout the nave provide perhaps the easiest guide to the developments within the work. The earliest, the aisle responds, have a simple rounded double bell, a polygonal pedestal, hollow chamfer plinth and a polygonal basement. The bases of the west porch and throughout the main arcades are more elaborate, with round double bell, polygonal pedestal, a polygonal bell undercut by a hollow chamfer and a polygonal basement. Yet another type can be seen against the west wall of the nave at the base of the mullion extensions. This design follows the same profile of the arcade bases until the second bell, which has become considerably larger and elongated and has additional necking which changes the emphasis of the whole profile. This base type, dating from 1396 in the nave, can also be found in the cloister and in all the works carried out in Canterbury Cathedral until *c.* 1430, and may therefore be associated with the arrival of Stephen Lote. For the sake of convenience, the series of Perpendicular base profiles at Canterbury can be enumerated 1 to 5: the first being the base type employed in the Black Prince's chantry and the chapel of Our Lady Undercroft, *c.* 1360; the second in the nave aisles from 1377; base type 3 the profiles of the main arcade bases; Stephen Lote's design becomes base type 4; while the last is the base type introduced from *c.* 1432 (Figures 123, 124, 125). As base type 4 continues to *c.* 1430, its appearance on part of the west window project would suggest

**123** (*below left*) The nave: arcade pier base
**124** (*below right*) Perpendicular base profiles: base type 1, Our Lady Undercroft, *c.* 1375; 2 nave aisle respond, *c.* 1380; 3 nave arcade bases, *c.* 1390; 4 cloister, *c.* 1395; 5 Lady Chapel, *c.* 1450

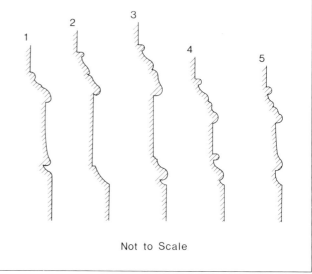

Not to Scale

that Stephen Lote had control of the work by that date. Lote, a local man probably from Newington near Hythe some twenty miles from Canterbury, worked extensively for the queen, Anne of Bohemia, between 1390 and 1394, and he and Yevele were responsible for her tomb in Westminster Abbey from 1395. Richard II took an active interest in the building of the west window of Canterbury and may have intended the window to be a memorial to his dead wife. If Lote built the west window, then the consequent construction of the high vaults is also likely to have been under his supervision, though the references to earlier vaults in the cathedral suggest that they may have been built to the original design of *c.* 1377. There remains the earlier work on the nave which, as we have seen, falls into two stylistic groups. The construction of the aisles from 1377 was undoubtedly executed by Thomas of Hoo. The design, however, could well pre-date the construction, for the new nave was already projected in 1369. Some of the archaisms of the aisles would be more easily explained if the designer were John Box, who must have trained during the early Perpendicular period of the 1330s and 1340s. Box could also provide the link so evident between the previous Perpendicular work at Canterbury and the first campaign in the nave. The second phase involving the construction of the arcade walls introduced a new monochrome style and significant changes in the treatment of wall surfaces as well as new moulding profiles. While the arcades continue the basic themes of the aisles, the stylistic repertoire has changed. With the arcade walls under construction during the 1380s, Thomas of Hoo is the only candidate that can be considered as its designer on present evidence.

The case for Yevele's authorship can rest on only one detail – the mouldings of the west porch. It has been pointed out elsewhere that the porches of Westminster Abbey, Westminster Hall and Canterbury Cathedral are similar in design. The mouldings found in both the Westminster porches are very similar indeed and they would appear to share the same workshop traditions. The date of the porch at Westminster Abbey is uncertain – Letheby thought as early as *c.* 1375, in which case it would have been the work of John Palterton, master mason of the Abbey until at least 1379,[21] but it is equally possible that it dates from post-1390 and is contemporary with the north porch of Westminster Hall which it so clearly resembles. The mouldings in the porch at Canterbury are not exactly similar to either of the Westminster examples, and the base type employed is quite different. It would be natural that Canterbury should adopt the general lines of the two important royal works, though any parallels are insufficiently close to claim anything but a family dependence upon Winchester.

On balance, Thomas of Hoo should be credited for building the nave of Canterbury Cathedral, and probably for the design of the greater part of it. The details of the vault may have been settled by Stephen Lote after his arrival in Canterbury, perhaps on Hoo's retirement, but the west window

21 W. Lethaby, *Westminster Abbey Re-examined*, pp. 139–40.

**125** The nave: aisle respond base

and the subsequent work of the early fifteenth century would all appear to come from a single hand – indicating that Lote had taken over design control by *c*. 1396.

## The cloister and Chapter House

The original intention of Archbishop Sudbury had been to rebuild only the nave of the cathedral, but the project became greatly enlarged; by the time Archbishop Courtenay died in 1396 it was envisaged that the cloister, Chapter House and possibly even the western transept of the church should be rebuilt in a similar manner to the nave. Much remained to be done, and Thomas Chillenden was plainly the man to do it. His energy and determination veritably transformed the priory. His term of office, from 1391 to 1411, saw not only the completion of the nave and crossing piers, but also the rebuilding of much of the cloister, the modernization of the Chapter House, the re-roofing and refenestration of the great dormitory, the extension of the Prior's Lodgings, the building of the Chillenden Chambers, the raising and re-edifying of the night passage and Water Tower, as well as a complete overhaul of the fresh-water system. Like Prior Wibert before him, Chillenden's building campaign was one result of a thorough reformation of the monastic finances, and by the year of his death, the revenues had reached around £4,000 – a sum hardly equalled in later years.

The cloister was rebuilt between *c*. 1395 and 1414. The luxuriant lierne vault is smothered with bosses – 864 in all – mostly heraldic (Figure 126). While little documentary evidence survives concerning the reconstruction, the heraldry provides an accurate dating scheme for the whole project. The outer walls of the cloister, common to so many of the monastic buildings, could not be rebuilt completely: 'consequently these walls, more especially in the east and north alleys resemble those of a museum of mediaeval architecture, against which examples of all the styles have been placed for the edification of students'.[22] The west wall was rebuilt as part of Chillenden's new cellarer's offices, and the south wall rebuilt or refaced as part of the reconstruction of the north aisle of the nave. The vault responds of the south alley have been inserted into this wall, showing at least two phases in the reconstruction.

The inner cloister arcades have regular bay divisions save at the angles where they are abbreviated to form the corners (Figure 127). The bays are defined by tall buttresses with crocketed spirelets, the set-offs have gables formerly filled with minute trefoils – regrettably, they did not reappear in the restorations in the 1930s. The whole exterior of the cloister has been thoroughly restored – renovated might be more exact. The first phase of this scheme in the early part of this century saw the restoration of the entire bay, but more recently, the original tracery has been left untouched

22  Willis, *Hist. Mon.*, p. 40.

26 (*above left*) The east walk
of the cloister
27 (*above right*) A cloister bay

23 Some of the cloister bays were
glazed later in the Middle Ages.

wherever possible. The reconstruction has one subtle but important difference from the mediaeval design. Each bay contains an ogee over-arch which rises just above the roof parapet. These arches were heavily crocketed, and this feature has been reproduced. However, the fourteenth-century finials appear to have been slighter and more elegant than their modern counterparts so that the interruption of the horizontal roof-line was minimal. Now, the ogee arches burst forcefully through the frame, which detracts from the Perpendicular quality of the original design.

The enclosed arcading within each bay takes the form of unglazed tracery[23] – the pattern based on the aisle windows of the nave. The arcade bases, like those of the vault responds, are base type 4, the design employed on the west wall of the nave interior from *c.* 1396 (Figure 128).

The interior of the cloister is dominated by its lush vaulting that sweeps along the walks and swirls around the corners. Seventeen ribs spring from each respond and no less than twenty-five at the angles. The complex lierne pattern relates to the high vaults of the nave with a greek cross and arrowheads from the axial apices. The number of liernes provides ample

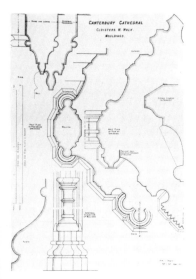

**128** Moulding profiles from
the west cloister walk

24 L. C. Duncan, 'The will of
William Courtenay, Archbishop
of Canterbury, 1396', *Arch. Cant.*,
23, 1898, pp. 55–67.

scope for the array of heraldic devices – a maximum of forty-two in each bay. Not surprisingly, the cloister of Canterbury Cathedral contains possibly the greatest collection of heraldry to survive from the Middle Ages. There are thirty-six bays in the cloister vault, including the angles. The numeration of the bays generally begin at the south-east angle near the door to the Martyrdom, and proceeds west, north, east and south, so that the south-west angle is bay 10, the north-west bay 19, the north-east bay 28, etc.

The south alley adjoining the nave is likely to have been rebuilt first. It also contains the least heraldry. Bay 1 contains the arms of Humphry de Bohun, the father of Mary de Bohun, first wife of Henry IV. Humphry died in 1372 and is the earliest person to be commemorated on the cloister vault. The remaining bays of the south alley before bay 8 are devoid of datable heraldry, save that of Archbishop Courtenay who died in 1396. There has been some confusion concerning the will of this archbishop, who left £200 for the building of the cloister walk between the Palace door and the church 'in a straight line'.[24] This reference is usually taken to mean the south walk, even though the only Palace door at this date was at the north-west angle of the cloister. A straight line reaching the church from that door would indicate the west walk, which tellingly is liberally spattered with the Courtenay arms. The present Palace door at the south-west angle appears to be a new entrance built by Cardinal Morton, *c.* 1490–1500, as part of a southern extension of the Palace. The identification of the Courtenay bequest as the west walk suggests that the south alley adjoining the nave was nearing completion by *c.* 1396. The vaults of bay 8 and bay 10 in the south alley display the arms of Archbishop Arundel, who succeeded Courtenay in 1397, and these may have been the last bays to be vaulted in that walk.

Bay 14, in the middle of the west walk, contains England and France modern, post 1405, and the arms of Edmund, second Duke of Kent (died 1407). The arms of Bishop Bokingham who was buried in Canterbury Cathedral in 1397–8 can be found in bay 18, and the presence of his arms probably denotes the bequest to the work made in his will. His arms are also found in bay 34 in the east walk, together with those of Lady Mohun, another benefactor of the cathedral, who died in 1404 and was buried in a tomb in the chapel of Our Lady Undercroft that she had prepared for herself. Another benefactor commemorated in bay 34 is John of Sheppey, a monk of Christ Church who gave £100 towards the building of the cloister. The last bay of the east walk, bay 36, which adjoins bay 1, contains the arms of England and France modern so that at least three bays of the east cloister walk had been started by *c.* 1405. From then on, the work appears to have concentrated upon the north walk, where Bishop Bokingham's arms are in bay 22 in the company of Henry Beaufort as bishop of Winchester and Henry, as Prince of Wales, that is before April 1413. The latter arms can also be found in bay 24.

Meanwhile, the east walk was taken up again after 1410, the progress probably having been arrested by the work on the adjacent Chapter House. Bay 33 contains Thomas, Duke of Clarence, married to Lady Margaret Holland, a liaison that occurred only in 1410, as well as the arms of Henry, Prince of Wales. This bay can therefore be firmly dated between 1410 and April 1413. Bay 30 displays the quartered arms of Mowbray and Neville, celebrating the marriage of Sir John Mowbray, second Duke of Norfolk, to Catherine Neville which took place in 1412. In bay 28, forming the north-east angle of the quadrangle, the arms of Archbishop Arundel are still found, indicating that the east walk was completed before his death in 1414, but the adjoining bay on the north walk, bay 27, contains the arms of his successor, Henry Chichele. This must have been the last bay to be vaulted and it marks the culmination of the two campaigns – northwards along the eastern walk and eastwards along the northern. The presence of the Mowbray–Neville arms in bay 30 of the east walk, those of Henry, Prince of Wales, in bay 24 of the west walk, and of Archbishop Arundel in the north-east angle indicates that the whole campaign must have drawn to a close in or soon after 1414. Some time after 1411, Thomas Hearne, a wealthy monk of Christ Church, donated £5 to the work of the cloister 'not yet finished'.[25]

The Chapter House was also transformed during the priorate of Thomas Chillenden (Figure 129). The building had been previously modernized and reshaped by Henry of Eastry and repaired once more after the earthquake of 1382. Nevertheless, it was deemed ruinous and dangerous in 1397, and reparation work involved the rebuilding of both gable end walls and the provision of new windows and a new roof. Chillenden's name was formerly inscribed under the west window, and the whole scheme was accomplished before his death in 1411. The cost was staggering – over £1,000 was spent in one year, and benefactions towards the work seem to have been accepted in much the same way as for the cloister. Thomas Fogge, who died in 1407, gave £20 to the work on the Chapter House – his wife, Lady Jane, had been one of the earliest subscribers to the new nave, and their family arms may also be found in the cloister.

The design of Chillenden's work in the Chapter House is intimately related to the work in the nave, then drawing towards its conclusion. The tracery of both the huge gable end windows and of the lateral windows represents simple variations on the design in the nave aisles. The roof is one of the most original creations of the period – a giant wagon vault made in wood, with seven canted sides and criss-crossed with a proliferation of ribs and liernes – all cusped and painted (Figure 130). The overall effect is similar to the choir vault at Gloucester with its inherent barrel profile and overlaid web of ribs. The roof was always painted – the present colour being a careful restoration of the late nineteenth century. The stained glass has not fared so well. In the eighteenth century much of the glass

25 W. G. Searle, ed., *The Chronicle of John Stone*, p. 18.

**129** (*above left*) The Chapter House interior from the east. The side walls and the arcading beneath the west window date from Eastry's time. The gable end wall, the side windows and roof are Chillenden's

**130** (*above right*) The Chapter House roof

remained, with the seven angelic Orders filling the head of the west window, and several heraldic panels – including the arms of Sudbury, Courtenay and Arundel – the latter also found in the 'stonework' and in the roof.

Chillenden died in 1411 and was succeeded as prior by John of Woodnesborough, who is reputed to have cleared the priory of all its debts – a remarkable achievement considering that extensive building works were still in progress. Early in his priorate, the king died. Henry IV had long expressed his intention to be buried in Canterbury Cathedral, and his uncle and executor, Archbishop Arundel, carried out his wishes. The king's body was laid to rest upon a hearse in the Trinity Chapel only yards from the Black Prince whose son he had so ruthlessly usurped. The Lancastrians avowed a deep reverence for Canterbury and St Thomas. Henry's half-brother, John Beaufort, Earl of Somerset, had already found his last resting-place in the Trinity Chapel, and in 1421 Henry's youngest son, Thomas, Duke of Clarence, was buried at the foot of his father's bier.[26] Henry's splendid tomb and chantry chapel, for which full provision was made in his will, were not undertaken until the 1430s and

26 Both husbands of Lady Margaret Holland were reburied in St Michael's chapel in 1440.

the king now lies with his second wife, Queen Joan of Navarre, who died in 1437.

The continual war with France occupied the new archbishop, Henry Chichele, who had succeeded Thomas Arundel in 1414. Very much a 'new' man of the fifteenth century, Chichele had risen to high office from the merchant classes rather than from the nobility. He was passionately concerned with education, and his foundation of All Souls in Oxford is as much his memorial as the lavish monument erected in the choir during his lifetime. He gave to Canterbury Cathedral his large collection of books which he housed in a new library built above the Prior's Chapel in the infirmary cloister. Chichele provided one of the most important stabilizing influences in the government of England during the minority of Henry VI. The boy king's father, the dashing Henry V of Agincourt, often visited the cathedral – most famously in thanksgiving for his crushing defeat of the French in 1415. But he did not choose the cathedral for his burial nor did any other monarch after him, and his entombment in Westminster Abbey in 1422 ended the brief expectation of a Lancastrian funerary church at Canterbury.

The priorate of John of Woodnesborough closed in 1425. It saw the continuation and expansion of the building projects of Chillenden; after the completion of the cloister, work began on the transformation of the south-west transept arm and of the south-west bell tower. Both works, in progress through the 1420s, evince the enormous importance to Canterbury of a group of major families centred upon the Beauforts, the Nevilles and, above all, the Hollands. These three families, inexorably linked by marriage, display their heraldic devices throughout the works. The Beauforts were Lancastrians, which explains their interest, and they were closely linked to the Nevilles by marriage. Similarly, the Hollands were kinsmen of both Richard II and the Beauforts and Lancastrians, and one of the vital elements in their continued interest in the cathedral appears to have been the successive marriages of Margaret, Countess of Holland.[27] Her first husband was John Beaufort and her second was Thomas, Duke of Clarence. The two other families represented in the heraldry of the south-west transept, the Percys and Mowbrays, were related to Lady Margaret by marriage, and the arms of yet more of her relations were formerly in the glass of the great transept window.

27 For details of their complex relationships, see F. Woodman, 'The Holland family and Canterbury Cathedral', *Cant. Cath. Chron.*, 70, 1976, pp. 23–8.

## The western transept and its chapels

The western transept did not figure in the rebuilding plans of Archbishop Sudbury, nor is it included in the list of achievements of Thomas Chillenden detailed in his orbit of 1411. The bays adjoining the central tower were fashioned, at least in part, when the crossing piers were recased towards the end of the nave campaign. The entrance arch from the south aisle of the nave was undertaken along with the south-west crossing pier, but the upper section of the bay, including the blind clerestory facing into the transept, is of a later date – there are clear breaks between the clerestory and the crossing pier (see Fig. 8). The Mowbray arms at the apex of the bay indicate a date of pre-July 1425. Thus the two separate phases of the work were accomplished between *c.* 1396 and 1425. The choir entrance bay opposite was rebuilt after the south-east crossing pier and its wall rib carried the arms of Archbishop Henry Chichele. The Percy arms at the apex of the southern crossing arch would seem to relate to the marriage of Henry Percy to Eleanor Neville in 1414. She was the sister of Catherine Neville, the wife of John Mowbray since 1412. If the heraldry of the aisle bay south of the crossing is reliable, then its construction should date between 1414 and 1425.

On the north side of the central tower, only the arch forming the entrance to the north choir aisle was rebuilt during the Chillenden's priorate, probably as part of a general re-ordering of the stairs under the central tower (see Fig. 9). The opposite arch formed the eastern end of the Lady Chapel that occupied the north aisle of the nave, and the chapel continued on this site until it was replaced by the present Lady Chapel in the middle of the fifteenth century. The existence of bonding breaks in both arms of the transept and the apparent inconsistency of the various builds would indicate that for some years, perhaps even decades, the sections of the transept contiguous to the central tower were partly rebuilt and stood as high as the new nave, while the projecting bays both north and south were Lanfranc's lower work from the eleventh century.

Eventually, when it was decided to rebuild the projecting bay of the southern arm, a more radical approach was adopted and the western and southern walls were demolished and rebuilt anew rather than the former piecemeal refashioning. Only the east wall of Lanfranc's work was suffered to remain standing – this due to the initial retention of the Romanesque double chapel and the complicated integration of the western transept with the choir aisle beyond. The whole southern bay of the transept, including the vault responds, was then rebuilt in a single campaign (Figure 131). The heraldry at the wall rib apices displays Arundel and two kings, the presence of Archbishop Arundel suggesting that the southern bay was begun before the upper part of the adjoining bay had been completed. The extensive bonding breaks that divide the Holland Chapel from the transept indicate that the work was completed before Lady Margaret Holland commissioned her chapel in 1437.

Documentary evidence concerning the rebuilding of the southern arm of the transept is slight, and is further complicated by its inclusion into the general fabric rolls of the period. The earliest reference to the work is probably that contained in the will of Thomas Waxchandler of 1418, who wished to be buried 'in the cemetery . . . before the porch of the new work'.[28] The date of the request would eliminate the possibility that it

28 Lambeth Wills, Chichele Reg. I.

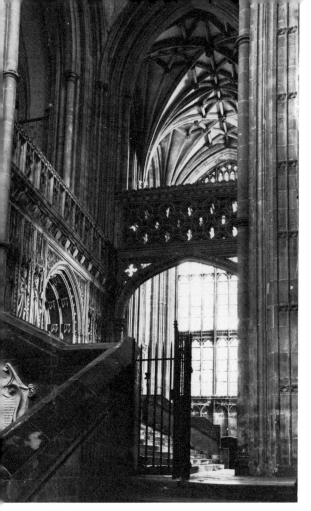

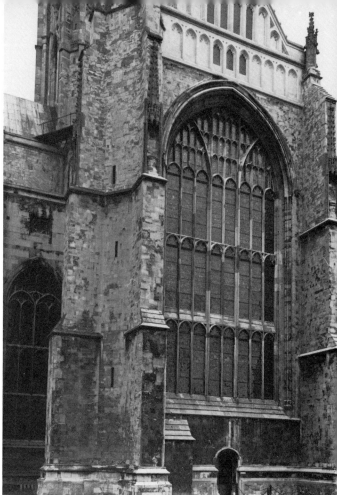

**31** (*above left*) Interior of the crossing and south-west transept from the north: the strainer arch by John Wastell after 1495

**32** (*above right*) The south-west transept exterior

29 Fabric Drawer Bundle XIX, Canterbury Cathedral Library. See E. Woodruff, 'The rebuilding of the south-west tower of Canterbury Cathedral', *Arch. Cant.*, 48, 1936, pp. 37–47.

referred to the south-west porch of the nave which was started only in 1424. The 'porch' referred to could be the door at the base of the great south window of the transept.

Further references appear to have found their way into the fabric rolls of the new south-west bell tower which was begun in 1424, for it is evident from these accounts that several works were in fact in progress, some of them outside the cathedral precincts.[29] The first roll is headed 'the new south bell tower', but from 1425 the rolls are for 'the new work of Christ Church'. In 1426 Overly, a carpenter, received 66s 8d in part payment 'for making the roof above the said new work', and in the same year Edward Duraunt, supervisor of the masons, and one Nicholas Hogges were paid 63s 4d for thirty-eight newels. The stair within the new tower contains only twenty-four steps, but the newels could have been for the stair turret within the angle pinnacle of the south-west transept arm. Furthermore, no roof can have existed over the new bell tower by 1426 – the building was still in progress in 1434 and was completed only *c.* 1460. The part-payment for a roof in 1426 is likely to be that over the transept.

The elevational design of the south-west arm of the transept continues the major themes of the nave, though with some modifications. The interior walls of the projecting bay are treated with tracery panels similar to the nave clerestory and gable end wall. In the choir aisle entrance bays on either side of the crossing, a frieze of blind panelling is introduced immediately above the spandrels and the blind triforium below the clerestory is pierced by single arched openings lighting a wall passage. The differences within the two bays of the southern transept arm reflect the original retention of the Romanesque double chapel against its eastern wall. The old tribune bridge was destroyed early in the rebuilding leaving the upper chapel entrance open to the transept interior. The Romanesque arch was enclosed within a grid-like tracery based on the pattern in the opposite window. The organ, formerly placed on the bridge, was transferred to a large bracket that projected into the transept from the upper chapel.

A later date for the southern bay of the south arm would explain the change in the base type from 3 to 4 (see Figure 124). The transept uses the slimmer design associated with the west window interior panelling, base type 4, which by the 1420s had become attenuated and spindly. The design of the great south window of the transept would also appear to date from about 1420 – it is larger even than the west window of the nave and is an exercise in grid pattern tracery (Figure 132). The major part of the window is made up of ranks of tall lights, eight across and three high. The lights are grouped 3–2–3 by thicker mullions which in turn support sub-arches within the head. The subdivided top lights are grouped into the three sections that result from the subarcuation, with two underlying transoms to enforce the regularity.

The exterior gable, rebuilt in 1978–9, reiterates the theme of the window in blind tracery and it also provides the first clue that the old central tower was about to be demolished – the pedestal finial at the apex of the gable was designed to carry the famous gilded angel from the central tower that had given it the name of Angel Steeple.

The design of the southern transept arm was probably by Stephen Lote and the work was continued after his death by Thomas Mapilton, referred to as master mason of Christ Church in 1423. Mapilton is best remembered at Canterbury for the south-west bell tower and porch and is frequently mentioned in the fabric rolls of that work, usually coming to the city with his servant. The reconstruction of the tower was really a remodelling, for much of Lanfranc's structure survives encased within the fifteenth-century ashlar (see Fig. 120). But the south-west porch was entirely new; indeed, St John Hope suggested that the previous south door of the Perpendicular nave stood somewhere along the south aisle and not at the base of the south tower.[30] The project for the new tower has always been associated with the patronage of Archbishop Henry Chichele, and between 1424 and 1434 he contributed nearly £500 towards the work. But this would hardly have been sufficient and it seems likely that private donations were accepted in much the same way as for

30  J. Legge and W. St J. Hope, *Inventories of Christ Church, Canterbury*, Corrigenda and Addenda. There would appear to be no evidence to substantiate their theory.

the cloister. The design of the south-west porch reflects the importance of the project and the heraldry decorating the entrance vault is one of the richest in England. The arms can provide an accurate dating for the construction of the porch – between 8 July 1425 and either 24 May 1426 or Lady Day of the following year.[31] The vault celebrates many of the same families who were instrumental in the rebuilding of the southern arm of the transept – Neville, Mowbray and Holland – and among the devices can be found Henry VI, Edmund Mortimer the son of Eleanor Holland, Thomas Montagu (one of Eleanor's many husbands), John Beaufort, husband of Lady Margaret Holland, Thomas, Duke of Clarence (another husband of Lady Margaret), and two of his brothers, Humphrey, Duke of Gloucester and John, Duke of Bedford.

As soon as the work began, carpenters and plasterers were hired to construct a lath and plaster enclosure 'about the new work' and hoisting tackle was purchased from Brother John of St Albans to lift the building supplies.[32] In 1426 the sum of 5s was paid for binding the 'great wheel', evidently a treadle wheel used for hauling stone – large quantities of which were floated upstream from Sandwich to Fordwich, just outside the city. When the prior's barge was available, only cranage dues had to be paid, otherwise the hire of a barge would cost a shilling a ton. The stone employed came predominantly from Caen in Normandy, but there were also purchases from Merstham in Surrey plus a rather mysterious 'northern stone', perhaps from Thefsdale or Huddlestone in Yorkshire. The work was expensive and demanding; the workforce employed in 1428 was actually greater than that involved in the rebuilding of the nave in 1396–7, and in deference to the high level of building at Canterbury Cathedral, the king allowed the prior to raise an additional £16 per annum from 1430. No obvious reason can be found for the abandonment of the work about 1434, unless it was the heavy expense coming at a time when the war in France was going badly.

The south-west tower stands in stark contrast to the elaborate porch, though its original severity has been somewhat softened by the addition of niches around the buttresses in the 1450s, and the overdressing of the spirelets and windows of the two principal facades in the late nineteenth century. The present pinnacles form part of the last campaign upon the tower which was concluded about 1459. The fan vault within the tower also dates from the mid-century.

Thomas Mapilton, the designer of the new tower, belonged to the same workshop tradition as Stephen Lote, indeed they were possibly partners. Yet Mapilton's work has none of the frailty of his predecessor at Canterbury. Lote took every opportunity to eliminate weight and mass – whole walls disappearing for giant essays in tracery and glass – whereas Mapilton's tower is solid and earthbound, with an excess of buttressing and small openings placed so high up as to recall military architecture. The west window at aisle-level is lost within the depth of the buttresses

31 The porch heraldry includes John Mowbray as Duke of Norfolk, i.e. post July 1425, and Henry Beaufort as bishop, i.e. pre 25 March 1427, when he received the cardinal's hat.

32 Fabric Drawer Bundle XIX, Canterbury Cathedral Library.

and its remoteness evidently encouraged Mapilton to break free from the nave tracery patterns with its subarcuation and lozenges. The aisle west window introduces more modern London forms with unbroken mullions dividing the opening into a series of narrow vertical strips. The horizontal transoms within the head, so typical of Lote's designs, were abandoned by Mapilton in favour of regular oval lozenges stacked in regimented ranks.

Despite an over-zealous restoration, the south-west porch is still a splendid piece (Figure 133). A great deal of decorative invention and display has been crammed into a very small object – more like a chantry chapel than the main entrance to England's Mother Church. The porch already embodies that tightness and minuteness of scale that so typifies the 'fantasy architecture' of the fifteenth century. Like the tower above, the porch walls maintain a solid aspect with no visible openings other than the entrance. There are in fact small windows lighting an upper chamber, concealed behind the fretted canopies on the south face. The division of the facades into two storeys provides a perfect setting for that favourite Perpendicular motif – the inset niche – the upper tier breaking into a profusion of gables and crockets. Originally the murderers of St Thomas occupied four of the principal niches, flanking a central scene above the door that must have contained the murder of the saint. From this, there survives only a depiction of the Altar of the Sword's Point. Erasmus describes only three knights 'in armour, carved in stone, who with their impious hands murdered that most holy man, their names, Tusci, Fusci and Beri being subjoined'. The fourth, de Mortville, seems to have been overlooked. The modern sculpture ignores the original iconography, choosing instead a selection of kings and archbishops; the evident discomfort expressed by St Anselm and Thomas Cranmer at their close proximity was apparently not intentional on the part of the sculptor.

If the south-west porch is a monument to the great patrons of the cathedral, then St Michael's chapel, off the south transept arm, is a memorial of the single most important of that group – Lady Margaret Holland. The chapel of St Michael occupied the ground-floor level of Lanfranc's south transept chapel. It had survived the reconstruction of the transept and for a time it must have resembled the equivalent transept chapels at Gloucester, glimpsed only through the Perpendicular overlay. Lady Margaret rebuilt St Michael's to house a tomb for herself and for her two husbands – both of whom were already buried in the Trinity Chapel. Lady Margaret Holland is one of the most significant figures in the architectural history of Canterbury Cathedral and she appears to have been central to the network of family patronage that was responsible for so much of the rebuilding of the fifteenth century.[33] Her prolific family had married their way into great power, though since the fall of Richard II, half-brother of Lady Margaret's father, their role had been less overtly political. Margaret's first husband was John Beaufort, Earl of Somerset

33 Woodman, op. cit.

and illegitimate brother of Henry IV. When Beaufort died in 1410, he was buried in the Trinity Chapel near the intended tomb of his brother. Margaret then married Thomas, Duke of Clarence, the youngest son of Henry IV and nephew of her late husband. He was killed in the French war in 1421 and his body brought back to Canterbury for burial. He was the last of the direct Lancastrian line to be buried in the cathedral; his brother had chosen Westminster, while Henry VI found sepulture at Windsor. For the rest of her life, Lady Margaret busied herself with her enormous family, especially with her husband's relatives the Beauforts, and those of her sister-in-law, the Nevilles. Margaret had many connections with Canterbury Cathedral – her mother, Alicia Fitzalan, was the sister of Archbishop Arundel, while her brother-in-law was Cardinal Beaufort, who shared her devotion to Canterbury Cathedral and resided for some of his life in the magnificent lodging called Meister Homers at the east end of the precincts. Margaret's sister-in-law had married Ralph Neville, and their son John was the husband of Margaret's own sister, Elizabeth. Another of Margaret's sisters, Eleanor, first married Roger Mortimer, fourth Earl of March, and later Thomas Montagu. Lady Margaret Holland was the key to the patronage of all these important families whose arms can be found throughout the cloister, the south-west transept and the south porch, and it is hardly surprising that the priory consented to her request for a funerary chapel for herself and her prestigious husbands.

The site adopted, St Michael's chapel, formed an extension of what was already a 'family transept', and work began in 1437 (Figure 134). The old Romanesque chapel was two bays long, plus an eastern apse, but the new chapel is square ended and is set at a slight angle to the body of the church in order to avoid a collision with the choir aisle which widened immediately after the apse of the old chapel. The notion of a double-storey chapel was preserved, though Lady Margaret died before the upper chapel of All Saints was completed. Construction of the lower chapel proceeded with great speed, and it was consecrated by the bishop of Ross on 18 December 1439. Within two weeks, on the Feast of the Martyrdom of St Thomas, Lady Margaret Holland died. On 28 January following, the young king wrote touchingly to the prior requesting that the bodies of 'Oor Oncle the Duk of Clarence and of our Cosyn Therl of Somersete' should be interred next to 'Our Aunte the Dutchese of Clarence just deceased'.[34] The king's wishes, expressing the will of Lady Margaret, were granted immediately, and all three were laid to rest in the sumptuous marble and alabaster tomb that almost fills the chapel.

St Michael's chapel, now called variously the Holland or the Buffs Chapel, must have been one of the earliest works of Richard Beke, master mason of Canterbury Cathedral from 1434–5. Beke replaced Thomas Mapilton in this position after the latter resigned in 1429. For some years he acted merely in a consultative role, no doubt to secure the continuation

34  Ibid., p. 28.

**134** (*opposite*) The Holland Chapel from the south-east prior to its restoration in 1979–80

35 L. Salzman, *Building in England down to 1540*, pp. 590–1.

of the south-west bell tower project, but in 1434–5 he was contracted for life as master mason for the priory of Christ Church.[35] Richard Beke was well known in London and had been chief mason of London Bridge. His style differs from both Lote and Mapilton, with a love of complexity and, perhaps, the tendency to over-decorate that was so typical of the 1430s. The Holland Chapel is no exception, with clustered vault responds, panelled socles and a lattice-work of ribs forming the most complicated vault in the cathedral. He also introduced a new base moulding – abandoning the aetiolated bases of Lote and Mapilton with their repeating polygonal bells and pedestals for a single polygonal bell and plain pedestal. This can be categorized as base type 5. The tracery in the Holland Chapel maintains the rigid verticality of the lower windows in the south-west tower – work that Beke must have continued for some years before it was halted in 1434.

The upper chapel of All Saints was completed after 1449 and is relatively simple – the most notable feature being the windows with their almost triangular profile. It has escaped the clutter that has overtaken the lower chapel with its array of flags and monuments. But even when it was first built, the Holland Chapel must have been a noisy affair, with the brilliant painted heraldry of the vault bosses and the glitter of its silvery glass. The present painted colour scheme by Tristram and the tattered flags still capture something of the panoply of its late mediaeval interior.

The architecture of the fifteenth century was dominated by the chantry chapel. The cathedrals, abbeys and parish churches of England sprouted private family chapels in all directions. Canterbury Cathedral already boasted the beautiful chantry of the Black Prince, and several more were built in the first half of the century. Archbishop Arundel built one under the north-west tower of the nave, and the chantry of Bishop Bokingham was finally constructed near the cloister door of the nave in 1433. The Brenchley family founded another chantry in the nave in 1447 – this time it was not an internal screened enclosure but a small chapel constructed between the buttresses outside the south aisle. One of the smallest, but arguably most significant, of these chapels was the chantry of Henry IV. The king had directed in his will of 1408 that he should be buried in Canterbury Cathedral at the discretion of his cousin, Archbishop Arundel, and that a chantry chapel should be established where priests could pray for the good of his soul. When Henry died in 1413, nothing was done about his wishes other than his burial in the cathedral. The coffin lay on a hearse to the north side of the shrine of St Thomas, surrounded by candles and, on certain days, decked out with flags. Thus the king lay through the reign of his son and long into the reign of Henry VI. But as the young Henry approached maturity, he began to interest himself in the tombs of his family. He continued the work on his father's chantry at Westminster and in 1438 the chantry chapel at Canterbury was begun in fulfilment of his grandfather's will. Preparation of the stone for the chapel began as early as 1435–6, while the alabaster tomb was built after the death of Henry's second wife, Joan of Navarre, in 1437. Little evidence has survived regarding the building of the chapel and nothing is known of who paid for it or who designed it. It was consecrated by the bishop of Ross on 1 March 1440, and was dedicated to St Edward the Confessor, the Lancastrian patron saint.[36]

The chapel projects from the north side of the Trinity Chapel and is constructed within two of the deeply projecting buttresses (see Fig. 35). It is supported by a pair of arches so arranged to avoid obscuring the windows of the Trinity Chapel crypt. The exterior of the chapel is severely plain and heavily restored, and has two small windows and a flat cornice. The tiny chapel measures only 14 ft by 8 ft – 427 cm by 244 cm (Figure 135). It is divided into two bays, each with a three-light window on the exterior northern side and is covered by an almost flat fan vault. The heraldry and colour have gone, but it doubtless displayed the Lancastrian arms, the arms of Henry's children, and the supposed device of Edward

36  *The Chronicle of John Stone*, p. 26.

135 Interior of the chantry chapel of Henry IV

the Confessor. The design of the vault has strong affinities with the fan vault in the chantry chapel of Henry's brother, Cardinal Beaufort, in Winchester Cathedral. Some of the details in the lower parts of the chapel suggest that it was designed by Richard Beke – the most telling motifs being the use of base type 5, the cluster of slim shafts forming the vault respond and the downward extension of the tracery to form a panelled socle. All these features can be found in the Holland Chapel. But the fan vault sits most unhappily on the vault responds, there being too many shafts for the single springing point required. This may indicate the presence of a second hand in the design, or at least a change of mind on the part of the first designer. The east wall of the chapel is now stripped bare, though it once contained an elaborate altarpiece. In Gostling's day there still remained 'a cornice . . . once adorned with such eagles as were on that monument [Henry's tomb] and over it some figures, now defaced, were painted on the wall'.[37] It is also reported that behind the present altar curtains is a scratching recording that 'Ye middel image was 19s. 11d', evidently referring to the statuary that once occupied the sculptured reredos.[38] The chapel is entered through a contemporary wooden screen and is still protected by its original ironwork.

Chantry chapels were not the only additions made to the fabric at this time, and one of the principal works of the late Middle Ages, the new Angel Steeple, was begun in 1433. John Stone records in his chronicle that the first stone of the new central tower was laid in that year.[39] The new work must have been commenced above the crossing as all the piers were recased in Perpendicular style during the priorate of Thomas Chillenden. The fifteenth-century work appears to have started at the lowest gallery within the lantern, on a level with the apex of the nave and south transept vault (see Fig. 8). The demolition of the old tower, which had become partially buried within the enhanced height of the new work, had been prepared in the preceding years. The old north-west tower next to the Palace was repaired in 1429 in order to accommodate the Arundel ring of bells presented to the priory by the archbishop before his death in 1414. Lanfranc's old north-west tower acquired the title of the Arundel Steeple as early as 1448. Little progress was made on the new central tower and it may have fallen victim to Prior Molash's expenditure cuts of the mid-1430s, when he was forced to 'put away his masons'.[40] The tower may have been under way again briefly, but all construction must have come to a halt in 1452 when the south-west crossing pier showed signs of collapse and substantial reinforcement became necessary to prevent a disastrous fall of the eastern end of the nave. The subsidence of the crossing piers may have been due to the effects of yet another earthquake, for as John Stone reports, the priory was shaken by a '*terre motus magnus*' in the middle of the night of 23 April 1449, between three and four in the morning.[41] The tremor lasted no longer than the space of one paternoster.

37  Gostling, *A Walk*, 1825, p. 281n.

38  G. H. Cook, *Mediaeval Chantries and Chantry Chapels*, London, 1963, p. 96.

39  *The Chronicle of John Stone*, p. 47.

40  Canterbury MS. Letters, Y143, Canterbury Cathedral Library.

41  *The Chronicle of John Stone*, p. 47.

Work on the new central tower came to a complete standstill for some years, and its subsequent history is given in chapter 6.

The new Lady Chapel was the next project undertaken by the Priory. It was begun in 1448 and formed part of the general transformation of the north-west transept arm, the famous Martyrdom, a work that took decades to complete – yet the Lady Chapel was finished in only seven building seasons. It was consecrated by the bishop of Ross on 18 October 1455, and was first entered by the monks on 21 December of that year.[42] Credit for the construction of the chapel is usually given to Prior Goldstone I, though it was begun shortly before his election. In his obit, the chapel is described with its stone vault, glazed windows and all its pertinent fittings. Goldstone also provided a vestry for the chapel, which he fitted between the north wall and the near-by Chapter House. The new Lady Chapel occupies the site of Lanfranc's double chapel on the eastern side of the Martyrdom (Figure 136). Unlike the Holland Chapel in the equivalent position on the southern arm of the transept, the Lady Chapel has a single storey and the dedication combines Our Lady with St Benedict – the shrine of St Blaise, whose chapel formerly occupied the upper chapel, was moved elsewhere.[43] The coupling of Our Lady and St Benedict may reflect a traditional devotion to the Virgin on this site, perhaps connected to the dying words of St Thomas, and the old Romanesque chapel of St Benedict had contained an image of her before which a light burned continually.

42  Ibid., p. 65.

43  The shrine of St Blaise had been removed to a beam over the throne of St Augustine some time prior to the enthronement of Archbishop Winchelsey in 1293.

**36**  Plan of the Martyrdom and Lady Chapel before the dissolution

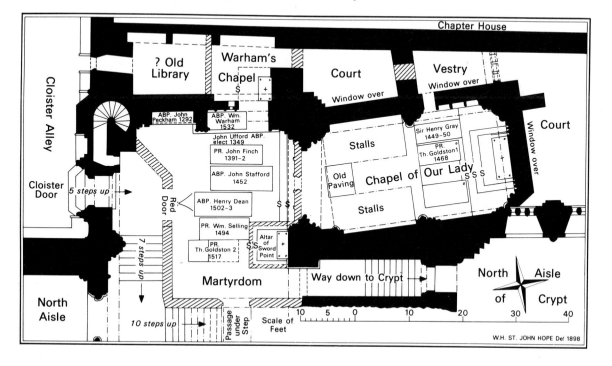

**137** South wall of the Lady Chapel

The chapel is two bays long and, like the Holland Chapel, is set obliquely to the church. Its southern wall is common to the adjacent north choir aisle and contains much of Lanfranc's masonry concealed beneath the later ashlar (Figure 137). The north and east walls are fifteenth century, and are taken up largely by windows. The eastern bay of the chapel contained the altar flanked by niches and backed by an elaborate reredos. The western bay contained wooden stalls, which account for the bare aspect of the lower walls.

The arch forming the western entrance to the chapel is part of the remodelling of the Martyrdom. It has type 5 bases, while the upper spandrels contain sculptured roses, no doubt the red rose of Lancaster hurriedly painted white after 1461. The chapel interior was cleaned in the mid-1970s and is now chillingly white. One must imagine its mediaeval splendour – the red and white of the Bourchier arms, the spectacular foliate sculpture, pretty demi-angels painted in naturalistic colours and the architecture rendered blue – the colour of the Virgin – with the details picked out in gilding. Much of the glass remains and in contrast to the stonework is pale and watery. The silver glass is almost transparent and contains the rebus of the Bourchier family – a love knot. The choice of such delicate glass was doubtless conditioned by the extreme problems of lighting a chapel squeezed between the great church and the tall Chapter House. The architecture of the Lady Chapel displays many of the motifs found in Beke's other works. The grouped bases are all type 5, the moulding profiles are similar to those in the Holland Chapel, as are the tracery patterns (Figure 138). The panelled treatment of the socle walls can also be paralleled in the Holland Chapel, but the richness of the Lady Chapel far exceeds anything in the cathedral prior to 1448 (Figure 139). The corner bay divisions melt away into a cascade of ribs, niches, angels, quatrefoils and vine scrolls. Most important are the niches that flank the vault responds – heavily sculptured and crocketed and excessively tall – they link the blinded areas of the lower walls with the glazed sections above. Among their minute ornamentation can be found angels, heads and tiny flowers. The canopy vaults also contain flowers forming the bosses for the minuscule ribs. The niche pedestals are faced with inset bracket mouldings, an early use of this favourite Tudor motif, while the niche bases have delicate floral patterns in both high and low relief. The east wall is especially enriched, with larger niches and a more complex traceried socle.

The Lady Chapel of Canterbury Cathedral contains the earliest large-scale fan vault surviving outside the west of England. This form of

**138** The Lady Chapel: base type 5 by Richard Beke

**139** South-east angle of the Lady Chapel and the tomb of Dean Boys

**140** Fan vaulting in the Lady Chapel

vaulting had already been employed in the tiny chantry chapel of Henry IV, but the Lady Chapel vault is radically different, with a sharper profile, twin-tier fans, and a complete absence of internal cusping (Figure 140). The first tier of each cone is divided by major and minor ribs which continue unbroken to the ridge rib. The second tier contains twice the number of panels by a simple subdivision of the panels of the first. The central vault spandrels are infilled with traceried circles. The vault design is very idiosyncratic, though in some ways it foreshadows the fan vaults of John Wastell of the early sixteenth century – including his crossing vaults of the new central tower at Canterbury.

At the entrance to the Lady Chapel is an elaborate stone screen which retains much of its original metal-work. The screen is clearly an afterthought for its imposition has resulted in some damage to it and to the surrounding stonework (see Fig. 9). The gabled and traceried design bears little resemblance to the Lady Chapel and its curious inverted top lobes and unusual dado tracery suggest a date nearer the end of the fifteenth century.

John Stone, in his chronicle, refers to the laying of the foundation stone of the new Martyrdom work on 9 September 1448.[44] Even the most casual

44 *The Chronicle of John Stone*, p. 44.

glance will reveal that the famous transept arm was refashioned and not rebuilt, and Stone's phrase is probably a standard convention indicating the commencement of a new campaign. The decision to remove the Lady Chapel from the nave and to rebuild it on the site of St Benedict's chapel also denotes a resolve to bring the Martyrdom into some accord with the new work of the crossing and south-west transept beyond. The work had been prompted by the project for a new central tower and quite obviously the Martyrdom had to be raised and vaulted if the new tower was to rise from a uniform roof-line.

But the Martyrdom was more than just the opposite arm of the south-west transept; it was the holiest, most venerated, spot in the cathedral – if not in England. How could this sacred structure be modernized without destroying its integrity? The solution seen today amply demonstrates how cautious was the approach, for little was touched, and much of Lanfranc's original work can still be seen inside and out. The dating evidence for the transformation of the Martyrdom is slight. John Stone refers to the 'new work in the Martyrdom' in 1418, though this was probably the continuing work on the entrance bay into the north choir aisle.[45] The bases employed, with the exception of the choir aisle entrance arch, are all base type 5, the profile introduced into Canterbury by Richard Beke in the 1430s. The Lady Chapel entrance is one build with the preceding bay of the Martyrdom, which suggests that at least the lower sections of the walls were complete by the time the Lady Chapel was consecrated in 1455. The Martyrdom vault, executed much later, contains the arms of Cardinal Beaufort who died in 1447, leaving the vast sum of £1,000 to the fabric of Canterbury Cathedral. This legacy may well have formed the basis for the initial reconstruction campaign. The completion of the work is well dated. The vault cannot have been constructed before 1476, for it carries the arms of John Russell as bishop of Rochester. The glazing that formerly filled the west window of the Martyrdom was given by John Barnwell before his death in 1478, and five years earlier £55 12s had been paid to various masons, plumbers and glaziers for the repair of the church in that year.[46] No other work is known to have been in progress at that time. Bequests of as much as £20 occur in 1461, 1462, 1468 and 1475, all of which were probably expended upon the Martyrdom. The last and most magnificent gift came in 1482, with the glazing of the Royal window – the great terminal window filling the north wall which was a personal gift of Edward IV.

The entrance bay into the north choir aisle is the most complex part of the Martyrdom. Like the equivalent bay in the southern transept arm, it contains entrances to both the choir aisle and to the crypt, but the Martyrdom was complicated by the requirements of the Altar of the Sword's Point, and as early as 1220 the various entrances had been rearranged (see Fig. 136). Chillenden relaid the floor in the north choir aisle, which continues right up to the screen at the western entrance. The

45  Ibid., p. 6.

46  Hussey, op. cit., p. 16.

screen is undated, but it contains a heraldic shield that occurs in the west
cloister walk of *c*. 1396–1405. The aisle entrance arch appears to be
bonded into the north-eastern pier of the crossing and may, therefore, be
the earliest work within the Martyrdom (Figure 141). At this stage it was
still intended to provide a passage at triforium level as in the opposite arm
of the transept, but this scheme was abandoned in the Martyrdom, with
only a short section built over the choir aisle entrance, and a section within
the west wall that was subsequently blocked. Both clerestory windows on
the eastern side of the Martyrdom appear to be of one build, and postdate
the construction of the Lady Chapel.

   The entrance arch leading into the north aisle of the nave was subject to
extensive remodelling as part of the emergency work to underpin the
crossing in 1452, and the character of the work corresponds with the Lady
Chapel bay of the Martyrdom. In the western wall, the main window and
the clerestory conform to those in the nave, whereas the eastern clerestory
windows present a radically different design, particularly the window
above the Lady Chapel which is the largest clerestory in any part of the
Perpendicular work. The walling below the clerestory is filled with five
niches, perhaps for St Thomas and his murderers, with wire-netting

vaults in the canopies and rather curious finals. The arch-heads in the panels above are segmental and uncusped, foreshadowing the more astringent Gothic of the post-Reformation period. Even the glazed panels forming the lower section of the window are uncusped, while the upper lights have trefoil cusping but no enclosing arch-heads. This strange style may not be that of Richard Beke, who died in 1458,[47] but that of his successor, Thomas Glazier, of whom little is known.[48] The great Royal window is more likely to be from Beke's designs with its regular grid pattern for the main lights and simple subdivided lights in tiers above (see Fig. 147). Many of the batement lights retain their original glass with figures of archbishops and saints, St Augustine and St Thomas occupying the central lower lights.

The Martyrdom vault follows the design of the opposite arm of the transept, though with heraldic shields in place of foliate bosses. It is the most decorated vault within the cathedral and is studded with the devices of the great and famous – Edward IV and his queen, Elizabeth Woodville, the Duke of Gloucester (the future Richard III), Warwick the Kingmaker, Clarence and Bedford, four cardinals – Beaufort, Stafford, Kemp and Bourchier – and two priors, Thomas Goldstone I and John Oxney.

In contrast to the high finish of the interior, the exterior of the Martyrdom is rather disappointing. The west face over the cloister is nearly all Lanfranc, with the single addition of the uppermost walling necessary to bring the transept up to the requisite height (see Fig. 6). The north face, almost hidden by the Chapter House, is filled with the Royal window. The gable above has a grid pattern of blind tracery set into a rough flint and rubble wall. The eastern wall is Lanfranc, broken up by the new clerestory windows, and the additional heightening is made up of re-used Romanesque ashlar and flintwork set into an approximate chequer pattern (see Fig. 17). The interior of the roof-space reveals a quantity of red brick which is first mentioned in the accounts of 1477.[49] The queen-post roof is the only mediaeval high roof to survive on the cathedral church.

Richard Beke probably completed another project before his death – the final campaign on the south-west bell tower which had been left in a half-built state since the 1430s. Prior Goldstone's obit of 1468 refers to this work and to the edification of the front of the church. The latter must refer to the niches that surround the west porch. The completion of the tower involved the pinnacles with their tiers of gabled spirelets recalling the niches in the Lady Chapel, as well as the construction of the vault within the tower. Beke built another in his series of fan vaults, with twin-tiered fans exhibiting the basic characteristics of his Lady Chapel vault (Figure 142). But unlike the Lady Chapel, the tower vault has cusping within the panels and the centre piece consists of a large circular trapdoor

47 *The Chronicle of John Stone*, p. 76.

48 Obit in BM MS. Arundel 68, f. 44v.

49 Hussey, op. cit., p. 6.

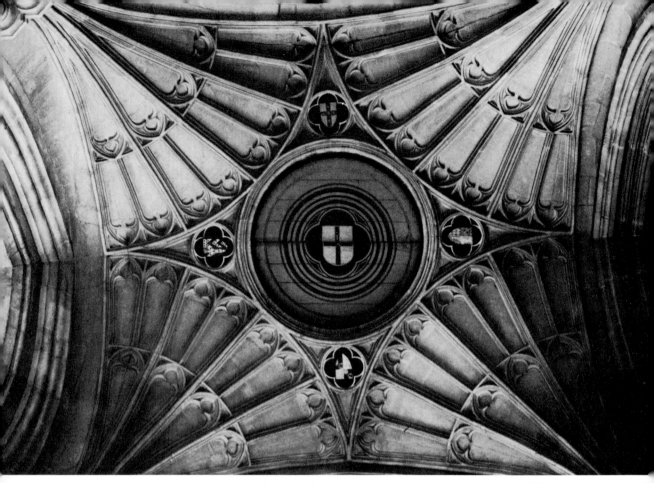

**142** Fan vaulting in the south-west tower by Richard Beke, c. 1455

through which the bells could be raised into position. The great bell, Dunstan, that had been recast for this tower in 1430, was finally raised into the tower in 1459 after standing for nearly three decades in the nave.

## The pulpitum

Richard Beke has never won the recognition he deserves, yet his architecture is superbly conceived and exquisitely wrought. One reason for the unjust treatment he has suffered is the failure to identify his greatest masterpiece which stands at the very heart of the cathedral. The pulpitum screen that forms the western entrance to the choir is one of the most sumptuous survivals from the English Middle Ages (Figure 143). It also appears to be totally misdated. The screen completely fills the eastern crossing arch under the central tower, but its bulk and solidity is tempered by its prodigious decoration and its fine sculpture. The only opening, the low central door, belongs to the earlier screen of Henry of Eastry – now inset within the deep splays of a later arch (Figure 144). The surrounding niches once contained figures of Christ and the Apostles. The rectangular frame of the entrance arch forms the centrepiece of the screen, and is flanked by groups of three elevated niches with exuberant canopies. Standing impassively amid all this activity are six kings, heavily draped and dignified. The kings remain as the only free-standing sculpture made for the screen; once a mass of tiny figures filled the niches that cling to the sides of the major pedestals and 'mytred saints' occupied the niches along the upper parapet. All were lost during the Commonwealth, if not before – the present uppermost figures were made soon after the Restoration for the tomb of Henry Chichele. Happily, more of the architectural sculpture remains, including the row of alluring demi-angels and a multitude of heads forming pendant drops for the hanging canopies.

The pulpitum stands at the top of a deep flight of stairs that begin west of the crossing arches and within the nave. The stairs extend across the aisle bay of the Martyrdom which they oversail by means of a bridge that connects the north aisle of the choir with that of the nave. The stairs break to form a platform immediately east of the western crossing piers providing access down to the south-west transept, and through the Martyrdom to the cloister door (see Fig. 131). A second platform at the summit allows a processional path from the north choir aisle to the pulpitum door. A tunnel runs beneath the upper flight providing a direct link across the transept without mounting the stair.

The name of Thomas Chillenden has erroneously become as inseparable from the pulpitum as that of Henry Yevele from the nave. St John Hope was perhaps the first to link the 'greteste builder of a prior' with the screen when he spotted the reference to 'the pulpitum of the nave' with its steps and '*stacione crucis*' in one of Chillenden's obituary notices. Hope interpreted these references as a choir screen and some form of rood for the nave, though the Latin indicates a new nave altar of the Holy Cross, with steps and screen. The whole assemblage probably stood

143 *(below left)* The pulpitum screen
144 *(below right)* The west door of the pulpitum. The inner door formed part of Eastry's pulpitum of *c.* 1304

50 Legge and Hope, op. cit., p. 108.

in the west arch of the crossing.[50] It is perhaps not without some significance that one of the most detailed of Chillenden's obits makes no mention of a pulpitum screen among his many works and, considering the rather trivial accomplishments that are included, the omission of such a great and expensive work as the present pulpitum would be difficult to explain. Hope's 'discovery' won instant acceptance and, ever since, antiquarians and others have searched for corroborative evidence. The problems raised by the style and iconography of the work have rarely been discussed, and the blind acceptance of a date earlier than 1411 has led to the 'stylistic' redating of other monuments by comparison with this 'firmly dated' piece. Yet antiquarians before Hope judged the pulpitum on style alone, and dated it to the mid-fifteenth century. What appeared to be a final confirmation of Hope's date of pre-1411 came in the 1930s when it was noted that Thomas Hearne, a wealthy monk of Christ Church, had donated two '*imagines*' for the nave: one of St Edward the Confessor and one of St Ethelbert.[51] These figures were identified immediately as those flanking the pulpitum door. The gift, recorded in John Stone's chronicle, was made some time during the priorate of John of Woodnesborough who succeeded Chillenden in 1411.[52] However, Stone goes on to list some eighteen other '*imagines*' that Hearne presented to the church, some described as 'pinctour', or painted. It is known that Woodnesborough collected a series of panel portraits of important patrons of Canterbury Cathedral that were hung in the choir on great occasions, and the references to Hearne's '*imagines*' would strongly suggest that he had presented many of these paintings.

51 C. Cotton, 'The screen of Six Kings', *Cant. Cath. Chron.*, April 1935, pp. 12–30.

52 *The Chronicle of John Stone*, p. 18.

The pulpitum is a document in its own right. Like all architecture, it contains evidence of style and authorship, and its highly decorative nature gave the designer full range to employ all his favourite motifs. The screen also contains sculpture, not figures chosen at random, but a clear and intentional iconography. Happily, the theme chosen was kingship – part of a general scheme that ran throughout the nave and west transept. Some of the figures can be identified as portraits of English monarchs, and their identity is vital for the establishment of a correct date for the whole work (Figure 145). All have been subject to some restoration in the early nineteenth century; the crowns have been remade and some patching can be seen here and there, but essentially the figures are original though the various emblems in their hands are modern and occasionally inappropriate. The king immediately north (left) of the door would appear to be St Ethelbert holding the church that he granted to St Augustine. The church emblem is new, but Gostling records a similar church before the restoration.[53] The king to the south of the door, now holding a sword, is usually identified as St Edward the Confessor – a likely candidate as he was the adopted patron saint of the Lancastrian family. Of the remaining kings, two are obvious portraits, the others less certain. Beginning at the northern end, the youthful king is identified as Richard II, the next as

53 Gostling, *A Walk*, 1825, p. 242.

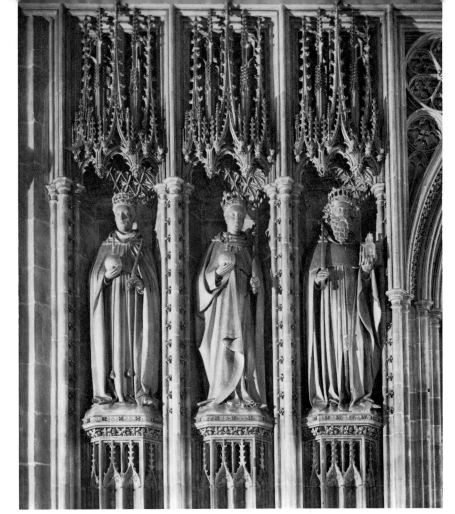

145 Three kings from the pulpitum, from left to right: Richard II, Henry V(?) and Ethelbert

Henry V, though this has also been considered to be Bertha, the queen of St Ethelbert! South of St Edward the Confessor is a good portrait of Henry IV, while the last and most significant figure is a portrait of Henry VI. The presence of Henry VI in the screen must raise serious questions about the date of the sculpture especially since he is shown in maturity. Thus the figure should postdate *c.* 1440, and it compares well with the statue of Henry VI made for All Souls, Oxford, in 1441, though at Canterbury Henry appears a little older. He was born in December 1421. The portrait of his grandfather, Henry IV, also appears to date from *c.* 1440, for it seems to be a copy of the recumbent figure of Henry's tomb in the Trinity Chapel, made some time after 1437.

Two arguments could be advanced in order to accommodate the problems raised by the sculpture in any justification of an earlier, i.e. pre-1411, date for the screen. The figures could be mid-fifteenth-century replacements of earlier sculpture, or the niches could have been left empty in *c.* 1410 to be filled only gradually. The latter argument is inherently weak; not only is it highly unlikely that such a splendid screen should be created without any clear idea of its iconography, but the

**146** The pulpitum screen: base
type 5

consistency of style evident in the six figure points to one workshop
if not a single hand. The former argument is more difficult to counter
though it would seem highly improbable that any sculpture made for the
screen earlier in the century, particularly if it were made during
Woodnesborough's priorate, 1411–25, should need replacing so soon.

The architecture of the screen is full of information regarding its
designer. As outlined above, the base types throughout the Perpendicular
work at Canterbury follow a discernable development which can be
numerated as base types 1–5 (see Fig. 124). Type 4, employed by Lote
and Mapilton, is the most convoluted and attenuated, and is found on all
the work at Canterbury between *c.* 1396 and 1430. The arrival of Richard
Beke is marked by a return to one of the simplest designs – the single
polygonal bell, base type 5. This can be found in the chantry of Henry IV
and the Holland Chapel, both begun in 1437, and in the remodelling of
the Martyrdom and the new Lady Chapel from 1448. It is also found
throughout the pulpitum screen (Figure 146). The bases on the screen are
clustered into groups responding to the major and minor shafts in exactly
the same way as those in the Lady Chapel – indeed their similarity is such
that they can easily be confused. The pulpitum has many other features in
common with Beke's Lady Chapel, the most important being the bracket
moulding flanked by tiny hollow chamfer fillets inset into the high
pedestals of the niches. This was to be a motif much loved by the court
architects of Henry VII, but is considerably rarer at this early date.[54] The
cornice mouldings of the pedestals in both the Lady Chapel and the
screen are treated with a band of shallow relief foliage, barely raised above
the surface and interspersed with high relief square flowers. In contrast,
the vine scrolls that surround the Lady Chapel windows and the door of
the pulpitum are three-dimensional. Diamond fleurons are liberally

54 The motif was probably
transmitted to Eton and on to
Oxford by John Smyth, who was
chief mason at Canterbury under
Beke. Smyth later became the
master mason at Eton, and was
master mason of Westminster
Abbey from 1453.

strewn over the pulpitum – a motif employed by Beke at the base of the Martyrdom window from 1448, and the screen and Lady Chapel both display ogeed canopies laid against a backdrop of regular panelling. It is details such as these that pinpoint the date of the screen to the mid-fifteenth century and made possible the attribution to Richard Beke.

The stairs preceding the screen can be dated to post-1452. The present arrangement completely fills the area under the central tower and the aisle bay of the Martyrdom. All the bases of the western crossing piers are buried beneath the stairs, yet some of them form part of the strengthening work carried out on the crossing in 1452. The bonding break caused by these additions can be seen on the Martyrdom side of the north-western pier. Further, the stair into the north aisle of the nave is unlikely to have existed prior to the removal of the Lady Chapel from that aisle, as the altar must have occupied the easternmost bay. The Lady Chapel was certainly replaced in the nave by Chillenden and was referred to as being in the nave in 1429. The new chapel was not begun before 1448 and was finished in 1455. The doors leading into the tunnel under the stair have type 5 bases, indicating that they, too, are the work of Richard Beke. The scale of the alterations of 1452 may indicate that the new stair and pulpitum formed part of the stabilizing scheme for the whole crossing.

It would appear that a date for the pulpitum and stair prior to *c.* 1450 would now be untenable, and that a date of *c.* 1450–60 is indicated by the available evidence. But if the pulpitum does date from the strife-torn years that marked the decline of Henry VI, then who paid for it and why does it not figure in any of the documentation of the period?

The theme of the iconography is Kingship and Canterbury, and a special emphasis has been placed on the continuity of monarchy from Richard II to the Lancastrians, an unlikely theme before the death of Henry IV in 1413. The legitimacy of the Lancastrian dynasty is stressed further by the allusion to Ethelbert, royal patron of Canterbury, and to Edward the Confessor, patron saint of both Richard II and the Lancastrians. Canterbury had become so inexorably tied up with the Lancastrian dynasty, both through the kings and through the close-knit group of families that bestowed their patronage upon the church, that the intended significance of the imagery would not have gone unnoticed especially during the 1450s when Henry's temporary insanity and the general malaise of the realm focused growing attention on his chief rival, Edward Duke of York. The support for the Yorkist cause finally erupted into open hostility towards Henry and his government at the Battle of St Albans in 1455, and while the king struggled on for a further six years, it is unlikely that the Metropolitical Church would have risked such an overt display of Lancastrian loyalty much after this event. The theme of the pulpitum and its obvious expense would tend to limit its donation to only a few people. The king would have been an obvious donor, were it not for his serious illness which rendered most decision-making impossible.

55 *The Paston Letters*, ed. J.
Gairdner, London, 1904, p. 270.

Further, the royal expenditure rolls of the period should give some
indication of the considerable cost that must have been involved. The
absence of any such record does not necessarily rule out the possibility
that Henry was the donor, for he often visited Canterbury, and his first act
upon his recovery after Christmas 1454 was to send his almoner to
Canterbury with a donation for the cathedral.[55] But while the omission of
small amounts from the royal accounts is understandable, the enormous
outlay involved in the creation of the pulpitum should have made some
appearance.

Another possibility is that the pulpitum was the gift of one of the
archbishops and for that reason the expense would not appear in the
priory accounts. When Henry Chichele died in 1443, he bequeathed
1,000 marks towards the fabric, but this was probably used up long before
the building of the screen: it may have been employed on the completion
of the south-west bell tower which had received considerable patronage
from the archbishop during his lifetime. Chichele's successor, Stafford,
died in 1452 and as a close relative of Henry VI he would appear to be a
likely choice. But as he died some years before the political insecurity
following the Battle of St Albans, the monks were perfectly safe to record
his munificence in his obit. No such credit was awarded to him.

Cardinal Kemp, who succeeded Stafford in 1452, died within two years
and was buried during one of Henry's fits of lunacy. Again, Kemp may
well have built the screen, but the monks were still safe to record his
generosity. His obit of March 1454 is silent on the matter. Thomas
Bourchier began his long archiepiscopacy in February 1455 but, as a
fervent Yorkist and uncle to Edward, Duke of York, he is hardly likely to
have paid for the construction of a monument to the greater glory of the
House of Lancaster.

If no suitable archbishop can be found, then surely the prior in whose
office the pulpitum was erected would earn some thanks after his death?
Thomas Goldstone I was prior from 1449 to 1463, throughout the period
proposed for the construction of the screen. His death occurred in the
troubled period early in the reign of Edward IV with Henry VI still alive
and very much a threat to the Yorkist usurper. Any work expostulating
the legitimacy of the last of the Lancastrians would have been a monstrous
embarrassment to Canterbury Cathedral at this time, yet Goldstone's
obit does contain some vague and enigmatic phrases that may well
indicate the delicacy of the situation. It acknowledges that the prior
'decorated the church with many ornaments' which were 'magnificent
works at such a troubled time'.

Two other candidates for the donor of the pulpitum stand outside the
obvious group of the king and archbishops. Cardinal Beaufort evinced a
great love for Canterbury and was granted Meister Homers in the
precincts as a residence for life. His brothers, Henry IV and John, Earl of
Somerset, lay buried in the church and although he chose his own

Cathedral of Winchester for his burial in 1447, he left Canterbury Cathedral £1,000 towards the work of the fabric. Some of this was expended upon the transformation of the Martyrdom where his arms can be seen on the high vault, but this substantial gift may have formed the basis for the financing of the great screen that depicts his brother Henry and his descendants.

The second candidate is also a Beaufort, one even more intimately connected with Canterbury Cathedral, a man of power but who aroused bitterness and hatred from his contemporaries. Edmund Beaufort became the second Duke of Somerset after his brother John committed suicide in 1447. His parents were John Beaufort, the brother of Henry IV and of Cardinal Beaufort, and Lady Margaret Holland. The young Edmund exercised an influence over Henry VI similar to that of his grandfather, Thomas Holland, over Richard II. It was to end with equal violence. Loathed for his power and ineffectual government, his destruction became the object of the Yorkist cause. Finally, he was slaughtered in the streets of St Albans in 1455. His affection for Canterbury showed a different side of his character. His fondness for the church stemmed from his parents who had chosen the cathedral for their burial. His mother, Lady Margaret Holland, had maintained an active interest in the rebuilding of the cathedral right up to her death, and Edmund appears to have continued this family tradition. When his own child Isabella died in 1453, Edmund buried her in St Michael's chapel, next to his own parents, and there can be little doubt that, had he died in less violent circumstances, he too would have found rest in Canterbury Cathedral. The rebuilding of the pulpitum may well have been regarded as an extension of the Holland commitment to the south-west transept. To the cathedral, Edmund Beaufort was a powerful and wealthy patron and one who gave liberally to the fabric. In 1453, shortly after his brief attainture in the Tower at the instigation of the Yorkist faction, the prior and convent granted Edmund the residence of Meister Homers for life, the former home of his uncle the cardinal. The deed of gift specifically refers to Beaufort's generosity towards the work already done and to other delayed works that they can now begin. The last phrase implies a recent gift towards a project not yet begun. No one could have had more interest in glorifying the Lancastrian line than Beaufort, whose very existence depended upon the continuation of the reign of Henry VI. He had the perfect motive for such a gift and he was exceedingly rich: both necessary qualifications for the donor of such a blatant piece of propaganda at such a delicate time. As the screen is unlikely to have been erected after the Battle of St Albans, and as the stairs appear to have been built after the strengthening of the crossing piers in 1452, the whole project would have been under construction when Beaufort's patronage at Canterbury was at its height. His bloody murder and the subsequent revolution in politics would more than justify the cathedral's silence – bad enough that the

**147** The Royal window in the Martyrdom, glazed *c.* 1482

screen extols the lineage of the deposed king, but worse still that it should have been paid for by his most evil henchman. What was intended as an apotheosis of the Lancastrian dynasty had become its memorial.

Fortunately the pulpitum survived the Wars of the Roses, though it must have caused the monks some embarrassing moments during the frequent visits of Edward IV. The new king chose to commemorate the founding of the Yorkist dynasty in an even more honoured place – the glazing of the great north window over the Martyrdom (Figure 147). Now Edward and Henry, the usurper and the usurped, stare impassively across that bloodstained floor, echoing the tombs of Henry IV and the Black Prince who lie in similar irony. The struggles of Plantagenet, Lancaster and York resolved in timeless silence amid the sacred stones of Canterbury.

The unsettled reign of Henry VI was a watershed in the history of

Canterbury Cathedral, as it was for the fortunes of England. The French war became a serious drain upon the state, with the added injury of almost continual defeat. In 1436 the Burgundians deserted the alliance, and Paris, that great prize of the war, had to be abandoned to the French. Crop failures at home led to further problems and the prior was forced to 'put away his masons'. Work on the new south-west bell tower came to a sudden halt and it was not taken up again for many years. The monastic income steadily declined. By 1437, it had dropped to £2,381 18s ¾d from a peak of over £4,000 in 1411. As revenues dwindled, so the debts mounted, and by 1456 they had reached £1,158 11s 1d, with an income of only £2,059 19s 3d. The Civil War between York and Lancaster frustrated the financial situation further, and by 1468 the income fell to £1,828 0s 7d, less than half that on Chillenden's death.

Paradoxically, the declining resources had only a passing effect upon the building work of the church. The main crisis seems to have happened around 1436, when only the essential work on the dormitory was continued. By 1448 the new Lady Chapel was in progress, and its building coincided with the transformation of the Martyrdom. The Lady Chapel was consecrated in 1455 and was decorated with the devices of the Bourchier family. Thomas Bourchier, bishop of Ely, had been elevated to Canterbury in that year and continued to occupy the throne of St Augustine for thirty-one years. He crowned both the Yorkist kings and the first of the Tudor dynasty, Henry VII. The wars of York and Lancaster posed unique problems for the priory, for both rival kings professed a devotion to St Thomas and his cathedral. Henry VI was a frequent pilgrim to the shrine, but the new archbishop was a fervent Yorkist and uncle to Edward IV. The monks, like the city, appear to have been evenly divided, and the prior and convent found themselves in the unenviable position of having to entertain both sides. For years the delicate political balance was kept by the prior, Thomas Goldstone I. But throughout the Civil War, visitors and pilgrims of all ranks continued to flock to the shrine, perhaps the most bizarre arrival being that of the patriarch of Antioch who appeared at the cathedral on 12 December 1466, accompanied by 'four dromedaries and two camels'. Neither Henry VI nor Edward IV were great benefactors of the fabric. The new pulpitum celebrates the glory of the Lancastrian dynasty though it was not apparently a royal gift. Henry's usurper, Edward IV, visited the shrine on a number of occasions and his arms, together with the leading members of his court, are powdered across the Martyrdom vaults. The transformation of the Martyrdom between 1448 and 1480 marked the end of the extensive campaigns that had begun a century before. Only the new central tower remained to be built. The 1470s had seen a marked improvement in the monastic finances and despite the several violent and bloody dynastic changes, the church continued to enjoy a high degree of royal favour.

But the peace exacted at such cost to the nation was short lived. The House of York rose and fell in a sea of blood. The brief reign of Richard III ended on the field of Bosworth, and a new house, Tudor, occupied the centre stage of English history. At some time before these momentous events, perhaps *c.* 1483, a serious fire swept through the cathedral and, though little is known of the blaze, the repairs of one year amounted to over £100.[56] The fragmented accounts of the period 1480–5 make reference to a new cloister on which £54 10s was spent,[57] and to another work 'to the east'. Neither work can now be identified.

56 Hussey, op. cit., pp. 16–17.

57 Possibly this refers to the glazing of some of the cloister bays.

# CHAPTER 6

# THE TUDOR CATHEDRAL, 1485-1540

The fall of the House of York before the rising star of Tudor hardly affected Canterbury Cathedral. Neither of the Yorkist kings had been great patrons of the church, and a new king, with the blood royal of Lancaster, promised a new age for the cathedral and the nation. The aged Cardinal Archbishop Bourchier lived just long enough to crown Henry VII, the third coronation of his archiepiscopacy. Bourchier had prepared a monument for himself next to the shrine of St Alphege on the north side of the presbytery, and there he was laid to rest after an archiepiscopacy spanning thirty-one years. He was succeeded in 1486 by John Morton, bishop of Ely, who was created a cardinal in 1493. The friend and chancellor of Henry VII, Morton became infamous for his financial policy known as 'Morton's fork'. His court glittered with the talent of a new age – with such men as Linacre and More – echoing the great age of the court of Theobald in the twelfth century. The cardinal was one of the most prolific builders of the late Middle Ages, donating large sums to projects throughout the country. In Canterbury he is best remembered for the building of the Angel Steeple, the new central tower that finally replaced Lanfranc's venerable structure.

## The central tower

The central tower of Canterbury Cathedral is one of the finest architectural achievements of the English Middle Ages (see Fig. 6). Erasmus was filled with religious awe at the majesty of it, and Gostling thought it 'the completest beauty of its kind anywhere to be seen'. It has more recently been dubbed 'the noblest tower in Christendom'. Its success is two-fold. It forms an almost perfect grouping with the short nave and the west towers, while at the same time its mass is sufficient to balance the disordered sprawl of the choir and Trinity Chapel. It achieves the near impossible task of drawing together all the various elements and styles of the great cathedral. It is truly a crowning glory.

The tower provides an unique insight into the vagaries of the mediaeval planning procedure as well as a rare glimpse of the role of patronage in the design process. This stems from the amount of surviving documentary evidence, mainly from the 1490s, which suggests that neither architect nor patron then had any fixed idea of the final appearance of the tower.

The new tower inherited the name of its predecessor, the Angel Steeple. During the sixteenth century it acquired its present name, Bell Harry, so called after a bell hung in the tower in 1498.

The present tower was begun in 1433 but little was achieved before the major period of construction in the 1490s. It is necessary to examine in some detail the lower stages of the tower above the crossing arches to define what debt, if any, the present tower owes to the first campaign from 1433. It is also important to explode the myth that the previous Romanesque central tower remains somehow encased within the present structure.

The idea that the old central tower remains inside the present Bell Harry was first propounded by C. E. Woodruff in 1912,[1] who talked of 'a stone casing built round the norman tower'. Woodruff confused the clocarium or great belfry recorded in various documents of the fifteenth century with the central tower, despite the fact that a free-standing bell tower on a mound south of the church can be shown to have existed until 1540 (see Fig. 24). The documentary evidence makes it quite clear that the clocarium was a building distinct from both the old and the new central tower, which is consistently referred to as the Angel Steeple.

The free-standing clocarium is believed to have collapsed during the earthquake of 21 May 1382, but it would appear that this *terre motus magnus*, like most monastic catastrophes, was not too serious. Only £11 was spent on repairing the Infirmary Chapel, which still displays a fine window of the first half of the fourteenth century, and a further £7 on the east cloister walk.[2] This last amount appears to have been spent on the quasi-thirteenth-century arcading flanking the Chapter House door, but neither the Chapter House nor any other surviving part of the earlier fabric shows any sign of damage or repair from this period.[3] It is clear that the clocarium survived the earthquake, for it is mentioned frequently in the Sacrist's Accounts throughout the fifteenth century. In 1415, there were 'repairs to the great belfry (*magno Clocario*) and clapper for Crundale [one of the bells in the clocarium in 1343] 10s'.[4] In the same account roll for 1429, there is an entry 'for various repairs in the bell tower and renewing the clappers there and in the Angel Steeple, £1 1s 0d', and in the same entry two masons were paid for repairing the bell tower next to the Palace – that is the north-west tower by the Archbishop's Palace. Thus, three bell towers are specifically mentioned in 1429 at a time when the south-west bell tower was being rebuilt.[5] The third bell tower of 1429 can only be the free-standing clocarium. In 1540 Leland noted that the detached bell tower was 'now a late clene pullid down',[6] and in the same year five bells were sold 'late in the grete belfrage of Christ Church'.[7] The weight of the bells was given as 24,646 lb, an average of nearly 2½ tons

1  C. E. Woodruff and W. Danks, *Mems CC*, p. 200.

2  S. A. Warner, *Canterbury Cathedral*, London, 1923, pp. 173–4.

3  *Thorne's Chronicle of St Augustine's*, ed. A. H. Davis, Oxford, 1934, ff. 2158–9 reveals that the damage caused by the earthquake to that abbey a few hundred yards from the cathedral was slight. Two windows appear to have been broken.

4  E. Woodruff, 'The Sacrist's Rolls of Christ Church, Canterbury', *Arch. Cant.*, 48, 1936, p. 35. Further references to the continued existence of the free-standing belfry occur in 1441–2, in the following year concerning the purchase and placing of shingles on the roof and, in the same year, the payments made for the repair of a wall next to the belfry. Bells in the great belfry were mended in 1446, 1452 and 1456, and two years later a great storm swept the city during which, according to John Stone, an evil spirit took possession of the clocarium. See W. G. Searle, ed., *The Chronicle of John Stone*, p. 74.

5  For the history of the south-west tower, see pp. 172–5.

6  J. Leland, *Itinerary*, pts VII and VIII, vol. 4, p. 41. John Leland, 'The father of English history', was an early graduate of Christ's, Cambridge. His contemporary record of the monuments of England in the 1530s and 1540s is of immense importance.

7  W. Somner, *Antiquities of Canterbury*, Pt III, p. 35.

**148** Bell Harry tower from the west

8 N. J. Davis, *Bells and Bellringers*, vol. 1, no. 1, 1966, p. 26.
9 *The Chronicle of John Stone*, p. 21.

each, far heavier than could prudently be hung in the present central tower.

Bell Harry tower is 235 ft – 7,163 cm – high, including the pinnacles, with about 100 ft – 3,050 cm – clear of the high roofs of the church (Figure 148). The design is dominated by the vertical rush of the corner turrets rising sheer from the high roofs to the pinnacles. The turrets are composed of groups of slim buttresses cutting across the corners of the tower and forming a series of sharp vertical lines and deep shadows which frame the two stages of the tower; the lantern and belfry above. There are three important features not easily visible from photographs. The corner turrets stand on a series of massive corbels which appear to have been inserted at a later date into the base walling of the tower. Approximately 26 ft – 792 cm – of the lower parts of the stone facing of the turrets are not bonded structurally into the tower facades, and further bonding breaks occur on all four sides for approximately 13 ft – 395 cm – below the sill-level of the belfry windows. These features provide crucial points to the constructional history of the tower.

In 1433, the bells given by Archbishop Arundel to the central tower were rehung in the north-west tower which became known as the Arundel Steeple.[8] In the same year, John Stone's chronicle records the laying of the foundation-stone of the new central tower.[9] The demolition of Lanfranc's central tower had become inevitable by the beginning of the fifteenth century. William of Sens had encroached upon its eastern face in the late twelfth century for his new higher choir roof, and from 1377 the transformation of the nave and west transept resulted in the gutting of the other facades of the tower for the higher vaults and roofs. The first stone of the new tower must have been laid at the level of the lower lantern gallery above the crossing arches, for all the walls supporting the high roofs of the church are of the fifteenth century. This indicates that the previous tower was demolished to the level of the internal string course immediately above the apex level of the crossing arches. Both the interior and exterior of the lantern were so altered in later campaigns that the only sure evidence for the progress of the work is contained within the stair turret in the south-west angle. It begins at the level of the lower lantern gallery as a stone-faced well 12 ft – 365 cm – high with eighteen steps, each an accurate 8 in. – 20 cm – in height. The stone well ends abruptly at step 19, where the material of the well changes from stone to vitrified brick. This section contains eight steps each approximately $6\frac{1}{2}$ in. – 16·5 cm – high before the upper lantern gallery, adding some 4 ft $3\frac{1}{2}$ in. – 131 cm – to the well, with a further 18 ft 2 in. – 554 cm – above the upper gallery with steps of uneven height ranging from 6 to 9 in. – 15 to 23 cm. The stair well then changes for the last time from vitrified to red brick, which continues to the top and can therefore be associated with the last phase of construction. The vitrified and red-brick sections are divided by a single stone course.

It would appear that there were three successive phases of the building; the stone well, changing to vitrified brick and the final red-brick campaign. While the transition from the stone well to brick shows no obvious relationship with any other architectural feature, the vitrified brick section of the stair well rises slightly higher than the level of the transoms of the lantern windows – significantly, the apex level of the high roofs of the church. Allowing for the fact that the stair-well construction is always likely to be a little ahead of the main walls, the two earlier phases of the work would have provided a stump of a tower with all the support necessary for the high roofs. This must have been the first concern of the tower-builders. The transition level from vitrified to red-brick in the stair well is also significant in the structure of the lantern and its galleries (see Fig. 151). The lower lantern gallery clearly formed part of the first campaign. The design has triple wall divisions and four angle vaulting shafts, whereas the final lantern design has double wall divisions and requires eight vault supports. The walling of the lower lantern gallery is haphazard in construction, with only the four lowest stone courses made up of regular well-cut blocks. The angle vaulting shafts are bonded into the walls at this level and so form part of the 1433 design. Above the first four courses, the shafts cease to be bonded until the last campaign work higher up. The stone coursing in the remainder of the gallery is quite arbitrary and consists mostly of small re-used blocks, perhaps salvaged from the previous tower. All the lower sections of the lantern windows have been inserted into this irregular-walling and become coursed into the wall only around their transom level. This is also the transition level from the blue to red brick in the stair well. This would indicate that the width and design of the lantern windows was determined only in the last phase of construction. A similar conclusion must be reached concerning the exterior angle turrets, which are not bonded into the tower facades for the first 26 ft – 792 cm.[10] This is even true of the south-west turret which contains the earlier sections of the stair well, so that the original face of that turret must either have been stripped or lies buried within the existing turret form. The south-west turret exterior received special attention and the new outer skin was carried across the face of the tower for several feet before the bonding breaks. This is not the case with the other angle turrets, which have obvious bonding breaks at the junctions with the main facades. The bonding evidence suggests that the interior walls of the earlier pre-1490s work survives some 4 to 5 ft – 122 to 152 cm – higher than the earlier exterior walls, except on the south-west corner where the stair turret rose as high as the transom level of the lantern windows. The evidence eliminates any suggestion that the final design of the tower owes a great debt to the earlier campaigns. The only inherited work was the interior lower lantern gallery with its angle vaulting shafts. Everything else, internally and externally, is of the last campaign.

In 1452 the south-west crossing pier under the tower showed signs of

10  Accurate drawings of the bonding patterns were made before the first restoration of the tower at the beginning of the century. Now in the Cathedral Archives.

11  Goldstone's Accounts 1452, Lambeth MS. 20.

collapse. Extensive reinforcements had to be introduced, and all work on the new central tower must have come to a halt.[11] The strengthening work involved the entrance arches from the nave aisles into the west transept and the first bay east of the nave. Such was the concern for the stability of the south-west crossing pier supporting the stair turret of the tower that the adjoining clerestory window was blocked up. The strainer arches were not built at this time but were inserted later with such care as to appear part of the same build.

The strengthening of the piers in 1452 could indicate the date of the change-over from the stone stair well in the tower to the lighter brick construction. Such substantial underpinning must have been the result of considerable concern for the new work, and must have caused some break in the building operations in case of further settlement. Construction could well have been in progress again by 1458, when bricks were purchased for an unknown purpose. If the blue brick section of the stair turret was built after 1452, then only 12 ft – 365 cm – of the earlier work survives. Stonework at a higher level may have been demolished in 1452 to prevent the collapse of the supporting south-west pier. Two bequests towards the work on the Angel Steeple occur in 1463 and 1471, and these may possibly represent the construction phase associated with the change of material in the stair turret from stone to blue brick.[12] Bricks first occur in the rather fragmentary accounts of this period in 1458, and 'redde brykes' are found in 1477.[13]

12  Charles Cotton, 'Churchwardens' Accounts of the parish of St Andrew, Canterbury, AD 1485 to AD 1625', *Arch. Cant.*, 32, 1917, p. 189.
13  R. C. Hussey, *Extracts from Ancient Documents*, p. 6.

The decision to continue and complete the new central tower was deferred for some years – no doubt because of the civil strife caused by the Wars of the Roses and the consequent decline in the revenue of the priory. The last campaign was begun under Prior William Sellinge, 1472–94, and Archbishop John Morton, 1486–1501. It saw the completion and vaulting of the stone lantern and the building above of a brick belfry clad in stone (Figure 149). There is a considerable amount of surviving documentary evidence from the period concerning the construction of Bell Harry, including letters from the prior and account rolls from several sources. Two building account rolls are known – one from autumn 1492 and the other more detailed roll from Easter 1494.

14  Ibid., p. 17.

The first of these rolls was recorded by R. C. Hussey in 1881, which he headed: 'An Account relating to the Angel Steeple beginning Anno Octavo H. Septimo' (that is the autumn of 1492).[14] On 17 June 1493, 39 tons of Caen stone was purchased at 6s 4d per ton: the consistent price throughout the account. On 8 October 1493 (Anno 9), another 39 tons was bought with a further 36 tons on 10 November. Another 72 tons of Caen stone was purchased for the workshop on 10 April 1494 (Anno 9) and 37 tons on 5 May. Two days later a large quantity of seacoal was purchased, and on 9 May an amount is entered for masons and sawyers working on the new tower. Payments for stone, including Merstham from Surrey, as well as for mason's costs and lead continue into 1498.

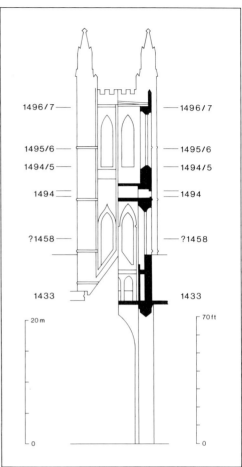

**149** (*above left*) Interior of the bell chamber and wheel loft. The upper section of the tower is built of red brick with stone dressings. The treadle wheel was used to haul materials from the floor below. It has been substantially renewed

**150** (*above right*) Bell Harry tower: the building seasons from the Account Rolls

15 Fabric Roll 20, Canterbury Cathedral Archives.

The second more detailed roll from Easter 1494 to Michaelmas 1497 contains a reference which provides a useful guide to the progress of the work.[15] In the account for 1496–7, it is recorded that the mason's work was being done at a rate of £8 per foot (30 cm), and as the mason's costs are also included in the roll, it is possible to convert this into actual building progress:

|  |  |  |  |  | feet | cm |
|---|---|---|---|---|---|---|
| 1494 | ½ year Easter–Michaelmas | £ 24 5s 4½d at £8 per ft | | | 3 | 91.5 |
| 1494–5 | | £107 16s 1 d | ,, | ,, | 13½ | 411.5 |
| 1495–6 | | £ 76 10s 11½d | ,, | ,, | 9½ | 289.5 |
| 1496–7 | | £188 0s 0 d | ,, | ,, | 23½ | 716 |
|  |  |  | | Total | 49½ | 1,509 |

It can be shown that these accounts cover only $49\frac{1}{2}$ ft – 1,509 cm – of the tower, which rises approximately 109 ft – 3,322 cm – from the lower lantern gallery floor level to the roof joist level, leaving some $59\frac{1}{2}$ ft – 1,813 cm – unaccounted for. The earlier campaign determined from the stair-turret evidence provides only $34\frac{1}{2}$ ft – 1,051·5 cm. Do the accounts for the missing 25 ft – 762 cm – come before Easter 1494 or after Michaelmas 1497, or perhaps some from either end? The answer lies in the accounts of costs paid out to bricklayers and carpenters.

The top half of the tower is built of red brick covered in stone, but the account for the full year 1494–5 has only £5 0s 1d to bricklayers and £10 4s 1d to carpenters. The following full year has £100 to bricklayers, and in 1496–7 £46 14s 4d was paid for 440,000 bricks. The fact that the half year Easter to Michaelmas 1494 has no reference to bricklayers must mean that work was still progressing in an all stone part of the building, whereas the small payment to bricklayers in 1494–5 suggests that the previous half year was the last all-stone section, which would be in the left above the vault and below the floor of the belfry wheel chamber.[16]

If the 49 ft 6 in. – 1,509 cm – of the building roll is measured from the tower roof joist level downwards, it would reach the approximate level of the vault loft floor. This would leave the half year of 1494 entirely within the all-stone loft, while the following full year, 1494–5, would proceed into the brick plus stone belfry chamber (Figure 150). This interpretation of the building roll allows for the progress of the construction to be outlined for the period 1494–7 as follows: the half year 1494, from the vault loft floor for about 3 ft – 91 cm; 1494–5, from the middle of the vault loft to the sill of the belfry windows;[17] 1495–6, from the sill of the belfry windows to just below the level of the transoms of the belfry windows; 1496–7, from just below the level of the transoms of the belfry windows to the roof ridge – that is the ledge supporting the roof joists which would provide the earliest opportunity to roof and weather-seal the building. By the late fifteenth century the pinnacles and battlements were most likely carried out under a separate contract, as was the case at King's College Chapel, Cambridge. The tower roof was certainly built by 1497–8, for in the Sacrist's Accounts of that year Ambrose Smith was paid 6s 8d for trussing three bells in the new tower.[18] This operation would not have been carried out before the construction of the roof which provided some support for the bells.

It would thus appear that the accounts for the missing 25 ft – 762 cm – of the tower come from before Easter 1494, and it is likely that three seasons of building had taken place by that time, as the all-stone tower would have proceeded at a slower rate than the brick plus stone construction. It is probable that the last campaign was under way by Michaelmas 1491, and perhaps as early as 1490. It is therefore notable that the cardinal's hat is not found on the exterior turrets until the base of the belfry. Morton was created a cardinal in 1493.

16  It has been demonstrated that the timbers of the belfry floor are those of a low-pitched roof. However, they cannot form an originally constructed roof-level as suggested (Cecil Hewett, 'New structural evidence regarding Bell Harry tower and the south-east spire at Canterbury', *Arch. Cant.*, 92, 1977, pp. 129–36), as it occurs within the brick section of the tower – that is about the summer of 1494. The decision to heighten the tower was already made by the beginning of that June. Further, there is no internal entrance to the vault-space under the 'roof', the only access being from the 'roof' through a trapdoor. Had this been constructed as an exterior roof, there would have been some provision for an entrance from the stair turret direct to the vault loft. It is most probable that the earlier roof had been constructed in the workshops and merely utilized for the belfry floor after the decision to extend the tower.

17  A tile levelling course occurs at this height in the north-east corner turret.

18  Miscellaneous Accounts, vol. 9, f. 120v., Chapter Archives.

19 Lambeth Court Roll, nos 1358 and 1360.

Work did continue after 1496–7, for in the following year John Colman, the archbishop's receiver, handed over £80 for the 'Angel stepill', and a further £62 was paid for 286 *dolia* of stone.[19] This stone must have been for the battlements and pinnacles. Two administrative letters have survived which deal with the construction of the tower. They explain many of the puzzling features of the structure of the tower, including the reason for the change from the all-stone lantern to the stone-clad brick technique of the belfry above. They also reveal an incredible change of mind on the part of either the architect or patron which raises fundamental questions concerning their attitudes and the mediaeval capacity to plan or even visualize a completed project.

The letters from the prior of Canterbury Cathedral provide datable evidence suggesting that the final design of the tower was decided upon only about half-way through the last campaign. The first is a draft letter, without date or signature, to the archbishop requesting that he choose one of two designs provided for the pinnacles of the new tower that will be finished by the next summer. It is not only of interest from the point of patronage, but it also confirms that the pinnacles were treated separately from the rest of the tower construction. The corrected text would read as follows:[20]

20 Christ Church Letters, vol. 1, f. 147, Chapter Archives.

Most Reverent father in God, and my most singler gode Lorde, after all due recommendation and humble obediens please it the same to understande that Master Surveyor and I have communed with John Wastell your mason, berer hereof to perceyve of hym what forme and shappe he will kepe in resyng of the pynacles of your new towre here; He drew unto us ij patrons of hem. The one was with doble fineall withowte crocketts, and the other was with croketts and single fineall. Thys ij patrons please y$^t$ your gode Grace to cammaunde the seyd Jo Wastell to draw and shew hem unto you, and uppon the sycht, your good Grace shew him your advise and pleasure whyche of them ij, or of any other to be devised, shall contente your gode Lordshyp to be appoynted. And furthermore if your gode Grace wolde require the seyd Jo Wastell so to do, I think that he might provide that these pynacles may be finished and accomplyshed this next somer folowing, the whyche if it mytt be so then your toure outwarde shuld appere a werke perfite.

The handwriting has been identified as that of Prior Sellinge, and W. G. Urry has said of the letter:[21]

21 W. G. Urry, *Cardinal Morton and the Angel Steeple*, p. 18. Urry, former archivist of Canterbury Cathedral, was the first to realize the importance of Fabric Roll 20.

There can be little or no question but that the document is in the characteristic humanist script which he must have acquired in sojourns in Italy. Sellinge, a conspicuous figure at the dawn of the English Renaissance, was not the only Canterbury monk who used this script. His successor, Prior Goldstone, wrote in a similar hand, while other monks employed it . . . There seems to be enough differences between Sellinge's known script (in signed letters) and that of Goldstone to assert that the letter about the pinnacles is in fact his. It bears Sellinge's characteristic cancellations and corrections in great profusion, and it would certainly be difficult to establish a case against it as a letter of his.

22 *Literae Cantuariensis*, vol. 20, p. 330. The 'other works' are unknown, only the Christ Church gate and an attempt to complete the Corona post-date the rebuilding of Bell Harry. Both projects are in brick, the gate being faced in Kentish rag and not Caen.

23 Hussey, op. cit., p. 6.

The identification of the handwriting is crucial to the history of the tower, for Sellinge died on 4 December 1494, making the latest possible 'somer folowing' that of 1495. Yet a second letter signed by Sellinge and dated 8 June 1494 is a request that William Feraunte of Caen purchase stone from that quarry for the next five years for the 'completion of a great tower, and other works'.[22] This second letter must post-date the correspondence concerning the pinnacles, as a further five years' work was then projected from June 1494 (that is, up to the summer of 1499); whereas the 'pinnacles' letter envisaged the completion of the tower in the following summer – 1495 at the latest, given that Sellinge was dead by the previous Christmas.

It would appear that shortly before June 1494 a major decision was made to extend the tower above the previous intended roof-line and that the brick plus stone belfry begun in the autumn of 1494 was an afterthought placed on top of what had been originally intended as only a new lantern tower.

In late May or early June 1494 a master mason, referred to only as 'magistro Lathamo', was paid for 'coming from the Cardinal'.[23] It is interesting that this entry comes before or on 7 June at the latest, for the following day Prior Sellinge wrote the letter to Caen requesting a further five years' supply of stone for the work. John Wastell may only just have brought back the cardinal's approval of an augmented scheme to include a whole new belfry above the lantern.

There is structural evidence within Bell Harry that a change of plan was put into operation from Michaelmas 1494, for the exterior turrets cease to be bonded into the main walls immediately above the Michaelmas 1494 date-line, and remain so for about 13 ft – 400 cm, that is, up to the level of the belfry windowsills. Above this point, the turrets are again bonded normally. This feature is consistent on all sides and indicates that either all the turrets were already free-standing with their pinnacles at the originally intended roof-line, or that walling previously built between the turrets was pulled down in order to build a link section to lead into the new belfry. The latter is perhaps more likely. The lantern must have been intended originally to stand as a low central tower half the present height, and when the decision was made to add a belfry above, a stone-clad brick construction was adopted to minimize the weight of the additional height.

To help with the additional weight, strainers were inserted into the southern and western crossing arches and into the easternmost bay of the nave arcades that had previously been strengthened in 1452 (see Fig. 7). The crossing strainers display the initials and rebus of Thomas Goldstone II, and therefore postdate his election as prior in January 1495 (see Fig. 131). The strainers have been meticulously set, and the small side arches even attempt to match the existing bonding lines. However, there are tell-tale vertical bonding breaks visible on them, and more obviously so on the larger crossing arches. The strainers are referred to in

24 *Anglia Sacra*, p. 147.

Goldstone's obit: 'He also with great care and industry annexed to the columns which support the same tower [the Angel Steeple] two arches or vaults of stonework, curiously carved, and four smaller ones to assist in sustaining the said tower.'[24] 'Curiously carved' refers to the fretted openwork pattern that lends the strainers their air of grace and elegance. They are so effortless and decorative that they could be taken as screens forming part of an extensive rood. The pattern on the small side strainers, a series of diamonds, is also found on the exterior of the tower below the belfry windows in part of the 1494–5 work. The large strainers have quatrefoils in circles – those on the upper and lower registers being elongated into teardrop lobes. The spandrels are also pierced and contain quatrefoil circles reminiscent of the contemporary chancel arcades at Thaxted, Essex.[25]

25 Thaxted chancel may well have been executed by the Wastell workshop while the men were working on the near-by church at Saffron Walden, *c.* 1491–1520. See F. Woodman, 'John Wastell of Bury, Master Mason', Ph.D. thesis, University of London, 1978.

With the pinnacles and battlements proceeding from 1497–8, there remained only the interior vault to construct. Vaults were commonly left until the end of a campaign, as their construction was easier under a completed roof and after initial settlement had taken place. This delay led to the many incomplete vaults in towers and gatehouses. Bell Harry has

**151**  The crossing vaults of *c.* 1504

the most famous and beautiful crossing vaults in Europe (Figure 151). A fan vault, not easily adapted to such a situation, springs from the corner shafts and the mid-points of the lantern walls. John Wastell had to insert corbel capitals for the latter, as the original provision from 1433 had only provided angle shafts for a standard rib vault. The fans have panels in two tiers which merge into one another in the corners. The decoration is rich but constrained, the edges of the fan cones having foliate cresting which is highlighted by chevron incisions on the webbing above. The fans create a large flattish central area which contains a series of concentric circles leaving four concave triangles in the angles. Each of these is filled with a large letter: T, G and P for Thomas Goldstone Prioris; the fourth angle containing the Goldstone rebus, three gold stones. The central circle has a large boss in the middle carrying the arms of the priory of the Holy Trinity, Christ Church, and this is surrounded by eight circles with trefoils. Around this is a band of diamond patterning and where the frame of the outer circle faces into one of the triangular spandrels, it is decorated with foliate cresting. This is also used to define the ridge ribs of the fans.

The capitals and corbels are decorated with two tiers of diamond fleurons, and the whole ensemble, beautifully repainted in the last century, is a work of richness and majesty.

The Bell Harry vault is particularly interesting as it is the earliest of Wastell's large fan vaults, and in style and decoration it is the forerunner of his vaults at King's College Chapel, Cambridge, completed in 1515. The date of the Canterbury vault can be ascertained from the four main bosses which carry the arms of Morton, died 1501, Henry VII, died 1509, Prior Goldstone II died 1517, and William Warham who became archbishop in November 1504. Warham provides the earliest date for the vault, with the latest at 1509.

Bell Harry is one of the most important buildings of the fifteenth century, not just for the excellence of the finished result but also because it provides sufficient evidence to create an unusually full picture of how major buildings were undertaken at this time: the strange disjointed process of design, which would be quite unacceptable by modern standards, and the position of the architect *vis-à-vis* his patron and committee in Canterbury. The cardinal, as patron, employed his own mason whom he no doubt paid, just as Chichele had first employed Mapilton on the south-west tower. Later this responsibility was taken over permanently by the priory. Morton was absent from Canterbury for considerable periods and appears to have regarded the successive priors as his 'man on the spot'. It is interesting to see how Goldstone assumed the responsibility for the new tower. His initials and rebus occupy the centre of each of the inscriptions on the large strainers, and he takes pride of place in the later crossing vaults. In his obit he is credited with almost the entire project: 'He, by the influence of Cardinal John Morton and Prior William Sellinge, erected and completed that lofty tower commonly called Angyll Stepyll in the midst of the church, between the choir and the nave, vaulted with a most beautiful vault, and with excellent and artistic workmanship in every part sculptured and gilt, with ample windows glased and ironed.'[26] Cardinal Morton, who began the last phase of the tower, has been relegated to the position of a mere helper according to Goldstone's biographer in *Anglia Sacra*, yet his rebus is found all the way up the exterior turrets. Morton contributed large amounts of cash and stone for the project, including 437 *dolia* of stone in 1495,[27] £100 from his Kentish manors in 1495–6, £80 from the same source in 1497–8, as well as a further 286 *dolia* of stone in 1497–8. Morton's obit states that, 'with his help, and at his expense great part of the tower in the middle of the church was erected'.[28] This puts his patronage more in perspective, for while the cardinal did not actually organize the construction and accounting of the work, he did pay for a great part of it and it was he who made the vital design decisions, no doubt after due consultation with Wastell.

The prior and the master surveyor acted as overseers in Canterbury – the prior controlling finance and administration and the surveyor dealing with costing, labour and day-to-day constructional problems. The master surveyor of the 'pinnacles' letter was a John Gudneston, master of the works, who on an unspecified Michaelmas Day was paid £4 in connection with the 'Campanile Angelicum'.[29] This was possibly a monk called John Goodnestone who entered the house in 1483 and who was appointed sacrist in 1510, though it would be unusual to find a monk performing so specialized a task at this late date.

In the Sellinge letter about the pinnacles, Wastell is referred to as 'your mason', that is the archbishop's, rather than the prior's. However Wastell was admitted to the fraternity of Christ Church as master mason on 7 April 1496,[30] and his new title almost certainly denotes a change in status to that of a permanent position usually commanding a regular salary.

Wastell was very much an architect in the modern sense, dealing directly with his patron and attending meetings with the committee in Canterbury. These meetings thrashed out the various options available: which design was preferable, the costing, available money, weight, support, supplies, etc., after which Wastell himself would go to the cardinal with a letter from the prior and discuss the options and draw the various designs. Morton would then make his decision, no doubt with Wastell's advice. Wastell paid only occasional visits to Canterbury, his practice being in Bury St Edmunds, and this emphasizes the need and importance of having a resident master of the works or warden who was known and trusted by Wastell and who may have been brought by him from Bury St Edmunds to act as 'mason inspector'. Wastell would hardly have left so important and prestigious a project in the hands of two monks.

There can be little doubt that Wastell got his way on all the major design decisions; the one known example – the pinnacles – though not

26 *Anglia Sacra*, p. 63.

27 E.404/82, Public Record Office.

28 *Anglia Sacra*, p. 63.

29 Urry, op. cit., p. 21.

30 BM MS. Arundel 68, f. 8.

executed at the original level, must have been Wastell's first choice. They are copied from Beke's pinnacles for the south-west tower of *c.* 1459, and the design was pre-empted by Wastell on Bell Harry in his complex angle turret design.

Bell Harry is of great importance not just to the cathedral but to the career of John Wastell. He was one of the leading architectural figures of the early Tudor period and his other works include the naves of the parish churches at Lavenham, Saffron Walden, St James', Bury St Edmunds, and Great St Mary's in Cambridge, and the more important works at Peterborough, the New Buildings, and the ante-chapel and vaults of King's College Chapel, Cambridge. He was perhaps the only great architect of his age not to have come out of the royal workshop centred upon Windsor and Westminster. Bell Harry is a perfect example of his rejection of the royal workshop style with its luxuriant, almost fantastic, creations such as Henry VII's chapel at Westminster. Wastell's style is one of clear lines, balance and restrained decoration. The crossing vaults of Bell Harry are brilliantly set off by the austerity of the lantern interior, and the horizontal elements of the facades are just sufficient to balance the vertical stress of the corner turrets. Wastell became master mason for the priory of Canterbury Cathedral in 1496 and probably remained so until his death about 1518.

The last years of the fifteenth century were tranquil and profitable for the cathedral. Peace brought prosperity back to the face of the land, and the contentment of the age found expression in the increasing comfort enjoyed by the monastic community. Draughty cloisters were glazed and panelled, the Palace was enlarged and modernized, and the prior moved out of his rambling lodgings into a splendid new mansion. Cardinal Morton died in 1501 and left 1,000 marks towards the fabric. His dazzling white tower was outwardly complete, though the vaults were not yet built. Some of Morton's legacy was spent on the last and most ornate project that was to be carried out by the monks, the Christ Church gate. Emeshed in panelling and studded with heraldry, it is the epitome of Tudor Perpendicular – yet amid the voices of the English court a foreign tongue can be heard. The Renaissance decoration that dribbles down the antique pilaster strips flanking the gates announce the advent of the sixteenth century.

## The Christ Church gate

The Christ Church gate, being on the south side and nearest to the city centre, has become the principal entrance to the cathedral precincts. It has suffered severely at the hands of despoilers and restorers alike, yet it remains a beautiful specimen of Tudor architecture. Like the age itself, the gate reflects the increasing interest in secular building that grew

**152** The Christ Church gate from the south, restored *c.* 1930

rapidly at the expense of ecclesiastical work (Figure 152). Typical of the early Tudor period, the facade is bedecked with heraldry proclaiming the arrival of the new dynasty.

The construction of the gate follows the basic form of Bell Harry, with a stone ground floor and brick upper parts faced with stone. To anyone visiting the cathedral for the first time since 1931 the gate would appear unrecognizable, for it has been thoroughly restored by the capable, if rather imaginative, hands of W. D. Caröe. The gate had been restored previously in 1803 but by 1900 the surface had weathered badly and most of the detail had mouldered away. The main culprit seems to have been the Kentish rag, the original facing-stone employed, and a totally unsuitable material for such fine and intricate carved surfaces. Of the present facade, little appears to be original work, or at least to date from earlier than 1803, but the many illustrations of the gate prior to the first restoration permitted a considerable degree of accuracy in the more recent renovation though some of Caröe's ideas were surely unsupportable.

The present turrets and battlements are replicas of those torn down by Jesse White, surveyor to the cathedral in the early nineteenth century, to satisfy a local bank manager who complained that he was unable to see the cathedral clock from his front door![31] Much of the facade recaptures the style of the original, though the central niche canopy is not in accord with representations made in the eighteenth century and the 'Angel frieze' lacks the charm and spirit of the early sixteenth century.

The documentary evidence for the construction of the gate is scant but significant. In 1504 John Nethersole left £66 in his will 'for the building of the gate of that church called Churchgate'.[32] In 1517 Prior Goldstone II bequeathed a sum of money for the completion of the gate, and in the accounts of 1519–21 it was noted that the income derived from the shops immediately inside it was reduced due to the work in progress for its completion. From this evidence alone, it would appear that the gate was in progress from at least 1504 until 1521, and Leland in his near-contemporary *Itinerary* comments that Prior Goldstone began the gate while his successor Thomas Goldwell 'performed it'.[33]

The exact date of the construction of the Christ Church gate has attracted more discussion than it could be said to warrant, though the dispute itself has now become almost as interesting as the gate, providing as it does an insight into the methods and observations of antiquarians over a period of over three centuries. Caröe was the first person to claim evidence *in situ* for a carved inscription across the front of the gate, though he failed to publish what he found. His wording in his restoration followed Somner's record of the inscription of 1640: '*Hoc opus constructum est Anno Domini Millesimo, Quingentesimo septimo*' ('This work was constructed in the Year of Our Lord 1507').[34] The exact wording of this inscription and the very date that ends it have been a subject for debate since the eighteenth century, and Caröe was perhaps a little hasty in his peremptory decision to include a new inscription with the date 1507, which is difficult to substantiate from the available evidence. Somner first recorded the inscription before the despoilation of the gate in 1642, but since 1772 every writer on the subject has claimed that it reads 1517 and that Somner had it wrong. What seems to lie at the heart of the problem is that no one indicated whether the inscription was carved, as at present, or merely painted on the gate. We shall never know the whole truth of the matter, but it is perhaps worth while to record some of the anomalies raised by the champions of both versions.

Somner states that the inscription of '1507' was 'hardly legible' in 1640.

31  Woodruff and Danks, *Mems CC*, p. 356.

32  Prerogative Court of Canterbury, 25 Holgrave. See A. Hussey, 'Further notes from a Kentish will', *Arch. Cant.*, 31, 1915, pp. 40, 41.

33  Leland, op. cit., pt VIII, p. 41.

34  *The Christ Church Gateway.*

35  J. Burnby, *An Historical Description of the Cathedral and Metropolitical Church of Christ, Canterbury*, Canterbury, 1772, p. 83.
36  Gostling, *A Walk*, p. 84.
37  E. Hasted, *History of Kent*, vol. 2, p. 506.
38  Z. Cozens, *An Ecclesiastical Topographical History of Kent*, 1800, vol. 1, p. 2. Copy in Christ Church Gate folder, Beaney Institute Library, Canterbury.
39  T. Hastings, *Vestiges of Antiquity*, London, 1813 (a book of plates).
40  J. Britton, *The History of Antiquities of the Metropolitical Church of Canterbury*, p. 43.
41  T. Willement, *Heraldic Notices of Canterbury Cathedral*, p. 1.
42  Gostling, op. cit., p. 84.

43  Ibid.

44  Property of the Friends of Canterbury Cathedral. Now in the Cathedral Library. Illustration in Caröe, *The Christ Church Gateway*, p. 30.

45  MS.162, Society of Antiquaries, London.

Burnby claimed in 1772 that it was in 'large letters', though he omits two words from Somner's legend and records a date of 1517.[35] Gostling gave the full inscription and a date of 1517, and commented that the letters were 'a span wide'.[36] In 1800 Hasted gave the date of 1517 but noted once again that the inscription was scarcely legible,[37] while in the same year Cozens had no trouble in recording the inscription 'on the cornice' or in reading the date of 1517.[38] Hastings remarked in 1813 that 'a few years since' the inscription was legible,[39] and Britton commented in 1821 that it 'formerly' existed.[40] Willement, writing in 1827, noted 'although much defaced it is still legible',[41] though between the comments of Hasted and Willement the gate had undergone a drastic refacing, according to Gostling, 'with Portland stone, nearly plain'.[42] This troublesome inscription that seems to have appeared and disappeared with the seasons was described in greatest detail by Gostling, one of the few eighteenth-century writers on the subject who lived in Canterbury. 'Age indeed has made the cornice and the inscription pretty near the same colour so that it does not take the eye, though it is legible enough with a little attention'.[43] The word 'colour' suggests that the inscription was painted, and not carved as at present; carving could become illegible only by physical damage. A painted inscription could indeed fade 'near the same colour as the stone itself'. Painted inscriptions were not uncommon in the sixteenth and seventeenth centuries, and a good example can be seen on the front of Trinity College gate in Cambridge. The Canterbury inscription may have been contemporary, i.e. 1507, or it may have been added in the early seventeenth century when a whole rash of painted 'Tables' were set up in the cathedral. The various disagreements over the wording and date of the inscription may have been the result of the repainting of the lettering after the Restoration, when the gate was refurbished, and at intervals thereafter as the paint simply faded. This would seem to explain the curious reappearance of the inscription between 1772 and 1827. Pictorial representations of the gate tend to confirm the absence of any carved inscription across the front. The 'Exact Model of the Christ Church Gate' of 1779,[44] Turner's exquisite illustration, and the precise drawings of F. Mackenzie give no indication of a sculptured frieze, indeed Turner drew a frieze of paterae along the cornice in question.

A date in the early seventeenth century for the original inscription would appear to be most appropriate, for not only were many others set up inside the church, but a detailed study of the heraldry on the gate was also made at this time.[45] The heraldry of the main facade includes the arms of Cardinal Morton, Archbishop Warham and Prior Thomas Goldstone II. Morton died in 1501, Warham succeeded Henry Dean in 1504 and Goldstone died in that most irritating year, 1517. The arms of Morton would suggest that at least some part of his generous bequest was expended upon the gate – it may well have prompted its commencement. The arms of Henry Dean would, therefore, be a curious omission, for his brief archiepiscopacy spanned the years 1501–2. The frieze above the entrance arches contains fifteen coats of arms of which the end two are modern. The central device is that of Henry VII, supported by a dragon and a greyhound. His arms are flanked by a Tudor Rose and a Beaufort Portcullis, the symbols of his parents. The next pair, moving out from the centre, are the Prince of Wales (left) and Catherine of Aragon (right), and herein lies yet another problem, for Catherine was married to Prince Arthur, the eldest son of Henry VII, who died in April 1502. Her subsequent marriage to Henry, Arthur's brother, took place only after his accession to the throne in 1509. In the early-seventeenth-century survey of the heraldry, Catherine is shown quartered with the Prince of Wales and not, as now, with only Aragon and Castile. Whoever is correct on this matter, and one would favour the seventeenth-century MS. as an original representation, the occurrence of the arms of Catherine of Aragon must pose significant problems for the heraldic date of the gate. The heraldry is further complicated by the remaining shields, which include that of Richard Guldeford, died 1506; Sir Henry Guldeford with the grant of the 'pommegranate proper' awarded to him by Ferdinand of Spain in 1511; and of Sir Thomas Howard, whose device carries an augmentation granted in 1513. Thus the frieze contains a mass of contradictory evidence, with the arms of Catherine of Aragon suggesting a date of *c.* 1500–2, Sir Richard Guldeford pre-1506, Henry VII pre-1509, the second Guldeford post-1511 and Sir Thomas Howard post-1513. But no date of post-1509 can be accepted, for Catherine was not married to Henry VIII while he was Prince of Wales. If the seventeenth-century depiction of her arms quartered with those of the Prince of Wales is correct, then her inclusion upon the gate must relate to her short marriage to Arthur until 1502.

One possible explanation for this clash of arms is that only the royal devices were carved when the gate was first commenced *c.* 1502, and that the additional arms were added during the final campaign, *c.* 1519. This could account for the uncarved shields and for the appearance of the Guldeford and Howard arms. Alternatively, Catherine may be present as dowager Princess of Wales, referring to Arthur, while the opposite device of the Prince of Wales may already refer to his successor, the future Henry VIII, who was Prince of Wales between February 1503–4 and April 1509. This solution would accommodate some of the other shields, though the Guldeford and Howard arms would still be too late.

The heraldry on the vault within the gate is much simpler, with the arms of Prior Goldwell establishing a date of post-1517. The vault bosses would be in accord with the known date for the completion of the gate, between 1519 and 1521.

The endless arguments surrounding the date of the Christ Church gate would be pedantic were it not for one extraordinary feature of its design. The entrance arches are flanked by pilasters decorated with Renaissance

**153** The Christ Church gate: detail of the side door and pilaster strips

motifs and supporting 'antique' capitals (Figure 153). If the gate were indeed to date from *c.* 1502, they would represent the earliest use of such Italianate forms in England. If the gate is 1517 they are no less remarkable but of less significance. It must be observed, however, that their relationship to the gate is far from convincing and that the remade exterior stonework cannot guarantee that they are not an addition. Nevertheless, the pilasters appear to be genuinely early and were perhaps added to the gate during the last campaign as a direct response to the similar pilasters that appear on the new hangings made for the cathedral in 1511 (Figure 154). Their relationship to the Perpendicular gate recalls the chapel of Henry VII at Westminster, where the early Renaissance altarpiece stood in glaring discomfort amid the filigreed extravagance of the Gothic chapel.

The parallel is well chosen, for the main facade of the Christ Church

**154** Aix-en-Provence: tapestries from Canterbury Cathedral made *c.* 1511. They were sold during the Commonwealth and were later hung in the cathedral at Aix. In 1978 they were stolen and have not yet (1981) been found

gate is strongly reminiscent of the royal work at Westminster and was probably executed by the same workshop. All the surfaces are panelled or treated as blind tracery, and the Windsor–Westminster 'Angel frieze' makes its almost obligatory appearance. The tracery design above the main arch reproduces the same design from the interior west door of the chapel. The rear of the gate is in complete contrast – severe and square, the only decoration being the traceried buttresses and the arms of the priory and the Tudor family. Within the gate, the plain walls support a striking lierne vault, its crown filled by a deeply carved Tudor Rose resting on a bed of foliage and flowers (Figure 155). It recalls the great Rose bosses of the high vaults of King's College Chapel, Cambridge, designed by John Wastell in 1512, but while Wastell may still have held his position as master mason for the cathedral, an office he acquired in 1496 during the building of the central tower, he did not design the new gate. It contains all the hallmarks of the Windsor–Westminster style, radically different from that employed by Wastell. There is every possibility that the gate became a royal project and Henry VII may well have provided one of his own master masons to design and supervise its construction. The most likely candidate would be Robert Vertue, who held property in Canterbury and was buried in St Augustine's Abbey in 1506.[46]

46 J. Harvey, *Gothic England*, pp. 183–5.

**155** The Christ Church gate:
interior vault

## The end of the cult of St Thomas

The first half of the new century saw Canterbury Cathedral at both its
zenith and nadir. The long archiepiscopacy of William Warham was a
time of twilight feasting, a tapestry of pageant and colour like the Age of
Tudor itself. The highlight of this idyllic masque was the state visit of the
Emperor Charles V in 1519. Accompanied by Henry VIII and Catherine
of Aragon, he paid homage at the shrine of St Thomas, and Henry's eyes
must have lingered long on the sight of that fabled wealth. When Warham
died in 1532, Henry was in the middle of his struggle with the papacy over
the dissolution of his marriage to Catherine of Aragon, and England had
entered a new phase of its history. Henry nominated Thomas Cranmer to
the see of Canterbury, and the prior and monks duly elected him
archbishop. It was to be the last time that they would ever exercise that
privilege. Cranmer was a man of the 'new learning' and a cautious
politician. Like many in the court of Henry VIII, he had no love for the

monastic system, which was considered effete and corrupt and, worse still, as owing a dual allegiance to the king and to Rome. The prior and monks dutifully signed the acknowledgment of the royal supremacy in 1534 but their fate was already sealed and the last years of the monastery were just a stay of execution.

The first move in the tragic end-game was the bizarre 'trial' of St Thomas. The martyr was accused of treason, contumacy and rebellion, a charge pronounced at his shrine for thirty days. The 'holy blisful martyr' refrained from any miraculous appearances at the judicial proceedings, with the result that St Thomas was found guilty as charged and sentence was passed. His bones were to be burned as a lesson to the living not to oppose the royal will, and all the offerings that enriched his shrine were declared to be the personal property of a traitor and therefore forfeited. In September 1538 the commissioners sent by Thomas Cromwell arrived to carry out the sentence. Their act of destruction brought to an end one of the most extraordinary aspects of the English Middle Ages – the cult of St Thomas of Canterbury. The violent death of an archbishop was not an uncommon event in mediaeval Europe, but the martyrdom of St Thomas in his own cathedral came as the culmination of a long drama that had been played out before the whole of Christendom. It was not a conflict between a tyrant and his subjects, nor was St Thomas fighting for even the remotest form of democracy – he died in an attempt to keep the Church separate from the State – and the memory of such a man had no place in the religious upheavals of Henry VIII. That the mass of the people should have so identified with the cause of St Thomas may have been due in some part to anti-Norman feeling still current in 1170, but it may also have been caused by the common feeling of 'over-government' in the reforming reign of Henry II. The murder of St Thomas redounded through Europe, 'so shocked was the Lord Pope at the news that for eight days he refused to discuss it even with his own people and issued a general order that no Englishman should have access to him.' The canonization of the martyr and the miracles reported at his tomb provoked a flood of pilgrims who came in search of spiritual and physical healing. His cult prompted a religious revival in England parallel to that devoted to the Virgin in France. The prior and convent acted swiftly to harness the momentum of events and, following the rebuilding of the choir, they had petitioned the pope in 1185 for permission to translate the body into the new shrine chapel elevated behind the high Altar. Nothing came of this at the time, but the great shrine was eventually commenced in 1216 and completed for the Translation of St Thomas in July 1220. That feast, celebrated on 7 July, became one of the great festivals of the Middle Ages and was a red-letter day throughout the Church. Kings, emperors and prelates made their pilgrimage along with the mass of common people. The popularity of the pilgrimage to Canterbury can be judged from the level of offerings made at the shrine and other holy places within the

47 E. Woodruff, 'The financial aspect of the cult of St Thomas of Canterbury', *Arch. Cant.*, 44, 1932, pp. 13–32.

cathedral. Treasurers' Accounts survive for most years between 1198 and 1337 from which the rise and fall of the level of donations can be gauged.

The early years before 1213 were patchy, partly because King John had exiled the monks. Nevertheless, offerings averaged over £425 p.a.[47] The Accounts, which cover the major sites in the Cathedral, omit the Altar of the Sword's Point in the Martyrdom, which certainly existed at this time and was extremely popular. The omission from the Accounts could be a simple oversight, or the income from that altar may already have been made over to one of the monastic officers.

The timing of the Translation was no accident. The fiftieth year after the murder provided an excuse for more than an ordinary anniversary, and Rome was petitioned for a jubilee at which a general pardon could be pronounced for all those present. The Translation provided the cathedral with a jubilee every fifty years, 1220, 1270, etc., so doubling the momentum of the cult. The offerings at the first jubilee achieved a staggering £1,142 5s, but this level could not be maintained and the average income derived from the various cult altars gradually diminished as the thirteenth century wore on (Table 1). The low-point occurred around 1260 when the average dipped to £102, and the worst year of all was 1258 when only £72 14s 10d was received. The civil strife associated with the reign of Henry III may account for some of this decline, but it would appear that the fever that had formerly gripped the populace was on the wane.

The second half of the thirteenth century saw a dramatic revival of the cult of St Thomas, which was maintained throughout the first three decades of the fourteenth century, or at least until the Treasurer's Accounts cease in 1337. One year only survives from the middle of the century, when it was recorded that over £800 was given in 1350. The fourth jubilee was held in 1370, when the Great Pardon was again available. The offerings made that year show that the increased level continued – £643 was raised compared with £670 at the previous jubilee of 1320. Apart from the £466 offered at the shrine, the most interesting figure is that of £50 raised at the Altar of Our Lady Undercroft in the crypt; in 1336, for example, only £5 was offered. Throughout the period 1370–84, the annual level of donations averaged £545, being highest in the year of the Black Prince's funeral, 1376, when nearly £700 was raised. During Chillenden's priorate, the income from the various shrines was transferred to the Prior's Accounts, most of which were lost after the dissolution, and so it is not possible to build up a complete picture of the cult of St Thomas during the fifteenth century. The donations made in 1396 totalled £503, whereas the figure for 1410 was only £265. The fifth jubilee held in 1420 was a marked success, with over 100,000 said to have attended to benefit from the Great Pardon – the offerings were £644. Between 1420 and the fall of Henry VI in 1461, the Prior's Accounts record the donations of only four years, revealing a remarkable decline in the offerings made at the shrine and other cult altars which is difficult to

Table 1    Offerings at the various shrines giving some indication of the rise and fall of donations

| | | | |
|---|---|---|---|
| 1200 | £620 4s | 1304 | £274 5s |
| 1203 | £248 18s | 1312 | £489 10s |
| 1213 | £76 | 1315 | £241 |
| 1214 | £380 19s 2d | 1318 | £577 |
| 1215 | £123 12s | 1320 | £670 13s 4d |
| 1216 | £88 14s 8d | 1329 | £351 |
| 1220 | £1,142 5s | 1335 | £461 |
| 1223 | £626 1s 10d | (missing from 1337) | |
| 1231 | £276 18s 2d | 1350 | £801 11s |
| 1236 | £312 17s | (missing) | |
| 1240 | £158 18s | 1370 | £643 |
| 1246 | £211 13s 8d | 1376 | £692 4s 7d |
| 1250 | £109 | 1381 | £362 10s |
| 1255 | £155 2s 10d | (missing) | |
| 1258 | £72 14s 10d | 1396 | £503 0s 10d |
| 1264 | £95 11s 3d | 1410 | £265 18s 4d |
| 1265 | £104 5s 6d | 1420 | £644 |
| 1270 | £204 2s 10d | 1436 | £66 15s |
| 1279 | £235 19s 6d | 1444 | £25 6s 8d |
| 1283 | £150 14s | 1453 | £31 1s |
| 1284 | £184 6s | 1455 | £25 6s 8d |
| 1294 | £203 12s | (missing) | |
| 1298 | £340 5s | 1532 | £13 13s 3d (excluding high Altar and altar of the Holy Cross in the nave) |

explain. It may be that only a proportion of the income was appropriated to the Prior's Accounts after 1420 with the bulk being paid into the revenue of another monastic officer. It may, however, reflect the waning of the whole cult of St Thomas or, at the very least, a change in attitudes towards financial donations. The fifteenth century had little of the religious fervour that had carried the cult of St Thomas to its former heights. People still came to the shrine, possibly in great numbers, but their motives were different from those early pilgrims. Most came to gawp and wonder – tourism had taken over from pilgrimage. The fabulous objects held sacred for so long became little better than curios to an altogether more cynical age. Gifts of gems and plate were still showered upon the shrine, but these presentations were tinged by the glory and prestige of patronage. By the late Middle Ages, the role of Canterbury had changed from a national shrine to a public spectacle. English and foreigners alike still marvelled at the cathedral and its contents. Two visiting Italians took back very different memories of the shrine: the Venetian ambassador, probably Andreas Tuerisano, arrived in Canterbury about 1500. His report to the Doge contains the typical reaction from those who saw the shrine at this time:[48]

48 *English Historical Documents*: vol. 5, *1485–1558*, ed. C. H. Williams, London, 1967, p. 196.

But the magnificence of the tomb of St. Thomas the Martyr, Archbishop of Canterbury, is that which surpasses all belief. This, notwithstanding its great size, is entirely covered over with plates of pure gold, but the gold is scarcely visable from the variety of precious stones with which it is studded, such as sapphires, diamonds, rubies, balas-rubies, and emeralds, and on every side that the eye turns, something more beautiful than the other appears. And these beauties of nature are enhanced by human skill, for the gold is carved and engraved in beautiful designs, both large and small, and agates, jaspers and cornelians set in relievo, some of the cameos being of such size that I do not dare to mention it, but everything is left far behind by a ruby, not larger than a mans thumb-nail, which is set to the right of the altar. The church is rather dark, and particularly so where the shrine is placed, and when we went to see it the sun was nearly gone down, and the weather was cloudy, yet I saw that ruby as if I had it in my hand. They say that it was the gift of a King of France.

The ruby was the Regale of France, donated by Louis VII in 1179 – one of the first gifts made to the tomb of St Thomas.

Andreas Franciscus, a fellow Italian, who saw the shrine of St Thomas on 17 November 1497, was rather less complimentary in his comments:[49]

49  Ibid., p. 188.

There seems to be nothing to be said about this town, unless anyone would like to know that it has a big cathedral dedicated to St. Thomas, which is very expensively and elaborately constructed and contains a stone tomb housing the body of the said Saint, which is decorated with many varied precious stones, brocades and gold in great quantity. There are also several objects of worship made of pure gold inlaid with many jewels, and a large number of sacred vestements also made of silk interwoven with gold and brocade. Everyone considers these very wonderful, owing to the lavish use of gold and precious stones, which all Englishmen boast of continually. The Bishop of this town is the Cardinal, with the title of St. Anastasius, and ranks first of all at the English Court in dignity and authority. He has a very large income from the Bishopric of Canterbury.

Most famous and revealing was the visit by Erasmus and Colet that occurred about 1513. The great man showed considerably more tolerance towards the whole business of relics than did his impatient friend. Erasmus recorded his pilgrimage in minute detail, 'the most pious of all pilgrimages' in Europe. He recounts it in the form of a dialogue between Ogygious, a pilgrim, and Menedemus who has never been to Canterbury. The discourse is worth quoting in part for its description and placing of the most important relics, and the manner in which important guests were escorted about the cathedral:[50]

50  Adapted from G. Smith, *Chron. Hist.*, pp. 212–21.

As we enter, the spacious majesty of the building displays itself. This part of the church anybody may visit . . . Iron pales prevent [further] entrance, but in such a manner that they allow a view of the space between the end of the nave and the place of the choir, as they call it. We ascend to the latter by many steps, beneath which a vaulted way leads to the North part. In this place is shown a wooden altar dedicated to the Blessed Virgin, of small size, and not worth notice, except as an ancient monument reproaching the excessive luxury of our own days. In the altar is the point of the sword by which the crown of the best of prelates was [pierced] and his brain scattered, the instrument of his death. For love of the Martyr we religiously kissed the sacred rust of this fragment of steel. Then, turning aside, we went down into the subterranean crypt, where there are priests in waiting. There, first of all, is exhibited the pierced skull of the Martyr; the relics are enclosed in silver, but the crown of the skull can be kissed, for it is bare. A plate of lead is also shown on which is engraved the title of Thomas of Acre. In the dark, there hang the hair shirt, the girdle, and the drawers, by means of which the Archbishop subdued the flesh; the very sight of them striking us with horror, and reproving our effeminacy and our luxuries . . . From this we went into the choir. On the north side are displayed the choice treasures; marvellous it is to tell of the store of bones brought out; skulls, jaws, teeth, hands, fingers, entire arms, upon all of which we, adoring, applied our kisses . . . After this we inspected the altar-piece and the ornaments of the altar, and then the things, all of the richest, which were stored under the altar. One would call Midas and Croesus beggars, in view of the power of gold and silver there to be seen . . . After this we were led to the Sacrarium. Ye Gods! What a show was there of silken vestments, what a power of golden candlesticks. I saw there the pastoral staff of St Thomas. The stem is covered with a coating of silver, of no great weight and quite unornamented, nor was it tall enough to reach beyond the waist . . . After these sights we were led still farther up the church; farther upwards, for behind the high Altar there is an ascent into, what one may call, still another Church. There, in a shrine, is shown the entire face of the saintly man, overlaid with gold, and made precious by jewels . . . the Prior himself opened for us the Shrine in which what is left of the Saint's body is said to lie . . . a wooden cover enclosed a golden one, which being drawn up by ropes, treasures beyond all calculations are displayed. The most worthless thing there was gold, every part glowed, sparkled and flashed with rare and large gems, some of which were bigger than a goose egg. Sundry monks stood reverently by, and when the other cover was withdrawn, we knelt in worship. The Prior pointed out several jewels, touching them one by one with a white rod; and, naming each in French, added the value and title of the giver, the chief of them having been bestowed by Kings . . . Leaving this place he brought us back to the underground place where the Virgin Mother has a station,[51] but a very dark one, here and there divided off by iron screens . . . I never saw any place more overloaded with treasures . . . when lanterns were brought we saw a display of more than royal splendour . . . These are not shown except to nobles or special friends.

Erasmus was clearly taken on the Grand Tour, visiting the most closely guarded treasures and altars in the church. Colet managed to upset the prior at nearly every turn, and it was only the tact of his friend and the letter of introduction from Archbishop Warham that prevented the prior from 'turning us out of the church, spitting upon, and reviling us'.

The last recorded visitor of rank was Madame de Montreuil, who saw the shrine only weeks before its destruction. Her visit followed roughly the same pattern as that of Erasmus and, once again, her reaction to the splendours is of considerable interest:[52]

By ten of the clock, she, her gentilwomen and the Ambassadour of France went to the Church, where I shewed her St. Thomas' Shryne and all other such things worthy of sight at which she was not a little marveilled of the great riches thereof,

51  The use of the term 'station' for the altar is relevant in view of the 'stacione crucis' in the nave mentioned in the obit of Prior Chillenden; i.e. it refers to the altar of the Holy Cross and not to a rood. See Legge and Hope, *Inventories of Christ Church, Canterbury*, p. 108.

52  *Calendar of State Papers of Henry VIII*, vol. 1, pp. 583–4.

saying to be innumerable; and that if she had not seen it, all the men in the wourlde would never made her belyve it. Thus ever looking and viewing more than an oure, as well the Shryne of St. Thomas' Hed, being at both sett cousshens to knyle, and the Pryour openyng Saint Thomas' Hed saing to her 3 times, 'This is Sainct Thomas' Hed', and offered her to kysse it, but she nother knyled not would kysse it, but still viewing the riches thereof. So she departed.

Madame de Montreuil's lack of respect for the precious relics appears to have been the common reaction of the day, for it in no way offended the prior who afterwards sent her quantities of 'capons, coneys, chickens and fruits'.

The shrine that was revealed to both Erasmus and Madame de Montreuil had changed considerably since it was first seen in 1220. The earliest depiction of the shrine, in the Trinity Chapel glass, shows a stylized golden box with a ridged roof and standing on slender columns.[53] In fact, the shrine appears to have stood on rather solid stone or marble arches – both Stow[54] and Franciscus refer to a stone construction, which was 'builded about a man's height'. Archbishop Langton had donated the iron coffer for the saint's remains, which was covered with gold and adorned with jewels. As the number of pilgrims increased, gifts of various kinds began to accumulate around the shrine, some being fixed onto it such as the famous Regale of France, a stupendous ruby that 'miraculously leapt' from the king's finger on to the shrine! This item was later to be transferred by less heavenly intervention to the fat thumb of Henry VIII. Stow also refers to 'plates of gold, damasked with gold wier, which ground of gold was againe covered with jewels of golde, as ringes – 10 or 12 cramped together with golde wier . . . many of those rings having stones in them, brooches, images, angels, precious stones, and great orient pearls'. The plates of gold encasing the metal coffer were doubtless originally embossed, perhaps with seated figures such as can be seen on Mosan shrines of the period. The Trinity Chapel representation shows quatrefoils along the length of the chest, though this may be a standard depiction of a shrine. However in 1372 the gold original plates were removed and sold, to be replaced no doubt by more modern and splendid designs.

The shrine was further enriched with precious objects given by rich and poor alike. In close proximity to the Regale of Louis VII could be seen the gold beads given by John Brown, the convent plumber in 1434. Edward I donated four images and two ships of pure gold to the shrine, as well as jewellery and gems, and in 1299 he presented his latest acquisition to St Thomas, the Royal Crown of Scotland. Henry VII left in his will a kneeling image of himself in silver gilt to be 'set before St. Thomas of Canterbury and as nigh to the shrine as may well be'.

The shrine was not always revealed – indeed, it seems to have been uncovered only once or twice a day. Normally the golden reliquary was concealed beneath a wooden cover that was, in turn, hidden under an

53 For recent views on the shrine, see N. Coldstream, 'English decorated shrine bases', *J. Brit. Archaeol. Ass.*, 129, 1976, pp. 28–30; A. J. Taylor, 'Edward I and the shrine of St Thomas of Canterbury', *J. Brit. Archaeol. Ass.*, 132, 1979, pp. 22–8; D. H. Turner, 'The customary of the shrine of St Thomas Becket', *Cant. Cath. Chron.*, 70, 1976 pp. 16–22.

54 For Stow's *Annals* of 1538, see G. Smith, *Chron. Hist.*, p. 236.

elaborate canopy. The latter was renewed in the late fourteenth century by Alicia Fitzalan, Countess of Holland, mother of Lady Margaret Holland and sister of Archbishop Arundel. She donated to the shrine, a 'new woven canopy with hangings'[55] that could be raised and lowered by means of a pulley fixed into the central boss of the apse vaulting. The ridge of the canopy was decorated with silver gilt ornaments, the central one weighing 80 oz, and each of the others 60 oz.

55 Turner, op. cit., p. 16.

Numerous battle-standards relating to the Crusades of the twelfth and thirteenth centuries were hoisted above the shrine, the sole survivor being the painted crescent still fixed to the vault. The standards recall of the dedication to St Thomas still known in Erasmus's day – St Thomas of Acre.

The dimensions of the shrine are difficult to estimate, as the broken area of the floor that marks the site of the shrine includes the total area taken up by the steps and railings. Stowe comments that the base was a man's height, and the shrine above may well have added half that height again. With the further addition of the canopy, the ensemble may have stood some 10 ft – 365 cm – above the floor of the Trinity Chapel. The stone base is unlikely to have exceeded 8 ft × 4 ft – 244 × 122 cm – square. The shrine stood on a marble floor patterned with large pink diamonds set into a background of blue-grey. At the western end was the altar of St Thomas which stood within the iron railings that protected the shrine and its treasures. Laid out like some great oriental carpet in front of the shrine is the superb mosaic floor of Opus Alexandrinum, probably a gift from Henry III made after 1220.[56]

56 The large mosaic floor has disrupted a previous scheme of four rows of inlaid roundels with scenes of the Labours of the Months, the Zodiac, Virtues and Vices, etc. The six central roundels from each row have been removed and gathered in two groups in the far corners of the pavement. The roundels probably date from *c.* 1213–20 and may have been the gift of the abbey of St Bertin in the Pas-de-Calais, where the monks spent their exile under John.

Three other cult shrines of St Thomas formed the route taken by the pilgrims. The Corona shrine, mentioned as early as 1213, contained a piece of the martyr's skull encased within a head reliquary known as the 'Caput Thomas', which stood either on or near the Trinity Altar within the chapel. The Altar of the Sword's Point in the Martyrdom stood against the wall where the saint fell. It was raised upon two wooden steps and above it was a canopy with hangings that could be opened to reveal an image of the archbishop and a reliquary containing the tip of Britto's sword that sheared off during the murder. Two rings were also displayed upon this altar: one contained a fragment of the saint's brain set under a crystal, the other was a ring that had been worn by St Edmund, the most recent archbishop of Canterbury to be canonized. The third shrine was the empty tomb which had lain open since 1220; the relics preserved at the altar there were described by Erasmus. These and many other relics associated with St Thomas were to fall into the hands of Henry VIII in 1538.

The king ordered that 'the said Thomas Becket should not be esteemed, named, reputed or called a saint, but Bishop Becket, and that his images and pictures throughout the whole realme, shall be put down and avoided out of all churches, chappelles and other places'. The destruction of the shrine and other objects associated with the saint produced nearly 3 cwt of gold, the same quantity of silver, nearly 5 cwt of silver gilt, 5 lb of parcel gilt, and countless precious stones. The spoil filled 'two great chests, such as sixe or seaven strong men could doe no more than carry one of them out of the church'.[57] The destruction of the shrine of St Thomas tore out the focal point of the choir. The Martyrdom reverted to its ancient role as the northern arm of the transept, still boxed up by redundant walls and bridges. The eastern crypt became empty and silent. But the orgy of vandalism had hardly begun, for within two years the whole cathedral would be ransacked and pillaged and the monastery dissolved.

57 For Stow, see G. Smith, *Chron. Hist.*, p. 236.

## The dissolution of the monastery

Canterbury Cathedral was probably the last great English monastic institution to fall prey to the commissioners of Henry VIII. The skill and devotion, the artistic achievements of centuries was to pass away in a moment. On 20 March 1540 Thomas Cranmer, archbishop of Canterbury, Richard Rich and Sir Christopher Hales drew up a form by which the monastery of Christ Church might be surrendered to the king. A few weeks later, on 10 April, a detailed inventory of the treasures of Canterbury Cathedral was taken which listed over 850 items ranging from an ivory table in Arundel's chantry, to 'the grete Rode covered with Sylver'. From this enormous list, it is possible to build up a vivid picture of the internal appearance of the cathedral in the last spring of its monastic life.[58]

58 For a complete list, see Legge and Hope, op. cit.

On entering the church, the nave was cluttered with tombs and chantries – that of Bishop Bokingham near to the north nave door and Archbishop Arundel's, nearer the crossing, with its rich ornaments. Both chapels were probably enclosed by stone screens fixed on to the adjoining nave piers. Other tombs in the nave included those of Archbishops Islip and Whittelsey and Priors Chillenden, Woodensborough, Elham and Salisbury. Somewhere in the nave stood a figure of St Thomas, clasping in his hands the four swords that slayed him, a gift to the cathedral from the early fifteenth century. At the east end of the nave strong iron grilles protected the crossing, a feature of the church that evidently went back to Lanfranc's day. By 1540 the north aisle had been freed of its obstructing Lady Chapel, but the western crossing arch was still blocked by a rood screen and its Altar of the Holy Cross. High above was suspended the great rood of the nave, with figures of the Virgin and St John. The crossing was reached as today, and from the raised platform under the tower the choir could be glimpsed through the pulpitum door. On great occasions the choir was hung with tapestries depicting the Life of Christ, of the Virgin and of St Alphege, while another showed the Life of Hester.

59 M. R. James, 'The tapestries at Aix in Provence and La Chaise Dieu', *Trans. Camb. Antiq. Soc.*, 11, n.s. vol. 5, 1907, pp. 501–14.

The most recent of these tapestries had been given in 1511 by Prior Goldstone II and the cellarer, Richard Deering (see Fig. 154).[59] The hangings may have been hung from the metal tie-rods which still exist between the main arcade capitals near the choir crossing, or they may have covered the blank wall space above the monastic stalls that forms the lower section of the Eastry screens.

The monastic stalls were contained between the pulpitum and the western piers of the choir crossing. The area beyond must have resembled an overstuffed museum crammed with precious objects and hangings. Even with the loss of the famous shrine beyond the high Altar, the sanctuary of Canterbury Cathedral must have been an astounding sight. It was dominated by three altars, with the high Altar in the centre flanked by the altar-shrines of Dunstan and Alphege. The altars were approached by three steps, a narrow platform and a further four steps. Beyond the group of altars ran the 'Auter Waule' of 'tabernacle work' built by Chillenden with donations from Richard II, Archbishops Courtenay and Arundel, and from Bishop Bokingham. The wall or screen contained two doors giving access to the steps up to the Trinity Chapel. In the centre of the screen was a silver *tabula* containing images of Christ and the Apostles, while on the top stood an 'Image of Our Ladie, four Aungells, and the holy ghoste for the Sacrament of Sylver and gylt'. The gilded pyx was held in the Virgin's hands, and the whole ensemble could be raised and lowered for access as well as for dramatic effect. The altar table itself, made at the time of Archbishop Courtenay, was of silver parcel-gilt upon which stood a 'Crucifix, Mary and John of sylver and gilte, with four Evangelists and a John sylver and gilt which weighed 149 oz'. Above the altar stood another rood covered with silver, and in front stood a large iron reading-desk that was placed on a semicircular platform that projected from the lowest step. Just to the north of the altar, on the site of the memorial to Archbishop Howley, stood the great relic-cupboard with its unbelievable objects seen only by the eyes of the privileged. Standing close to the cupboard was a brazen eagle desk for the gospel reading, given by Prior Goldstone II, and in the corresponding place to the south stood the huge pascal candlestick of copper and gilt. The Lenten veil could be drawn right across the sanctuary from just east of the tomb of Cardinal Kemp – one castle-shaped bracket for this still survives almost hidden by the wooden canopy of the cardinal's tomb. Even the air around the high Altar was filled with objects suspended from the vault, including Archbishop Arundel's three silver bowls which were doubtless used as sanctuary lamps, and running through this myriad of pendant gems passed a relic beam that supported the reliquaries of various saints, including St Blaise.

The throne of St Augustine stood behind this clutter, apparently in stark isolation. What view the archbishop could have had from the far side of the altar wall and its accompanying contraptions is hard to imagine, but it probably indicates that the screen was of no great height. Behind the throne, a tall iron grille known as the 'Hake' shut off the ritual sanctuary from the shrine chapel beyond. The subsidiary altars within the transept were also richly decorated; a picture of the Annunciation graced the south-east transept as well as the 'godly tumbe' of Archbishop Winchelsey. The various chapels contained relic beams that supported caskets and reliquaries with the remains of saints and archbishops. In the north-east transept was a figure of the Virgin, as well as the rather enigmatic 'Height of Our Lady'.[60] Even the aisles were filled with obstructions – huge cope-chests ranged along both aisles of the choir, as well as cult images of assorted saints such as St Osyth and St Appollonie in the south aisle, at which offerings were occasionally made. These two images stood on either side of the tomb of Prior Henry of Eastry. St Anselm's shrine could be glimpsed in the chapel of SS. Peter and Paul, whereas the opposite chapel of St Andrew had been divided up since Chillenden's time by the insertion of an intermediate floor to provide additional vestry space. The easternmost chapel of the Corona, now stripped of its head reliquary of St Thomas, still contained the Altar of the Holy Trinity and the shrines of St Wilfrid and St Oda. Over the entrance to this chapel was another relic beam carrying the remains of St Feologild. The crypt contained a multitude of altars and chapels, with the nine altars mentioned by Gervase plus St Clement, St Edmund of Canterbury, St Thomas the Apostle and St Bartholomew. Two of these altars occupied the aisles of the eastern crypt where the scars of their reredos beams can still be seen.

At the time of the dissolution, the cathedral also retained its full complement of stained glass, including the Life and Passion of Christ in the choir aisles, and untold quantities of fifteenth-century glass in the nave and west transept. It was also equipped with extensive panel paintings, screens and images with at least eighteen in the choir alone.

All this incomparable magnificence survived until 20 March 1540. The preceding night, the monks performed their services, well knowing the fate that awaited them on the morrow. A few stayed on as members of the New Foundation. Most accepted a pension and left. The demise of the prior and convent was dignified and without rancour. On a cold March day, it just ceased to exist, and with the dissolution of the Priory of the Holy Trinity, Christ Church, the great age of English monasticism passed quietly away.

60  Legge and Hope, op. cit., p. 111; Woodruff and Danks, *Mems CC*, p. 283.

# CHAPTER 7

# THE POST-REFORMATION CATHEDRAL, 1540-1980

## Reform, revolution and restoration, 1540–1825

The post-Reformation history of the architecture of Canterbury Cathedral forms a miserable postscript to the preceding chapters. Three centuries of neglect rendered the cathedral fabric desolate and the monastic buildings ruined. Much of the damage was the deliberate policy of 'reformers' of all shades, and was followed by the various 'improvers' of the eighteenth and early nineteenth centuries. But at no time was the very existence of the cathedral itself seriously at risk – even the Commonwealth which treated it with contempt spent considerable sums upon maintenance and repair. The fittings fared less well. Altars, books, tombs, chantry chapels and stained glass were all ruthlessly vandalized in the name of God, the king or parliament. From the earliest days of the New Foundation, objects of 'superstition and popery' were sought out and destroyed together with the last vestiges of the monasticism that had maintained them. Cranmer and the king did not agree on the exact format of the new regime following the dissolution of the monastery on 20 March 1540. Henry VIII proposed a large quasi-academic institution that was not favoured by the archbishop.[1] Finally a Charter of Foundation was drawn up on 8 April 1541, allowing for a dean, twelve prebendaries, six preachers, twelve minor canons, one deacon, etc., but eliminating the professors and academics. Despite assurances, Thomas Cromwell overlooked the former prior, Thomas Goldwell, and nominated Nicholas Wooton for the post of dean. The aged prior declined a secondary position in the new establishment and retired with dignity and a pension. A great deed of settlement was made, dispersing the vast complex of monastic buildings among the new members;[2] the dean received the prior's mansion, while sections of the infirmary, the Aula Nova and other ancient buildings of the convent were divided up between the prebends, canons and other officers. Considerable destruction was entailed, not only for the conversion of mediaeval institutionalized buildings for modern commodious residences but also for the profit to be had from their salvage. Between 1541 and 1547 the 'long hall of the Infirmary', 'the Frater', and 'ye great Dortor' were taken down 'for ye treasure of the

[1] For details, see G. Smith, *Chron. Hist.*, p. 243.

[2] Willis, *Hist. Mon.*, pp. 192–6.

3 C. E. Woodruff and W. Danks, *Mems CC*, p. 330.

church'. The huge dormitory was only partially demolished, for six families still lodged in it in 1649,[3] and sections of the refectory and infirmary survived buried within, or left adjacent to those buildings suffered to remain. In the midst of all this destruction, disaster of another kind stalked the precincts. In 1544, during preparations for the visit of the viceroy of Sicily, the great Hall of the Archbishop's Palace was consumed by fire. The Hall stood blackened and derelict, and was rebuilt only partially by Matthew Parker after 1559.

The death of Henry VIII in 1547 let loose a new wave of Protestant fanaticism upon the cathedral, but six years later the reign of the Catholic Mary Tudor witnessed a brief revival of the former practices and the refitting of the church with roods, images and altars. The revolutions of the Tudor dynasty ended with the accession of Elizabeth I in 1558 and the establishment of the Anglican Church – mostly Protestant but with sufficient breadth for the less ardent and politically-minded Catholic. The cathedral entered the Elizabethan era with whitewashed confidence. The Palace was rebuilt, music and bells rang out on Sunday mornings and, once again, royalty and foreign dignitaries were entertained with mediaeval lavishness.

But throughout Elizabeth's long reign, extreme elements within and without the Church grew alarmingly strong. At first, the Huguenots, those French Protestants who fled from the wars of religion, were given a cautious welcome by the astute queen. Thousands settled in Canterbury, where they assisted in the great revival of the cloth trade. Their numbers were such that by about 1575 the whole crypt had been granted to them for their services. But their arrival coincided with the growth of the Puritan movement; nonconformists of all kinds who believed only in the word of scripture and who loathed the established Church with its bishops, cathedrals and other Romish institutions. The Puritans, little more than a nuisance in Elizabeth's day, were to dominate the early seventeenth century and came close to destroying many of England's great churches. The plight of Canterbury was made worse by the attitude of William Laud, archbishop 1633–45. His attempts to restore something of the mediaeval panoply to Christ Church earned him the hatred of the Puritans and an untimely end. Laud refitted the choir with an altar, candlesticks and other dressings, a rich carpet and a 'Glory-cloth'

4 See R. Culmer, *Cathedrall Newes from Canterburie*, 1644, in G. Smith, *Chron. Hist.*, p. 288.

decorated with golden rays emanating from the name of Jehovah.[4] Further offence to the Puritan party came in 1639 when Dr John Warner, bishop of Rochester, presented the cathedral with a handsome black and white marble font fitted with classical figures and a fantastic cover; 'so that none can look up in prayer there, but hee shall behold those tempting images in the place of Divine Worship, against the Law of God and the Doctrine of the Church of England'.[5] The activities of Laud and his

5 Ibid., p. 289.

supporters continued to outrage the Puritans: 'they have a long time caused the godly neare them to groane under their tyranny, superstition

6 Ibid., p. 287.

7 Ibid., p. 302.

and scandall'.[6] In 1639 Laud erected four great iron flags on the pinnacles of Bell Harry emblazoned with the arms of the king, Prince Charles, the Church and of himself. But in December,[7]

> in the midst of their Cathedral Iovialities and Christmas Gamballs, there was a Gamball plaid by the flag, which had the Archbishops armes on it, which had a rumbling cast from the top of the steeple, being strucken down by a stroake from heaven, in a fearfull tempest, on Innocents day early in the morning: And the Archbishops arms pulled down the top of the pinnacle, which upheald them, and were carryed (partly against the wind) a good distance from the steeple, on which they stood, and fell upon the roofe of the Cloyster, in which Cloyster, the Armes of the Archbishop of Cant. were carved and painted on the lower side, or concave of the Arch, or seeling of the Cloyster; which Armes in the Cloyster, were dashed in pieces by the Armes which fell from the pinnacle of the steeple; The Arms of the present Arch-Bishop of Canterburie, brake downe the Armes of the Arch-Bishoprick, or Sea of Canterburie: The fall was so violent, that it brake through the leads, plancks, timbers, and stone-Arch of the Cloyster and made an impression in the pavement of the Cloyster, as if it had been done with canon shot, which impression is partly to be seene at this day, though repayred. And this prodigious fall of the Arch-Bishops Armes, was very near the place, where that proud Prelate, Thomas Becket, Arch-Bishop of Canterburie, and Arch Traytor, was cast down headlong in that Cathedrall, for his Treason and Rebellion; And very neere the unparallel'd Idolatrous window in that Cathedrall.

The damage was made good with some haste, though the arms of the archbishopric were not replaced in the cloister, nor were the arms of Laud put back on the tower. The great storm also damaged the roof of the 'Idolatrous Quire' which required attention. These sinister events gave rise to a popular verse:[8]

8 Ibid., p. 303.

> Cathedrall Church of Canterbury,
>     Hath taken mortall harmes:
> The Quire and Cloyster do want a plaister,
>     And so doe the Arch-Bishops Armes
> The heavens just stroake the Prelates Armes broke
>     and did Cathedrall maule;
> 1.6.3.9. Brought forth this signe,
>     Heaven foretells Prelates fall.

The fall of Archbishop Laud was not long delayed.

Meanwhile, events moved with calamitous speed. In 1641 the images around the new font were smashed and in August 1642, with England on the brink of civil war, the keys of Canterbury Cathedral were handed over to Colonel Sandys of the Parliamentary army. The troops looted the church and burnt and desecrated the books, altar-ware and all the trappings of 'the Whore of Rome'. This incident preceded a 'more orderly and thorough Reformation in that Cathedrall' which began on 13 December 1642:[9]

9 G. Smith, *Chron. Hist.*, pp. 311–14.

**156** The destructions of 1642: an angel from the Lady Chapel

When the Commissioners entred upon the execution of that Ordinance, in that Cathedrall, they knew not where to begin, the Images and Pictures were so numerous, as if that Superstitious Cathedrall had been built for no other end, but to be a stable for Idolls. At last they resolved to begin with the window on the East of the high Altar, beyond that Sainted-Traytor, Arch-Bishop Beckets shrine, at which shrine to this day may be seen, how the stones of the pavement on the sides, and ends of that shrine, were worn with the kneeling of the Idolatrous people, which came on Pilgrimage, to offer there, to that Pope-holy saint.* But the Commissioners knew not what pictures were in that Easternmost window of that Cathedrall, and comming to it, the first picture they found there, was of Austin the Monke, who (as is said before) was the first Arch-Bishop of Canterburie that ever was, and so it casually fell out, that the image of this Arch-Prelate of Canterburie was the first that was demolished in that Cathedrall; many window-Images or pictures in glasse were demolished that day, and many Idolls of stone, thirteen representing Christ and his twelve Apostles standing over the West doore of the Quire, † were all hewed down, and 12 more at the North doore of the Quire, and 12 Mytred-Saints fate aloft over the West doore of the Quire [see Fig. 143],‡ which were all cast downe headlong, and some fell on their heads, and their Myters brake their necks: While this worke was in hand, in comes a Prebends wife and pleaded for the Images there, and jeered the Commissioners viragiously: but when she saw a picture of Christ demolished, she skreekt out, and ran to her husband, who (after shee was gone) came in, and asked for their Authoritie to doe those things: and being answered that there was the Ordinance of the KING and PARLIAMENT, he replyed, not of the King, but of Parliament if you wil, he also pleaded for the Images there, and spake in justification of his bowing towards the Altar, yea he would maintain his bowing three times that way because there were three Persons in the Trinity; a poor argument for a Cathedrall Doctor, he might as wel have argued, because he did give thanks for the three parishes or steeples he enjoyed. But after he had disputed awhile with the Ministers, that assisted the Commissioners in that work; the grand Priest complained for want of breath, saying he was ready to faint, and desired to be let out: And indeed he looked very ill; 'tis true he stood very neere the place where Arch-Bishop Becket was cast over headlong; but this man had no cause of fear, not a distastefull, or disrespective word: and he quietly let out, as he desired. And then the work of Reformation went on; the Commissioners fell presently to work on the great Idolatrous window [the Royal window in the north wall of the Martyrdom], standing on the left hand, as you goe up into the Quire [see Fig. 147]: for which window (some affirm) many thousand pounds have been offered by out-landish Papists. In that window was now the picture of God the Father, and of Christ, besides a large Crucifixe, and the picture of the Holy Ghost, in the form of a Dove, and of the 12 Apostles; and in that window were seven large pictures of the Virgin Marie, in seven several glorious appearances, as of the Angells lifting her into heaven, and the Sun, Moon, and Stars under her feet, and every picture had an inscription under it,

---

* This almost suggests that the shrine, or at least its stone base, still existed.
† Christ and the Apostles occupied the niches surrounding the central door.
‡ The saints filled the upper niches of the pulpitum. The present figures of *c.* 1660 were taken from the Chichele tomb 'at the north door'.

beginning with gaude Maria: as gaude Maria sponsa dei, that, Rejoice Mary thou Spouse of God. There were in this window, many other pictures of Popish Saints, as of St. George etc. But their prime Cathedrall Saint – Arch-Bishop Thomas Becket – was most rarely pictured in that window, in full proportion, with Cope, Rochet, miter, Crosier, and all his Pontificalibus, And in the foot of that huge window, was a title, intimating that window to be dedicated to the Virgin Mary. In laudem &c. honorem beatissime Virginus Maria matris dei &c. But you have a register of the Cathedral Idolls in a late book mentioned in the recited Canterburie Petition:* In that Prelaticall book, thanks are given to the piety of these times, that the altar in that Cathedrall was so richly adorned, there is a project for the discovery to what Saint every parish church is dedicated: that Church-Ales, and wakes, and parish-feasts may be better kept: This booke was a card and compasse to sail by, in that Cathedrall Ocean of Images: by it many a Popish picture was discovered, and demolished. It's sure working by the booke: But here is the wonder, that this booke should be a means to pull down Idols, which so much advanceth Idolatory. But as that window was the superstitious glory of that Cathedrall; as it was wholly superstitious, so not it more defaced than any window in that Cathedrall. Whilst judgement was executing on the Idols of that window: the Cathedrallists cryed out againe for their great Diana, hold your hands, holt, holt, heers Sir &c. A Minister† being then on the top of the Citie ladder, near 60, steps high, with a whole pike in his hand ratling down proud Beckets glassy bones (others then present would not adventer so high) to him it was said, 'tis a shame for a Minister to be seen there; the Minister replyed, Sir, I count it no shame, but an honour, my Master whipt the living buyers and sellers out of the Temple; these are dead Idylls, which defile the worship of God here, being the fruits and occasions of Idolatory. Some wisht he might break his neck, others said it should cost bloud. But he finished the worke and came downe well, and was in very good health when this was written. Many other Images were defaced in other windows there, severall pictures of God the Father, of crucifixes and men praying to crucifixes, and to the Virgin Marie; and Images lay on the tombs, with eyes and hands lifted up, and right over them was pictured God the Father, embracing a crucifix, to which the Image seemed to pray. [The reference is to the tomb of the Black Prince.] There was a Cardinalls hat, as red as blood, painted in the highest window in that Cathedrall within Bell-Harry steeple, over the Quire doore, covering the Arch-Bishops Armes [the arms of Cardinal Morton], which Hat had not so much respect shewed it, as Cardinall Wolseys hat had at Court, it was not bowed to, but rattled downe: There were also many huge crosses demolished, which stood without the Cathedrall, four on Bell-Arundel steeple: and a great Idoll of stone, [this was the Angel that formerly stood on the central tower], which stood on the roofe of that Cathedrall, over the South dore, under Bell Harry steeple, was pulled down by 100 men with a rope: in the fall it buried itselfe in the ground, it was so heavy, and fell so high. This Image held a great brazen Crosse in his hand; it was the Statue of Michael the Arch-Angel, looking straight to a lane right over against it, in Canterburie, called Angell-lane [now called Butchery Lane]. There was demolished also, a very large stone Image of Christ, over which was the Image of the Holy Ghost, in the forme

*Evidently a list of dedications and the like drawn up for Archbiship Laud.
†This was Richard Culmer, rector of Hackington, Canterbury, and a notorious vandal of mediaeval art.

of a Dove: this Idoll stood right over the great Cathedrall South-gate next the Bull-stake [the Christ Church gate in the Buttermarket]: this Image was pull'd down with ropes: at first the head began to shake and nod to and fro, a good while: at last it fell off two houres before the body, which was riveted to the wall with iron barres. The Papists report it was a miracle, that the Image nodded the head to reprove those that pull'd it downe, one said then, it was a shame they should pull it downe in such a base manner. This Image (amongst the rest) was the meanes of much Idolatory; men, now living, testifie, that they have seen travellers kneele to it in the street, as they entered the Cathedrall, which is continually visited by Outlandish Papists, who daily commit Idolatory in that Cathedrall; and yet how many that profess love to true Religion, and hatred of Idolatory, are now zealous for these Images, which are monuments, and instruments, and occasions of Idolatory, the continuance whereof hath bin our great sin, shame, and misery?

Most of this lamentable destruction was carried out by Richard Culmer, 'one of the greatest villains in the Kingdom',[10] of whom Gostling recounts the following story:[11]

While he was laying about him with all the zeal of a renegado, a townsman, who was among those who were looking on, desired to know what he was doing. 'I am doing the work of the Lord,' says he. 'then,' replied the other, 'if it please the Lord I will help you', and threw a stone with so good a will, that if the saint had not ducked he might have laid his own bones among the rubbish he was making; and the place, perhaps, had been no less distinguished by the fanatics for the martyrdom of St Richard Culmer, than by the Papists for that of St Thomas Becket, though his relics might not have turned to so good an account.

Culmer later appeared as a witness against the ill-fated Laud whose life ended on the scaffold on 10 January 1645. The cathedral and its precincts now fell into the hands of the Puritans. Its properties were plundered and the church used as a stable and armoury. Yet despite their lack of respect for the cathedral, it was still deemed necessary to maintain its fabric. In 1646, £109 was spent on repairs to the roof of the church while, in the following year, £80 was laid out 'for a great repair to the arch over the body of the church with much expense of masonry', and a further £16 for repairs to the clerestory.[12] It was proposed to demolish many of the subsidiary buildings of the cathedral in 1649, including the vestiarium, night passage, Water Tower and the cloister – fortunately these intentions were stillborn. For the next ten years the great church echoed to the tramp of military boots and horses' hooves. The organ was silent, the bells hung still. Wind whistled through the shattered glass, lifting the torn shreds from the songbooks and tossing them amongst the battered tombs. While spoken services were held in the Chapter House, now styled the 'Sermon House', the cathedral stood empty, idle and derelict, a mere shadow of its former glory.

The Rebellion ended almost as suddenly as it began. On Sunday 26 May 1660 King Charles II entered Christ Church to attend to his

10 Ibid., p. 317.

11 Gostling, *A Walk*, p. 227.

12 Woodruff and Danks, *Mems CC*, p. 329.

**157** The Juxon gates, *c.* 1660

13  Clarendon, *History of the Rebellion*, 1819, vol. 3, pt 2, p. 1021.

devotions. The cathedral was 'much dilapidated and out of repair, yet the people seemed glad to hear the Common Prayer again'.[13] An enormous task faced the new Dean, Dr Thomas Turner, and during the next decade nearly £8,000 was expended upon the church for its 'reparations, utensils and ornaments'. Among the many items purchased at this time were the splendid carved doors of the Christ Church gate and the superb eagle lectern of the choir. A new organ was set up in the choir, standing on the north side with a wooden stair traversing the aisle – the latter involving the removal of the Virgin window in the north choir aisle.* The thirteenth-century Prior's Chapel near the Water Tower was rebuilt in red brick and fitted out as a library (see Fig. 47). The old building had been damaged in 1580 by a fire that had broken out in the Chichele Library above the chapel, and evidently no repairs had been made, for the building was a complete ruin.

In the 1670s it was decided to improve the choir and its seating. In 1675, Roger Davis of London was employed to panel the choir to a height of 12 ft – 366 cm – the work to be modelled on 'that lately set up in the hall

14  Woodruff and Danks, *Mems CC*, p. 342.

of the Mercers Company in London' (Figure 158).[14] The panelling was of exquisite execution, with fluted pilasters, corinthianesque capitals and elegant carvings, yet it covered the Eastry screens and blotted out the vista into the aisles; for this crime the woodwork was unceremoniously ejected in the nineteenth century and converted into cupboards in the crypt.† The return stalls and accompanying screen fared rather better. This extravagantly Baroque work was commissioned from Roger Davis in 1682 at a cost of £320. Sir Gilbert Scott argued for its removal in 1879 in order to reveal the remains of Eastry's pulpitum – his advice was gratefully ignored, and the screen remains *in situ* as one of the finest products of English carpentry.

In 1703 the old monastic stalls were replaced by more comfortable seating which was to be 'finished as well and in as good workmanlike

15  Ibid., pp. 346–7.

manner as the pews and benches are in the Cathedral of St. Pauls.[15] Archbishop Tenison made his own 'seat' rather more splendid by the addition of a gigantic Baroque canopy, the design of which has been attributed to Nicholas Hawksmoor and the execution to Grinling Gibbons. By the 1830s it was felt to be an unsuitable ornament for a Gothic church and was put into storage, but later in the century it was brought out again and redeployed as an organ case in the south-east transept. It now stands somewhat forlornly at the west end of the nave. The refitting of the choir was completed by the erection of a new altar-piece and screen to replace the previous screen that may still have retained much of Prior Chillenden's work. The architect James Burrough was commissioned in 1730 to produce a classical altar-piece 'of grand

---

* The westernmost window of the north choir aisle. It is still blocked.

† They have now (1981) been removed. Sections of the woodwork have since been incorporated into the Guildhall in Canterbury.

**58** The choir interior in the eighteenth century

appearance', and it was probably he who completed the panelling in the crossing and presbytery in the style of the earlier panels of the choir. In preparation for the erection of the new screen, the mediaeval altar steps were taken up and new black and white marble steps put down slightly further to the east – the work carried out at the expense of Dorothea Nixon. The choir also acquired new lighting. The first of a series of brass chandeliers had been presented in 1692 by Sir Anthony Aucher and was hung under the eastern crossing. A second was hung in the presbytery in 1726, a gift of Dr Edward Tenison, while yet another was hung near the Chichele tomb in 1747, donated by Dr Shuckford.

By 1750 the working area of the choir and presbytery had been cased up in modern panelling which was draughtproof, commodious and well lit and with more spacious and comfortable seating.

Work of a more structural nature was also carried out at this time. In

1703, the wooden spire that Eastry had placed on the old north-west tower was severely damaged in a storm and the next year it was removed and the top of the tower made good. In 1718 the mediaeval audit house was rebuilt upon its old undercroft, but now in red brick.* A grave was dug in 1734 in the Martyrdom, but as it was too close to the wall that contained the famous Red Door, the latter was undermined and demolished. After this, the transept arm was laid open to the crossing as at present. The Corona was the next to receive attention – evidently the Tudor attempts to complete the eastern tower chapel were now considered unsightly, and in 1748 Captain Humphrey Pudner provided the funds for the present Gothic battlements (see Fig. 93). The embrasures appear to be the reveals for an additional fenestrated storey, executed in red Tudor brick. The steps of the nave and the long iron screen that divorced it from the crossing were the next items to disappear; the steps were relaid in 1750 but the grill was never seen again. In the next year, the gable of the south-east transept was restored under the direction of George Dance the Elder – the rather dry 'Romanesque' design is perhaps preferable to the shanty weatherboarding that had covered the gable for many decades.

The post-Restoration organ that had been placed in the north choir aisle was removed in 1784 and placed on top of the pulpitum, where it appears in Britton's account of the cathedral of 1821. But whereas some of the activities of the eighteenth century were undoubtedly improvements, none was so outrageous as the clearing of the nave in 1787. Tombs, chapels and screens were ruthlessly swept away, so that a pleasant prospect could be provided from the west door.[16] Not everyone approved of this action, nor of the whitewashing of the choir interior that followed. Horace Walpole wrote in 1794: 'I wish you had seen Canterbury some years before they whitewashed it, for it is coarsely daubed and so few tombs remain for so vast a map that I was shocked at the nudity of the whole'.[17] The destruction within the nave also claimed the tiny Brenchley Chapel, and in 1796 the chantry chapel of Archbishop Warham squeezed between the Martyrdom and the Chapter House was similarly 'improved away'.

The turn of the new century saw the advent of Jesse White, surveyor to the cathedral, whose infamous reputation has survived to this day. His attitude and that of his fellow-citizens, was wholly typical of the period. George Gilbert, who lived with his family in the precincts at this time, recounts the circumstances of White's most notorious achievement:[18]

I saw a letter from him† to Dean Powys in which he earnestly deprecated the removal of the two turrets from the great gate of the churchyard. It was

16  A plan of the tombs and chapels was made about 1786; see ibid., p. 195.

17  *Walpole's Correspondence*, ed. P. Cunningham, vol. 9, London, 1891, p. 441.

18  Woodruff and Danks, *Mems CC*, p. 356.

---

* Sections of the undercroft survive against the west wall of the vestiarium.

† A reference to Dr Luxmore, prebend of Canterbury Cathedral and later dean of Gloucester.

unavailing. The true story of their removal is this. My father was one day in the bank of Simmons and Gipps at the corner of St Margaret's Street; Alderman Simmons and Jesse White (then Cathedral surveyor) were present. The exact time of day was asked by the Alderman, who said, 'if those turrets of the cathedral gate were away we should see the church clock from the bank door. Can't you pull them down, Jesse?' 'It shall be done,' replied Jesse; and it was done. They were reported to be insecure and too heavy for the gate, and down they came. Jesse White put up wooden pinnacles to the nave of the Cathedral. The plea was economy, yet wood was then as dear as stone. He was clever as a surveyor, and a man of substance in body and in pocket.

## The last 150 years

In 1825 Canterbury awoke from a long slumber. The city burst with new energy; trade and industry were on the move and the world's first passenger railway was commenced to improve communications with London; even a canal was proposed to link the city with the open sea. In the cathedral a new regime was established that was to have a profound effect upon the architecture. On 2 June Hugh Percy became dean of Canterbury, a man of strong will and deeply rooted ideas, especially when it came to Gothic architecture. Percy determined to rid the cathedral of its 'classical' excrescences and to restore the beauty and harmony of the mediaeval building – notions that were to mutilate many of England's churches. Canterbury was fortunate to have a new surveyor, George Austin, whose skill and enthusiasm for mediaeval architecture enabled the momentum of reform at Canterbury to continue beyond the brief office of Percy. The eighteenth-century panelling of the presbytery and crossing were thrown out and the Eastry screen and the various tombs restored to view. Next, the dean determined to remove James Burrough's altar-piece, and actually built a new 'Gothic' screen behind it while awaiting the approval of the chapter to remove the 'antique' intruder. The altar-piece duly disappeared in 1826, exposing the new screen; 'the specimen in confectionary perpendicular which the late Mr Austin inflicted on Canterbury Cathedral'.[19] Percy's devotion to the Gothic was more theatrical than accurate, and for the first time since 1180 the high Altar was removed from its ancient site to a more remote position:[20]

19 G. Smith, *Chron. Hist.*, p. 345.
20 W. Caröe, 'The choir of Canterbury Cathedral', *Archaeologia*, 62, pt 2, 1911, p. 362.

They [the choir screens] were both destroyed by Austin in about 1825, when the present piece of spurious Gothic synchronized with the falsification of the medieval scheme for this part of the church. This, which had survived with dignity all the changes and chances of Reformation, Renaissance and Revolution, had to succumb at last to the milk and water of restoration, and all the indignity and inanity attaching thereto. The altar was elevated to the top of the ascent, where it has no business to be. The patriarchal chair had been dethroned somewhat earlier. The disposition of the steps was also altered for the worse.

The dean had even less regard for Romanesque architecture, for he permitted the bricking up of the south aisle of the crypt in order to provide the Huguenots with a more convenient chapel, incorporating the aisle with the Black Prince's chantry. But one undoubted improvement of this period was the removal of the organ-pipes out of sight and up into the south choir tribune. This action was accompanied by Austin's expert repair of the columns and capitals of the north choir arcade damaged by the erection of the organ of 1663. The remaining sections of the seventeenth-century panelling in the choir were removed in 1836 when the Eastry screens were restored and glazed.

A contemporary account of the Cathedral and the activities of Dean Percy is given by the last editor of Gostling's *A Walk in and about the City of Canterbury* in 1825 :[21]

21   *A Walk*, pp. 346–9.

The present Dean of Canterbury (the Honourable and Very Reverend Doctor Hugh Percy), has been chief promoter of the repairs and decorations which this venerable cathedral has lately undergone; and, to his unwearied attention may be attributed the vast improvement which has taken place in the interior. It was ascertained after some trifling renovations, that the groins of the roof, in many places, had given way, and that considerable danger might ensue, if they were suffered to remain without repair: the shafts of the columns of the nave, were unsightly in consequence of the numerous iron bolts which had been driven in them by the soldiers of Oliver Cromwell: the reformists, at the same time, likewise greatly injured the plinths by lighting fires against them: and the thick coatings of white-wash, with which the whole was covered, hid many imperfections, besides numerous beautiful frescoes, which could not be preserved by reason of the adhesive nature of the coating.

The plan of rendering the interior of the building uniform, was commenced with Becket's Chapel. The dingy superfices of the columns were carefully cleansed, and every indentation, however trifling, was filled up: in the next place, the ceiling underwent the same process, and the fresco-paintings were substituted by stirious ornaments. The small pillars, extending round the triforium, were rendered of one hue; and where age had diminished their size, they have been repaired with a composition called mastic.

The beautiful mosaic or tesselated pavement, rich in varied colours, is a fine specimen of masonic skill. This pavement is formed in circles, each circle consisting of semi-circles and various triangles; the ensemble is complete; and since its restoration, we know not whether to admire most the beautiful architecture of the edifice, or the exquisite workmanship below.

Before we leave this spot, it is necessary to observe, that a new altar piece has been erected, in unison with the Gothic architecture of the choir, built of Caen stone, which has withstood the pelting of the pitiless storm for ages in Saint Augustine's monastery. It was deemed preferable to abandon the site of the old screen, in order to give a lengthened appearance to the choir, which it will have the effect of doing; and, when the wainscoting, extending from the stalls to the present altar, is removed, and the interstices of the columns filled up with glass sashes, it will present, on the north side, the beautiful stained windows, and the ancient monuments on the south; and we believe the intention of the projector will then be complete.

The pinnacles have been taken from the Organ, and, in order to save manual exertion, a pair of horizontal bellows have been added, and the effect is such as was anticipated. The rich tone of this powerful instrument, is not surpassed by any one in England. It was the one used at the commemoration of Handel, in Westminster Abbey.

We now arrive at the screen, but we omitted to mention that the north and south aisles of the choir, have undergone the same process as the choir itself. It has been asserted by competent judges, that the screen or entrance is the finest part of the whole building, and as far as the eye or judgment of a casual observer, is capable of discriminating, we think they will yield to that opinion. The length of time this portion occupied in completing, is incredible; but the workmanlike manner in which it has been executed, and the splendour of its appearance, sufficiently repay the liberality of the chapter, who have erected an iron barrier, in order to preserve its beauty; and to prevent the hand of curiosity from defacing the delicate touches of the chisel.

Without descending the steps leading to the nave, the ceiling of the great tower, and its ornaments, sufficiently engross attention. This part was completed before the alteration of the choir, and is calculated to fill the spectator with admiration and wonder.

The aisles of the nave, replete with emblazonment, were left until the completion of the choir. Mr. Austin, the superintendent, has here displayed considerable skill and taste, not only in repairing the dilapidations of time, but in decorating the ornaments in a manner that calls forth expressions of satisfaction from every visitor.

The north as well as the south cross aisle, will be executed in a similar manner, and the thousands of pounds which have been expended in restoring to its pristine grandeur, a building consecrated to devotion and the worship of God, will be repaid by its lasting magnificence.

This seemingly callous attitude towards the ancient fabric and the surviving remnants of its mediaeval decoration was shared by the dean and chapter. Archaeological interest and considerations came a poor second to the possibility of presenting a neat and tidy interior to the casual visitor. No better example of this official attitude can be found than the tragic saga of the old north-west tower (see Fig. 20). As early as 1824, Lanfranc's venerable tower was thought to be in a dangerous state and Thomas Hopper, a London architect, was brought in to give his advice. His report provides an interesting account of the structure – then 750 years old:[22]

22 Woodruff and Danks, *Mems CC*, pp. 360–1.

The foundations are sound, also are the inner ashlar and pillars. The external ashlar, excepting the part above the top water table, is flawed in many places and the surface is nearly gone. The rubble work, composing the core, is very defective, and split in many parts. The projecting angle of the tower is cracked in several places, and many of the stones are crushed. The upper part of the tower is split on each of its four sides, and the angle next to the side aisle is not perpendicular. The outer wall on the sides has several cracks and the columns and jambs of the windows are crushed. Part of the staircase is broken by the settlement in the outer wall. Many of the steps have fallen, and several more are in a crippled state . . . The wall on the west side has been much injured by the iron tie-bar . . . Much of the present defective state of the tower is owing to the manner in which it was built. The core is composed of small stones mixed with bad lime and rubbish, without binding stones or through courses . . . Injury has been done to the tower by the introduction of the pointed arches. A sufficient substance of wall was not left at the angles to form a butment to resist the pressure of the arches, and the effect of that deficiency has been increased by the removal of the spire, the weight of which pressing down upon the angles of the tower acts as a butment for that purpose . . .

23  Ibid., p. 361.

Hopper concluded his report with the following recommendations:[23]

Under all circumstances, the surveyors do not recommend the taking down of the tower, which, notwithstanding its defects, is an interesting relic of the most ancient style of ecclesiastical architecture.

Despite this advice, the old tower was doomed. Not only did it arouse the consternation of those who thought it dangerous but it offended the taste of early nineteenth-century correctness by its uncompromising barbarism and stern appearance. It simply failed to match the Perpendicular prettiness of its fellow and, as every contemporary student of mediaeval architecture knew, west fronts had to balance. And so, in 1831, the tower was demolished by Act of Parliament and £24,515 laid out for its replacement (see Fig. 120). The new tower was designed by George Austin and was an attempt at a copy of the adjoining Chichele tower. The work involved rebuilding the entire western and northern walls – those against the church were left standing as they had been incorporated into the Perpendicular nave (see Fig. 19). Hence the eastern wall of the tower retains important features from Lanfranc's work. The new tower is serviceable enough, though the Caen stone facing was soon eaten away by coal pollution from the near-by cathedral gas-works, and by about 1900 the tower had to be extensively refaced. Austin could not resist a few added frills of his own – attenuated crocketed pinnacles and heavy crockets over the windows – embellishments that soon appeared on the adjacent fifteenth-century tower. The rebuilding of Lanfranc's tower robbed the cathedral of its most venerable relic and an outstanding example of early Romanesque architecture. The new regularity of the cathedral rendered it thoroughly English, whereas the previous quaint asymmetry had added a gallic touch to the Kentish landscape.

By 1834 the cloisters were sufficiently dilapidated to require a thorough repair, unfortunately carried out in rather poor stone. Two years later another irreparable loss was inflicted upon the cathedral when the houses infilling the south aisle of the infirmary were swept clear to reveal the Romanesque arches. Evidently the intruders were thought to be post-

Reformation; in fact, they were the lodgings of the sub-prior erected within the aisle in the early fifteenth century. The visual release of the arcade from such magnificent trappings was a sour reward. Further 'tidying up' resulted in the removal of the Cemetery gate in 1841. This was taken down from its twelfth-century site between St Anselm's chapel and the plumbery and re-used as an entrance to the garden south of Meister Homers. The destruction of the mediaeval boundary between the lay and monastic burial-ground threw open the southern precincts and created the 'park' setting so loved by the nineteenth century.

Several 'Gothic' improvements inside the church were undertaken in the 1840s, so undoing most of the achievements of the previous centuries. The Tenison throne canopy was ejected and replaced by a 'wedding-cake' designed by Austin and erected in 1844. Greater discretion was displayed when Butterfield was commissioned to design the choir pulpit in 1846, an eloquent explanation of his high reputation. A large section of the Eastry screen was cut down to provide space for Archbishop William Howley's vacuous monument – its dismal design introduces the single bland note into the choir interior – but it does mark a new interest in the cathedral by its archbishops. Few of the eighteenth- and early nineteenth-century archbishops of Canterbury ever set foot in the city. They were enthroned by proxy and thereafter chose to reside at Lambeth. While Howley was interred at Adisham outside Canterbury, his monument within the cathedral tokens a new relationship between the Primate and his cathedral.

The economic changes within the Church of England left the financing of any restoration work within the cathedral almost entirely in the hands of the Church Commissioners, and in 1862 some £20,000 was granted to the dean and chapter for various repairs, including work on the choir roof, the strengthening of the south-west tower and the restoration of sections of the west front. The repairs were under the direction of the architect Christian, assisted by the ageing George Austin:[24] 'The Dean and his architects set to work with much energy and the best intentions . . . but it is to be feared that the mantle of the mediaeval builders had not fallen evenly on this galaxy of virtue and ability.' During this period gas lighting was installed within the church, a comfort purchased at the expense of much of the exterior stonework that perished in the fumes that belched forth from the gas-works outside the west door!

The office of Dean Alford, 1857–71, saw the usual mixture of good and bad work. The ancient and picturesque Chequer building perched above the infirmary cloister was ruthlessly torn down in 1868, the exquisite stair turret of the south-east transept was saved from disintegration, the fifteenth-century refitting of St Andrew's chapel was ripped out while a new entry to the north-east transept was erected. Alford also encouraged the building of a modern cathedral library, albeit in a pseudo-Italo-Romanesque style. He, too, was responsible for the present lead parapets

24  Ibid., p. 366.

around the choir roof, modelled on those at Lincoln. A year after his death in 1871, calamity struck the church. The roof of the choir and of the Trinity Chapel was set ablaze during repairs, an awesome fire that threatened the entire fabric. By a mixture of chance and immense courage the church was saved, but the blaze had destroyed the ancient roof and had blackened the east face of Bell Harry. Despite this serious setback, restoration work went on apace, mostly under the direction of Sir Gilbert Scott and Sir Reginald Blomfield. Scott replaced the Queen Anne pews in 1879 with Gothic stalls of a ponderous nature, while Blomfield expertly restored the crypt, Chapter House and cloister from 1896. Caröe began work at Canterbury in the same year, beginning with the building of a new 'Old Palace' in which he incorporated every remaining scrap of the mediaeval ruin. How attitudes had shifted in so short a space of time!

In the early years of the twentieth century, the exterior stone cladding of Bell Harry was meticulously repaired, again by Caröe, while the south-west tower was extensively restored by him immediately prior to the First World War. By the summer of 1914 the fabric of Canterbury Cathedral was sound and the interior swept and orderly. The transformation over the previous century had seen the elegant comfort of the Age of Reason replaced by an academic correctness that was coldly 'right and proper'. The First World War, with its disruption of convention and threat of air attack, brought with it a new awareness of the human and artistic value of England's historic monuments, and post-war financial problems encouraged the cathedral authorities and those private individuals concerned for the future of the fabric to exploit this new feeling amongst the general public. Canterbury led the nation in its concern for a permanent base which would ensure, as far as was humanly possible, the preservation of the cathedral. Thus in 1929 the Friends of Canterbury Cathedral was formed – the first such 'Friends' organization in the world. Under the initial guidance of Dean Bell, and later of the inimitable Margaret Babington, the zest of the 1920s and early 1930s was channelled into the precincts. Money-raising for restoration projects was, of course, the principal concern, but the Friends also encouraged the arts within the cathedral. Eliot's *Murder in the Cathedral* was just one of the many plays commissioned by the Friends to be performed at an annual arts festival, as they sought to establish a new relationship between cathedral and city, and with the entire English-speaking world. It must be said that, in its early years, the Friends was an extension of English society – within the context of the economic background of the 1930s it could hardly have been otherwise – but it did raise large sums of money, as well as pioneer the participation of the general public in areas from which they had been previously excluded. The principal achievements of the 1930s were the restoration of the Water Tower and the rather enthusiastic reconstruction of the facade of the Christ Church gate.

The Second World War brought about a revolution in almost every aspect of Canterbury Cathedral. The daily threat of aerial bombardment placed a severe strain on the church and on the citizens of Canterbury. Many were killed and untold destruction wrought upon the city. Yet despite repeated attack, the cathedral escaped unscathed. No major damage was inflicted upon the fabric of the church, and thanks to the vigilance of the firewatchers the incessant shower of incendiaries was swept clear of the roofs. The stained glass was removed and buried before the declaration of war – indeed some was removed as early as the Munich crisis of 1938. Sandbags filled the nave and crypt and smothered the fragile monuments in the choir and Trinity Chapel. The precincts fared less well during the nightly bombings. The Victorian library received a direct hit in 1942 and the deanery was half demolished on the same night. Serious damage was inflicted upon the Eastry buildings of the Green Court, while others were lost in the southern precincts. But despite all this, and the destruction of much of the adjoining city, the cathedral church had a miraculous deliverance.

Since the war, extensive work has maintained the fabric of the church. The south-east transept stair turret and the south-west tower were repaired and cleaned and the cloister has been dramatically renewed. The library was rebuilt in a singularly awful style, a kind of Tudorbethan on Romanesque legs, while a new library was built over the infirmary cloister in a similarly bland expression. How sad that the cathedral no longer encouraged the work of the best contemporary architects – John Wastell was not chosen for his ability to design a faceless sham. With due regard for proportion, materials and the monastic plan, the most modern and innovative architecture could complement the achievements of the past.

The cathedral must now face all the problems of the modern world, most especially pollution and tourism. The extensive replacement of exterior fabric that has occurred in recent years may prove an over-hasty reaction to the problems of increasing decay as well as a regrettable development from an archaeological viewpoint. The cathedral is of value because its very fabric is ancient, and that value decreases with every stone that is removed and replaced by modern work. The future will not thank us for preserving the mere appearance of our great historic monuments – the attitude of the nineteenth century that cost us so dear. The phenomenal growth of tourism has brought a new and appreciative audience to Canterbury. Millions flock to the church every year – their motives mixed, perhaps some have none at all, for many it is just on the 'tourist map'. The tourist machine is a curious monster, its trappings are inconvenient and often unsightly, yet it has created a new role for the cathedral not unlike the one that it played throughout the later Middle Ages. Once again the cathedral has become a source of wonder, of interest and admiration. Then it was for the thousands of believers, now it serves the whole world. Exposure to such a magnificent monument must have some affect on the individual, and if there is to be any hope of changing the attitudes and values of modern society towards its economic and environmental victims, it is through public awareness of the problem and of the rich artistic and spiritual rewards that must be handed on.

# THE STAINED GLASS

Canterbury Cathedral is justly famous for its mediaeval glass. The history of this collection and its important place in the study of painting in the Middle Ages lies outside the scope of an architectural history of the building,[1] but as the iconography of the windows was a major concern of the patron, some consideration of the glass-painters' requirements must have influenced the decisions of the master masons. Master mason and master glazier worked in close co-operation to integrate structural necessity with iconographic desirability, and a change in plan from one could cause serious problems for the other; for example, the extended Trinity Chapel of William the Englishman. Until 1540, the cathedral retained most of the glass that had been made for the various architectural campaigns. Only the surviving section of St Anselm's choir had lost its original glass of c. 1110–30, and was then filled with windows from about 1175 to 1200. The whole of the choir, with its eastern transept, presbytery, Trinity Chapel and Corona, still contained its late Romanesque and early Gothic glass. No windows are known to have been lost, except in the chapel of St Anselm where the twin southern windows had been replaced by the large Kent school window of 1336; this, no doubt, was filled with glass from that period.

The western parts of the cathedral contained glass from the later Middle Ages. The nave was glazed from c. 1390, the west window from c. 1396, while the transept received its glass between about 1425 and 1485. In addition there were considerable quantities of stained glass in the Chapter House dating from the fifteenth century, and probably more in other claustral buildings such as the Prior's Chapel which was refenestrated c. 1250, the infirmary chapel with windows of c. 1330 and 1450. The largest collection of glass found today in the cathedral dates from the later years of the twelfth and early decades of the thirteenth centuries, while important panels survive from the fifteenth-century glazing together with yet more glass that has appeared since the dissolution that does not necessarily belong in the cathedral.

The stained glass from the Gothic choir has survived well – perhaps because of its relative inaccessibility. There were originally three main iconographic schemes in the William of Sens building, with a fourth theme added, or at least expanded, when the Englishman decided upon an even larger eastern chapel. The choir aisles and the western and terminal walls of the eastern transept contained twelve windows depicting the Life and Passion of Christ. The cycle began at the western end of the north choir aisle with the Life of the Virgin (destroyed seventeenth century) and continued to the western end of the southern aisle with the Crucifixion, Entombment and Resurrection.[2] The

1 The most important and detailed study of the early glass to date is M. Caviness, *The Early Stained Glass of Canterbury Cathedral.* This will soon be joined by Caviness's study of all the mediaeval glass at Canterbury to be published by the British Academy as part of the *Corpus Vitrearum* for England. The other major study is B. Rackham, *The Ancient Glass of Canterbury Cathedral.*

2 M. R. James, *The Verses formerly inscribed on Twelve Windows in the choir of Canterbury Cathedral,* Cambridge Antiquarian Society, Octavo Pubs, no. 38, 1901.

sequence was interrupted on the eastern faces of the transept by four windows depicting the lives of those saints in whose honour the apsidal chapels were dedicated, St Martin of Tours and St Stephen (north) and St Gregory and St John the Evangelist (south). The two windows of the presbytery aisles may have continued this theme with the Lives of St Alphege (north) and of St Dunstan (south) – these being the nearest windows to the shrines of those saints. This would seem to be a more appropriate arrangement for the iconography than has been suggested elsewhere.[3]

The third iconographic theme occupied the clerestory windows throughout the choir, the transept, presbytery and most of the Trinity Chapel – a chronological representation of the ancestors of Christ. The first window, containing the figures of God the Father and Adam, filled the westernmost clerestory window on the north side, and the cycle was completed directly opposite with the Virgin and Christ. In the apse of the Trinity Chapel, the series was broken by three or five windows containing biblical subjects and the major scenes from the Life of Christ, and it is here that the enlargement of the building post-1179 affected the original genealogical sequence.[4]

The aisles of the Trinity Chapel contained twelve windows with scenes from the Life and posthumous miracles of St Thomas. The five windows of the Corona contained a Tree of Jesse (?) and at least one typological window depicting the Passion, Resurrection, Ascension and Pentecost.

The surviving glass from the period 1175–1220 has been subjected to serious loss, various restorations and substantial rearrangements, especially in the eighteenth and nineteenth centuries. Most of the Geneaology figures were moved into the nave and west transept in 1799, and later, Victorian copies were substituted in the clerestory. Much of the work of the restorers, especially Samuel Caldwell, is of high quality and will provide knotty problems for the glass experts for centuries to come. The original arrangement of most of the glass in the choir aisles can be determined with the help of earlier writers and from a correct identification of the various scenes and figures. Fortunately, the subjects depicted in the twelve windows of the Life of Christ were detailed in an early fourteenth-century manuscript in the Cathedral Library MS. 246,[5] which confirms that glass from a number of windows has found its way into the two surviving windows of the north choir aisle. The subjects were arranged typologically: that is, the scenes selected from the Life of Christ were accompanied by biblical parallels which commented or explained the primary subject. These commentaries were often subtle and academic – i.e. the Marriage Feast of Cana and the Ages of Man and of the World – and their complexity raises serious doubts that the windows were ever intended as the 'poor man's bible' of popular imagination. In the first surviving window, north choir aisle II, the first fourteen scenes from the top are in their original position, the rest were moved from other windows in the cycle and relate to the parable of the Sower. The adjoining window, III, contains the early life of Christ, with a few additions from other windows to make up for the losses. No glass survives *in situ* from the Christ cycle within the transept or the south aisle – the scenes of the Ascension, etc., now in the south aisle triforium may have come from the windows below or from the similar cycle that occupied the apse clerestory in the Trinity Chapel.

3  Professor Caviness places these cycles elsewhere.

4  See pp. 116–17.

5  James, op. cit.

Of the Lives of the saints, only a few scenes survive: one from the Life of St Martin, and several from the Lives of Alphege and Dunstan now collected in the north aisle triforium.

The Trinity Chapel glass depicting the miracles of St Thomas has suffered similar deprivations, with much lost or restored. By 1912, several scenes relating to the miracle of Adam the Forester and that of William Kennet had found their way into the north choir aisle triforium, while other pieces have 'travelled' overseas. But the north aisle of the Trinity Chapel preserves much of its original glass and illustrates the general effect gained from a complete series, albeit made up with modern additions.[6] The texture and colour of the north aisle provide a perfect complement for the rich tones of the architecture. Little survives in the Corona other than the majority of the axial window and two figures from a Tree of Jesse.

No original glass from the cathedral has survived from the years between 1220 and 1396. The first glass from the late Middle Ages can be found in the upper tracery of the west window which includes the arms of Richard II and of his wives, Anne of Bohemia and Isabella of France, shields that should pre-date 1399. The remaining lights contain apostles and saints which, according to Woodruff, came from the tracery of the Chapter House.[7] A similar provenance is accorded to the seven kings in the main lights below, beginning with Canute (Fig. 159) and ending with Stephen, but despite the claims of Westlake that they were moved about 1800,[8] Gostling plainly refers to them as being present in the nave in 1774. Had all twenty-one lights of either the nave or the Chapter House west windows been filled with the successive kings of England, the line would have extended to Henry VII, with William the Conqueror, Henry III and Henry VI occupying the three central lights. However, a date of post-1485 might be considered too late for these figures.

The south window of the western transept contains many original fragments, probably dating from post-1425, together with the majority of the remaining Genealogy figures from the choir. Much of the fifteenth-century glass from this window was heraldic, and it included the arms of Lord Cromwell, granted in 1433. The glass in the Royal window over the Martyrdom dates from *c.* 1482, though it may have been completed only after 1485.[9] All the tracery lights have survived, though two have been removed to the Water Tower. Beneath are portraits of Edward IV and his family, magnificently realized and delicately coloured. The window once contained the seven glorious appearances of the Virgin as well as depictions of St Thomas, and this window was the particular object of Puritan hatred in the 1640s. When Culmer smashed out the various figures, he zealously recorded that he had 'rattled down proud Becket's glassy bones'.[10] Despite its position over the Martyrdom, the Royal window was dedicated to the Virgin, whose chapel stands against the eastern wall of the transept. The east window of the elegant chapel also retains much of its glass, made after 1495 as a memorial to Archdeacon Bourchier. This window was repaired in 1544, and the lower sections made up again in recent years.

The Water Tower contains two panels from the tracery of the Royal window with the figures of St Martin and St Wilfrid, together with other glass from unknown sources. The quality of the two removed panels, possibly German

6 Four shillings was spent in 1544 'mending the windows and casements where the shryne was and in our Lady chapell', Woodruff and Danks, *Mems CC*, p. 299.

7 Ibid., p. 430. Also G. Smith, *Chron. Hist.*, p. 381 who quotes Westlake.

8 G. Smith, *Chron. Hist.*, p. 381.

9 Two heraldic devices point to a late completion date. The arms of Henry VII now appear between Edward IV and his queen, though the device is clearly inserted and may have come from elsewhere. Above the first group of daughters, including Elizabeth of York and Cecily, is the device of Welles, generally taken to be for Viscount Welles who married Cecily in 1487. Why her marriage should be commemorated by the replacement of the Welles arms for those of the king of Scotland, her first husband, is a mystery. After all, her sister beside her was, by 1485, Queen of England.

10 See pp. 232–3.

159 (*opposite*) Head of Canute from the west window, fifteenth century

work of about 1480, makes one regret the relative inaccessibility of the remaining tracery lights. The exaggerated drawing of the faces recalls the grotesque images of contemporary Flemish artists, and their style might provide some support for later dating of the apostles, saints and kings in the nave west window.

Little modern glass of note can be found in the cathedral, with the exception of the remarkable copies of the twelfth-century clerestory glass which includes an amount of re-used mediaeval pieces. Of the subsequent glass, one window deserves attention – the Nativity window in the south-west transept, made in 1903 by C. Whall. The style retains vestiges of the Arts and Crafts movement while expressing more than a passing interest in Art Nouveau. Three other donations must be singled out for their sheer inappropriateness: the vulgar and painful glass lurking up in the nave clerestory, the insipid and pathetic portraits of the Windsor family over the Martyrdom door, and the aggressive glass that shouts out from the Oxenden window in St Anselm's chapel. Their only justification is that they increase appreciation of the splendid work that surrounds them.

# THE TOMBS AND MONUMENTS

As might be expected, Canterbury Cathedral contains a wealth of mediaeval and later monuments, the earliest dating from the thirteenth century. The relics of the pre-Conquest archbishops, many of whom were revered as saints, were collected carefully into the Romanesque church, but sadly not one tomb or shrine has survived. The first tomb-sites within the present church are those of Lanfranc in the north-east transept chapel of St Martin, and of St Anselm, who probably lies under the apse floor in the chapel commonly dedicated in his memory. The bodies of SS Dunstan and Alphege may have been reinterred after the destruction of their shrines in 1540, though the altar steps that supported their tombs have been relaid twice since the dissolution without any recorded discovery of their remains. Their burial may have occurred elsewhere. Of the post-Conquest archbishops, seven lie in the church under unmarked graves: Lanfranc, St Anselm, Theobald (north aisle of the nave), Robert Winchelsey (probably under the floor of the south-east transept), Simon Islip, William Whittlesey, Thomas Arundel (nave – tombs destroyed 1787). Three more lie under matrix stones from which the brasses have been torn – Cardinal John Stafford and Henry Dean, both in the Martyrdom, and Cardinal John Morton in the crypt.

The tombs of fifteen archbishops still survive distributed throughout the church. They form the greater part of the collection of the mediaeval monuments at Canterbury, to which can be added the tomb of one prior, one king, one queen, a duke, an earl, a countess and several other important lay people. Many of the tombs were prepared long before the death of the 'occupyer': i.e. Chichele, 1425, died 1443; Bourchier, 1480, died 1486; Warham, 1507, died 1532; whereas some of the archbishops were not buried according to their last wishes and their tombs will post-date their deaths, i.e. Reynolds, 1327, and Courtenay, 1396.

The following list summarizes the most important tombs, including some from the post-Reformation period.

*Hubert Walter, archbishop, died 1205* – south aisle, Trinity Chapel.
Identity established by examination 1897, though correctly identified in Corpus Christi, Cambridge, MS. 298 (a Canterbury MS. of *c.* 1520 detailing the position of all the major tombs of the church). Purbeck tomb chest with gabled roof. Roof decorated with circles and lozenges, filled with magnificent series of carved heads. Sides of chest with trefoil arcade. Tomb contained complete set of vestements, etc., and chalice and patten of *c.* 1200.

*Stephen Langton, cardinal archbishop, died 1228* – St Michael's chapel.

Plain tomb chest now pushed under the altar of the Holland Chapel so that it projects into the churchyard. Great scholar and theologian, divided the Bible into books, chapter and verse. Archiepiscopacy noted for the exile under John, Magna Carta, and the Translation of the relics of St Thomas in 1220. Rebuilt the Palace at Canterbury.

*John Peckam, archbishop, died 1292* – north wall of Martyrdom.

Franciscan theologian and scholar. Accorded great honour of burial in the Martyrdom. Originally tomb was tucked into the corner formed by inner wall that screened the cloister door from the Martyrdom. Fine gabled monument, chest with niches and weepers, side pilasters decorated with ogee headed gables – an early instance of this motif – and a large gable with rich foliate carving. Tomb one of a series by the Kent school, including that of Edmund Crouchback in Westminster Abbey and Bishop Louth in Ely. Painting restored 1825. Fine oak effigy.

*Walter Reynolds, archbishop, died 1327* – south choir aisle.

Desired to be buried at the foot of his predecessor, Winchelsey, in the south-east transept. For some reason, he was buried in the south choir aisle. Tomb chest set into socle of the most westerly window in the aisle. Originally surmounted by an openwork (?) gable against the window. Chest decorated with ogee arcade. Fine foliate capitals only remains of canopy. Small effigy, not that of Reynolds but of a prior, possibly Richard Oxenden, moved from St Michael's chapel.

*Henry of Eastry, prior, died 1331* – south choir aisle.

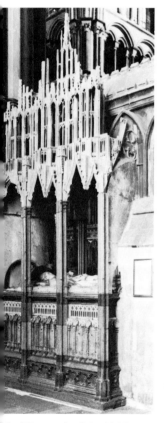

Only prior of Christ Church to be accorded a standing monument. Tomb in next bay east of Reynolds. Treasurer's Accounts of 1331 record £21 3s 4d as payment for the tomb. Canted chest with elaborate gabled wings and niches for the figures of SS Sythe and Apollonie. Side gables with 'wire-netting' tracery. Main gable against window lost. Fine effigy of prior under vaulted canopy with painted decoration. Figure appears to have been made as a floor monument, reset into a standing tomb. The identity of this tomb has long been a subject of confusion.

*Simon Meopham, archbishop, died 1333* – entrance to St Anselm's chapel.

Ambitious monument all but barring the entrance. Tomb in form of a sarcophagus, enclosed within a pierced double screen, with twin doors. Black painted tomb and surrounding arches decorated with a display of tracery and angels, very well preserved. Interior face of screen has elegant sculpture filling the spandrels. Original ironwork.

*John Stratford, archbishop, died 1348* – south side of presbytery (Figure 160).

Perhaps the finest stone monument in the church. A fantasy of fretting and filigree spun round a splendid alabaster effigy. The quality of the work, its many early Perpendicular details and its uncomfortable setting within the Eastry screen suggest a London product, perhaps from the royal workshop, shipped to Canterbury and assembled on site. Faultless display of architectural elements and polychrome materials – Purbeck, Caen and alabaster. Tragically, the three spires proved too easy a target for the despoilers, who inflicted cruel damage upon them.

*Thomas Bradwardine, archbishop, died (of plague) 1349* – south wall, St Anselm's chapel.

Simple tomb chest beneath Oxenden window.

**60** The tomb of Archbishop Stratford in the eastern crossing, *c.* 1340

*Edward of Woodstock, Prince of Wales, died 1376* – south arcade, Trinity Chapel.

Famous tomb of legendary Black Prince, consisting of a Purbeck tomb chest, latten gilt effigy and painted wooden tester. Suspended above are copies of the funeral achievements preserved elsewhere in the church. The tomb chest is austerely simple, showing the magnificent effigy to advantage. The underside of the tester retains fragments of elaborate painted depiction of the Trinity. There may have been a small altar opposite this tomb; the step is very worn, and the Black Prince's arms were formerly in the base of the window. Iron surround of the tomb (?) fifteenth century.

*Simon Sudbury, archbishop, murdered 1381* – south side of high Altar (see Fig. 70).

Elaborate monument with low arcaded tomb chest and high vaulted canopy – a design that allowed daylight to pass through the tomb and on to the high Altar. The monument is really a reworking of the Stratford tomb, only larger and less elegant. A feature is made of the cornice, based on the Eastry screen that formerly crossed the site. Rather precocious angle pilasters with trapped necking peeping through. No effigy.

*Lady Mohun, benefactress, died 1404* – Our Lady Undercroft.

The tomb was already built when Lady Mohun founded a chantry at this altar in 1395. The canopied tomb interrupts the superb screens of the chapel, but as they too are undated the evidence of the tomb is unhelpful. Tomb and figure very much mutilated.

*William Courtenay, archbishop, died 1396* – south arcade, Trinity Chapel.

Curiously dry alabaster monument to a great benefactor of the cathedral. Founder of All Saints College, Maidstone, where he intended to be buried. Richard II, arriving at Canterbury the day following the archbishop's death, ordered that his friend be buried at the foot of the king's father. The tomb therefore post-dates the archbishop's death. There are certain resemblances between the effigy and that on the tomb of William of Wykeham in Winchester.

*Elizabeth Swynbourne, Lady Tryvet, died 1433* – entrance to St Gabriel's chapel. Sadly damaged tomb of a benefactress of the cathedral, who requested burial in the church in her will of 1421. Dart shows her tomb in a better state than it is seen today. Figure of an elderly woman dressed rather like an abbess.

*Henry IV and Joan of Navarre, died 1413 and 1437* – north arcade, Trinity Chapel.

Spectacular alabaster double tomb of Henry and his second wife. On his death in 1413, the king's coffin was laid on an elaborate hearse next to the shrine of St Thomas, draped in a rich cloth. Thus it remained for many years, being occasionally decked out with flags. Eventually, in the reign of his grandson Henry VI, the elaborate tomb was erected, probably between 1437 and 1439 when the adjoining chantry chapel was built and the magnificent hearse sold. The twin figures lie under identical canopies, though the effigies appear to be by different hands. Possibly the king's figure was made for a single tomb, *c.* 1436 prior to the death of Joan, and the tomb then redesigned for them both. Lavish tomb chest, niched and painted, exquisite canopies and figure sculpture, all executed in alabaster with painted and gilded highlights. Wooden tester with some painting, and one or two original wooden angels. Fifteenth-century ironwork.

*Lady Margaret Holland, Countess of Somerset, Duchess of Clarence, died 1439* – St Michael's chapel.

Enormous monument erected in 1439 by Lady Margaret for herself and her two husbands, John Beaufort, Earl of Somerset, brother of Henry IV, and Thomas, Duke of Clarence, brother of Henry V. Both were previously buried in the Trinity Chapel. Marble tomb chest with three majestic alabaster figures; their remarkable preservation due, no doubt, to the remoteness of the chapel.

*Henry Chichele, cardinal archbishop, died 1443* – north side of presbytery.

The tomb was already built in 1425 and may have been designed by Thomas Mapilton. Open tomb chest revealing rotting (wooden?) corpse, while above is the effigy of the archbishop dressed in his full pontificals. The tomb stands under a wooden tester supported by ornate wooden piers, all restored. Chichele founded All Souls, Oxford, which is responsible for the upkeep of his tomb – hence its pristine state and appalling statuary. The sculpture made for it after the Restoration has found its way to the top of the pulpitum.

*John Kemp, cardinal archbishop, died 1454* – south side of presbytery.

Kemp's archiepiscopacy was so brief that he can hardly have finished his monument before he was put under it. Marble chest, no effigy, elaborate wooden canopied top, restored, with three spires under a wooden tester – a carpentry reworking of the adjoining Stratford tomb. The door west of the tomb appears to have been remade at this time, in a 'period' style evidently thought to be like early fourteenth-century Eastry work.

*Thomas Bourchier, cardinal archbishop, died 1486* – north side of high Altar.

Tomb erected by agreement with convent in 1480, that specified it should allow light to reach the adjoining altar. Hence it repeats the Sudbury design with low chest and high canopy, only now everything is bigger and better. Result is splendid, if a little top-heavy. Purbeck chest raised above the aisle to compensate for height of sanctuary floor – Sudbury's does not do this. Was there a change in the altar steps about 1400 as part of Chillenden's rearrangement of the high Altar? Niches with iron hooks for weepers, and delicately carved love-knots, the Bourchier device, and difficult to cut in Purbeck. Stone end piers supporting large flat-topped canopy, almost the size of a chantry chapel. Niches with fine vaults and tiny figures of female saints. The designer of this work should be identifiable, but is not. It is first-rate work, with a number of indications of a Windsor or Westminster provenance.

*John Morton, cardinal archbishop, died 1501* – south aisle of crypt.

Morton is actually buried under a matrix stone in the chapel of Our Lady Undercroft; tomb in the aisle is only a cenotaph. The tomb chest fills one of the arcade arches, while the arch soffit has been transformed into an elaborate niched tester. The tomb is very mutilated. It was probably erected *c.* 1495, when John Wastell was the cardinal's mason for the new central tower. However, the tomb may not be by him but another master, perhaps from the royal workshop. There are tragic remains of high quality sculpture.

*William Warham, archbishop, died 1532* – north wall of Martyrdom.

The tomb, together with its tiny chantry that lay outside the north transept wall, was built in the summer of 1507. Chapel destroyed and tomb altered early in the nineteenth century. Tomb chest with recumbent figure, within a huge architectural frame with gabled canopies. The chest is now central but was originally to the west, there being a small door into the chapel. Tiny window remains over figure. Restoration by (?) Austin. Design of tomb recalls contemporary tomb of Bishop Redmond in Ely, and several motifs indicate that both may have been designed by John Wastell.

*Reginald Pole, cardinal archbishop, died 1558* – north side of Corona.

Remains of a splendid early Renaissance ensemble with sarcophagus and extensive painted cycle, best seen in Gostling's *A Walk . . .* of 1774. The 'Marble' tomb is in fact wooden, while the paintings were scraped off in 1825. Needless to say, the loss of a large English religious painting of this period is tragic.

A number of post-Reformation monuments are worthy of note. Outstanding among them is the Renaissance set-piece for Nicholas Wooton, the first dean, died 1567, who is seen kneeling in prayer. The head is truly remarkable and was often attributed to Bernini! The cathedral is well stocked with Jacobean and Carolean monuments, including the remains of the Neville family tombs rescued from the demolition of the Brenchley Chapel in 1787, and now placed in the south choir aisle. Notable amongst them is Dean Neville, died 1619. The Lady Chapel contains three splendid pieces, the thoroughly nasty tomb of Dean Fotherby, died 1619, emerging from a veritable carnary; the dramatic monument to Dean Boys, died 1625, who is caught in pensive mood in his study (see Fig. 139), and the portrait memorial to the unfortunate Dean Bargrave, died 1643, painted on copper. A fourth monument, the memorial tablet to Alexander Chapmen, died 1629, placed over the site of the Martyrdom, was removed in 1970 to a more discreet position at the top of the north choir aisle stairs.

The Holland Chapel is so bursting with monuments that it is all but impossible to see where one ends and the next begins. The Thornhurst family tombs occupy most of the north wall, including Lady Thornhurst, died 1609, Dorothy, died 1620, and Thomas, died 1627. The group is completed by a monument to William Prude, died 1632. The chapel also contains a brave monument to Sir George Rooke, died 1708, conqueror of Gibraltar.

The aisles of the nave recall those of Westminster Abbey – littered with monuments of an awful variety. With the tombs and chantry chapels pre-1787, the nave must have been in a turmoil. Some fine memorials survive caught up in the general chaos, particularly on the north side: the Hales tomb of 1596 depicting a burial at sea; the superb head of Orlando Gibbons, 1625, by Nicholas Stone; the elegant tablet to Dr Thomas Lawrence by Flaxman, 1806, and the small plaque to Edgar Evelyn Ravenhill of 1907 with lettering by Eric Gill. One other modern tomb that cannot be avoided is the monument in the Corona to Archbishop Temple, died 1902. The impressive bronze effigy of the archbishop in prayer was by F. W. Pomeroy, who should be better known. The frenetic architectural setting was by W. D. Caröe, who should have known better.

# THE PAINTINGS

The mediaeval paintings of Canterbury Cathedral represent one of the finest collections in the country, with important works surviving from the twelfth to the fifteenth centuries. The Romanesque mural paintings are of outstanding interest, both for their quality and state of preservation. The following summary can provide only an indication of the range and extent of these works.

## The twelfth century

St Anselm's choir was famous for its painted decoration, but the fire of 1174 destroyed all but one work – the St Paul in the south ambulatory tower chapel. Another more extensive fresco remains in the crypt, while yet another cycle from the twelfth century was preserved until some time between c. 1920 and 1970 in the Infirmary Chapel. The St Gabriel cycle within the crypt chapel commonly dedicated to that archangel has deteriorated since 1945. The surviving scenes depict the naming of St John the Baptist, to whom the chapel was originally dedicated. Other fragments can be seen within the apse, including sections of a Christ in Majesty surrounded by flying angels, and the ghost of a nativity cycle. Cleaning and restoration work since 1970 has revealed further paintings on the interior of the apse entrance wall, while yet more painted decoration may survive beneath the plaster around the main windows of the chapel. Further work exists above the chapel entrance that once formed part of a complete vault cycle in the main chapel.

The style of the apse painting illustrates the strength of Byzantine influence on Romanesque work of the period, with damp folds, nests of Vs and white 'comb' highlights. Tristram judged that 'these paintings should certainly be ranked amongst the finest examples of Western European art of the twelfth century'.[1] In the apse of the chapel above, now called St Anselm's but dedicated originally to SS Peter and Paul, one panel from a double cycle of the lives of those saints survives almost hidden behind the apse entrance arch. The scene of St Paul and the Viper on the island of Malta was concealed behind a buttress inserted by William of Sens during the rebuilding of the choir (Figure 161). The painting was discovered only in the nineteenth century when the additional masonry was removed. The elegant pose, the rich colour and exquisite quality of the work place it at the height of artistic achievement. The strong Byzantinizing style recalls the mid-twelfth-century MS. of the Canterbury scriptorium – the Lambeth and Dover Bibles – and parallels have also been drawn between the

1 E. W. Tristram, *The Paintings of Canterbury Cathedral*, p. 4.

**161** St Paul and the Viper
from St Anselm's chapel,
*c.* 1160

2 See pp. 52–4.

Canterbury painting and the Bury Bible. Certainly, the figure of St Paul has all
the ease and subtlety of that great work. The plaster base and parts of the
decorative frieze above the figure extends around the angle formed by the apse
and the entrance arch, indicating that the fresco was painted after the
strengthening of the tower chapels. The structural alterations within the south
ambulatory tower chapel are crucial to the dating of the paintings of St Paul and
St Gabriel. The first major alterations occurred *c.* 1100, while the Romanesque
choir was still under construction. At this point, the windows of the tower
chapels were raised in accordance with the scale of the aisle entrance arch and the
entry into the apse. Subsequently, it was discovered that these arches were too
high and wide for the weight of the towers above, and additional strengthening
was introduced. This involved the extension of the piers of the apse entry and the
thickening of the arch mouldings of both major arches. A similar strengthening
occurs in the crypt chapels. The date of this exercise was discussed earlier,[2] and a
date of *c.* 1150–60 for the alterations to the main level chapels can be proposed by
comparisons with the sculpture, rib vaults and mouldings from the buildings of
Prior Wibert. The exact date of the extension of the crypt apse piers is impossible
to determine – it may form part of the earliest reconstruction of the chapels of *c.*
1100, but its precise alignment with the additional work in the chapels above
could question their sequence of construction. The base plaster for both sets of
paintings runs unbroken across the additional masonry and herein lies the

problem. Stylistically the Gabriel paintings should pre-date the St Paul. The latter is more refined, and displays a complete integration of those Byzantine elements that appear so consciously in the lower work. Yet the base plaster under St Paul continues over the additional masonry within the apse, work that sits exactly on the added pier buttresses in the crypt. If different dates are demanded on style, then it has to be proposed that the crypt additions were part of the first alterations, of *c.* 1100, and that in the second phase, *c.* 1160, great care was taken to ensure that the new work above fitted precisely onto the existing work in the crypt. However the evidence might be interpreted, a date of 1160 would seem entirely appropriate for the painting of St Paul; indeed it was the accepted date for the work long before any attempt was made to establish the dating sequence of the architectural alterations. A date nearer to *c.* 1120 would appear to satisfy the stylistic analysis of the Gabriel cycle. But certain elements in the fragments exposed against the interior face of the apse entrance arch have caused some comment that could cast doubt on this early date. As with so many problems at Canterbury, the lack of English material of this quality in the twelfth century renders all opinion difficult.

Other paintings of a twelfth-century date were discovered in the Infirmary Chapel in the early years of the present century, but it is to be feared that they have perished due to inadequate protection.[3]

## The thirteenth century

The thirteenth century was represented by an extensive cycle throughout the choir and the Trinity Chapel. The high vaults of the choir were decorated with demi-figures in niches that radiated from the central bosses. Tristram recalled that as recently as 1935 'on the low walls and on the lower part of the columns may still be seen large painted chevrons which probably formed part of this scheme of decoration'.[4] They have since disappeared. The ambulatory of the Trinity Chapel contained full-length figures, and in the early nineteenth century St Blaise, St Andrew, an apostle, a king, St Mary Magdalene, St Dunstan, St Thomas, St Peter, St Leonard and several others were noted on the vaults. An inscription subjoined to a figure of Henry III recorded that the cycle was painted in 1220, doubtless in time for the Translation.[5] All these paintings were scraped off, according to Gostling, some time before 1825: 'in order to render the interior uniform'. The door from the cloister into the Martyrdom and the near-by tomb of Archbishop Peckam still show traces of their former colour schemes, basically architectural painting in red and green, with occasional gilding. The colouring of the Peckam tomb was restored in 1825.

## The fourteenth century

Several of Prior Eastry's works from the early fourteenth century show fragments of paint. The east face of the pulpitum was brightly coloured and gilded, and the tiny vault within the northern screen door is still painted red and green. The Chapter House colouring was restored in the late nineteenth century, on the evidence of considerable remains. The throne is particularly brilliant, with

3 For a report on the discovery of these paintings, and a coloured depiction, see W. D. Caröe, 'Wall paintings in the Infirmary Chapel' *Archaeologia*, 63, 1911–12, pp.51–6.

4 Tristram, op. cit., p. 9.

5 For a discussion of these paintings, see M. Caviness, 'A lost cycle of Canterbury paintings of 1220', *Antiq. J.*, 54, pt 1, 1974, pp. 66–74.

its gilding and enamels, and the canopy provided a frame for a major Crucifixion scheme. Faint traces of painted designs can be found throughout the choir-shadows of sunbursts on the north side of the Eastry screens, and painted arcading on the prior's tomb in the south aisle. Many of the tomb figures were painted, particularly the alabaster effigies, and restored decoration of this nature can be seen on the Courtenay tomb of 1396. The adjoining tomb of the Black Prince retains the battered fragments of perhaps the finest panel painting of the century – the Trinity painted on the underside of the hanging tester. Despite its damaged state, the figure of God the Father can be made out, holding the Crucified Christ with the Holy Ghost perched on the cross-bar. The ensemble is enclosed within an elongated split-cusped quatrefoil, with the tetramorph filling the remaining angles.

### The fifteenth century and after

One major mural painting survives from late in the fifteenth century – the legend of St Eustache in the north choir aisle. It appears to be painted in oil straight on to the ashlar. The cycle relates the hectic and somewhat unlikely episodes of the life of the early Christian martyr, charmingly detailed and dressed in fifteenth-century attire. The date is probably *c.* 1480–1500; perhaps it was executed after the fire of *c.* 1483. It is not well lit, nor should it be in its present condition. Tristram reported that in 1929 further cycles concerning the lives of SS Christopher and George were discovered in the choir, but no trace of them survives.

The chapel of Our Lady Undercroft in the crypt has an extensive vault painting depicting the heavens. The background was blue – it now appears black, but this may be dirt – and the whole vault is powdered with sunbursts or stars. These once contained tiny concave mirrors that twinkled in the reflected candlelight – a similar motif can still be seen in the roof of St Mary's, Bury St Edmunds, of *c.* 1460. A slightly earlier date, *c.* 1450, can be proposed for the Canterbury roof, for among the coats of arms crammed into the lower sections of the paintings are those of Archbishop Stafford, 1444–52. It might be argued that the arms are a later addition to an earlier, i.e. *c.* 1380, scheme. The architectural painting scheme in the Holland Chapel was restored by Tristram in the early 1930s, though his evidence for this restoration is not at all clear. He has adopted a fourteenth-century colour contrast – red and green – that may not be entirely appropriate for *c.* 1440. At the entrance to the chapel hang two odd panel paintings depicting ecclesiastics. They are executed in a monochrome style, similar to the mural paintings in Eton College Chapel of *c.* 1480. However, the mere mention of Eton places the Canterbury works in the third or fourth rank of English art, a fact that has been emphasized in their recent cleaning. For some reason it was decided to plug certain holes in them that traditionally were the wounds of Parliamentary muskets – perhaps they were knotholes. The curious curved profile of the panels suggests that they once covered the coving of the great bracket that projected above the Holland Chapel entrance. This supported an organ, and was still in position when Britton detailed this transept arm in 1821.

The most important panel paintings of the fifteenth century, and tragically the greatest loss, were the pictures made for the tomb of Henry IV, *c.* 1440. The Coronation of the Virgin and the Murder of St Thomas once hung at either end of the alabaster tomb. Tristram painted reconstructions of both that are now hanging in the church. When faced with the minute fragments of the originals, it is difficult to accept Tristram's claim that 'they are sufficient to enable a reconstruction to be made, the accuracy of which is almost indubitable'.[6] Henry's tomb is also painted – this time blue, red and gold – and the earlier tomb of Archbishop Chichele has similar colouring, though repainted so often that nothing can be original. Cardinal Morton's tomb of *c.* 1495 also retains extensive colouring, all renewed by Tristram. It is said that the Lily panel at the eastern end once contained an Annunciation scene. There remain in the church two panel paintings whose provenance and date remain obscure. One is a side panel from a Flagellation scene, perhaps late fifteenth century,[7] and the other is a portrait of Queen Ediva, a Saxon queen and benefactress of the cathedral. The painting contains a long inscription relating the munificence of Ediva, though the present legend has the appearance of being an addition. Perhaps the portrait was one of the series made for Prior Woodnesborough between 1411 and 1425 depicting all the great patrons of Canterbury Cathedral. They were intended to be displayed in the choir on festive days. The style of the work is difficult to assess – it is both dirty and behind glass.

In the eastern crypt, and in other parts of the church, curious and undatable inscribed drawings can be made out, some of which have now been protected by glass. Those in the eastern crypt, including a Christ in Majesty with the Evangelists, a Virgin and Child, two bishops and a Coronation of the Virgin, may be the underdrawing of a lost painting cycle. The Jesus chapel under the Corona has an initial series of M and J picked out in black.

The only major painting cycle known from the sixteenth century was that over the tomb of Cardinal Pole, *c.* 1558. The tiered decoration included cherubs supporting a wreath, more cherubs hovering over a sarcophagus and a large figure of the Virgin ( ?) holding out a Crucifix. The mural was clearly Renaissance in style, and is a tragic loss. The rest of the Corona chapel was painted with a repeated pattern showing a phoenix rising from the flames. The date is unknown. There were also painted full-length figures within the blind arcading above the windows. The chapel was scraped clean *c.* 1825.

6  Tristram, op. cit., p. 11.

7  It was found during the demolition of the Chequer Building in the nineteenth century.

# NOTES ON THE HIGH ROOFS

The high roofs of Canterbury Cathedral have not fared well, compared with cathedrals such as Winchester or Lincoln. Only one major roof is known to survive from the Middle Ages, that over the Martyrdom of *c*. 1473. The north and south aisles of the nave may have their original roofs of *c*. 1395, while St Anselm's chapel has a flattish roof probably of the fourteenth century. The spire of the south-east transept stair turret is undoubtedly early mediaeval, perhaps late twelfth or early thirteenth century, while the wheel loft within the central tower is made up from sections of a flat roof, possibly that made for the lower crossing tower of *c*. 1494.

Most of the main roofs were rebuilt in the eighteenth and nineteenth centuries. The south-east transept roof in *c*. 1771, and the opposite transept arm was probably reroofed at the same time. The choir roof between the central tower and the eastern transept was rebuilt in 1863, while the whole roof between the chapels of St Anselm and St Andrew and the Corona was rebuilt after a fire of 1872. The aisle roofs throughout the choir and Trinity Chapel also appear to be nineteenth century. Possibly the flat roof over the south choir aisle tribune is of an early date, though without the removal of the lead it is impossible to investigate.

The nave and south-west transept roofs were rebuilt *c*. 1900. Cross-sections of both the nave and choir roofs were depicted by Britton in 1821,[1] and were remarkably similar in form: i.e. ashlar pieces standing well out on the tie-beams and quite divorced from the wall plates, and scissor braces with intervening collars. If Britton is correct, it would appear that both roofs were of a similar date – the nave must have been roofed *c*. 1400 when the high vaults were commenced. Alternatively, both the nave and choir roofs may have been destroyed in the mysterious fire of *c*. 1483, a time when the absence of a central tower could have allowed a fire to jump the crossing space. This fire has left no trace in the cathedral, though the repairs were expensive.[2] The reign of Richard III might be considered too late for the use of scissor braces, though the Martyrdom roof of *c*. 1473 has scissor braces mixed with double purlins, queen struts, arch braces and wind braces. One other roof in the monastic complex might throw some light on the date of the lost nave and choir roofs – the Chapter House. This remarkable roof has not been examined, though it is undoubtedly mediaeval and is most likely to be that built *c*. 1405. The boarded shape seen inside and the exterior profile would suggest that the roof has long scissor braces with a collar intersecting below the scissor. This construction would provide the seven canted sides necessary for the boarded ceiling and could be built without interior tie beams. The basic structure would be similar to the losts roofs of the nave and choir, and a date early in the fifteenth century could suggest that Prior Chillenden rebuilt the choir roof to match the new high roof of the nave.

1 J. Britton, *The History and Antiquities of . . . Canterbury*, Plates III, IV, V.

2 See p. 198.

# NOTES ON THE MASTER MASONS
# OF CHRIST CHURCH

1 I am indebted to Eric Fernie for
pointing this out to me.

Nine architects or master masons of the mediaeval Cathedral (indicated*) can be
positively identified, ranging from the twelfth to the sixteenth centuries. At one
time, the master of St Anselm's choir was identified as Blithere, mentioned in a
MS. of *c.* 1090, but this appears to refer to St Augustine's abbey and not to the
cathedral.[1] Hence William of Sens becomes the first master known by name.

## William of Sens, 1174–9*
Known only through Gervase. Arrived at Canterbury after the fire of September
1174, when all the other masters were sent away. Fell from scaffolding
September 1178. Continued operations from his sick-bed, but soon returned
home to France. Nothing is known of his background save his name. The
architecture of the choir suggests that he was well versed in the style of Arras and
Cambrai, and aware of the Channel school of the mid-twelfth century. Gervase
refers to him as 'active and ready, and as a workman most skilful both in wood
and stone' and he speaks of his 'lively genious and good reputation'.

## William the Englishman, 1178/9–84*
Known only through Gervase. Took over the building of the new choir after the
departure of William of Sens. Completed the presbytery, refashioned the eastern
transept and designed the Trinity Chapel and Corona. Gervase calls him 'small
in body but in workmanship of many kinds acute and honest'. His architecture is
diverse, pointing to Laon, Reims and England. Nothing known after 1184.

## John Pikenot, *c.* 1236
Named in the Sacrist's Accounts as Master John Pikenot and paid for 'work on
the refectory'. His position is unclear, but may have been master mason.

## Michael of Canterbury, *c.* 1275
One of the leading masters of the Kent school in the reign of Edward I. Paid from
1275–6 for work on the London house of the prior of Christ Church, and referred
to in a Canterbury document of 1284 as 'master Michael le macun'. He entered
royal service *c.* 1291, when he began the Eleanor Cross at Cheapside, and in the
following year was employed on the first phase of St Stephen's chapel,
Westminster. His work at Canterbury may include the Peckham tomb, *c.* 1292,
the Eastry remodelling of the Chapter House, *c.* 1304, and the Eastry choir
screens. Michael was an important and innovative architect who contributed to
the revolution in English architecture in the late thirteenth century.

### Thomas of Canterbury, *c.* 1325–35

No known connection with the cathedral other than his name, and that he succeeded Michael in the royal service at St Stephen's. Links between the probable design of the great east window of that chapel and the Oxenden window at Canterbury of 1336 might suggest that Thomas did indeed work for the cathedral.

### John Box, from *c.* 1350*

In service of the prior in 1350. Entered royal service in the same year. Little else is known; his name disappears from Canterbury after 1356, though he may have remained master mason for the cathedral while involved in the building of Queenborough Castle between 1361 and his death in 1376. He may have designed the tiny Gloriet porch, the Black Prince's chantry and the chapel of Our Lady Undercroft at Canterbury, and may have provided the first design for the new nave, projected in 1369.

### Thomas of Hoo, 1380–98*

Named first among those 'masons of Canterbury at work on the fabric of the church' in an exemption from jury service granted in 1380. He was still listed among the masons and artificers in the Prior's Livery List of 1398. His long association with the cathedral might suggest that he was the master mason responsible for the design of the nave.

### Henry Yevele, 1386–1400

Variously attributed with the design of almost every important building in southern England between 1365 and 1400. His connection with Canterbury Cathedral is related to the rebuilding of the city wall around the precincts, completed soon after his death. The cathedral contains at least two 'portraits of the dead Henry Yevele', one at least carved four years before he died. His connection with the nave is examined in greater depth in chapter 5.

### Stephen Lote, 1396–1417*

Named as an esquire in the Prior's Livery List in each of the surviving grants between 1398 and 1416. No other known connection with Canterbury, but likely to have been the designer of the nave west window, the south-west transept arm, cloister and Chapter House remodelling. Worked at St Paul's Cathedral, then at Westminster Abbey in the royal service. Later at Westminster Palace and at the Tower. Made a bequest to a monk of Christ Church in his will of 1417.

### Thomas Mapilton, 1423–32*

Named as master mason of Christ Church in 1423 and 1429. Younger partner (?) of Lote. Previously master mason at Durham, and appointed king's master mason in 1429. His work at Canterbury includes the south-west tower and porch from 1424, the completion of the south-west transept and probably the Chichele tomb of *c.* 1425. Evidently Mapilton resigned his post in 1429.

### Richard Beke, 1432–58*

Formerly chief mason of London Bridge, he appears at Canterbury from 1432. Appointed master mason for life in 1434–5, the deed of contract being one of the

2 The contract can be found in L. Salzman, *Building in England down to 1540*, pp. 590–1.

most complete and interesting from the English Middle Ages.[2] Beke's work at Canterbury includes the Holland Chapel, the Lady Chapel, the strengthening of the crossing piers and the lower gallery of the central tower, the completion of the south-west tower and its vault, the decoration of the west front, the commencement of the Martyrdom remodelling and the pulpitum. Beke may also have designed the chantry of Henry IV. In his will of 1458, Beke left £2 towards the building work in the cathedral.

### John Smyth, 1429–60

Not a master mason of the cathedral, but first mason between 1433 and 1441. He was overlooked by Prior Molash for the position of master mason in 1434–5 in favour of Beke. Smyth moved to Eton College, where he became royal master mason in 1448. He was responsible for the enlarged design for the chapel. In 1453 Smyth became master mason of Westminster Abbey, a position he retained until 1460, when he probably died. His career coincided almost exactly with that of Richard Beke at Canterbury, and while he remained for nearly a quarter-century, he could never rise to the master masonship. Nevertheless, after he left Canterbury, he quickly rose to the position of prominent architect. It is possibly through Smyth that some of the motifs employed at Canterbury in the 1430s and 1440s, entered the royal repertoire later in the century.

### Thomas Glazier, 1458–66*

Master mason of the cathedral after the death of Richard Beke. Glazier had worked there between 1432 and 1442, and then at Eton under John Smyth. He returned to Canterbury in 1454, perhaps to work on the pulpitum, for he was described as a 'carver' at Eton. Glazier was probably responsible for the completion of Beke's work at Canterbury – the south-west tower, pulpitum and upper section of the Martyrdom. The curious tracery in the clerestory above the Lady Chapel is likely to date from his time.

### Thomas Redman, 1466

Named as a mason of Canterbury Cathedral in 1466. There is no evidence as to his status at the cathedral.

### John Wastell, *c.* 1490–1518*

3 F. Woodman, 'John Wastell of Bury, master mason', Ph.D. thesis, University of London, 1978.

Named as master mason of Canterbury Cathedral in 1496, but worked on the new central tower from at least 1491.[3] One of the great figures of late mediaeval architecture in England. A Hertfordshire man, trained at Cambridge, where he rose to prominence in the late 1480s. Master mason of King's Hall (later Trinity College), where he designed the first stage of the great gate. Moved his architectural practice to Bury St Edmunds in or soon after 1489, perhaps on his appointment as master mason for the abbey. Visited Canterbury occasionally during his period as master mason, for he had several projects in Cambridge and elsewhere to oversee. From 1508 he was king's master mason for the final campaign on King's College Chapel in Cambridge, where he designed the antechapel, the high vaults and many of the exterior enrichments. He died *c.* 1518.

Several buildings can be attributed to him on stylistic or documentary grounds: they include part of Great Barton church in Suffolk, the nave of

Lavenham (Suffolk), Great St Mary's in Cambridge, the nave of Saffron Walden, St James', Bury St Edmunds, the inner chapel of Our Lady Redmount in King's Lynn, the New Buildings at Peterborough and the tombs of Redmond at Ely and Warham at Canterbury. Wastell's career approximated to that of a modern architect, sending out plans and drawings to his clients and relying on trusted wardens to supervise the work on the spot.

Not referred to in Canterbury after 1496, though the completion of Bell Harry and the building of the crossing vaults post-1504 were certainly executed by him. The 'widow of John Wastell' was living in Canterbury in 1518, though it is not an uncommon name in Kent.

### Robert Vertue, *c.* 1500–6

No known connection with the cathedral, but owned property in the city, in St Paul's parish, and asked to be buried in St Augustine's Abbey. While this does not signify that he worked in the city, as a leading member of the 'Windsor–Westminster' school of masons he is the most likely candidate as architect of the Christ Church gate, a royal work from *c.* 1502. Vertue may also have been the Windsor–Westminster mason who designed the set of doors throughout the cathedral built by Cardinal Morton (?). These include the doors of the north-east transept, the Water Tower passage to the crypt, the Martyrdom and west cloister door. There was also the considerable work carried out on the Palace, *c.* 1500. While these works indicate a Windsor–Westminster mason, Vertue's authorship can remain only speculative.

# ARCHBISHOPS OF CANTERBURY TO 1558

| | | | |
|---|---|---|---|
| St Augustine | 597–604 | St Anselm | 1093–1109 |
| St Laurence | 604–19 | Ralph d'Escures | 1114–22 |
| St Mellitus | 619–24 | William de Corbeuil | 1123–36 |
| St Justus | 624–27 | Theobald | 1138–61 |
| St Honorius | 627–53 | St Thomas of Canterbury | 1162–70 |
| St Deusdedit | 655–64 | Richard of Dover | 1174–84 |
| St Theodore of Tarsus | 668–90 | Baldwin | 1185–90 |
| St Berhtwald | 693–731 | Hubert Walter | 1193–1205 |
| St Tatwin | 731–4 | Stephen Langton, Cardinal | 1207–28 |
| Nothelm | 735–40 | Richard Grant | 1229–31 |
| Cuthbert | 741–58 | St Edmund of Canterbury | 1234–40 |
| Bregwin | 759–65 | Boniface of Savoy | 1245–70 |
| Jaenberht | 766–90 | Robert Kilwardby, Cardinal | 1273–9 |
| Ethelheard | 793–805 | John Peckam | 1279–92 |
| Wulfred | 805–32 | Robert Winchelsey | 1293–1313 |
| Feologild | 832 | Walter Reynolds | 1313–27 |
| Ceolnoth | 833–70 | Simon Meopham | 1327–33 |
| Ethelrede | 870–89 | John Stratford | 1333–48 |
| Plegmund | 890–922 | Thomas Bradwardine | 1349 |
| Ethelm | 922–3 | Simon Islip | 1349–66 |
| Wulfhelm | 923–42 | Simon Langham, Cardinal | 1366–8 |
| St Oda | 942–58 | William Whittlesey | 1368–74 |
| Alfsin | 959 | Simon Sudbury | 1375–81 |
| St Dunstan | 961–88 | William Courtenay | 1381–96 |
| Athelgar | 988–89 | Thomas Arundel | 1397–1414 |
| Sigeric | 989–94 | Henry Chichele, Cardinal | 1414–43 |
| Aelfric | 995–1005 | John Stafford, Cardinal | 1443–52 |
| St Alphege | 1005–12 | John Kemp, Cardinal | 1452–4 |
| Living | 1013–20 | Thomas Bourchier, Cardinal | 1455–86 |
| St Ethelnoth | 1020–38 | John Morton, Cardinal | 1486–1501 |
| St Eadsige | 1038–50 | Henry Dean | 1501–2 |
| Robert of Jumièges | 1051–2 | William Warham | 1504–32 |
| Stigand | 1052–70 | Thomas Cranmer | 1533–56 |
| Lanfranc | 1070–89 | Reginald Pole, Cardinal | 1556–8 |

# DEANS AND PRIORS OF CHRIST CHURCH TO 1540

## Anglo-Saxon deans, some dates unknown

| | | | |
|---|---|---|---|
| Aelfric | | Heahfrith | *c.* 813 |
| Aelfsige | | Ceolnoth | *c.* 830 |
| Aelfwine I | | Athelwine | *c.* 860 |
| Aelfwine II | | Edmund | *c.* 871 |
| Kynsige | | Ethelnoth | *c.* 1015 |
| Maurice | | Godric | *c.* 1020 |
| Cuba | *c.* 798 | Ethelric | *c.* 1055 |
| Beornheard | *c.* 805 | Henry | 1070 |

## Priors of Christ Church

| | | | |
|---|---|---|---|
| Henry | 1080–96 | Nicholas of Sandwich | 1244–58 |
| Ernulph | 1096–1107 | Roger of St Alphege | 1258–63 |
| Conrad | 1108–26 | Adam of Chillenden | 1264–74 |
| Geoffrey I | 1126–8 | Thomas of Ringmere | 1274–84 |
| Elmer | 1129–37 | Henry of Eastry | 1285–1331 |
| Jeremias | 1137–43 | Richard Oxenden | 1331–8 |
| Walter Durdent | 1143–49 | Robert Hathbrand | 1338–70 |
| Walter Parvus | 1149–50 | Richard of Gillingham | 1370–6 |
| Wibert | 1153–67 | Stephen of Mongeham | 1376–7 |
| Odo | 1167–75 | John Finch | 1377–91 |
| Benedict | 1175–7 | Thomas of Chillenden | 1391–1411 |
| Herlewin | 1177–9 | John of Woodnesborough | 1411–25 |
| Alan | 1179–86 | William of Molash | 1425–37 |
| Honorius | 1186–8 | John of Salisbury | 1437–46 |
| Roger Norris | 1189 | John of Elham | 1446–9 |
| Osbert of Bristol | 1190 | Thomas Goldstone I | 1449–68 |
| Geoffrey II | 1191–1213 | John of Oxney | 1468–71 |
| Walter | 1213–22 | William of Petham | 1471–2 |
| John of Sittingbourne | 1222–32 | William of Sellinge | 1472–94 |
| John of Chatham | 1232–8 | Thomas Goldstone II | 1495–1517 |
| Roger of Lee | 1239–44 | Thomas Goldwell | 1517–40 |

# BIBLIOGRAPHY

## Essential sources

*Anglia Sacra* (ed. H. Wharton), 2 vols, 1691. Vol. 1 for obits of archbishops and priors. See also Stephen Birchington, *Historia de Vitis Archiepiscoporum Cantuariensiem*, ibid., vol. 1, pp. 1–48; *Historia Priorum Cantuar*, ibid., pp. 135–49; *Vita Simonis Sudbury, ex Speculo Parvulorum Lib.5.cap.27*, attributed to William of Chartham, ibid., pp. 49–50.

BEDE, *Historia Ecclesiastica Gentis Anglorum*, see *Venerabilis Baedae Opera Historica* (ed. C. Plummer), Oxford, 1896.

BRITTON, J., *The History and Antiquities of the Metropolitical Church of Canterbury*, London, 1821.

DART, J., *The History and Antiquities of the Cathedral Church of Canterbury*, 1726.

EADMER, *Historia Novorum in Anglia, 960–1122* (ed. M. Rule), Rolls Series, 1884; see also *Vita Sancti Anselmi* in ibid.

EADMER, *The Life of St Anselm, Archbishop of Canterbury* (ed. R. W. Southern), London, 1962.

GERVASE, *The Historical Works of Gervase of Canterbury* (ed. W. Stubbs), 2 vols, Rolls Series, 1879, 1880. For the *Burning and Repair of Christ Church Canterbury* see *Chronica Gervasii*, ibid., vol. 1, pp. 3–29.

GOSTLING, W., *A Walk in and about the City of Canterbury*, 1774; 1825 ed. with prints.

GRANSDEN, A., *Historical Writing in England*, London, 1974.

GROSE, F., *Antiquities of England and Wales*, 3 vols. For Canterbury, vol. 3, 1783.

HASTED, E., *History of Kent*, 2nd ed., 2 vols, Canterbury, 1800.

HUSSEY, R. C., *Extracts from Ancient Documents relating to the Cathedral and Precincts of Canterbury*, privately published, 1881.

LEGGE, J. and ST JOHN HOPE, W., *Inventories of Christ Church, Canterbury*, London, 1902.

LELAND, J., *The Itinerary of England and Wales* (ed. L. Toulmin Smith), 4 vols, London, 1909, reprinted 1971. For Canterbury, vol. 4.

*Literae Cantuariensis* (ed. J. Brigstocke Sheppard), Rolls Series, 2 vols., 1889.

MESSENGER, A., *The Heraldry of Canterbury Cathedral : the Great Cloister Vault*, Canterbury, 1947.

PHILLIPS, C. S., *Canterbury Cathedral in the Middle Ages*, London, 1949.

SMITH, G., *A Chronological History of Canterbury Cathedral*, Canterbury, 1883.

SMITH, R. A. L., *Canterbury Cathedral Priory*, Cambridge Studies in Economic History, Cambridge, 1943, reissued 1969.

SOMNER, W., *Antiquities of Canterbury*, 1640 (ed. N. Battely, 1703, with prints and additions).

SOUTHERN, R. W., *St Anselm and his Biographer*, Oxford, 1963.

STANLEY, A., *Memorials of Canterbury*, 1854.

URRY, W. G., *Canterbury under the Angevin Kings*, London, 1967.

WILLEMENT, T., *Heraldic Notices of Canterbury Cathedral*, London, 1827.

WILLIAM OF MALMESBURY, *De Gestis Pontificum* (ed. N. Hamilton), Rolls Series, 1870.

WILLIS, R., *The Architectural History of Canterbury Cathedral*, London, 1845.

WILLIS, R., *The History of the Monastery of Christ Church Canterbury*, London, 1869.

WOODRUFF, C. E. and DANKS, W., *Memorials of the Cathedral and Priory of Christ in Canterbury*, London, 1912.

WOOLNOTH, W., *A Graphical Illustration of the Metropolitical Cathedral Church of Canterbury*, 1816.

## Artistic background material

### 1 The Anglo-Saxon cathedral

*Canterbury*

R. GEM, 'The Anglo-Saxon cathedral church at Canterbury', *Archaeol. J.*, 127, 1970, pp. 196–201.

W. ST JOHN HOPE, 'The first cathedral church of Canterbury', *Proc. Society of Antiquaries of London*, 2nd ser., 30, 1918, pp. 136–58.

D. D. KNOWLES, 'The early community of Christ Church Canterbury', *J. Theological Studies*, 39, 1938, pp. 126–31.

D. PARSONS, 'The pre-Conquest Cathedral of Canterbury', *Arch. Cant.*, 84, 1969, p. 175.

J. ARMITAGE ROBINSON, 'The early community of Christ Church Canterbury', *J. Theological Studies*, 27, 1926, pp. 225–40.

H. M. TAYLOR, 'The Anglo-Saxon cathedral church at Canterbury', *Archaeol. J.*, 126, 1969, pp. 100–21.

*Comparative material*

G. BALDWIN BROWN, *The Arts in Early England*, vol. 2: *Anglo-Saxon Architecture*, London, 1903.

A. W. CLAPHAM, *English Romanesque Architecture before the Conquest*, Oxford, 1930.

K. J. CONANT, *Carolingian and Romanesque Architecture, 800–1200*, Penguin, 1959.

D. JACKSON AND E. FLETCHER, 'Excavations at Lydd basilica', *J. Brit. Archaeol. Ass.*, 31, 1968, p. 19.

E. KIRSCHBAUM, *The Tombs of St Peter and St Paul*, London, 1959.
H. M. TAYLOR, 'Corridor crypts on the Continent and in England', *North Staffordshire J. Field Studies*, 9, 1969, p. 17.
H.M. and J. TAYLOR, *Anglo-Saxon Architecture*, Cambridge, 1965.
J. TOYNBEE and J. WARD PERKINS, *The Shrine of St Peter*, London, 1956.


## 2 The Romanesque architecture

*Canterbury*
J. BILSON, 'The Norman school and the beginnings of Gothic architecture: two octopartite vaults: Montivilliers and Canterbury', *Archaeol. J.*, 74, 1917, pp. 1–35.
W. G. URRY, *Canterbury under the Angevin Kings*.
F. WOODMAN, 'Lanfranc's cathedral at Canterbury', *Cant. Cath. Chron.*, 71, 1977.

*Caen*
M. ANFRAY, *L'Architecture normande*, Paris, 1931.
M. BAYLE, *La Trinité de Caen*, Geneva, 1979.
CAEN, Congrès archéologique tenu à, LXXVième session, 2 vols, Paris, 1909.
E. G. CARLSON, 'Excavations at Saint-Etienne, Caen (1969)', *Gesta* (New York), 10, no. 1, 1971, p. 23.
E. LAMBERT, *Caen, roman et gothique*, Caen, 1935.
L. SERBAT, 'Eglise de la Trinité et Abbaye aux Dames', *Congrès Archéologique*, vol. 76, 1908.

*Comparative material*
T. BOASE, *English Art, 1100–1216*, Oxford, 1955.
J. BONY, 'La technique normande du mur épais à l'époque romane', *Bull. Monumental*, 1939.
A. W. CLAPHAM, *English Romanesque Architecture after the Conquest*, Oxford, 1934.
S. COLLON-GEVAERT, J. LEJEUNE and J. STIENNON, *Art roman dans la vallée de la Meuse au XIe et XIIe siècle*, Brussels, 1962.
K. J. CONANT, *Carolingian and Romanesque Architecture, 800–1200*, Penguin, 1959.
K. J. CONANT, *Cluny, les Eglises et la Maison du Chef d'Ordre*, Cambridge, Mass., 1967.
J. EVANS, *The Romanesque Architecture of the Order of Cluny*, Cambridge, 1938.
E. GALL, *Die gotische Baukunst in Frankreich und Deutschland*, Brunswick, 1955.
L. GENICOT, *Les Eglises mosanes du XIe siècle*, Liège, 1972.
L. GRODECKI, *L'Architecture ottonienne*, Paris, 1958.
E. KUBACH, 'Die frühromanische Baukunst des Maaslandes', *Zeitschrift für Kunstwissenschaft*, 7, 1953.
E. KUBACH, *Romanesque Architecture*, New York, 1975.
R. DE LASTEYRIE, *L'Architecture religieuse en France à l'époque romane*, ed. M. Aubert, 2nd ed., Paris, 1929.

R. Liess, *Der Frühromanische Kirchenbau des 11 Jahrhunderts in der Normandie*, Munich, 1967.

V. Rupprich-Robert, *L'Architecture normande*, 1885–9.

J. Vallery-Radot, *Eglises romanes*, Paris, 1931.

G. Zarnecki, *English Romanesque Sculpture, 1066–1140*, London, 1951.


## 3 The Gothic choir

*Canterbury*

C. Cave, *The Roof-Bosses of the Cathedral Church of Christ, Canterbury*, Canterbury Papers, No. 4, Canterbury, 1934.

P. Frankl, *Gervase of Canterbury : the Gothic, Literary Sources and Interpretations through Eight Centuries*, Princeton, 1960.

K. Severens, 'William of Sens and the double columns at Sens and Canterbury', *J. Warburg and Courtauld Insts*, 33, 1970, pp. 307–13.

F. Woodman, 'The "re-opening" of the choir, 1180–1980', *Cant. Cath. Chron.*, 74, 1980.


*Sens*

R. Branner, *Burgundian Gothic Architecture*, London, 1960.

E. Chartraire, *La Cathédrale de Sens*, Paris, 1934.

J. Hubert, 'La construction de la cathédrale de Sens au XIIe siècle', *Bull. Société nationale des Antiquaires de France*, 1965.

F. Salet, 'La cathédrale de Sens et sa place dans l'histoire de l'architecture médiévale', Académie des Inscriptions et Belles-Lettres, *Comptes-rendus*, 1955.


*Comparative material*

J. Bilson, 'The beginning of Gothic architecture', *JRIBA*, 6, 1899.

T. Boase, *English Art, 1100–1216*, Oxford, 1955.

F. Bond, *Gothic Architecture in England*, London, 1906.

J. Bony, 'French influences on the origins of English Gothic architecture', *J. Warburg and Courtauld Insts*, 12, 1949, pp. 1–15.

J. Bony, 'The resistance to Chartres in early thirteenth century architecture', *J. Brit. Archaeol. Ass.*, 3rd ser., 20–1, 1957–8.

J. Bony, 'Origines des piles gothiques anglaises à fûts en délit', *Gedenkschrift Ernst Gall*, Berlin and Munich, 1965, pp. 95–122.

R. Branner, 'The transept of Cambrai Cathedral', ibid., pp. 69–86.

L. Demaison, 'Reims, Eglise St-Remi', Congrès archéologique tenu à Reims, 1911.

E. Gall, *Die gotische Baukunst in Frankreich und Deutschland*, Brunswick, 1955.

E. Lambert, 'La cathédrale de Laon', *Gazette des Beaux-Arts*, I, 1926.

E. Lambert, 'L'ancienne abbaye de Saint-Vincent de Laon', Académie des Inscriptions et Belles-Lettres, *Comptes-rendus*, 1939.

C. H. Moore, *The Medieval Church Architecture of England*, London, 1912.

H. Oursel, 'Quelques éléments sculptés nouvellement identifiés de l'ancienne cathédrale d'Arras et remarques sur les débuts de la sculpture romane dans le nord de France', *Bull. Commission départementale de Monuments Historiques du Pas de Calais*, vol. 3, 1978.

F. Salet, *La Madeleine de Vézelay*, Melun, 1948.

L Serbat, 'Quelques églises anciennement détruites du nord de la France', *Bull. Monumental*, 88, 1929.

C. Seymour, *Notre-Dame of Noyon in the Twelfth Century : a Study in the Early Development of Gothic Architecture*, New Haven, 1939.

O. V. Simpson, *The Gothic Cathedral*, Princeton, 1974.

G. Webb, *Architecture in Britain in the Middle Ages*, London, 1956.

## 4 The architecture from Richard I to Edward III

*Canterbury*

W. Caröe, 'The choir of Canterbury Cathedral', *Archaeologia*, 62, 1911.

A. Reader-Moore, 'The liturgical chancel of Canterbury Cathedral', *Cant. Cath. Chron.*, 73, 1979, pp. 25–44.

F. Woodman, 'Two tombs in the south choir aisle', *Cant. Cath. Chron.*, 69, 1975, pp. 15–22.

*Comparative material*

P. Biver, 'Tombs of the school of London at the beginning of the fourteenth century', *Archaeol. J.*, 67, 1910.

T. Boase, *English Art, 1100–1216*, Oxford, 1955.

H. Bock, *Der Decorated Style*, Heidelberg, 1962.

F. Bond, *Gothic Architecture in England*, London, 1906.

J. Bony, *The English Decorated Style*, Oxford, 1979.

R. Branner, *St Louis and the Court Style*, London, 1965.

P. Brieger, *English Art, 1216–1307*, Oxford, 1957.

H. Colvin, *The History of the King's Works : the Middle Ages*, 2 vols, ed. R. Brown, H. Colvin and A. J. Taylor, London, 1963.

J. Evans, *English Art, 1307–1461*, Oxford, 1949.

P. Frankl, *Gothic Architecture*, London, 1963.

J. Harvey, 'St Stephen's chapel and the origins of the Perpendicular style', *Burlington Magazine*, 88, 1946.

J. Harvey, 'The origin of the Perpendicular style', in *Studies in Building History*, ed. E. M. Jope, London, 1961.

J. Hastings, 'The Court style', *Arch. Rev.*, 105, 1949.

J. Hastings, *St Stephen's Chapel and its Place in the Development of Perpendicular Style in England*, Cambridge, 1955.

N. Pevsner, 'Bristol–Troyes–Gloucester : the character of the early fourteenth century in architecture', *Arch. Rev.*, 113, 1953.

L. Stone, *Sculpture in Britain in the Middle Ages*, London, 1955.

A. H. Thompson, 'Master Elias of Dereham and the King's Works', *Archaeol. J.*, 48, 1941.

## 5 The Perpendicular cathedral

*Canterbury*

J. Legge and W. St J. Hope, *Inventories of Christ Church, Canterbury*.

A. Oswald, 'Canterbury Cathedral, the nave and its designer', *Burlington Magazine*, 75, 1939.

W. G. Searle, ed., *Christ Church Canterbury : 1. The Chronicle of John Stone*, Cambridge Antiquarian Society. Octavo Pubs no. 34, Cambridge, 1902.

F. Woodman, 'The Holland family and Canterbury Cathedral', *Cant. Cath. Chron.*, 70, 1976, pp. 23–8.

*Comparative material*

J. Evans, *English Art, 1307–1461*, Oxford, 1949.

J. Harvey, *Henry Yevele*, London, 1944.

J. Harvey, *The Perpendicular Style*, London, 1978.

D. Knoop and G. Jones, *The Medieval Mason*, Manchester, 1933.

W. Lethaby, *Westminster Abbey Re-examined*, London, 1925.

A. McLees, 'Henry Yevele, disposer of the King's Works of masonry', *J. Brit. Archaeol. Ass.*, 36, 1973, pp. 52–71.

L. Salzman, *Building in England down to 1540*, Oxford, 1952.

G. Webb, *Architecture in Britain : the Middle Ages*, London, 1956.

C. Wilson, 'The original design of the City of London Guildhall', *J. Brit. Archaeol. Ass.*, 129, 1976.

## 6 The Tudor cathedral

*Canterbury*

W. Caröe, *The Christ Church Gateway*, Friends of Canterbury Cathedral, 5th Annual Report, Canterbury, 1932.

J. Legge and W. St J. Hope, *Inventories of Christ Church, Canterbury*.

A. J. Taylor, 'Edward I and the shrine of St Thomas of Canterbury', *J. Brit. Archaeol. Ass.*, 132, 1979.

D. H. Turner, 'The Customary of the shrine of St Thomas Becket', *Cant. Cath. Chron.*, 70, 1976.

W. G. Urry, *Cardinal Morton and the Angel Steeple*, Friends of Canterbury Cathedral, 38th Annual Report, 1965.

*Comparative material*

N. Coldstream, 'English decorated shrine bases', *J. Brit. Archaeol. Ass.*, 129, 1976.

H. Colvin, D. Ransome and J. Summerson, *The History of the King's Works*: vol. 3, *1485–1660*, London, 1975.

J. Harvey, *Gothic England*, 2nd ed., London, 1948.

W. St J. Hope, *Windsor Castle*, London, 1913.

R. Willis and J. Clark, *The Architectural History of the University of Cambridge*, Cambridge, 1886.

## Appendix I  The stained glass

*Canterbury*
T. BORENIUS, *St Thomas Becket in Art*, London, 1932.
M. CAVINESS, *The Early Stained Glass of Canterbury Cathedral*, Princeton, 1977. The Canterbury volume of the *Corpus Vitrearum* will be published by the British Academy.
B. RACKHAM, *The Ancient Glass of Canterbury Cathedral*, London, 1949.

*Comparative material*
P. BRIEGER, *English Art, 1216–1307*, Oxford, 1957.
J. LE COUTEUR, *English Medieval Painted Glass*, 1926.
J. EVANS, *English Art, 1307–1461*, Oxford, 1949.
M. RICKERT, *Painting in Britain : the Middle Ages*, London, 1954.

## Appendix II  The tombs and monuments

*Comparative material*
P. BIVER, 'Tombs of the school of London in the beginning of the fourteenth century', *Archaeol. J.*, 67, 1910.
P. BIVER, 'Westminster tombs', *Bull. Monumental*, 68, 1909.
J. BONY, *The English Decorated Style*, Oxford, 1979.
P. BRIEGER, *English Art, 1216–1307*, Oxford, 1957.
J. EVANS, *English Art, 1307–1461*, Oxford, 1949.
E. PRIOR and A. GARDNER, *An Account of Medieval Figure Sculpture in England*, Cambridge, 1912.

## Appendix III  The paintings

*Canterbury*
W. CARÖE, 'Wall paintings in the Infirmary Chapel', *Archaeologia*, 63, 1911–12, pp. 51–6.
M. CAVINESS, 'A lost cycle of Canterbury paintings of 1220', *Antiq. J.*, 54, part 1, 1974, pp. 66–74.
C. DODWELL, *The Canterbury School of Illumination*, Cambridge, 1954.
E. TRISTRAM, *The Paintings of Canterbury Cathedral*, Friends of Canterbury Cathedral, Canterbury, 1935.

*Comparative material*
E. MILLAR, *English Illuminated Manuscripts from the 10th to the 13th Century*, Paris, 1926.
M. RICKERT, *Painting in Britain, the Middle Ages*, London, 1954.
E. TRISTRAM, *English Medieval Painting*, Paris, 1927.
E. TRISTRAM, *English Medieval Wall Painting*, Oxford, vol. 1, 1950, vol. 2, 1954.

**The master masons**

*Canterbury*
J. HARVEY, *English Medieval Architects*, London, 1954.
D. KNOOP and G. JONES, *The Medieval Mason*, Manchester, 1933.
L. SALZMAN, *Building in England down to 1540*, Oxford, 1952.


**The high roofs**

C. HEWETT, *English Cathedral Carpentry*, London, 1974.

# INDEX